Teach Yourself VISUALLY Fire™ Tablets

This is a gift from the:

Danville Library Foundation

Elaine Marmel

WITHDRAWN

Teach Yourself VISUALLY Fire™ Tablets

Published by
John Wiley & Sons, Inc.
10475 Crosspoint Boulevard
Indianapolis, IN 46256

www.wiley.com

Published simultaneously in Canada

Copyright © 2015 by John Wiley & Sons, Inc., Indianapolis, Indiana

No part of this publication may be reproduced, stored in a retrieval system or transmitted in any form or by any means, electronic, mechanical, photocopying, recording, scanning or otherwise, except as permitted under Sections 107 or 108 of the 1976 United States Copyright Act, without either the prior written permission of the Publisher, or authorization through payment of the appropriate per-copy fee to the Copyright Clearance Center, 222 Rosewood Drive, Danvers, MA 01923, 978-750-8400, fax 978-646-8600. Requests to the Publisher for permission should be addressed to the Permissions Department, John Wiley & Sons, Inc., 111 River Street, Hoboken, NJ 07030, 201-748-6011, fax 201-748-6008, or online at www.wiley.com/go/permissions.

Wiley publishes in a variety of print and electronic formats and by print-on-demand. Some material included with standard print versions of this book may not be included in e-books or in print-on-demand. If this book refers to media such as a CD or DVD that is not included in the version you purchased, you may download this material at http://booksupport.wiley.com. For more information about Wiley products, visit www.wiley.com.

Library of Congress Control Number is available from the Publisher.

ISBN: 978-1-118-9192920-3 (pbk); ISBN: 978-1-118-91964-4 (ePDF);
ISBN: 978-1-118-91930-9 (ePub)

Manufactured in the United States of America

10 9 8 7 6 5 4 3 2 1

Trademark Acknowledgments

Wiley, Visual, the Visual logo, Teach Yourself VISUALLY, Read Less - Learn More and related trade dress are trademarks or registered trademarks of John Wiley & Sons, Inc. and/or its affiliates. Kindle Fire is a trademark of Amazon Technologies, Inc. Kindle Fire is a trademark of Amazon Technologies, Inc. All other trademarks are the property of their respective owners. John Wiley & Sons, Inc. is not associated with any product or vendor mentioned in this book.

LIMIT OF LIABILITY/DISCLAIMER OF WARRANTY: THE PUBLISHER AND THE AUTHOR MAKE NO REPRESENTATIONS OR WARRANTIES WITH RESPECT TO THE ACCURACY OR COMPLETENESS OF THE CONTENTS OF THIS WORK AND SPECIFICALLY DISCLAIM ALL WARRANTIES, INCLUDING WITHOUT LIMITATION WARRANTIES OF FITNESS FOR A PARTICULAR PURPOSE. NO WARRANTY MAY BE CREATED OR EXTENDED BY SALES OR PROMOTIONAL MATERIALS. THE ADVICE AND STRATEGIES CONTAINED HEREIN MAY NOT BE SUITABLE FOR EVERY SITUATION. THIS WORK IS SOLD WITH THE UNDERSTANDING THAT THE PUBLISHER IS NOT ENGAGED IN RENDERING LEGAL, ACCOUNTING, OR OTHER PROFESSIONAL SERVICES. IF PROFESSIONAL ASSISTANCE IS REQUIRED, THE SERVICES OF A COMPETENT PROFESSIONAL PERSON SHOULD BE SOUGHT. NEITHER THE PUBLISHER NOR THE AUTHOR SHALL BE LIABLE FOR DAMAGES ARISING HEREFROM. THE FACT THAT AN ORGANIZATION OR WEBSITE IS REFERRED TO IN THIS WORK AS A CITATION AND/OR A POTENTIAL SOURCE OF FURTHER INFORMATION DOES NOT MEAN THAT THE AUTHOR OR THE PUBLISHER ENDORSES THE INFORMATION THE ORGANIZATION OR WEBSITE MAY PROVIDE OR RECOMMENDATIONS IT MAY MAKE. FURTHER, READERS SHOULD BE AWARE THAT INTERNET WEBSITES LISTED IN THIS WORK MAY HAVE CHANGED OR DISAPPEARED BETWEEN WHEN THIS WORK WAS WRITTEN AND WHEN IT IS READ.

FOR PURPOSES OF ILLUSTRATING THE CONCEPTS AND TECHNIQUES DESCRIBED IN THIS BOOK, THE AUTHOR HAS CREATED VARIOUS NAMES, COMPANY NAMES, MAILING, E-MAIL AND INTERNET ADDRESSES, PHONE AND FAX NUMBERS AND SIMILAR INFORMATION, ALL OF WHICH ARE FICTITIOUS. ANY RESEMBLANCE OF THESE FICTITIOUS NAMES, ADDRESSES, PHONE AND FAX NUMBERS AND SIMILAR INFORMATION TO ANY ACTUAL PERSON, COMPANY AND/OR ORGANIZATION IS UNINTENTIONAL AND PURELY COINCIDENTAL.

Contact Us

For general information on our other products and services please contact our Customer Care Department within the U.S. at 877-762-2974, outside the U.S. at 317-572-3993 or fax 317-572-4002.

For technical support please visit www.wiley.com/techsupport.

Credits

Acquisitions Editor
Aaron Black

Project Editor
Maureen S. Tullis

Copy Editor
Scott D. Tullis

Manager, Content Development & Assembly
Mary Beth Wakefield

Publisher
Jim Minatel

Editorial Assistant
Jessie Phelps

Project Coordinator
Erin Zeltner

Proofreading
Debbye Butler.

Indexing
Broccoli Information Mgt.

Printer
Command Web Missouri

About the Author

Elaine Marmel is President of Marmel Enterprises, LLC, an organization specializing in technical writing and software training. Elaine has an MBA from Cornell Universtiy and previously worked on projects building financial management systems in both New York City and Washington, DC. She has authored over seventy books predominantly on business productivity software. Elaine left her native Chicago for the warmer climes of Arizona (by way of Cincinnati OH; Jerusalem, Israel; Ithaca, NY; Washington DC; and Tampa, FL) where she basks in the sun with her PC, her latest cross stitch project, and her dog, Jack.

Author's Acknowledgments

My sincere thanks go to Katie Mohr, who gave me the opportunity to write this book — and here's to many more, Katie, because it has been a pleasure to work with you. And Maureen and Scott Tullis are the best project team ever. . .I can't thank you enough for your dedication to this project.

How to Use This Book

Important Note About Fire Tablet Versions

Please note this book was written using the Fire HDX 7-inch model. Although the steps presented in this book can be used for most Fire tablets, your tablet's appearance may differ.

Who This Book Is For

This book is for the reader who has never used this particular technology or software application. It is also for readers who want to expand their knowledge.

The Conventions In This Book

1 Steps

This book uses a step-by-step format to guide you easily through each task. Numbered steps are actions you must do; bulleted steps clarify a point, step, or optional feature; and indented steps give you the result.

2 Notes

Notes give additional information — special conditions that may occur during an operation, a situation that you want to avoid, or a cross reference to a related area of the book.

3 Icons and Buttons

Icons and buttons show you exactly what you need to click to perform a step.

4 Tips

Tips offer additional information, including warnings and shortcuts.

5 Bold

Bold type shows command names, options, and text or numbers you must type.

6 Italics

Italic type introduces and defines a new term.

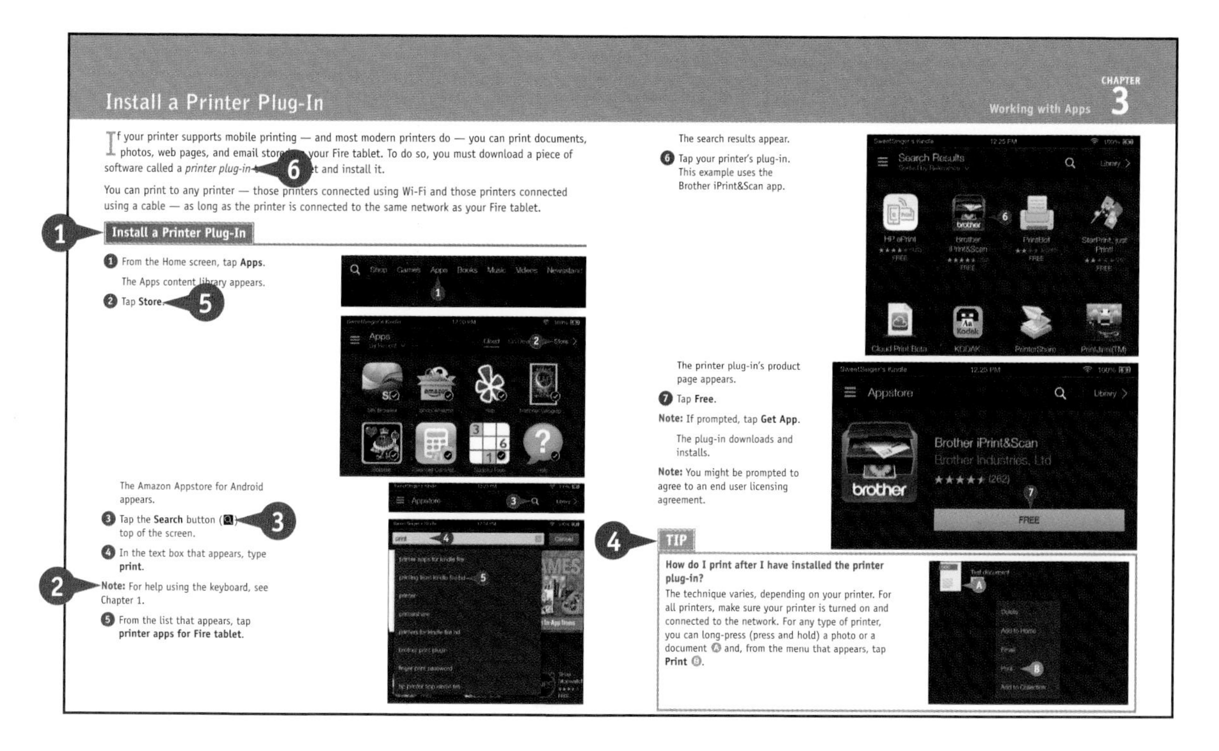

Install a Printer Plug-In

CHAPTER 3

Working with Apps

If your printer supports mobile printing — and most modern printers do — you can print documents, photos, web pages, and email stored on your Fire tablet. To do so, you must download a piece of software called a *printer plug-in* and install it.

You can print to any printer — those printers connected using Wi-Fi and those printers connected using a cable — as long as the printer is connected to the same network as your Fire tablet.

Install a Printer Plug-In

1. From the Home screen, tap **Apps**.

   The Apps content library appears.

2. Tap **Store**.

   The Amazon Appstore for Android appears.

3. Tap the **Search** button at the top of the screen.

4. In the text box that appears, type **print**.

Note: For help using the keyboard, see Chapter 1.

5. From the list that appears, tap **printer apps for Fire tablet**.

   The search results appear.

6. Tap your printer's plug-in. This example uses the Brother iPrint&Scan app.

   The printer plug-in's product page appears.

7. Tap **Free**.

Note: If prompted, tap **Get App**.

   The plug-in downloads and installs.

Note: You might be prompted to agree to an end user licensing agreement.

TIP

How do I print after I have installed the printer plug-in?

The technique varies, depending on your printer. For all printers, make sure your printer is turned on and connected to the network. For any type of printer, you can long-press (press and hold) a photo or a document Ⓐ and, from the menu that appears, tap **Print** Ⓑ.

Table of Contents

Chapter 1 Getting Started

Understanding Fire Tablet Functionality 4
Unbox and Charge the Fire Tablet 6
Create an Amazon Account 8
Examine the Hardware 10
Turn the Tablet On and Off 11
Set Up the Fire Tablet 12
Explore the Tablet Home Screen 18
Understanding the Fire HDX Mayday Feature 19
Navigate a Content Library 20
Using Quick Settings 22
Display Battery Charge Percentage 24
Handle Notifications 26
Using the On-Screen Keyboard 27
Copy and Paste Text 28
Dictate Text 30
Using the User Guide 32

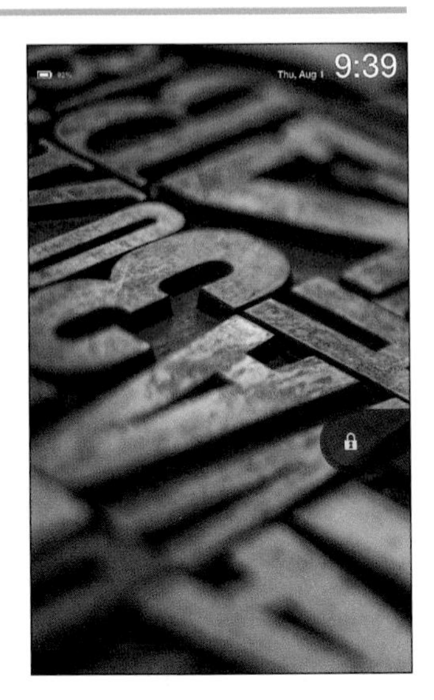

Chapter 2 Shopping for Content

Buy Amazon Coins 36
Shop for Physical Products 38
Shop for Games 40
Shop for Apps 42
Buy Books 44
Buy or Subscribe to Publications 46
Buy Music 48
Buy or Rent Movies 50
Buy Audio Books 52

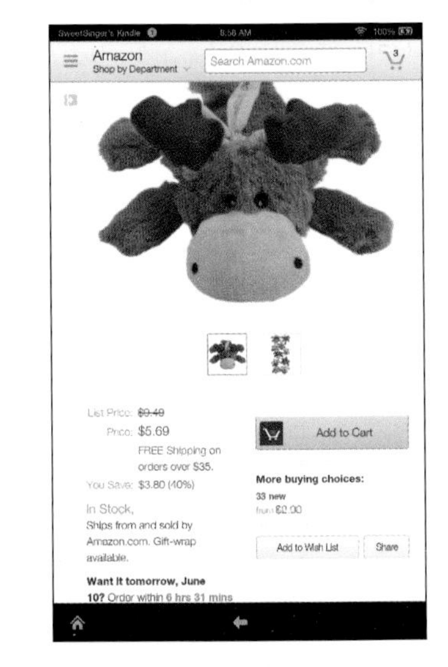

Chapter 3 Working with Apps

Add an App to Favorites.. 56

Remove Fire Tablet Content.................................. 57

Install a Printer Plug-In.. 60

Using Goodreads on the Fire Tablet 62

Set Clocks and Alarms... 64

Using Other Clock Features.................................... 68

Set Up Kindle FreeTime.. 72

Using Kindle FreeTime 78

Explore the IMDb Movies & TV App 80

Find Movie Times and Buy Tickets 82

Read about Celebrities... 84

Examine Yelp 86

Chapter 4 Playing Games, Music, and Movies

Work with Amazon GameCircle 90

Turn Off In-App Purchasing.................................... 92

Listen to Music.. 94

Transfer Music from Your PC 96

Watch a Movie or a TV Show 98

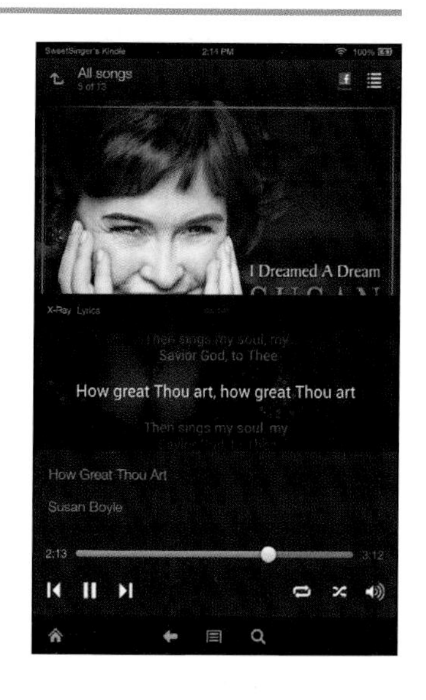

Table of Contents

Chapter 5 Managing Photos and Personal Videos

Upload to Cloud Drive via PC 102
Copy Media from Your PC 106
View Photos or Personal Videos 108
Edit Photos 110
Take Pictures or Videos 112
Delete Photos or Videos 114
Share Photos 116

Chapter 6 Reading Books

Read a Book 120
Change the Reading View 124
Listen to Books with Text-to-Speech 128
Experience Immersion Reading 131
Using X-Ray to Explore a Book 134
Look Up Information While Reading 136
Add, Edit, or Remove Highlights 138
Add, Edit, or Remove Notes 140
Add or Remove Bookmarks 142
Read without Buying 143
Work with Cloud Collections 144

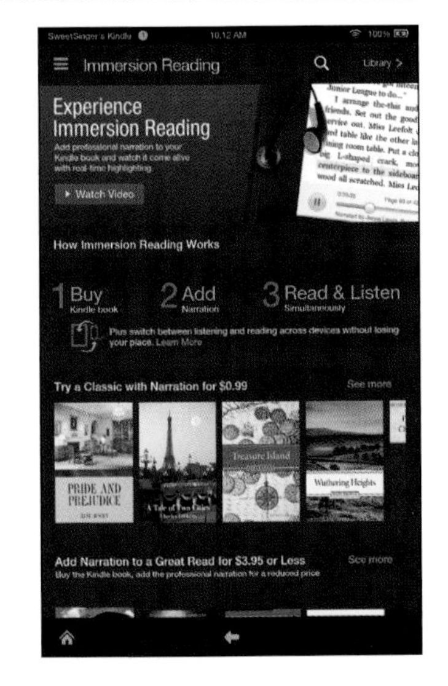

Chapter 7 Reading Magazines and Newspapers

Learn about Subscriptions 150

Manage Magazine or Newspaper Subscriptions 152

Change Privacy Settings for Subscriptions 154

Keep an Issue on Your Device 155

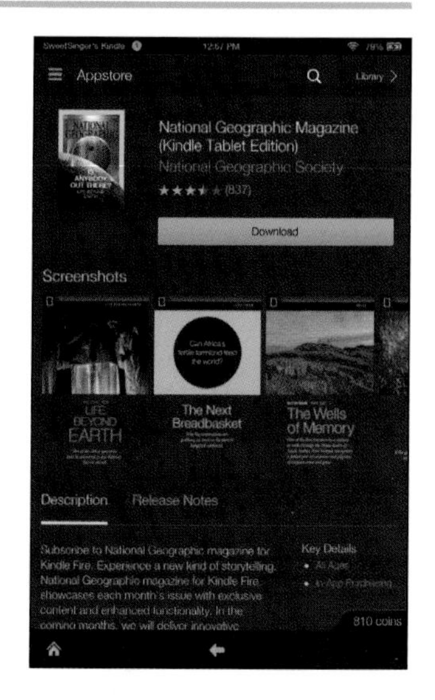

Chapter 8 Working with Email

Set Up an Email Account 158

Set Up an Email Account Manually 160

Explore the Email app 162

Work with Multiple Email Accounts 164

Read a Message 166

Delete Messages 167

Move a Message to Another Folder 168

Search for an Email 170

Manage Messages from the Inbox 171

Create and Send an Email Message 172

Check for New Messages 174

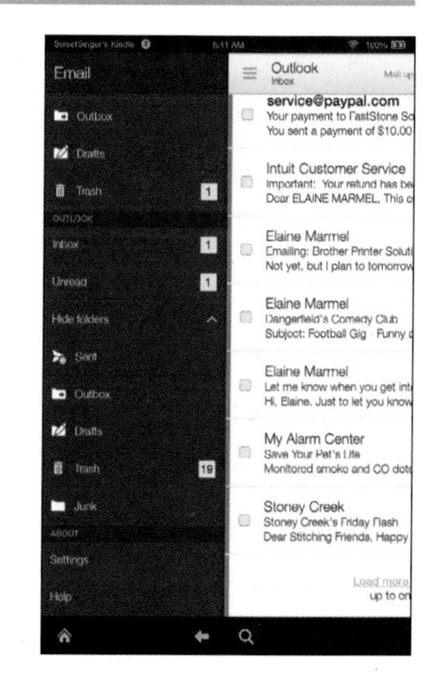

Table of Contents

Forward an Email Message 175
Add an Attachment to an Email 176
Reply to an Email 178
Open an Email Attachment 180
Receive Documents via Email 182
Review General Email Settings 184
Review Settings for Specific Accounts 186

Chapter 9 Maintaining Contacts

Open the Contacts App 190
Set Up Your Contact Profile 192
Add a Contact 194
Add a Contact from an Email Message 196
Import Contacts 198
Edit or Delete a Contact 200
Combine Contacts 202
Search for a Contact 205
Establish Settings for Contacts 206

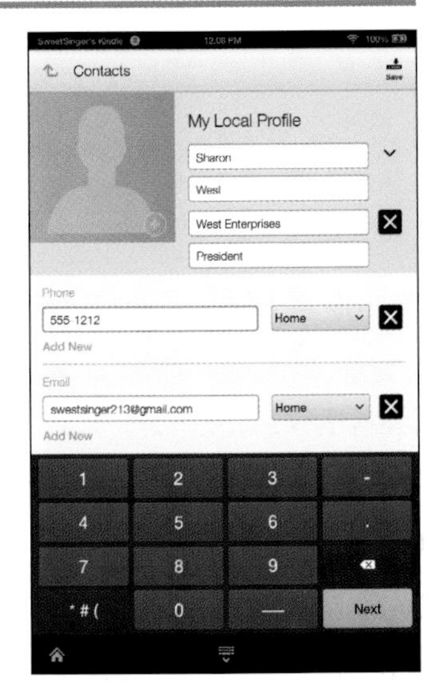

Chapter 10 Using the Calendar

Open the Calendar App 210
Change Calendar Views 212
View or Hide Calendars 214
View an Event 215
Create an Event 216
Edit an Event 218
Include Facebook Events 220

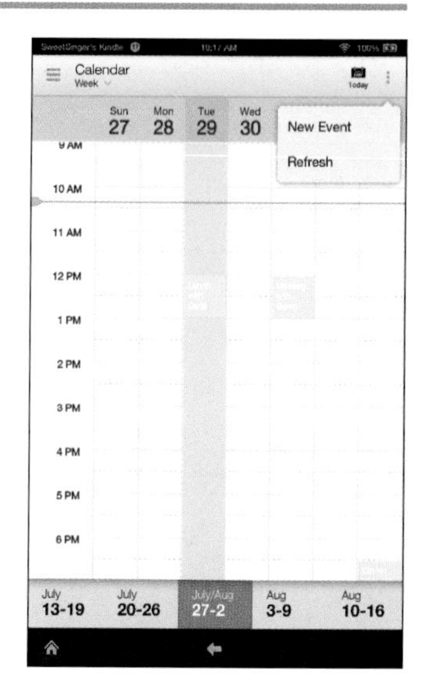

Chapter 11 Going Online

Open Silk 224
Understanding the Silk Screen 225
Open a New Tab 226
Bookmark a Page 227
Navigate Using a Bookmark 228
Using Reading View 229
Request Another View 230
Search a Page 232
Search the Web 234
Set the Default Search Engine 236
View Browsing History 238
Review Silk Settings 239

Table of Contents

Clear Browser Information..240

Download and Open a Document..............................242

Make Phone Calls Using Skype 244

Connect to Social Networks 246

Chapter 12 Customizing Settings

Open Settings 250

Manage Display and Sounds Settings 251

Show or Hide Home Screen Recommendations...........252

Manage Notifications 254

Connect to a Wireless Network 258

Work with a Lock Screen Password..........................260

Check for Software Updates....................................262

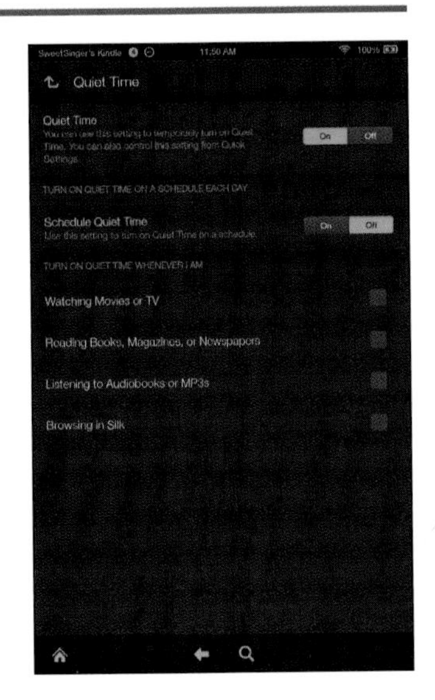

Index... 264

CHAPTER 1

Getting Started

In this chapter, you get started using your Fire tablet. You examine the hardware, review the functionality available on the Fire tablet, and set up and register it to your Amazon account. This chapter also covers basic tasks you need to use your tablet.

Understanding Fire Tablet Functionality 4
Unbox and Charge the Fire Tablet 6
Create an Amazon Account 8
Examine the Hardware 10
Turn the Tablet On and Off 11
Set Up the Fire Tablet 12
Explore the Tablet Home Screen. 18
Understanding the Fire HDX Mayday Feature. 19
Navigate a Content Library 20
Using Quick Settings 22
Display Battery Charge Percentage 24
Handle Notifications 26
Using the On-Screen Keyboard 27
Copy and Paste Text 28
Dictate Text 30
Using the User Guide. 32

Understanding Fire Tablet Functionality

The Fire is a *tablet computer*, which is a mobile device with its display, circuitry, and battery stored in a single device. Tablets in general and the Fire tablet in particular include a camera, microphone, and touchscreen. You use gestures to navigate on a tablet instead of a mouse and keyboard. When you need to type, an on-screen, pop-up virtual keyboard appears. Most people use tablets primarily to play games and view published content such as books, videos, and news. The Fire tablet offers you a variety of functionality.

Device Basics

The Fire tablet comes in two screen sizes, measured diagonally across the viewing area: 7 inch and 8.9 inch. The 7 inch size uses a 2.2 GHz quad-core processor, and the 8.9 inch size uses a 2.5 GHz quad-core processor and both units support a fast and fluid gaming and video experience. Both devices use gorilla glass; the resolution of the 7-inch Fire tablet display is 1920 pixels x 1200 pixels, with a pixel density of 323 pixels per inch (PPI). The resolution of the 8.9-inch Fire tablet is 2560 pixels x 1600 pixels, with a pixel density of 339 PPI.

Weight, Storage, and Battery

The 7-inch Fire tablet weighs approximately 10.7 ounces, and the 8.9-inch model weighs approximately 13.2 ounces. You get almost the same amount of life from the battery for either device: 11 to 12 hours of mixed use and 17 to 18 hours when reading. You use the USB port on the device to charge it.

Each model is available with 16, 32, or 64GB of storage space, but you are not limited to the storage space on the device; you can store up to 5GB of content for free on your Amazon Cloud Drive, with the option to purchase additional storage space.

Sound and Camera

Both devices come with Dolby Audio, dual stereo speakers to which you can attach a 3.5 mm stereo headset, and a built-in microphone. The 7-inch Fire tablet comes with a front-facing camera intended primarily for use on video calls. The 8.9-inch Fire tablet comes with both a front- and a rear-facing camera.

Connectivity

Both Fire tablet devices can connect to any public or private wireless network that uses the 802.11a, 802.11b, 802.11g, or 802.11n standard, and both devices support WEP, WPA, and WPA2 wireless networking security. You can also purchase either model with support for 4G LTE connectivity. If you have added your Fire tablet to your cell phone plan, you can use 4G LTE connectivity when wireless networks are not available; most people use wireless connectivity with their Fire devices.

Software Functionality

Fire tablets come with preinstalled apps that offer a variety of functionality, including the Amazon ereader software you use to read books, and apps for email, calendar functions, tracking contacts, opening and reading documents, playing music, videos, and audiobooks, and browsing the Internet. All these apps are covered in various parts of this book.

If you do not find an app for a function you need, you can visit the Amazon Appstore for Android; many of the apps in the store are free, and others are typically available for a small fee.

Accessibility Features

Fire tablets support a variety of accessibility features to improve the experience of those with vision or hearing impairments. For example, Screen Reader provides spoken feedback that describes actions taking place on your screen; you can even control the speed of Screen Reader. The Explore by Touch feature recognizes five accessibility shortcut gestures to help you navigate on your Fire tablets; this feature also comes with tutorials. Fire tablets also support Braille; you can download the free BrailleBack app from the Amazon Appstore for Android. The Closed Captioning feature enables you to watch Amazon Instant Videos using closed captioning on videos for which closed captioning is available.

Whispersync

Whispersync is a feature that enables you to use the same content on multiple devices. For example, if you buy a book and start reading on your Fire tablet, Whispersync enables you to pick up on your phone where you left off on your Fire tablet. Similarly, you can start watching a movie on the tablet and then pause it and resume watching it on your TV.

Amazon Prime

Fire tablets come with a free, one-month subscription to Amazon Prime. Amazon Prime includes free two-day shipping on millions of items, with overnight shipping for only a few extra dollars. Although Amazon Prime is not available for every item on Amazon, it is available for enough items that you might find it worth the annual cost of $99. In addition to the shortened shipping time, Amazon Prime gives you the ability to stream, for free, thousands of movies and TV shows; Amazon calls them “Prime Instant Videos.” The free month of Amazon Prime begins as soon as you register your Kindle, not from your first purchase using Prime.

Unbox and Charge the Fire Tablet

Before you try to use your Fire tablet, you should charge it. The box containing the Fire tablet also contains an electric power adaptor and a USB cable. The USB cable has a standard USB connector on one end and a micro-B USB connector on the other. The standard USB connector plugs into the electric power adaptor, and the micro-B USB connector plugs into the Fire tablet.

Although you might be eager to start using your Fire tablet, take the time to fully charge the device to get the best battery life from the device.

Unbox and Charge the Fire Tablet

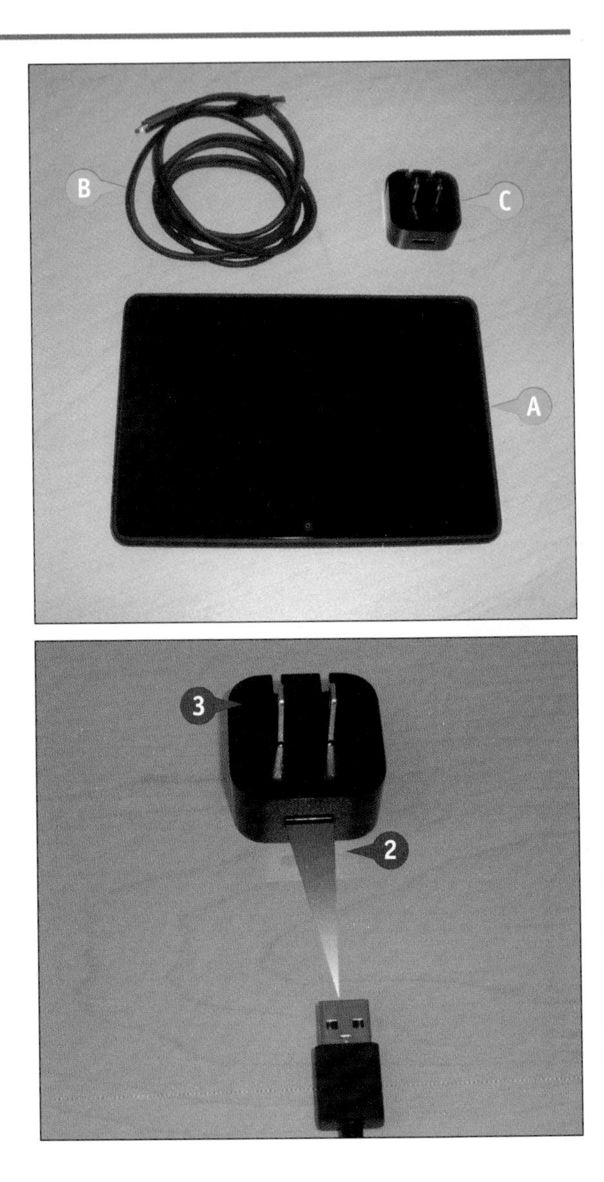

1. Open the box and remove its contents.

   A The Fire tablet looks like this.

   B The box also contains a USB cable.

   C Make sure you see a power adaptor.

2. Connect the USB end of the USB cable to the power adaptor.

Note: Check the orientation of the USB connector and the power adaptor; the USB connector fits into the power adaptor in only one direction.

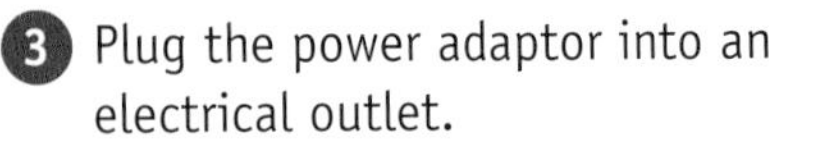

3. Plug the power adaptor into an electrical outlet.

4 Connect the opposite end of the USB cable to the Fire tablet.

Note: The opposite end of the USB cable contains a micro-B USB connector that fits into the tablet in only one direction; the micro-B USB connector appears slanted when connected to your Fire tablet.

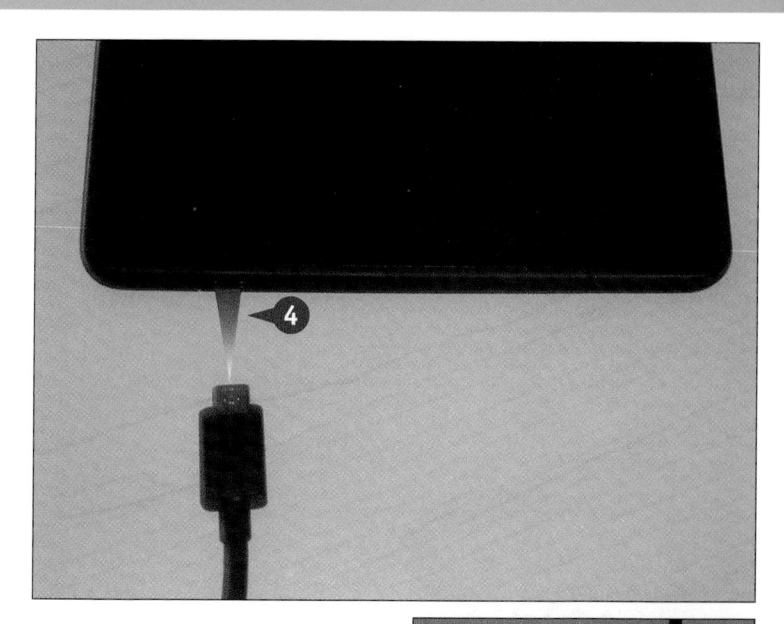

D When the Fire tablet is properly connected to an electrical outlet, the lock screen appears.

E The date and time appear.

F The battery indicator contains a lightning bolt to indicate the device is charging and shows the amount of charge the device currently has.

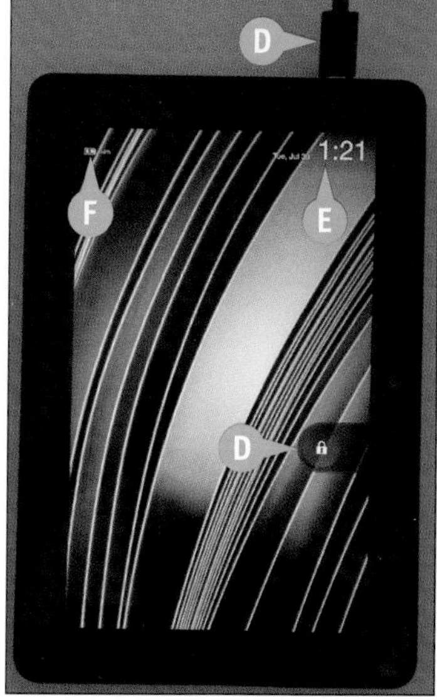

TIP

Can I charge my Fire tablet using any USB cable that has a standard USB connector on one end and a micro-B USB connector on the other?

You can, but Amazon recommends that you use the USB cable that came with your device because using another USB cable could increase the charging time. Also be aware that, whereas you can connect the standard USB cable to your computer and charge the tablet, charging from your computer also increases charging time.

Create an Amazon Account

To use your Fire tablet, you need to set it up and register it, and registering the device involves connecting it to an Amazon.com account. If you already have an account at Amazon.com, you can skip this section. If you do not yet have an Amazon.com account, follow the steps in this section to establish one before you set up the Fire tablet and register it. Although you can register either on your Fire tablet or the Internet, it's easier to see the registration screens on a monitor. For this reason, this section assumes an Internet registration.

In addition, you must set up a payment method for your Amazon account by identifying a credit or debit card you intend to use for Amazon purchases.

Create an Amazon Account

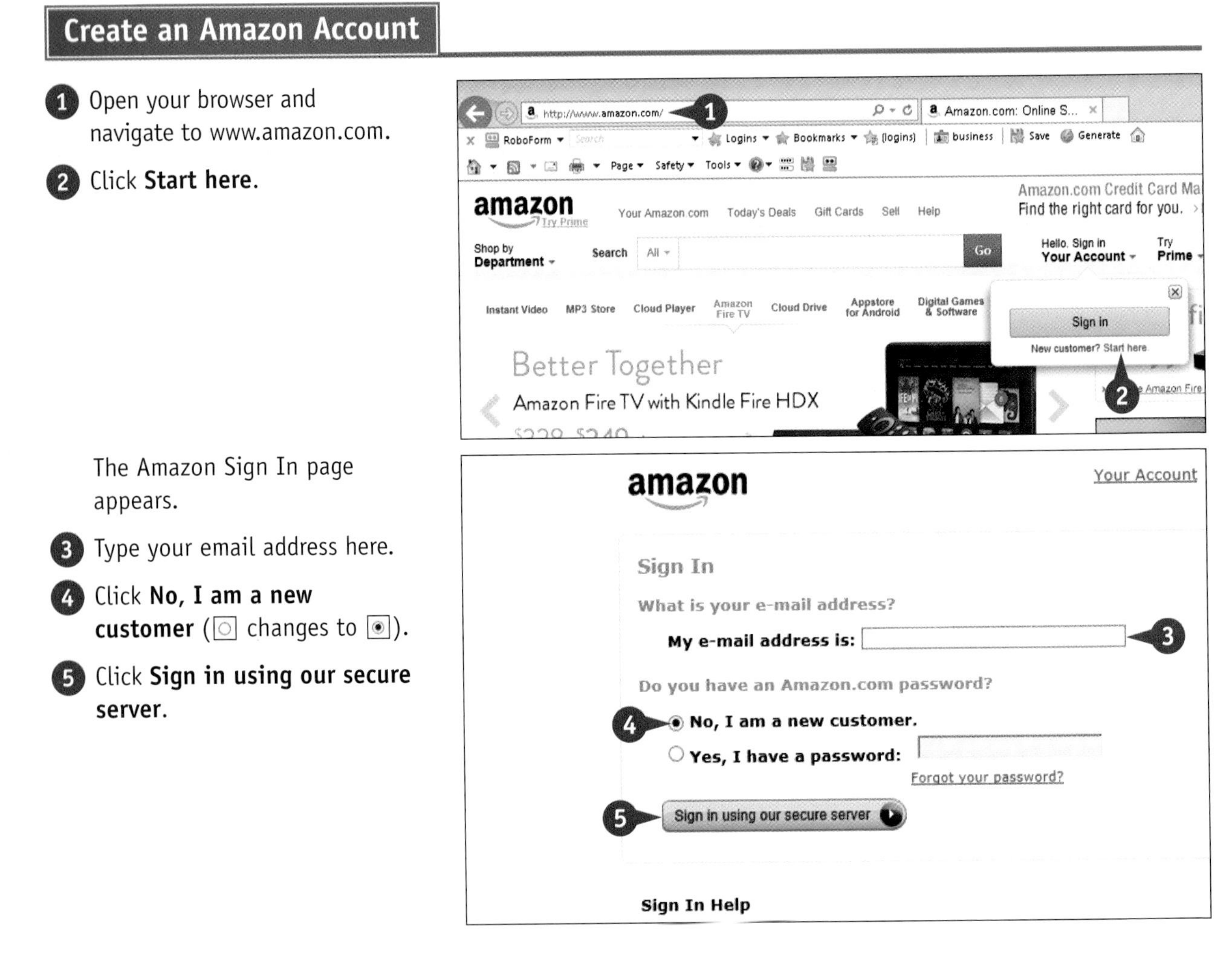

1. Open your browser and navigate to www.amazon.com.
2. Click **Start here**.

The Amazon Sign In page appears.

3. Type your email address here.
4. Click **No, I am a new customer** (○ changes to ◉).
5. Click **Sign in using our secure server.**

The Registration page appears.

6. Type your name.
7. Retype your email address.
8. Type a password.
9. Retype your password.
10. Click **Create account**.

The Amazon home page reappears.

A. You can see that you are signed in to Amazon because the name you supplied while creating your account appears here.

B. When you position the mouse pointer over your name, a menu appears showing you options that help you navigate your Amazon account, orders, content, and more.

C. You can search for things you want to buy by typing here.

D. You can click here to shop Amazon by department.

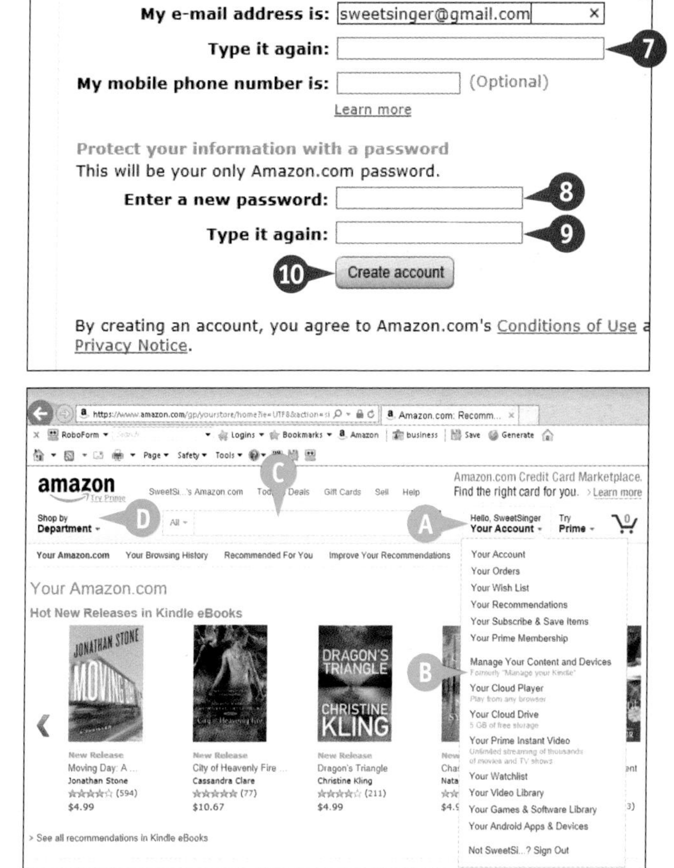

TIP

How do I set up a payment method?

After you click your name to display the Your Account page, click **Add a Credit or Debit Card** (A) and supply the requested information.

Examine the Hardware

You can examine the Fire tablet and identify its controls. The front of the tablet has a highly reflective black surface, and the front-facing camera appears on one of the long sides. On the back of the device, you find the Amazon logo, the volume control buttons, and the Power button.

Periodically, you may want to clean the device's screen; use a soft dry cloth or purchase wipes designed for touchscreens. You might also consider purchasing a case to protect your Fire tablet; some cases also double as stands so that you can read hands-free.

Examine the Hardware

1. Position the device in landscape orientation as you view it from the front.

   A. This is the aperture of the front-facing camera.

   B. The microphone is here.

2. Turn the tablet over so that you can see the back of the device.

3. Position the device in landscape orientation so that you can read the Amazon logo.

   C. This is the Power button; for details on turning the device on and off, see the next section.

   D. You can press these buttons to increase or decrease the volume of audiobooks, music, or videos.

   E. The stereo speakers are here.

   F. You can plug a 3.5-mm stereo headset into the Fire tablet here.

Turn the Tablet On and Off

You can turn the Fire tablet on and off as needed. For example, if you begin to experience slow screen response or the screen freezes, you might want to restart the Fire tablet, which involves shutting it off and then turning it back on.

You can make the tablet go to sleep by locking it, which is similar to putting a laptop computer to sleep. The Fire tablet locks automatically if you do not tap or swipe the screen. You can lock or unlock the Fire tablet by gently pressing the Power button.

Turn the Tablet On and Off

Turn On the Fire Tablet

1. Press and hold the Power button on the back of the Fire tablet for two seconds to display the lock screen.

Note: To find the Power button, see the section "Examine the Hardware."

A. You can swipe here from right to left to unlock the Fire tablet.

Note: The first time you unlock the Fire tablet, the setup process starts. See the section "Set Up the Fire Tablet."

Turn Off the Fire Tablet

1. While the Fire tablet is on, press and hold the Power button.

2. Tap **Power off** to turn off the Fire tablet.

Note: If the Fire tablet screen is frozen, press and hold the Power button for 20 seconds until the screen goes blank. Then, press the Power button again to turn the Tablet back on.

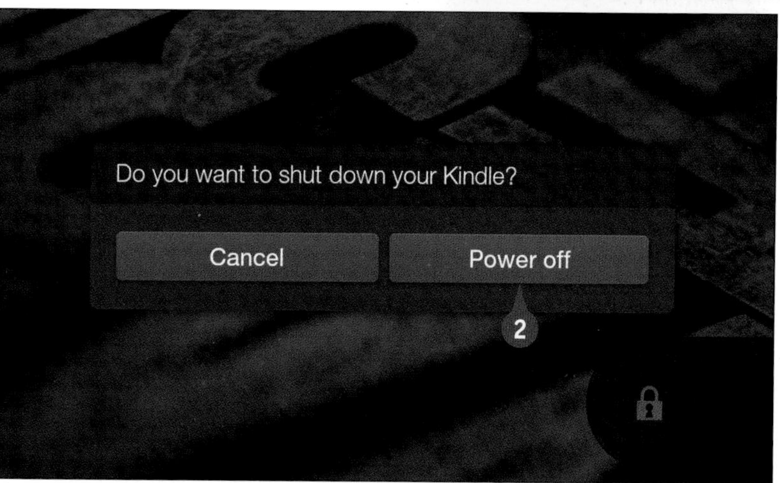

Set Up the Fire Tablet

The first time you turn on your Fire tablet, a series of screens walks you through setting up and registering the device. During this process, you are prompted to choose the language you want to use on your Fire tablet and to connect to your wireless network, for which you need your wireless network name and password.

Although you can connect to your wireless network later, setting up the connection when you set up the device makes using your tablet easier.

Set Up the Fire Tablet

1. Turn on the Fire tablet to display the lock screen.

Note: See the section "Turn the Tablet On and Off" for details.

2. Swipe here from right to left.

Note: Your Fire tablet displays different images each time the lock screen appears.

The first setup screen appears.

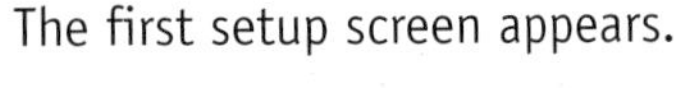

3. Tap your language (■ changes to ☑).

This example uses English (United States).

4. Tap **Next**.

A list of available wireless networks appears.

5 Tap the name of the wireless network to which you want to connect.

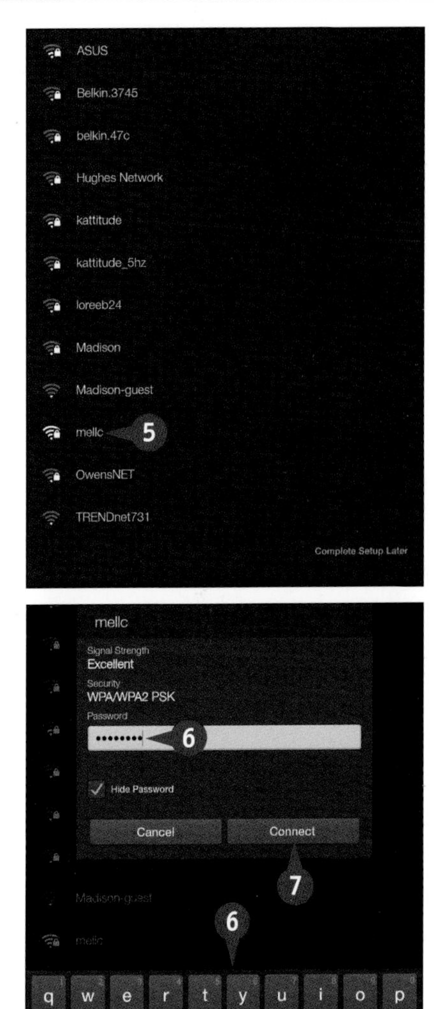

6 Tap keys on the keyboard to enter the password to your wireless network.

A You can type numbers or symbols by tapping **?123**. ?123 changes to ABC, which you tap to switch back to letters.

7 Tap **Connect**.

TIP

Where do I find the name of and password for my wireless network?

The name of and password for the wireless network were established when you installed your wireless router. If someone installed your router for you, he probably handed you a piece of paper and said, "Do not lose this." If you do not know the information associated with your wireless network, you can visit the site of your router's manufacturer and download the router's manual for directions on resetting the router to its factory settings; then you can establish a new name and password for your wireless network.

continued ►

When you register a Fire tablet, you connect it to an Amazon account. Connecting a Fire tablet to an Amazon account is simple; when prompted, you supply the email address and password associated with the account.

Also during the setup process, you are prompted to connect to the Facebook, Twitter, and Goodreads social networks. If you have accounts with these social networks and want to connect your tablet to these accounts, you can supply the information during setup or you can connect to these accounts at any time as described in Chapter 11.

Set Up the Fire Tablet (continued)

The Register Your Kindle screen appears.

8. Type the email address you use for your Amazon account.
9. Type the password you use for your Amazon account.
10. Tap **Register**.

Note: If you do not have an Amazon account and did not create one as described in the section "Create an Amazon Account," you can tap **Create Account** and follow the on-screen prompts.

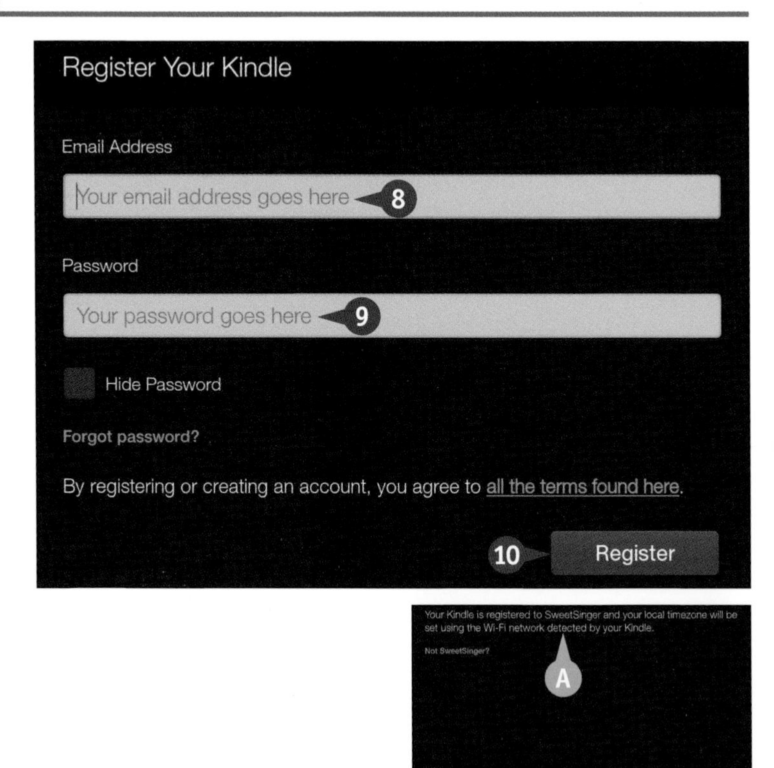

A. Amazon completes the registration process and asks you to confirm your account.

11. Tap **Next**.

The Connect Social Networks page appears.

B You can tap any arrow (>) beside a social network to set up the account.

Note: You can set up social network connections at any time; see Chapter 11.

12 For this example, tap **Next** without setting up social network connections.

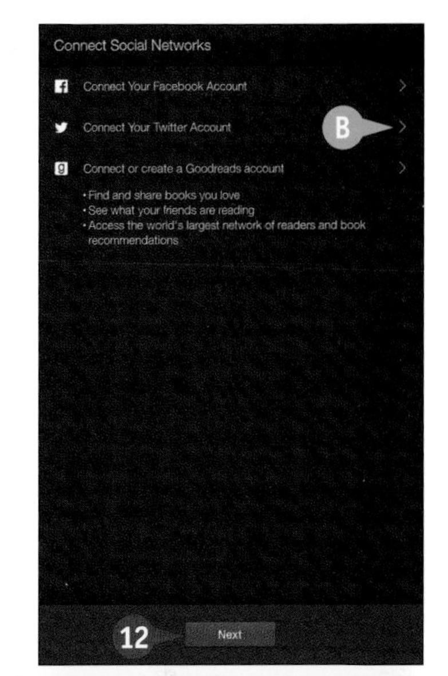

A short tutorial begins to show you how to navigate around your Fire tablet.

 Tap **Get Started**.

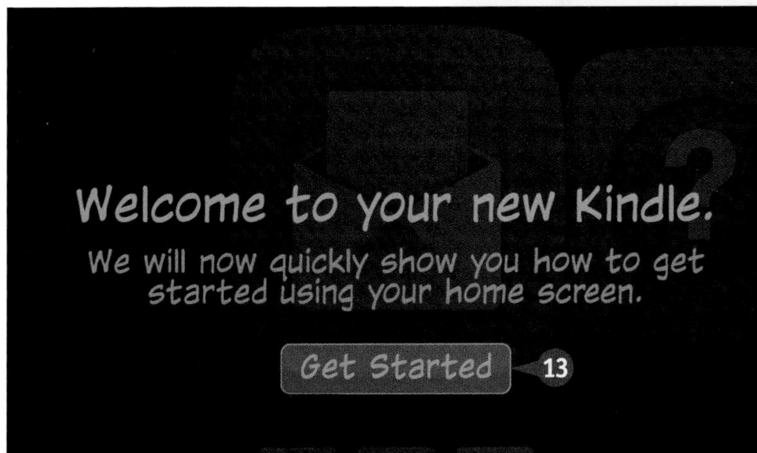

TIP

Why do I have to register my Fire tablet to an Amazon account?
Amazon stores the content you purchase to use on your Fire tablet on its cloud servers; when you want to use some of that content, you download it. That way, you store only content you need at a given point in time and do not fill up your Fire tablet. Amazon uses your account to keep track of your content and to associate your content with any of several Amazon devices. You are not limited to associate only one device with one Amazon account.

continued ►

After you have supplied all the information needed to set up and register your Fire tablet, Amazon provides a brief tutorial that shows you how to navigate on the Fire tablet Home screen. The tutorial is just a few steps and focuses on showing how you can swipe up, down, left, and right on the Home screen. Once you complete the tutorial, your Home screen appears and you are ready to start using your Fire tablet.

For more information on the Home screen, see the section "Explore the Tablet Home Screen."

Set Up the Fire Tablet (continued)

14 Swipe left following the tutorial arrow to view recently used apps, books, and other items in your Carousel.

Note: See the section "Explore the Kindle Home Screen" for more information.

15 Swipe up following the tutorial arrow to view your Favorites.

Note: See Chapter 3 for details on adding to the Favorites section.

14
Swipe left
To view recently used items and recommendations.
Swipe up
To see your apps and favorite content.
15
Silk

 Swipe down following the tutorial arrow to redisplay recently used items and your Carousel.

The tutorial ends.

17 Tap **Finish**.

The Home screen of your Fire tablet appears. See the section "Explore the Tablet Home Screen" for more information.

TIP

What is the Carousel?

The Carousel appears on the Home screen and contains images that represent recently used content such as books you have opened, games you have played, and music you have listened to. If you check email on your Fire tablet, the Email app appears in the Carousel. You can swipe left or right to view the items in the Carousel, and you can tap any item to reopen it. The Fire tablet stores images in the Carousel chronologically, with the item you used most recently appearing on top.

Explore the Tablet Home Screen

The Home screen appears the first time you start your Fire tablet, and you can return to it whenever you want. The Home screen contains information you can use to navigate around your Fire tablet as well as status and other helpful information.

A Status Bar

Contains useful information about your Fire tablet. The name of your device appears at the left edge of the Status bar, and the current time appears in the center. At the right edge, you see symbols that represent, for example, that your device is connected wirelessly to the Internet as well as the level of the device's battery charge.

B Navigation Bar

Runs across the top of the Fire tablet, just below the Status bar, and contains links to various content libraries, which are described in the section "Navigate a Content Library."

C Carousel

The Carousel runs across the center of the screen and contains images that represent recently viewed books, games, music, videos, and other digital content. The item you viewed most recently appears at the left edge of the Carousel. Swipe from right to left to review Carousel items and tap any item to open it. You can remove any item from the Carousel — without removing it from the Fire tablet — by pressing and holding the item and then tapping **Remove from Carousel** from the menu that appears.

D Recommendations

When you hold your Fire tablet in portrait orientation, recommendations appear beneath the Carousel. The recommendations you see are based on content you view and purchase, and they change as you use your Fire tablet. You can hide recommendations; see Chapter 12 for details.

E Favorites

The Favorites section appears at the bottom of the Home screen and contains links to commonly used apps, books, music, videos, and other content. You can add items to and remove items from the Favorites section; see Chapter 3 for details.

Understanding the Fire HDX Mayday Feature

Using the Mayday feature and a wireless connection, you can directly connect to an Amazon Tech advisor to get assistance on using any Kindle feature. Note that the Mayday feature is only available with the Fire HDX.

Availability and Requirements

Mayday is free service and available 24-7, 365 days a year. Most calls are answered within 15 seconds. To use the service, your Fire HDX must be registered to an Amazon account and have an active, strong Wi-Fi connection so that your Amazon Tech advisor can access your device and help you.

Start a Session

To start, from Quick Settings on your Fire HDX (see the section "Using Quick Settings"), tap **Mayday**. On the Mayday screen, tap **Connect**; a small window appears in the lower-right corner of the Home page screen indicating your Fire HDX is connecting to the cloud. Then, your Amazon Tech advisor appears in the window.

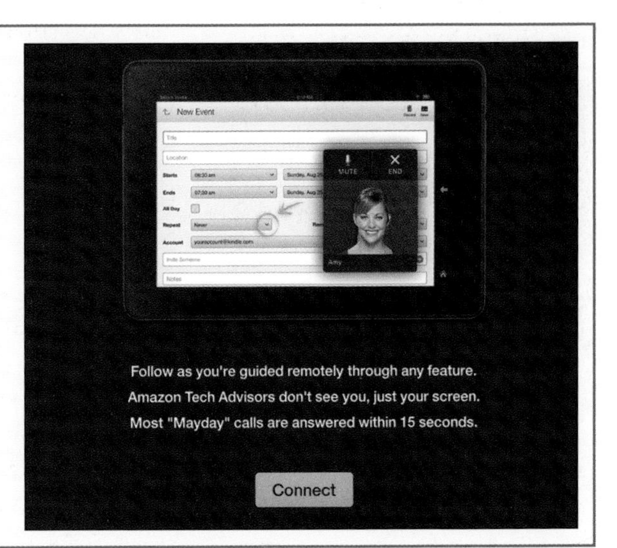
New Event
MUTE
END
Follow as you're guided remotely through any feature.
Amazon Tech Advisors don't see you, just your screen.
Most "Mayday" calls are answered within 15 seconds.
Connect

Mayday Facts

You cannot get help registering a device because Mayday works only with already-registered devices. Also, you can see the Amazon Tech advisor, but the advisor sees only what appears on your screen, so she can draw on your screen to illustrate how to complete various tasks. At this time, Amazon provides support in English for customers in the U.S. and the U.K. The quality of the Mayday feature depends on the wireless connection's signal strength, which is secure because it uses industry-standard authentication and encryption.

Disable Mayday

To disable the Mayday feature, open Quick Settings as described in the section "Using Quick Settings" and then tap **Mayday**. Display the Mayday Navigation panel by swiping to the right from the left edge of the screen. In the Navigation panel, tap **Settings**. On the Mayday Settings screen, tap **Off**.

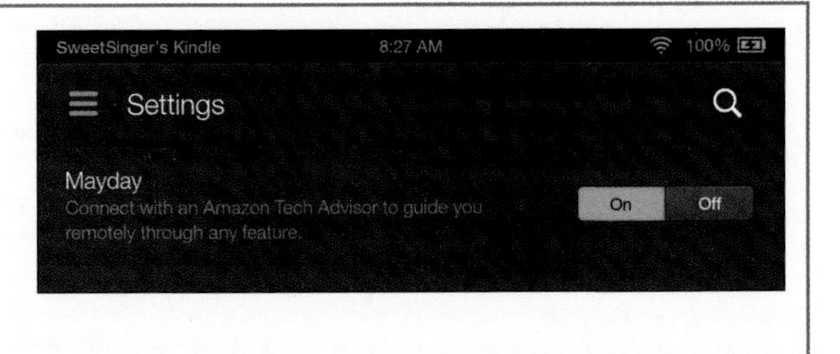
SweetSinger's Kindle
8:27 AM
100%
Settings
Mayday
Connect with an Amazon Tech Advisor to guide you remotely through any feature.
On
Off

Fire tablets use *content libraries* to organize the information stored on your device. You can think of these as folders that contain a category of information. When you tap a content library, the tablet opens it and displays its content as well as tools you need to navigate the content library.

To switch to a different content library, you can return to the Home screen. Or, if the content you want to use appears in the Carousel, you can switch to the content directly without switching back to the Home screen.

Navigate a Content Library

Opening a Library

1. From the Home screen, tap a content library.

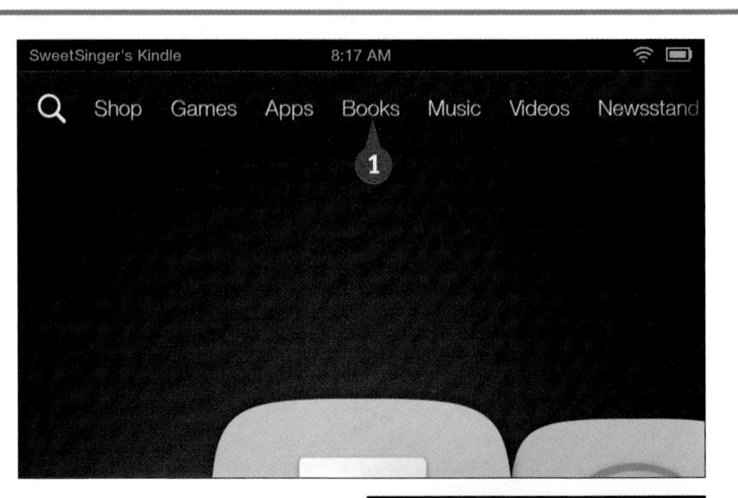

The selected content library appears.

- A You can use the content library's Options bar to navigate.

Note: In landscape orientation, the Options bar appears on the right side of the screen.

- B You review available content by swiping from right to left or from the bottom of the screen to the top.
- C You can search a library by tapping the **Search** button (🔍). A keyboard appears on-screen. See the section "Using the On-Screen Keyboard" for details.
- D Once you purchase and download content, Cloud and On Device appear here, so that you can view content stored in the cloud and content stored on the device.

2. Tap the **Navigation** button (☰).

Ⓔ The content library's Navigation panel appears.

Note: You can use the Navigation panel to view selections for purchasing and accessing content.

Note: The choices in the Navigation panel vary, depending on the content library you are viewing.

3. Tap the **Navigation** button ( ) to close the panel.

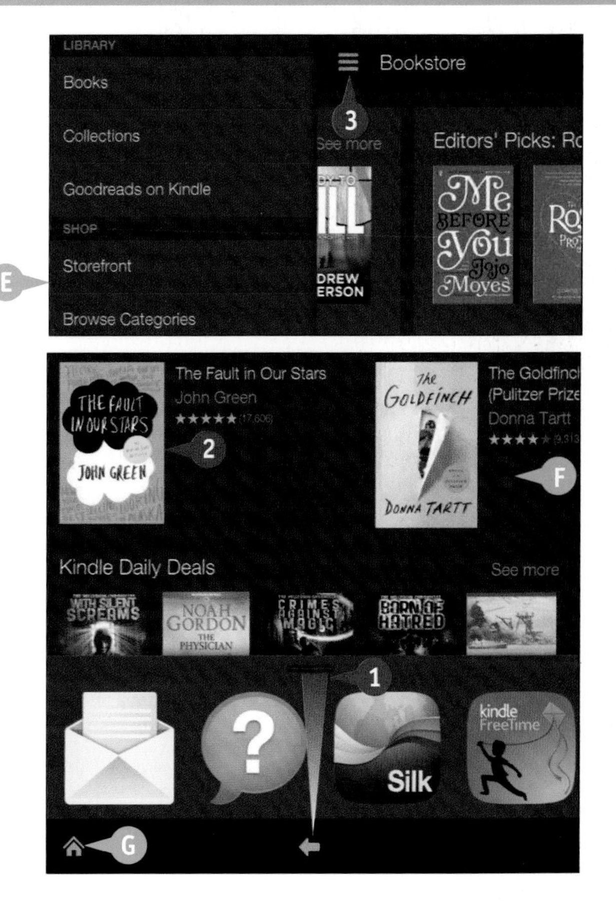

Switch to Other Content

1. Swipe up from the **Back** arrow ( ).

Note: If you are viewing the Fire tablet in landscape orientation, swipe the Back arrow in the Options bar from right to left.

Ⓕ The Carousel appears.

2. Scroll and tap any item.

Ⓖ To redisplay the Home screen, tap the **Home** button ( ).

TIP

What buttons can I expect to see in the Options bar?

The buttons change, depending on what you are viewing. The table shows the most common buttons ones.

Button	Purpose
	Displays the Home screen.
	Displays the previous screen you viewed.
	Appears with the on-screen keyboard; tap it to close the keyboard.
	Displays a search text box at the top of some content libraries.
	Tapping this button opens a menu of choices.
	Navigates to the previously viewed page in the Silk browser app.
	Navigates to the next page in the Silk browser app.
	Displays a Silk browser web page in full-screen mode.
	Tap to exit full-screen mode in the Silk browser and redisplay the Options bar.

Using Quick Settings

Using Quick Settings, you can configure commonly used settings. You can control the Fire tablet's rotation and screen brightness as well as switch to Airplane mode, which stops your Fire tablet from searching for available wireless networks. You also can turn on Quiet Time, which stops notifications to your device, during the night or when you need to concentrate. You schedule Quiet Time from the Notifications & Quiet Time settings menu; see Chapter 12 for details. You turn on Quiet Time from Quick Settings, as shown in this section.

Using Quick Settings

1. Swipe down from the top of the Fire tablet.

   The Quick Settings panel appears.

2. Tap **Auto-Rotate**.

- A The Fire tablet is locked in the current position and does not rotate if you physically change the device's orientation.

  You can tap Auto-Rotate again to unlock the device's rotation.

3. Tap **Brightness**.

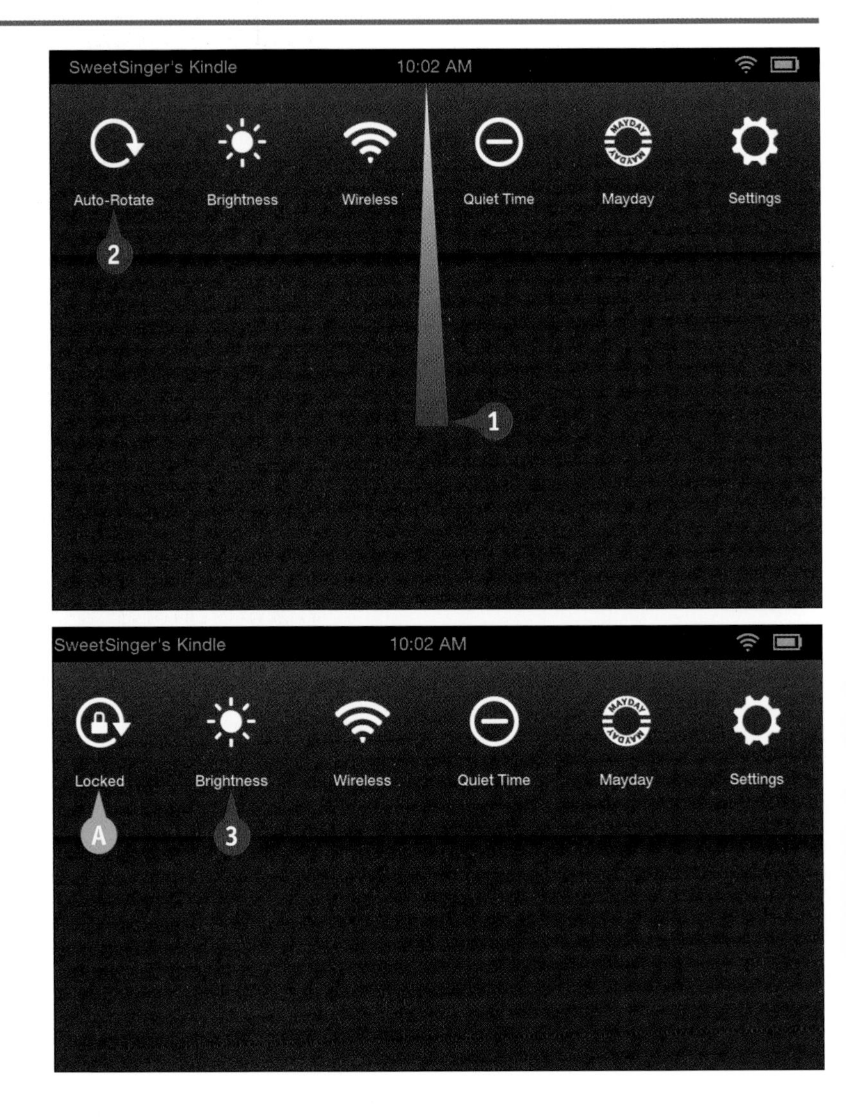

The Brightness controls appear.

B You can drag the slider or tap **On** or **Off** to control Auto-Brightness.

4 Tap **Brightness** again to hide the Brightness controls.

C You can tap **Quiet Time** to engage quiet time. A symbol like the Quiet Time symbol appears in the Status bar. Tap **Quiet Time** again to disengage it.

5 Tap **Wireless**.

The Wireless settings page appears.

D You can tap **On** to set the device to Airplane mode.

E You can tap ▶ to connect to a different wireless network; see Chapter 12 for details.

F You can tap the Location-Based Services button to **On** to show your location via Wi-Fi.

You can tap the **Home** button (🏠) at the bottom of the screen to redisplay the Home screen.

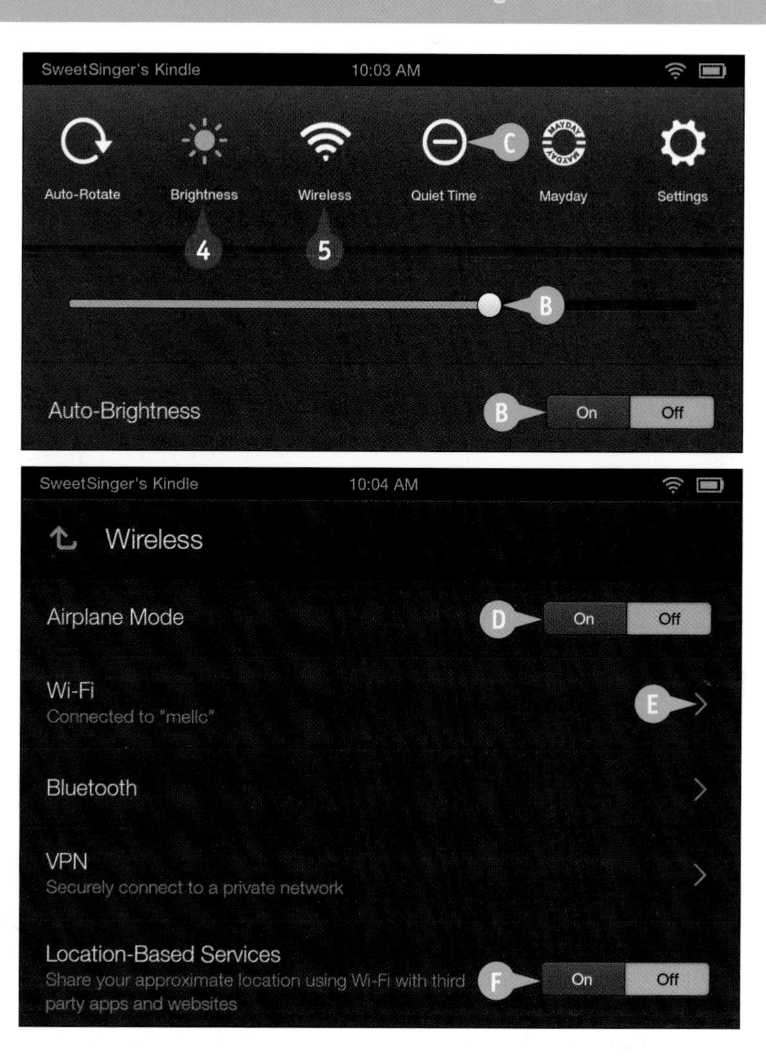

TIP

When would I turn on Bluetooth?

You turn on Bluetooth if, for example, you want to pair a Bluetooth headset to your Fire tablet so that you can listen to music or an audiobook via your Bluetooth headset. With Bluetooth activated, you can tap an option to pair a Bluetooth device, which then opens on-screen directions that both show the device is turned on and help you find other Bluetooth-enabled devices. You can then scan for the device and choose it from the list that the Fire tablet finds.

Display Battery Charge Percentage

By default, a battery icon appears at the right edge of the Status bar; this icon gives a visual representation of the remaining battery charge for your device. You can, in addition, display this amount as a percentage. Displaying a percentage amount gives you a more specific idea of the remaining battery charge.

You get approximately 11 hours of mixed use and 17 hours of reading from the battery on the 7-inch Fire tablet. On the 8.9-inch Fire tablet, you get 12 hours of mixed use and 18 hours when reading.

Display Battery Charge Percentage

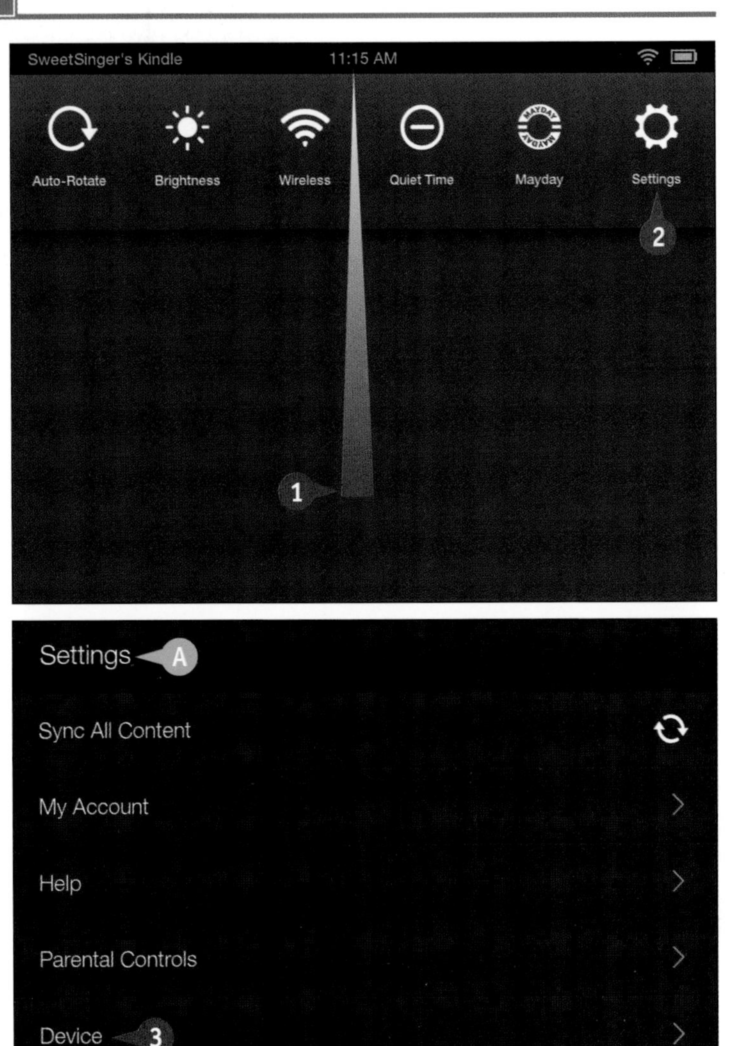

1. Swipe down from the top of the screen to open Quick Settings.
2. Tap **Settings**.

A The Settings menu appears.

3. Tap **Device**.

(B) The Device menu appears.

4. Tap the **Show Battery Percentage in Status Bar** button to **On**.

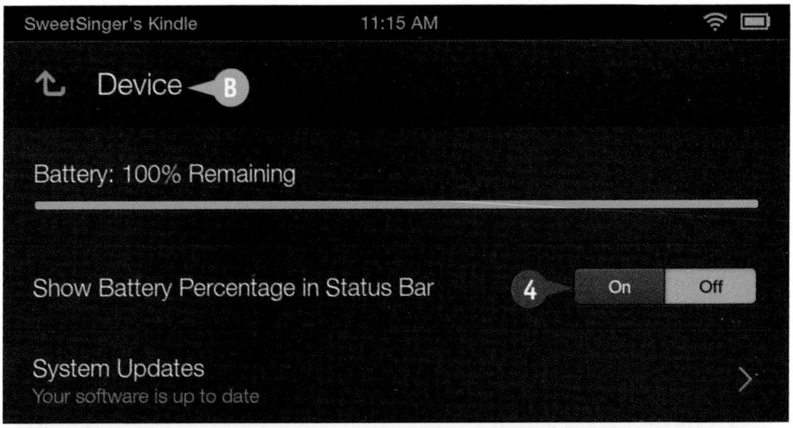

(C) The percentage of remaining charge for the battery appears in the Status bar.

You can tap the **Home** button (🏠) at the bottom of the screen to redisplay the Home screen.

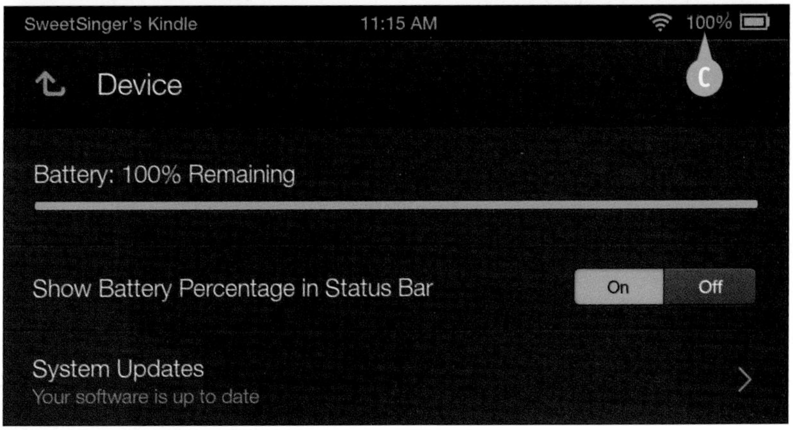

SweetSinger's Kindle 11:15 AM
Device
Battery: 100% Remaining
Show Battery Percentage in Status Bar On Off
System Updates
Your software is up to date

SweetSinger's Kindle 11:15 AM 100%
Device
Battery: 100% Remaining
Show Battery Percentage in Status Bar On Off
System Updates
Your software is up to date

TIP

Is there a way to conserve battery life?

Yes, there are several settings you can adjust. For example, you can use Quick Settings to disable notification alerts, lower screen brightness, and turn off wireless networking. While watching a video or listening to music or an audiobook, you can use headphones to avoid broadcasting through the tablet's speakers. And, if you set up email, you can reduce the frequency with which the Email app checks for new mail. See Chapter 8 for details on working with the Email app on your Fire tablet.

Handle Notifications

Periodically, notifications appear; you might hear a sound or just visually observe the Notifications icon in the Status bar at the top of the Fire tablet screen. Notifications appear when you, for example, download an app or when Amazon has a system update for your Fire tablet. You can review the notifications from the Quick Settings panel and interact with them either individually or as a group.

You can control the behavior of any program's notifications from the Notifications & Quiet Time settings screen; see Chapter 12 for details.

Handle Notifications

A This symbol appears when you have notifications and indicates the number of notifications you have.

1 Swipe down from the top of the Fire tablet.

The Quick Settings panel appears (see the section "Using Quick Settings" for details).

B Notifications appear here, below the Quick Settings buttons.

Note: You can tap and hold any notification to interact with it.

Note: You can swipe any individual notification from left to right to dismiss it.

2 Tap **Clear All**.

All notifications disappear.

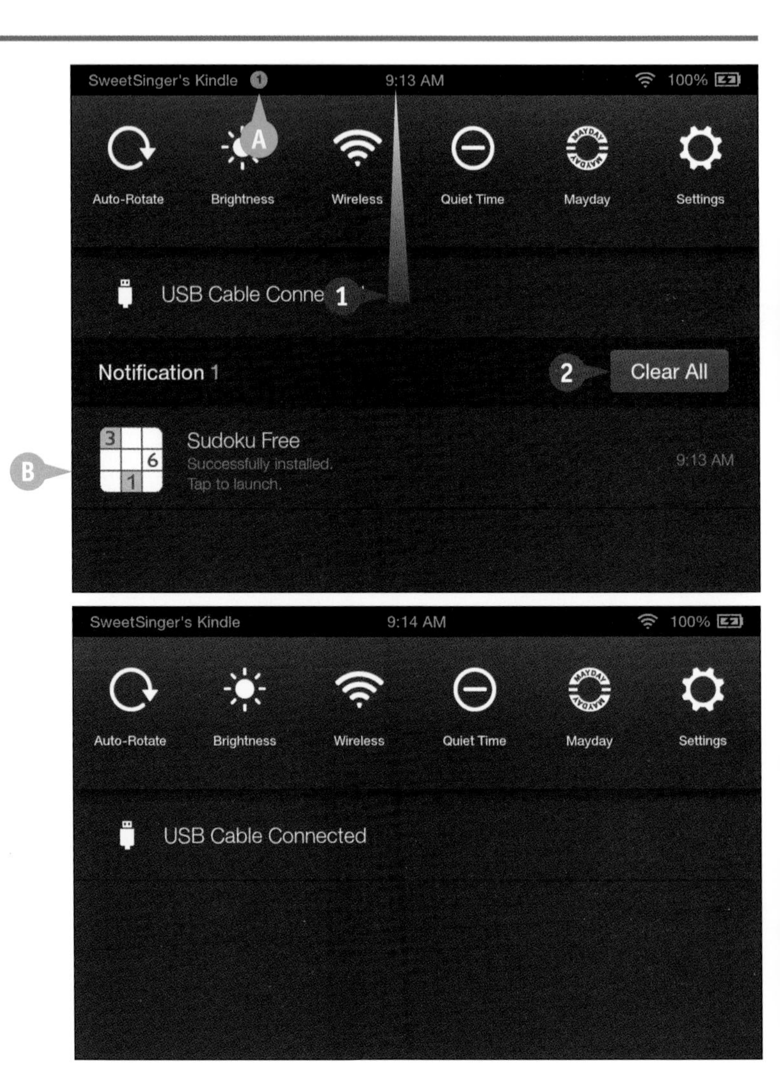

Using the On-Screen Keyboard

Some features on your Fire tablet enable you to use an on-screen, virtual keyboard from which you can enter text and numbers. Some keys also contain alternate characters, which you can access by tapping and holding over a character until a panel of choices appears. As you type, the tablet suggests words for you.

You can change the location where you are typing, or correct a mistake, by tapping in the text. You can then location-drag the marker to the position where you want to type.

Using the On-Screen Keyboard

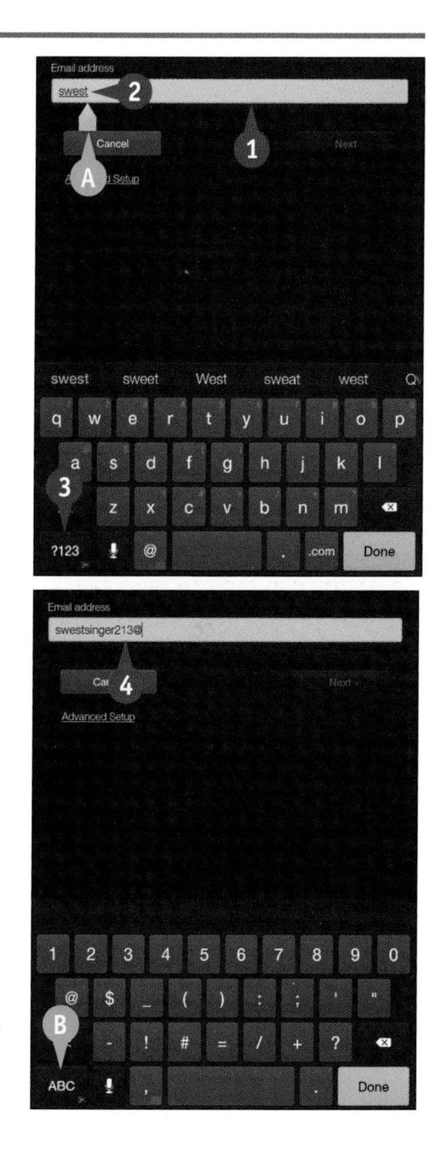

1. Tap in any text field to display the on-screen keyboard.
2. Type text.

Ⓐ If you tap again in the text field, the insertion point marker (■) appears, which you can drag to a new position.

Note: To type an alternative character, tap and hold the main character; when the panel of choices appears, you can tap the one you want.

As you type, suggestions appear; you can tap any suggestion to use it.

3. Tap **?123**.

The number pad for the on-screen keyboard appears.

4. Type numbers or symbols as needed.

Ⓑ You can tap **ABC** to redisplay letters on the keyboard.

You can tap the **Keyboard** button (⌨) at the bottom of the screen to hide the keyboard.

Copy and Paste Text

As you edit your writing, you might find that you need to cut or copy text to either move it to a different location or to duplicate it.

Whatever text you cut or copy is temporarily stored on the *clipboard*, an invisible holding area. You can paste the text on the clipboard as many times as you want; the copied text remains there until you cut or copy other text.

Copy and Paste Text

1 Type text in a text field.

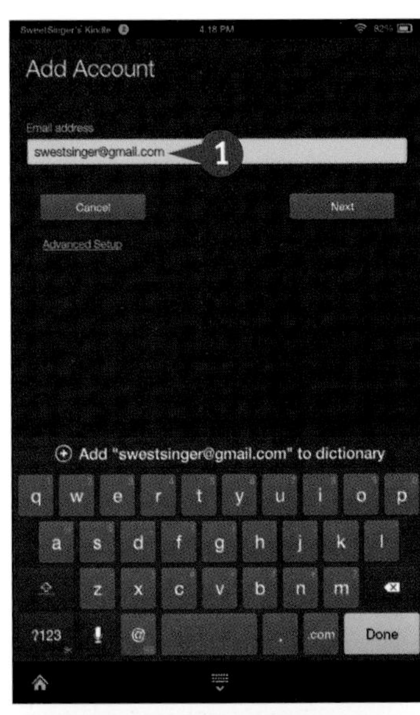

2 Tap and hold the text to select all the text in the field.

A toolbar appears.

A You can drag either of these markers to change the selection.

3 Tap **Cut** to remove the text or **Copy** to duplicate it; for this example, tap **Cut**.

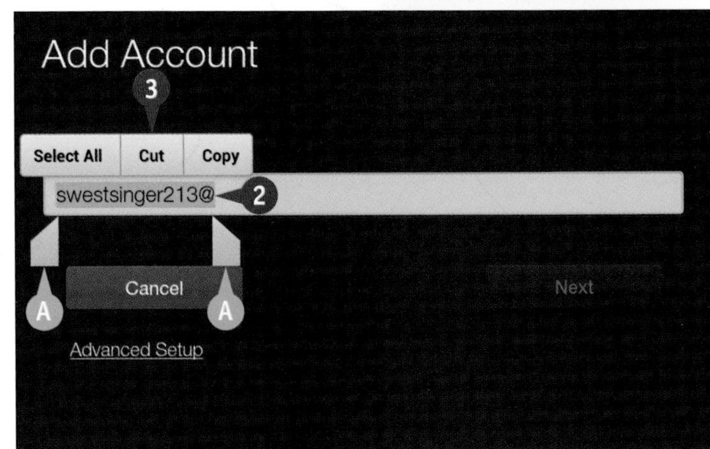

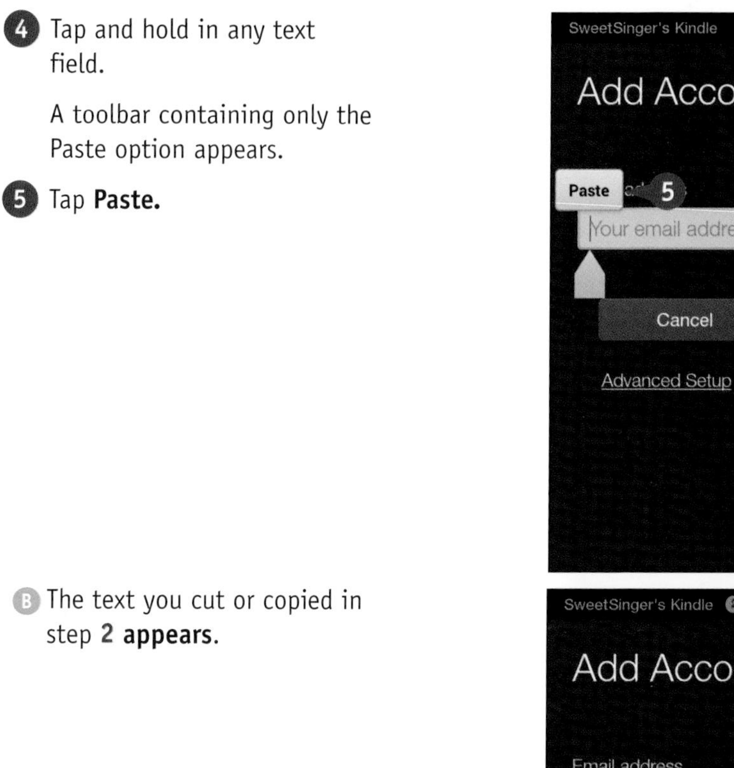

4. Tap and hold in any text field.

   A toolbar containing only the Paste option appears.

5. Tap **Paste.**

B. The text you cut or copied in step **2 appears**.

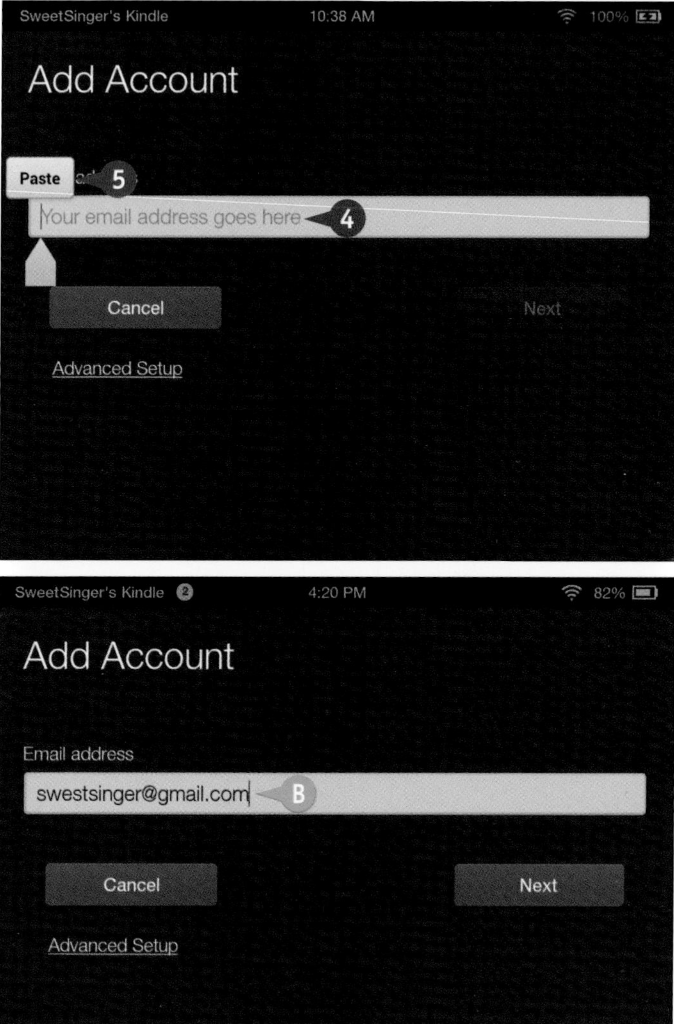

TIP

Can I cut or copy more than one selection to the clipboard?

The clipboard holds only one selection of cut or copied text. You can select several paragraphs and cut or copy them to the clipboard, but, to store all the text in those paragraphs on the clipboard, you must select all of them and then cut or copy. If you select one paragraph and cut or copy it and then select another paragraph and cut or copy it, the second selection overwrites the first selection on the clipboard.

Dictate Text

In any app that uses text fields and a keyboard, you can record text instead of typing it. For example, you can dictate an email message, a calendar event, and even contact information. Be aware that the Fire tablet's voice recognition software is fairly accurate at recognizing common words, but it does not do as well with unusual names. If you opt to record, you activate a dictation service in the cloud that transcribes what you say and displays it on your Fire tablet.

Dictate Text

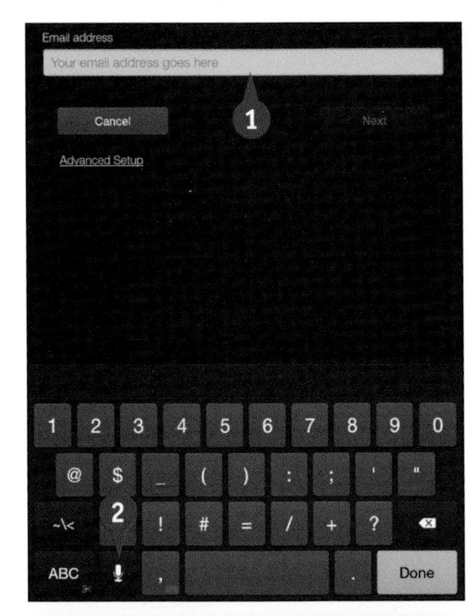

1. Tap in any text field.

   The keyboard appears.

2. Tap the **Microphone** button (🎤) to start recording text.

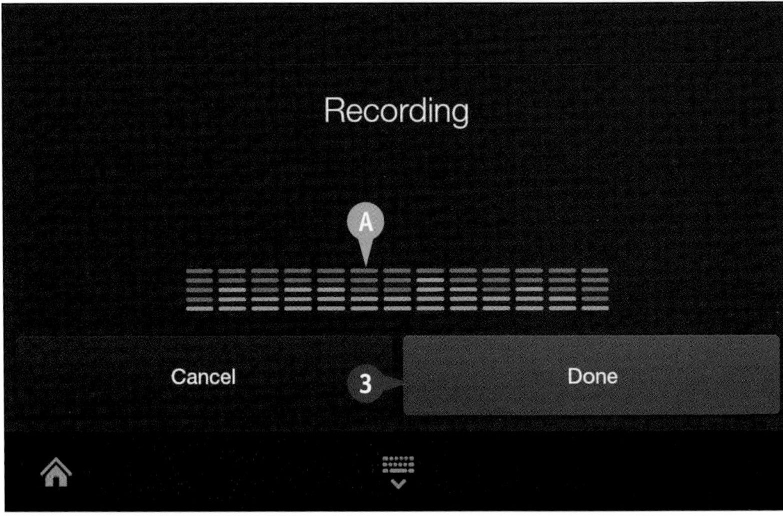

- A As you record, you see a recording level meter on-screen.

3. Tap **Done** when you finish speaking.

The cloud dictation service processes your speech.

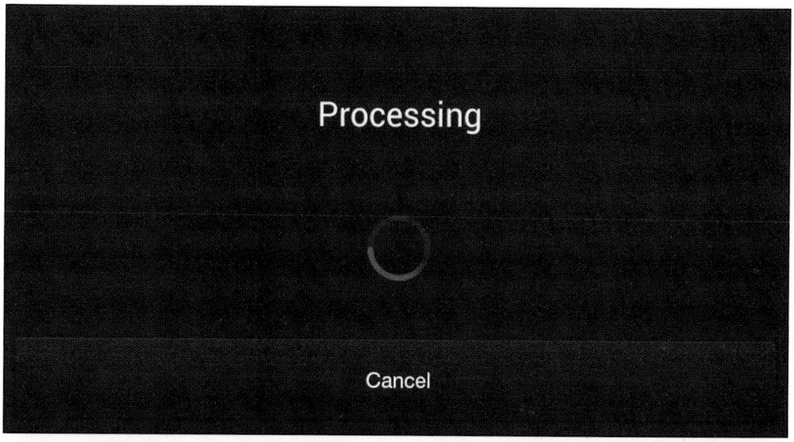

B When processing finishes, the text you recorded appears in the field and the on-screen keyboard reappears.

You can tap the **Keyboard** button (⌨) at the bottom of the screen to hide the keyboard.

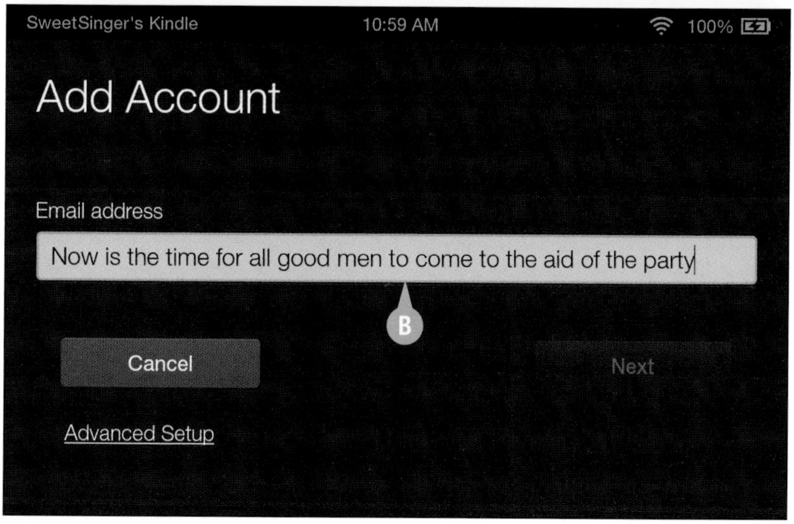

TIP

How do I handle punctuation marks while dictating?

As you speak, you can include common punctuation, such as a comma (,), period (.), exclamation point (!), ampersand (&), at sign (@), and more. Just say the name of the punctuation mark at the point in the dictation where you want the punctuation mark to appear; when you finish dictating, the punctuation appears in the correct location.

Using the User Guide

You can get help using your Fire tablet in a variety of ways. As discussed in the section "Understanding Fire HDX the Mayday Feature," you can contact an Amazon Tech advisor who can connect to your Fire HDX device to assist you.

If you prefer to try to find answers on your own, you can use the onboard user guide that comes with all Fire tablets. You can search through the guide, or you can view topics as listed in its table of contents.

Using the User Guide

1. From the Favorites section on the Home screen, tap **Help**.
2. On the screen that appears, tap **User Guide**.

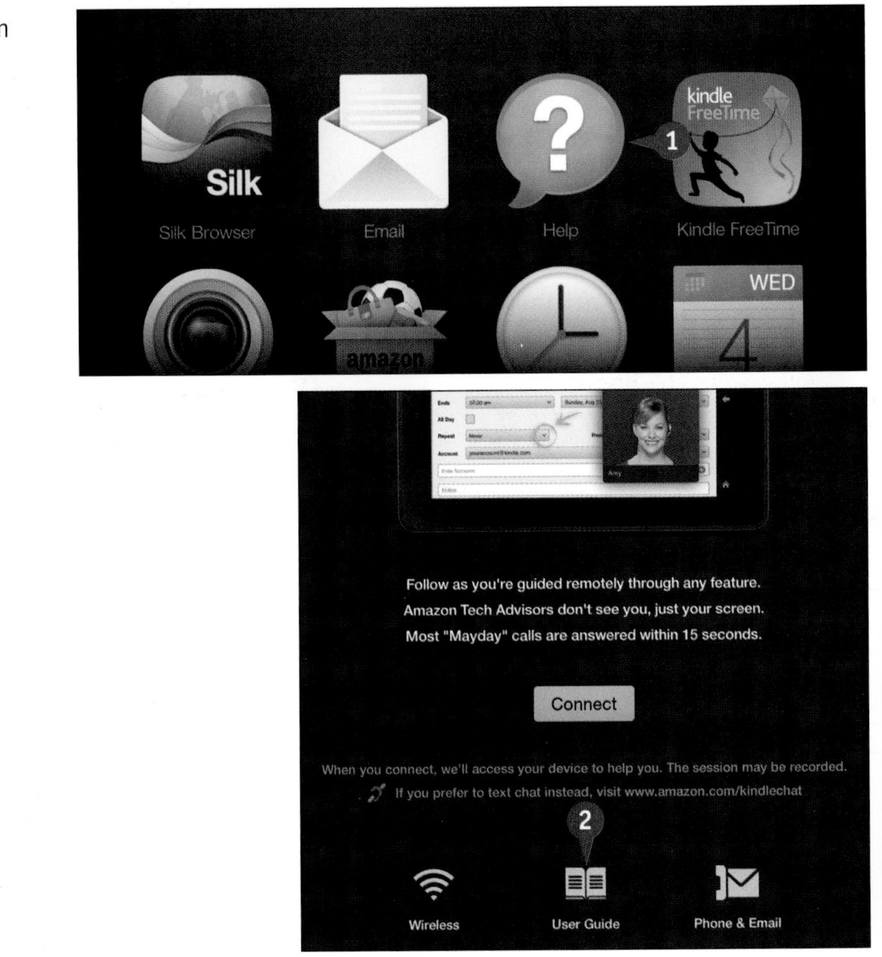

The table of contents of the onboard user guide appears.

Ⓐ You can tap the **Search** button (🔍) and type to search for a topic.

❸ Tap any topic to display its associated subtopics.

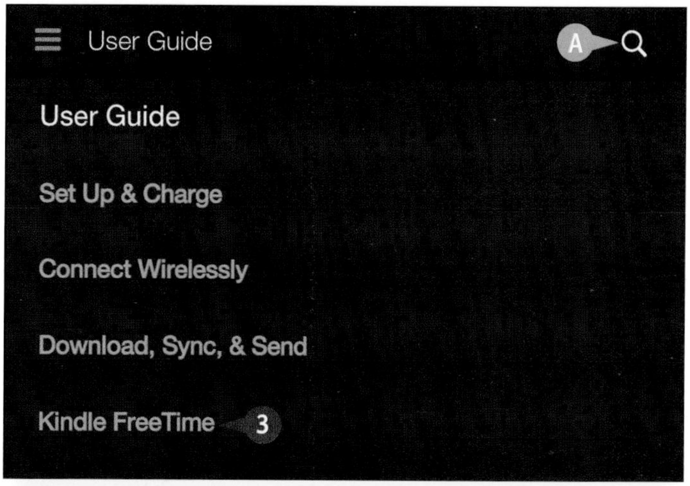

Ⓑ You can tap any blue link to view the information for that topic.

Ⓒ You can tap **User Guide Main Menu** to redisplay the table of contents.

You can tap the **Home** button (🏠) at the bottom of the screen to redisplay the Home screen.

TIP

What happens if I tap Phone & Email on the Mayday screen?

You can contact customer service by phone or by email, or you can provide feedback and rate features on the Fire tablet. When you contact customer service, you identify your issue and then opt to be contacted by phone or email.

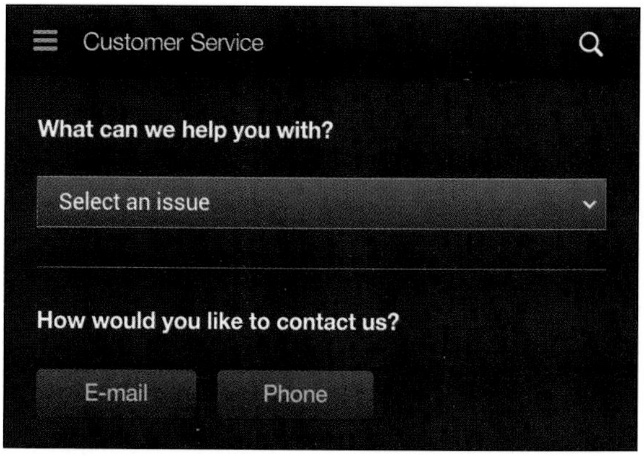

CHAPTER 2

Shopping for Content

You can buy digital content to use on your Fire tablet directly from its interface; you also can use your Fire tablet to buy physical goods such as garden supplies or computer accessories. You use money or Amazon Coins — a form of virtual money — to make purchases at Amazon.com.

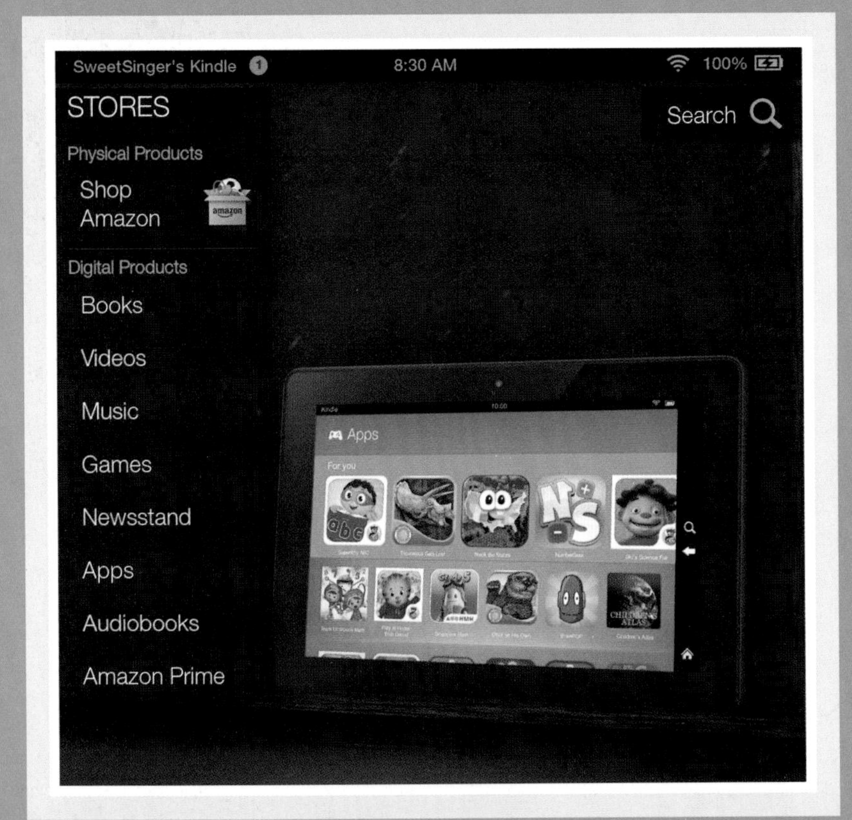

Buy Amazon Coins 36
Shop for Physical Products 38
Shop for Games 40
Shop for Apps 42
Buy Books 44
Buy or Subscribe to Publications 46
Buy Music 48
Buy or Rent Movies. 50
Buy Audio Books. 52

Buy Amazon Coins

To purchase apps and games, you can use Amazon Coins and save money. Amazon Coins are prepaid credits that reduce the price of apps and games by as much as 10 percent. You automatically earn Amazon Coins when you purchase certain Fire tablet apps and in-app items, or you can buy Amazon Coins directly.

Although Amazon Coins that you purchase do not expire, coins that you earn from purchases do expire 12 months after you receive them, and are used first when making purchases with them.

Buy Amazon Coins

1. Tap **Games** or **Apps**.

Note: This example uses Games.

The appropriate content library opens.

2. Tap the **Navigation** button (☰) to display the Navigation panel.
3. Tap **Amazon Coins**.

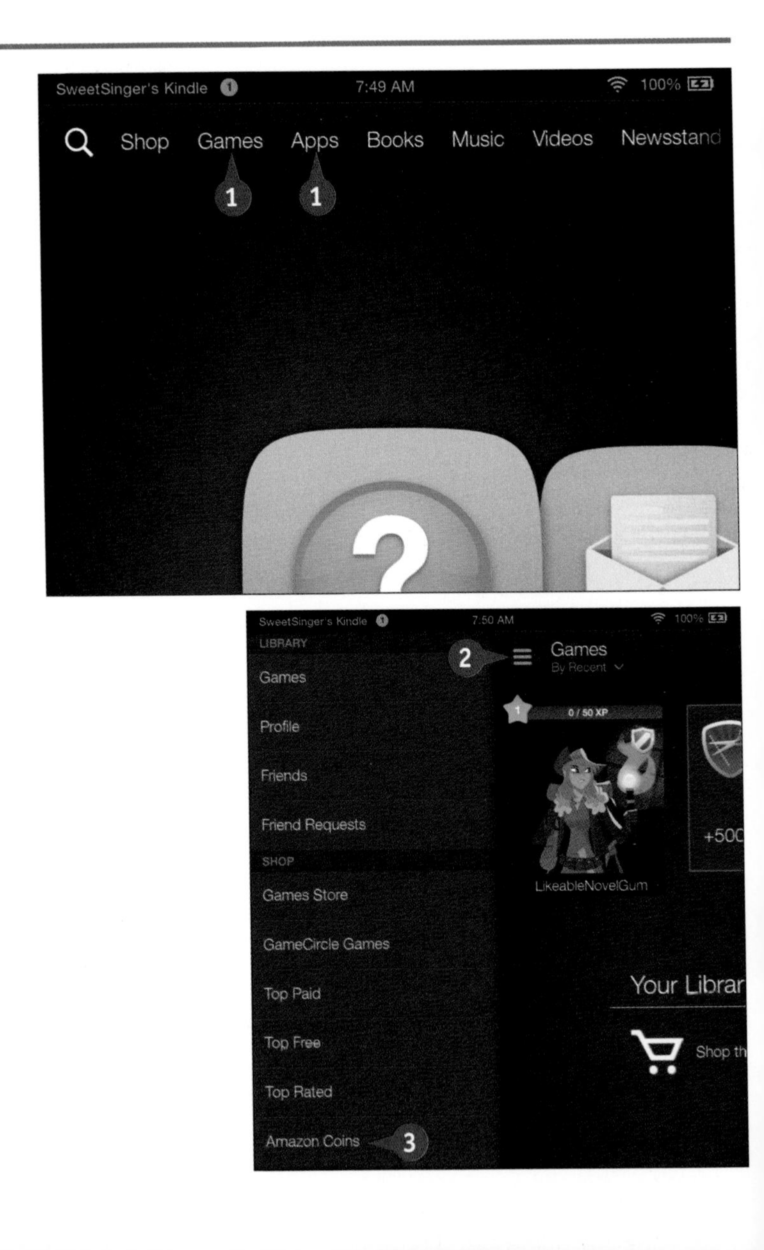

The Amazon Coins screen appears.

Ⓐ The number of coins you currently have appears here.

4 Tap **Buy More Coins**.

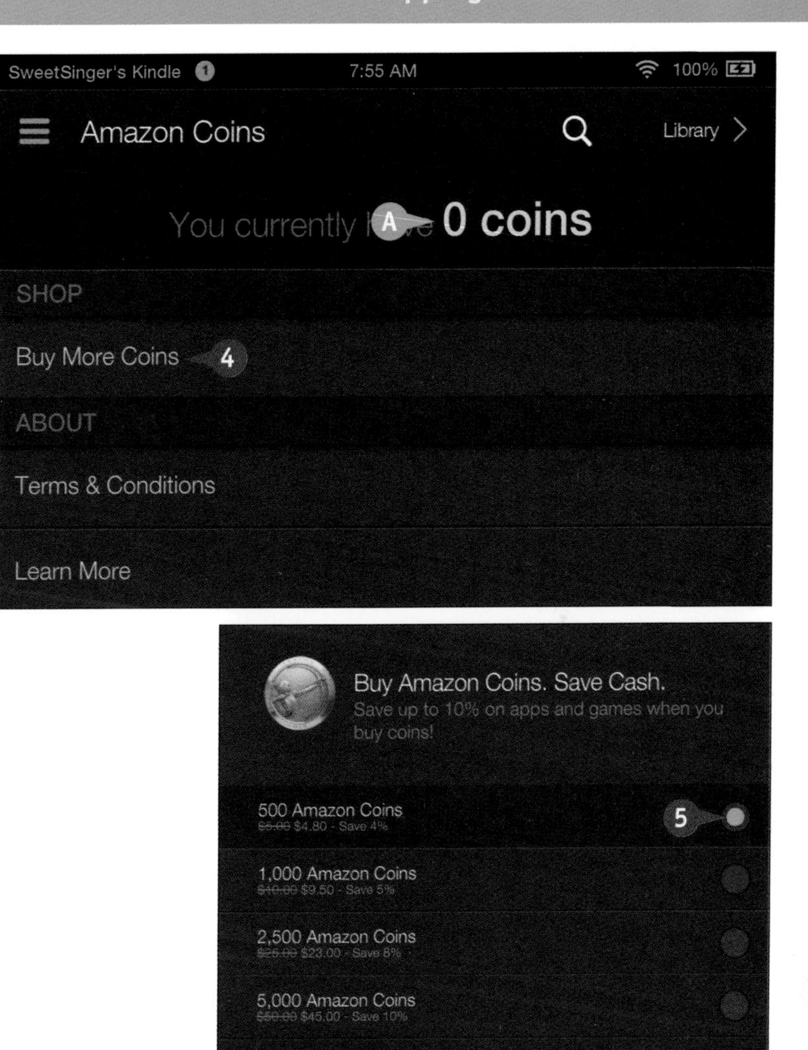

5 Select the option for the number of coins you want to buy (■ changes to ▣).

6 Tap **Buy coins**.

Amazon completes your purchase using a payment method established for your Amazon account.

TIPS

How much is each Amazon Coin worth, and how do I use them?
Each Amazon Coin is worth $0.01, and you can use them when you purchase an eligible app or game, as described in the sections "Shop for Apps" and "Shop for Games." Amazon Coins follow the same parental controls available for other payment methods.

Can I redeem Amazon Coins for cash?
At this time, you cannot redeem them for cash or transfer them to another Amazon account.

Shop for Physical Products

You can use your Fire tablet to shop for physical products — ones you do not use on your Fire tablet. Suppose, for example, that you want to purchase a toy or some treats for your dog. No problem; just grab your Fire tablet and use the information in this section to make your purchase.

Buying physical products requires that you visit the www.amazon.com website and sign in to your Amazon.com account. You make purchases using a payment method established in your account.

Shop for Physical Products

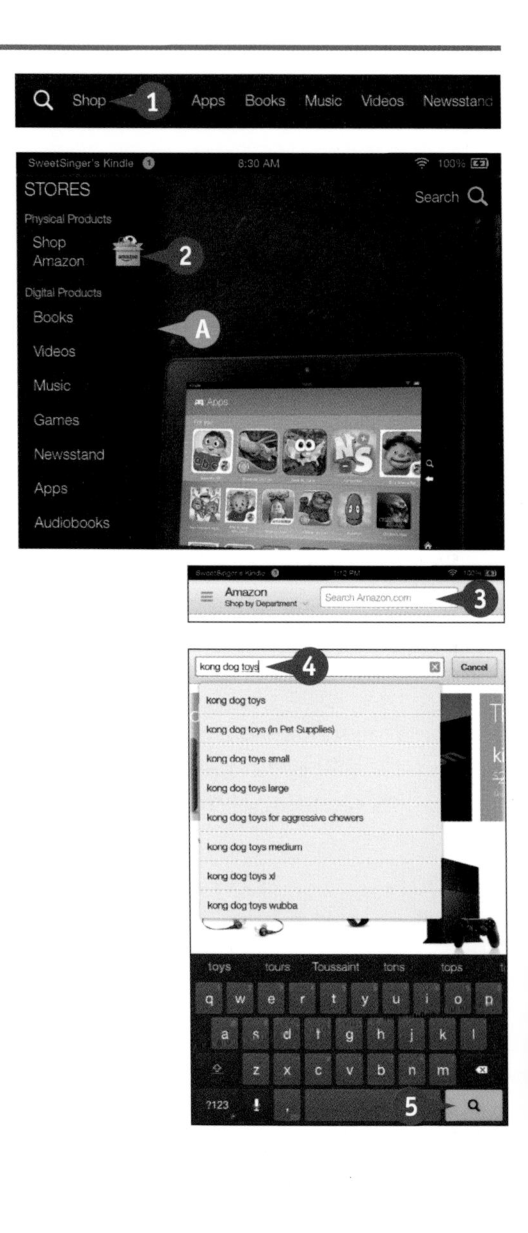

1. From the Home screen, tap **Shop**.

   The Shop content library appears.

   A. Various Amazon stores appear in the Navigation panel.

2. Tap **Shop Amazon**.

   The Amazon Shop by Department page appears.

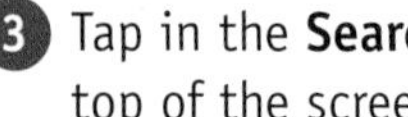

3. Tap in the **Search** text box at the top of the screen.

4. Type a phrase that describes what you want to buy.

Note: For help using the keyboard, see Chapter 1.

5. Tap .

Products that meet your criteria appear.

6. Tap a product to view its details.

B You can swipe up to scroll down and read more.

C You can tap **Add to Wish List** to save the item and purchase it at another time.

7. Tap **Add to Cart** to purchase the product.

A prompt appears, asking if you want to continue shopping or check out; you can tap **Continue Shopping** or **Go to Cart** ( ).

If you tap **Continue Shopping**, repeat steps **3** to **5**.

When you tap **Go to Cart**, a summary of the items in your cart appears; follow the on-screen prompts to complete the purchase.

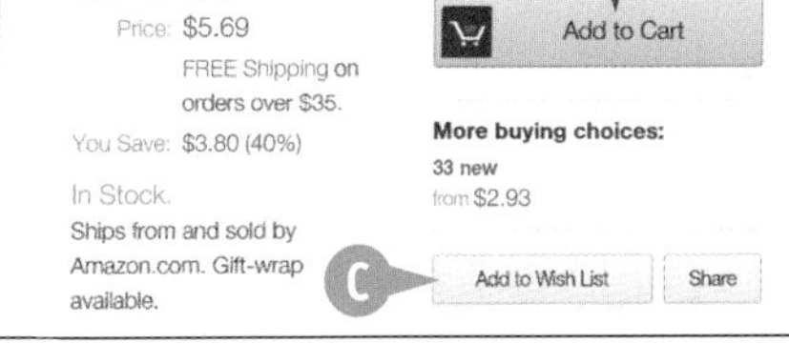

TIP

How can I view the items in my cart?

At any time, tap the shopping cart icon A in the upper-right corner of the screen. You see the same summary that appears when you tap **Go to Cart** after placing an item in the cart.

Shop for Games

You can shop for games to play on your Fire tablet. You start in the Games content library and then enter the Amazon Appstore for Android. Initially, you see available games organized into categories, such as Top Free Games, Top Paid Games, and New Releases. But, you also can search for a particular game by typing its name in the Search text box.

When you see a game that interests you, you can view its details and decide if you want to buy it. You can purchase games using money or using Amazon Coins.

Shop for Games

1. From the Home screen, tap **Games**.

   The Games content library appears.

2. Tap **Store**.

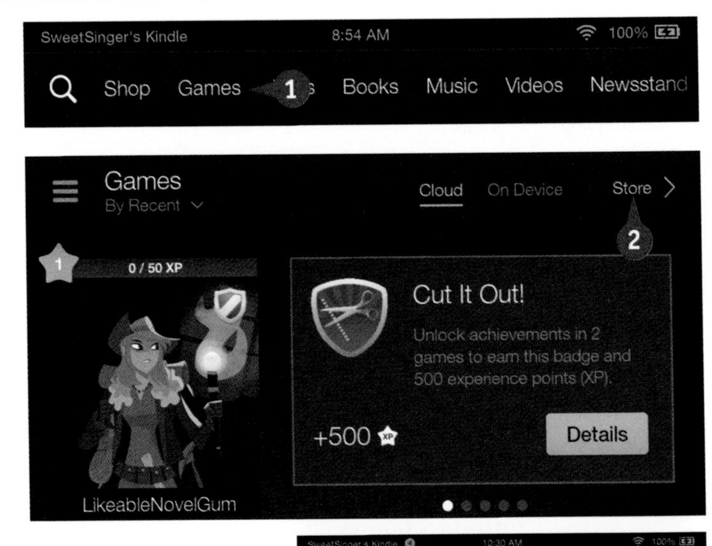

The games available in the Amazon Appstore for Android appear.

- A You can tap the **Search** button (🔍) to type a phrase to search for a game. For help using the keyboard, see Chapter 1.
- B You can swipe up to scroll down and find games.

3. Tap a game to review its details.

The product page for the game appears.

Ⓒ You can swipe up to scroll down and review details.

4 Tap here to purchase the game.

5 Choose to use Amazon Coins or money to pay for the purchase (■ changes to ◙).

6 Tap **Get App**.

The app downloads and installs on your Fire tablet.

A link to the game appears in the Games content library and on the Home screen's Carousel.

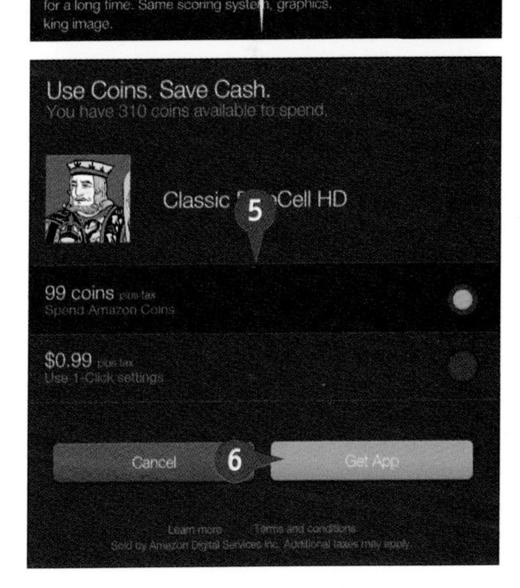

TIP

How do I start the game?

Tap the image for the game in the Games content library or on the Carousel as shown here.

Shop for Apps

You can shop for apps to enhance your Fire tablet. You start in the Apps content library and then enter the Amazon Appstore for Android. Initially, you see apps organized into categories, such as featured or free apps and games, apps inspired by your browsing history, apps recommended for you, and more. You can also search for apps by describing them.

When you see an app that interests you, you can view its details, decide if you want to buy it, and purchase it using money or Amazon Coins.

Shop for Apps

1. From the Home screen, tap **Apps**.

   The Apps content library appears.

Note: Because games are also apps, games appear in the Apps content library.

2. Tap **Store**.

   The apps available in the Amazon Appstore appear.

   A. You can tap the **Search** button (🔍) to type a phrase to search for an app. For help using the keyboard, see Chapter 1.

   B. You can swipe up to scroll down and find apps.

3. Tap an app to review its details.

The product page for the app appears.

Ⓒ You can swipe up to scroll down and review details.

4. If the app costs money, follow steps **5** and **6** in the section "Shop for Games."

5. For free apps, tap **Free**.

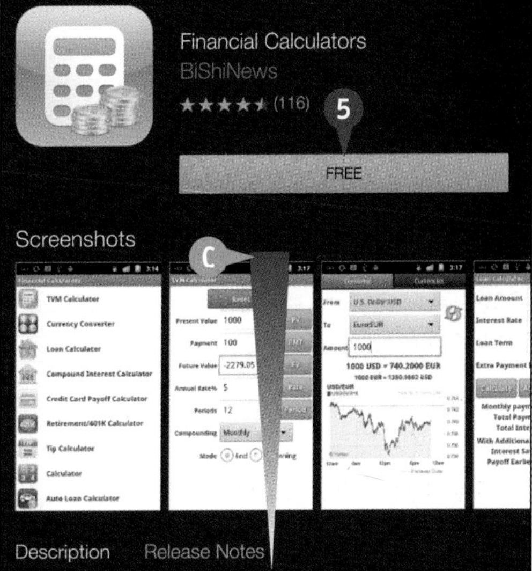

The Free button changes to the Get App button.

6. Tap **Get App**.

The app downloads to your Fire tablet.

A link to the app appears in the Apps content library and on the Home screen's Carousel.

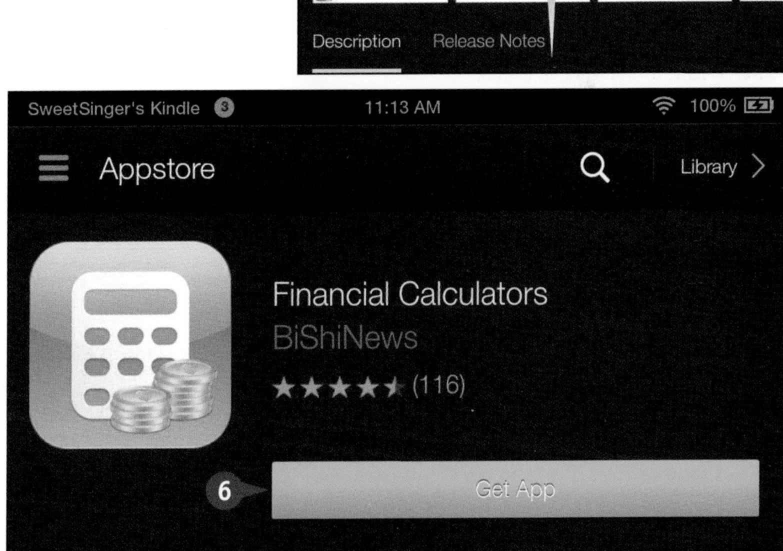

TIP

Is there an easy way to view all apps in a particular category, such as the Featured Apps category?

Yes. Tap the **Search** button (🔍) at the top of the Appstore for Android screen and type "featured" in the search box. From the suggestion list, tap **featured apps and games** Ⓐ.

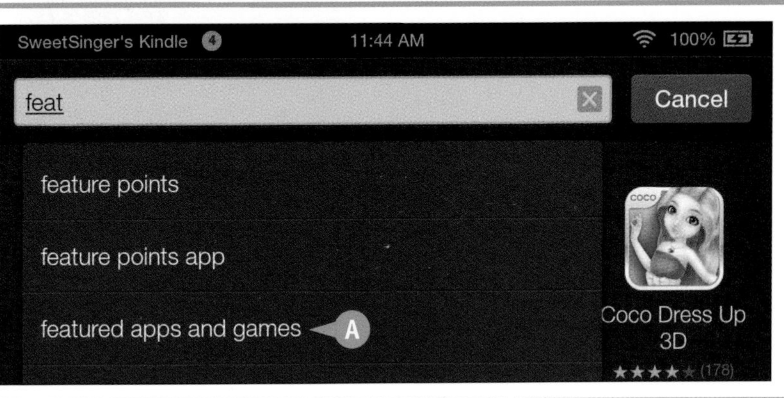

Buy Books

You can buy ebooks and read them on your Fire tablet. Books in the online bookstore are organized into categories such as those books recommended for you, Daily Deals, Monthly Deals for $3.99 or Less, Editor's Picks, Popular Singles — typically a chapter of a book that you can read as a sample — and more. You can search for books by title, author, or genre. You also can find free books, and some books offer sample chapters that you can download for free before purchasing.

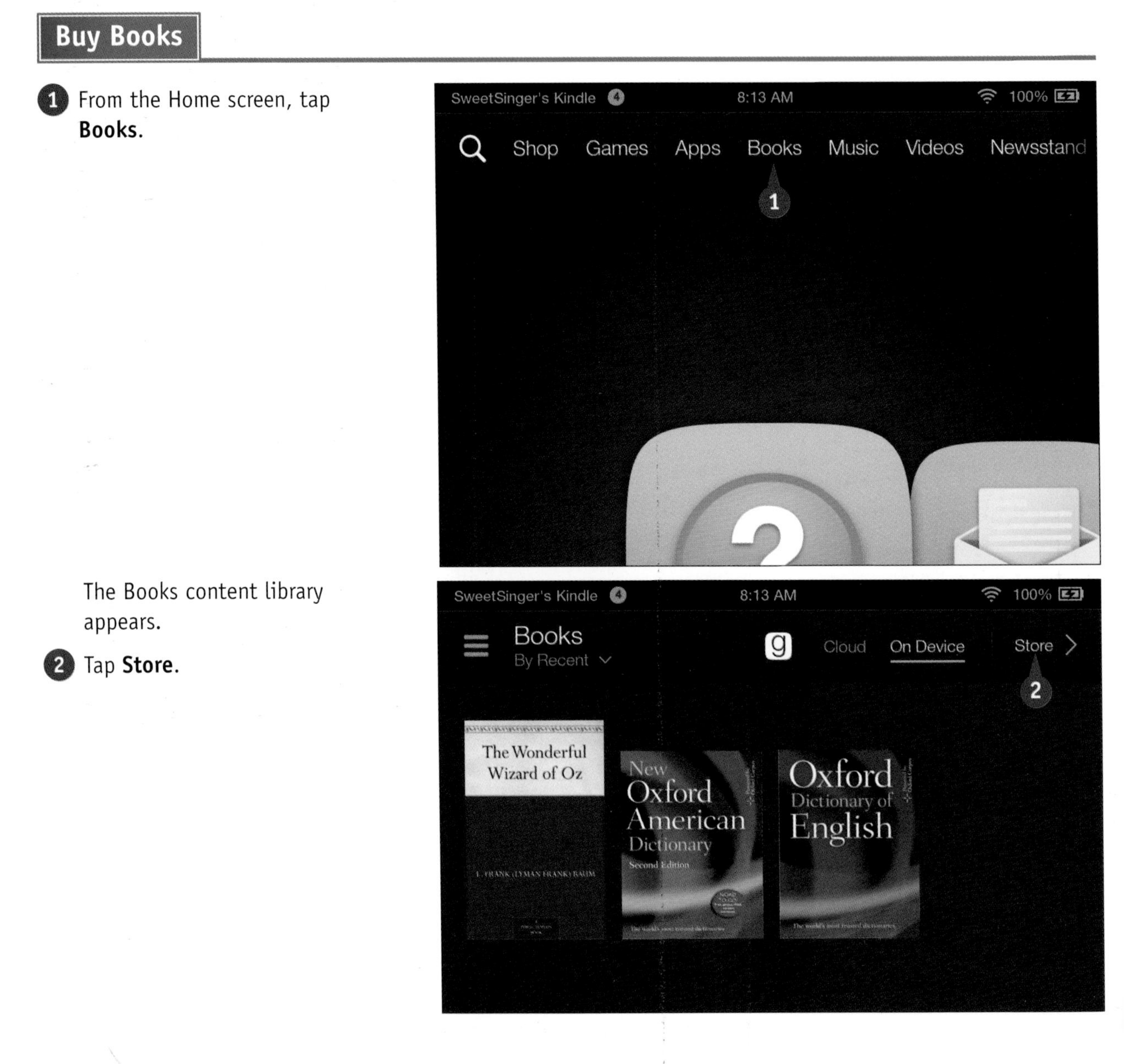

Buy Books

1. From the Home screen, tap **Books**.

   The Books content library appears.

2. Tap **Store**.

The online bookstore appears.

Ⓐ You can tap the **Search** button (🔍) to type a phrase to search for a book. For help using the keyboard, see Chapter 1.

Ⓑ You can swipe up to scroll down and find books.

3 Tap a book to review its details.

The product page for the book appears.

Ⓒ You can swipe up to scroll down and review details.

4 If the book costs money, follow steps **5** to **6** in the section "Shop for Games."

5 For free books, tap **Buy for Free**, and the book downloads to your Fire tablet.

A link to the book appears in the Books content library and on the Home screen's Carousel.

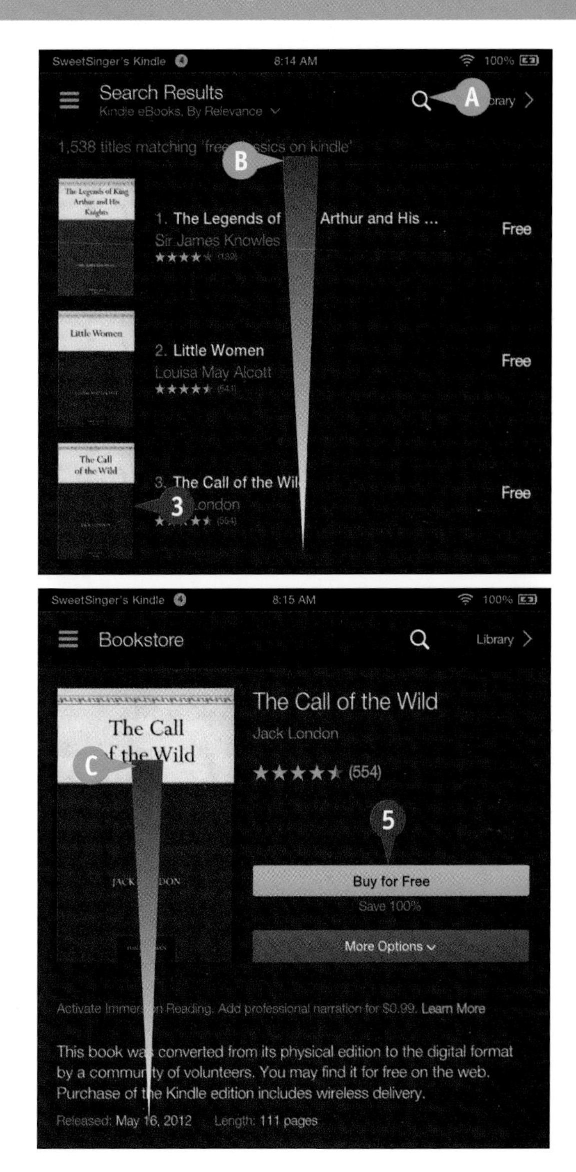

TIP

What is Immersion Reading?

Some ebooks have enhanced features like *X-Ray* and *Immersion Reading*. When Immersion Reading is available for an ebook, you can simultaneously read and listen to your book as a professional narrator reads it. As the narrator reads, the words are highlighted in your book. For more information on Immersion Reading and other enhanced features you find in some ebooks, see Chapter 6.

Buy or Subscribe to Publications

You can buy single issues of a publication or, as described in this section, you can subscribe to a magazine or newspaper. Any subscription you purchase includes at least a 14-day free period, and you can cancel at any time during the free period. After the free period, your subscription continues at the regular price using the default payment method in your Amazon account. The publication's product page tells you how often you will receive issues.

Issues of your subscription download using a wireless connection, so you must connect your device to a wireless network to receive the latest issue.

Buy or Subscribe to Publications

1. From the Home screen, swipe the Navigation bar to the left and tap **Newsstand**.

   If you have not yet purchased publications, the Newsstand content library automatically displays the online storefront.

Note: If you own publications and want to shop, tap **Store** in the upper-right corner of the screen.

2. Tap the **Search** button (Q) to search for a publication.

3. Type a search phrase. For help using the keyboard, see Chapter 1.

4. From the list of suggestions, tap a phrase.

Note: This example uses **free subscriptions**.

5. Tap Q.

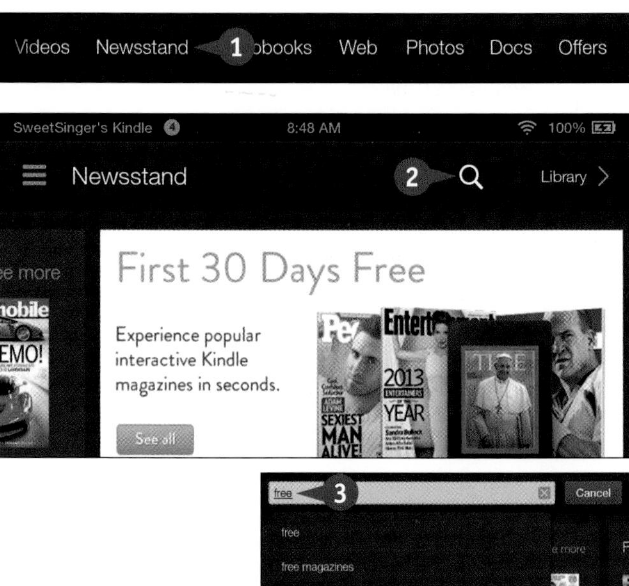

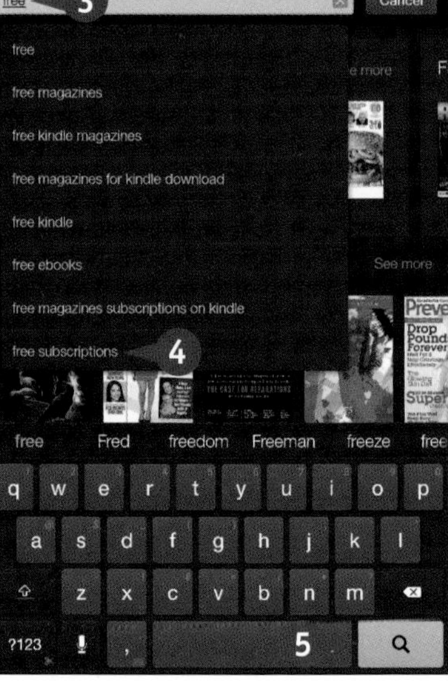

The results of your search appear.

6. Tap a publication.

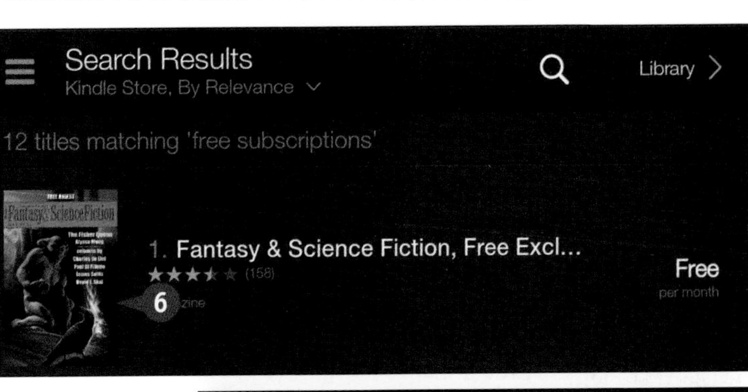

The product page for the publication appears.

A You can swipe up to scroll down and review details.

B If single issues are available and you want to buy the available issue, tap **Buy Issue**.

C The available issue appears below the button.

7. Tap **Subscribe now**.

The publication downloads to your Fire tablet.

A link to the publication appears in the Newsstand content library and on the Home screen's Carousel.

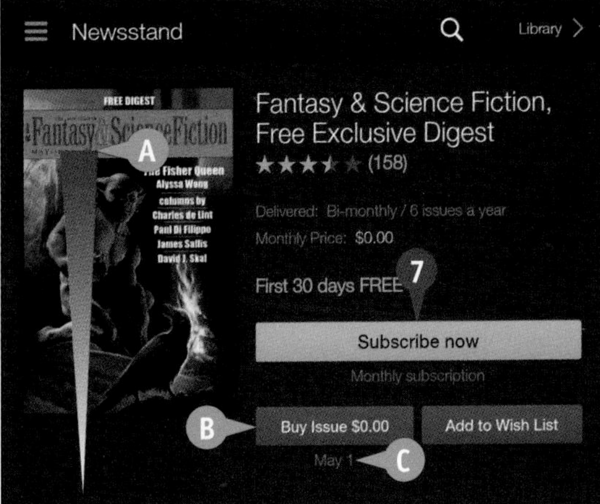

TIP

How do I cancel a subscription?

Return to the product page for the publication and scroll to the bottom. Click **Manage Your Content and Devices**, and the Fire tablet automatically opens the sign-in page to your Amazon account. After signing in, your content appears. Tap **Magazines** A, tap the **Action** button (…) B, then tap **Cancel Subscription** C.

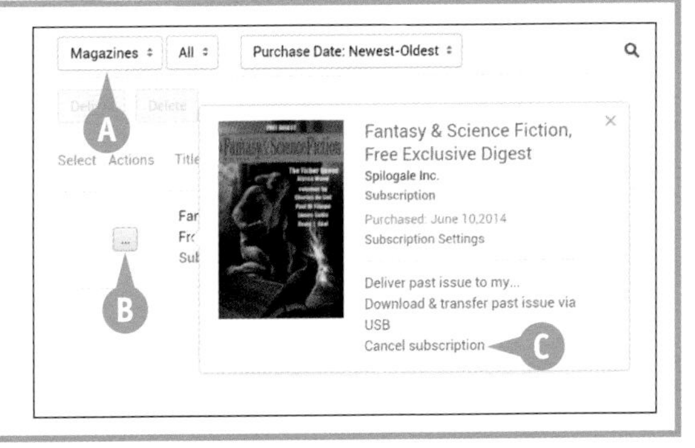

Buy Music

From the Music content library, you can visit the online store at Amazon to shop for music. You can buy individual songs or entire albums using the payment method stored in your Amazon account. The music you buy is stored free of charge in the Amazon Cloud Player and does not count against the storage limits associated with your Amazon account. You can play back your music from the Amazon Cloud Player, or you can download your music to your Fire tablet.

Buy Music

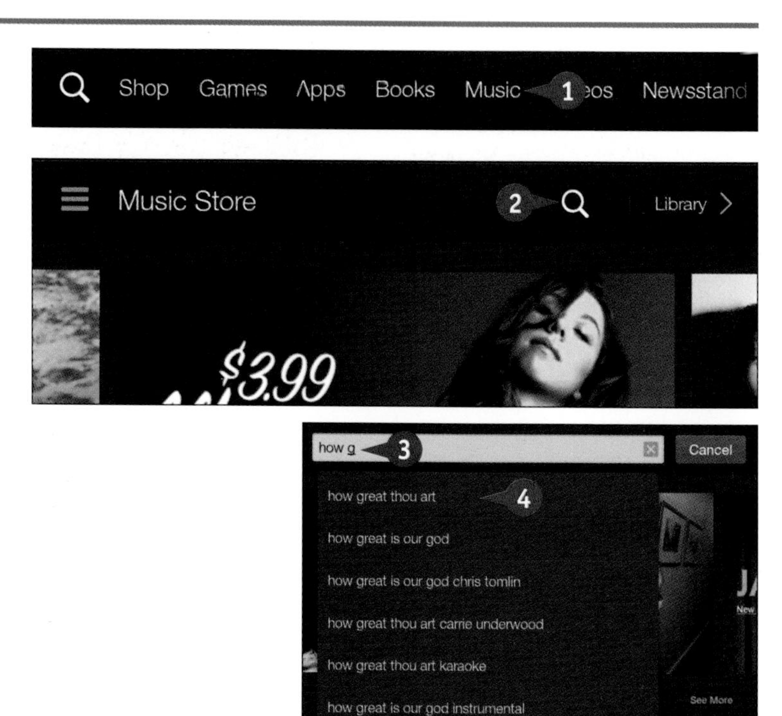

1. From the Home screen, tap **Music**.

   If you have not yet purchased music, the Music content library automatically displays the online storefront.

Note: If you have music on your device and want to shop, tap **Store** in the upper-right corner of the screen.

2. Tap the **Search** button (🔍) to search for music.
3. Type a search phrase. For help using the keyboard, see Chapter 1.
4. From the list of suggestions, tap a phrase.

Note: This example uses **how great thou art**.

5. Tap 🔍.

The results of your search appear.

Ⓐ You can tap any **Play** button (▶) to listen to a sample of the song (▶ changes to ■).

6 Tap a song title to view its product page.

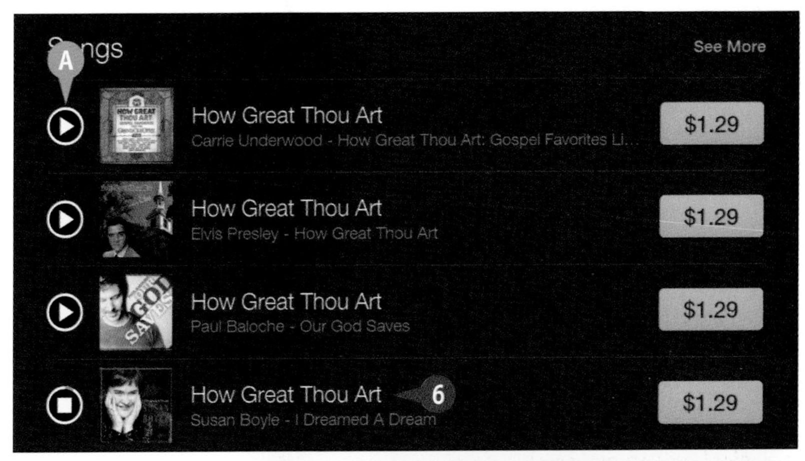

Ⓑ You can swipe up to scroll down and review album and artist details.

Ⓒ You can tap any **Play** button (▶) to preview songs on the album (▶ changes to ■).

Ⓓ You can tap **Buy Album** to purchase the entire album.

7 Tap any song's price to purchase that song (the price button changes to Buy).

8 Tap **Buy**.

Note: A "Terms of Use" screen appears; tap **Continue** to download the music to your Fire tablet.

TIP

Can I transfer music stored in the cloud at Amazon to my computer?

You can download music from the Amazon Cloud to your device (and ultimately to your computer). In the Music content library, tap **Cloud** Ⓐ and tap a song. On the screen that appears, tap **Download All** Ⓑ. Then, see Chapter 4 for details on transferring the song to your computer.

Buy or Rent Movies

From the Videos content library on your Fire tablet, you can visit the Amazon Instant Video store to rent or buy movies and TV shows and even watch some for free. You can watch a rented video for a specified time period and a purchased video as often as you want.

After you rent or buy a video, you can watch it either by streaming it over a wireless network or by downloading it to your Fire tablet; if you download it, you can watch without being connected to a wireless network.

Buy or Rent Movies

1 From the Home screen, tap **Videos**.

If you have not yet purchased or rented videos, the Videos content library automatically displays the online storefront.

Note: If you have purchased or rented videos and want to shop, tap **Store** in the upper-right corner of the screen.

2 Tap the **Search** button (Q) to search for movies.

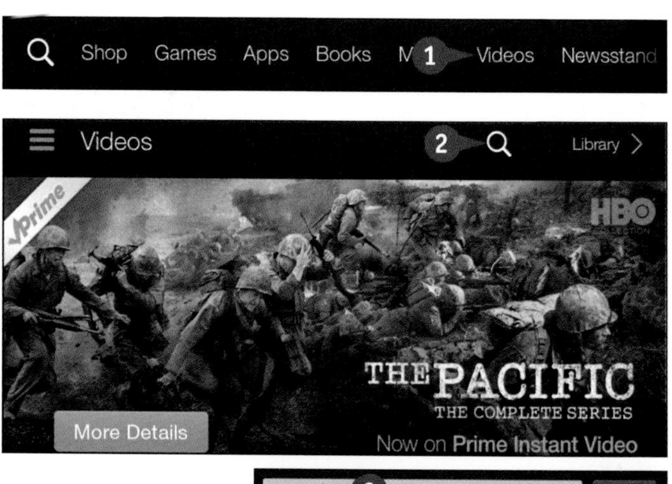

3 Type a search phrase. For help using the keyboard, see Chapter 1.

4 From the list of suggestions, tap a phrase.

Note: This example uses **my cousin vinny**.

5 Tap Q.

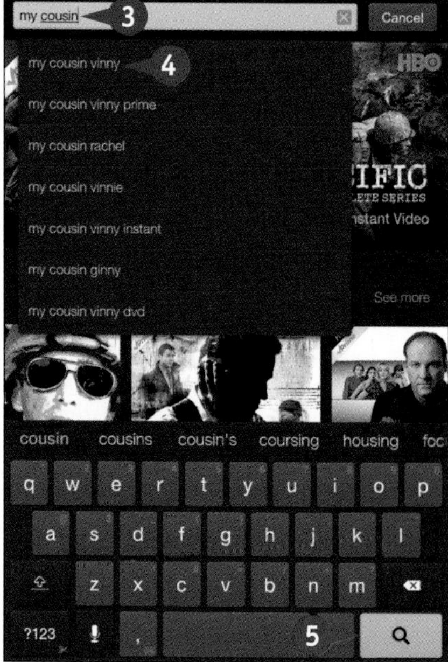

The results of your search appear.

Ⓐ You can swipe up to scroll down and review the list.

6 Tap a title.

The product page for the title appears.

Ⓑ You can swipe up to scroll down and review the video's details.

Ⓒ You can tap here to watch a movie's trailer.

7 Tap either **Rent** or **Buy** to rent the movie or buy it.

Your purchase is processed, and you are then offered the option to watch now or download the movie to your Fire tablet.

A link to the movie appears in the Videos content library and on the Home screen's Carousel.

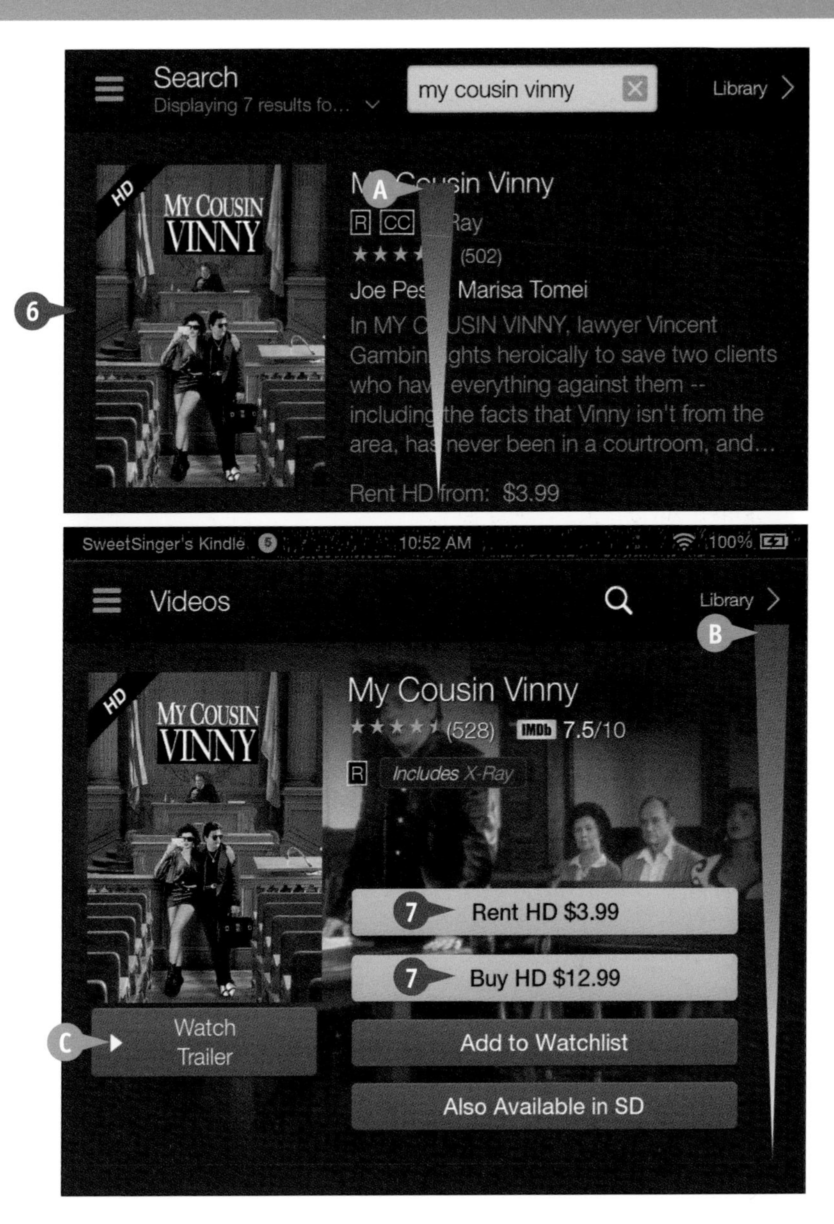

TIP

Are free movies and TV shows available?

Yes. You can search for "free movies" or "free TV." In many cases, you can watch the first episode of TV shows for free. Tap the **Navigation** button (☰) in the Videos content library and then tap **First Episode Free** Ⓐ in the Navigation panel.

Buy Audio Books

In the Audiobooks library on your Fire tablet, you can shop for, purchase, and listen to audiobooks from Audible.com. Although it is nice to have an Audible.com account, you do not need one to purchase and listen to an audiobook. If you do have one, you can link it with your Amazon account and use any Audible.com credits to purchase audiobooks for your Fire tablet. If you want to sign up for an Audible.com account, visit www.audible.com.

You can listen to audiobooks even when your Fire tablet is not connected to a wireless network.

Buy Audio Books

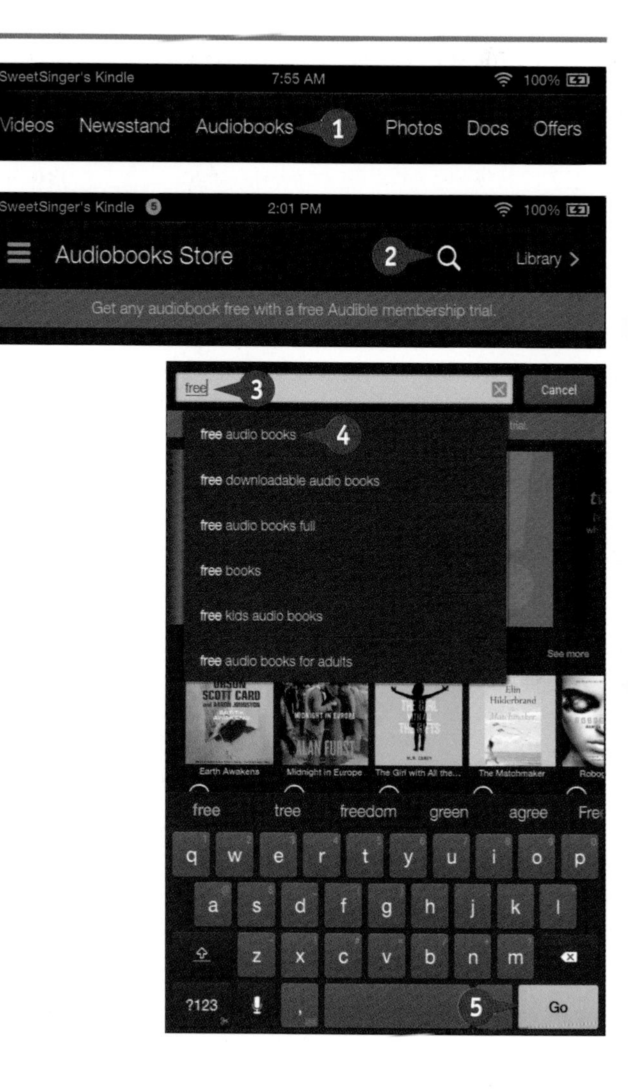

1. From the Home screen, tap **Audiobooks**.

   If you have not yet purchased any audiobooks, the Audiobooks content library automatically displays the online storefront.

Note: If you have purchased audiobooks and want to shop, tap **Store** in the upper-right corner of the screen.

2. Tap the **Search** button (🔍) to search for audiobooks.

3. Type a search phrase. For help using the keyboard, see Chapter 1.

4. From the list of suggestions, tap a phrase.

Note: This example uses **free audio books.**

5. Tap .

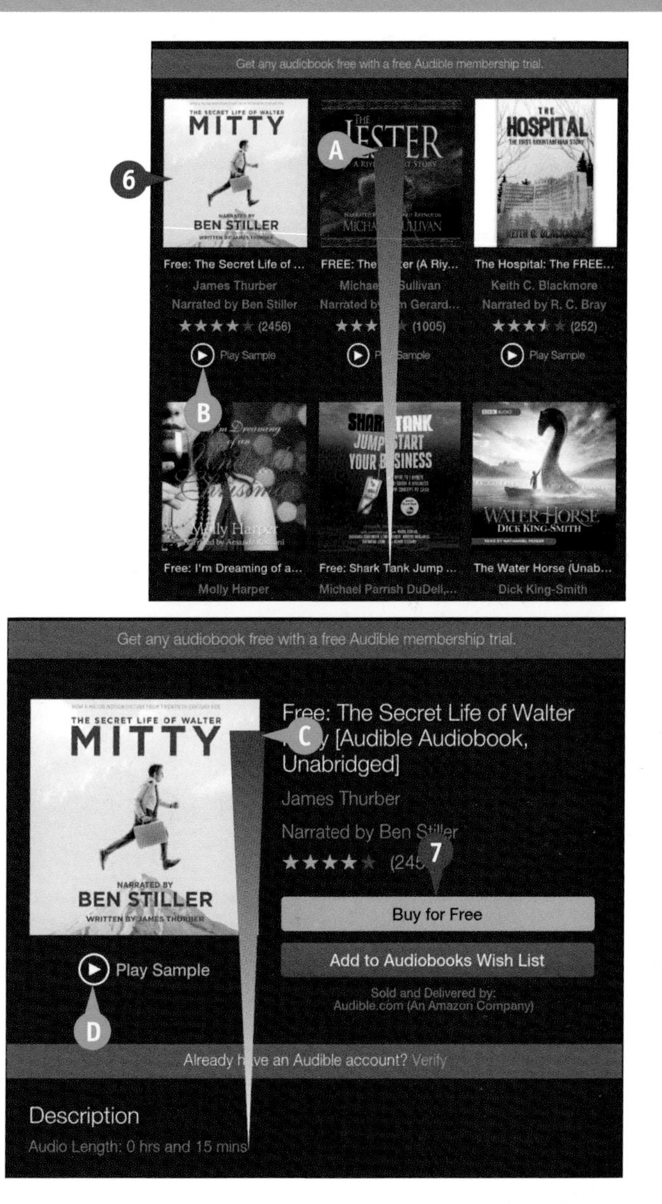

The results of your search appear.

Ⓐ You can swipe up to scroll down and review the list.

Ⓑ You can tap any **Play** button (▶) to hear a sample of the audiobook (▶ changes to ■).

6 Tap a title.

The product page for the title appears.

Ⓒ You can swipe up to scroll down and review details.

Ⓓ You can tap the **Play** button (▶) to hear a sample of the audiobook.

7 Tap here to buy the audiobook.

Your purchase is processed and you are then offered the option to listen now.

A link to the audiobook appears in the Audiobooks content library.

TIP

How do I link my Amazon and Audible.com accounts?

Sign in to www.audible.com. You are prompted to connect your Audible account with your Amazon account; click the **Link Now** button. Then, type your Audible.com password and your Amazon email address and password when prompted. Last, identify the credit or debit card you want to use as the default card for Audible purchases and membership charges. After you link your Amazon and Audible accounts, your Audible audiobooks appear on your Fire tablet, and you can access Audible member discounts. Going forward, use your Amazon email and password to sign in to Audible.com.

CHAPTER 3

Working with Apps

As discussed in Chapter 2, you can easily buy apps to use on your Fire tablet, but you can also take advantage of the apps that come with it too. You can also add or remove apps and content to and from the Favorites section of the Home screen.

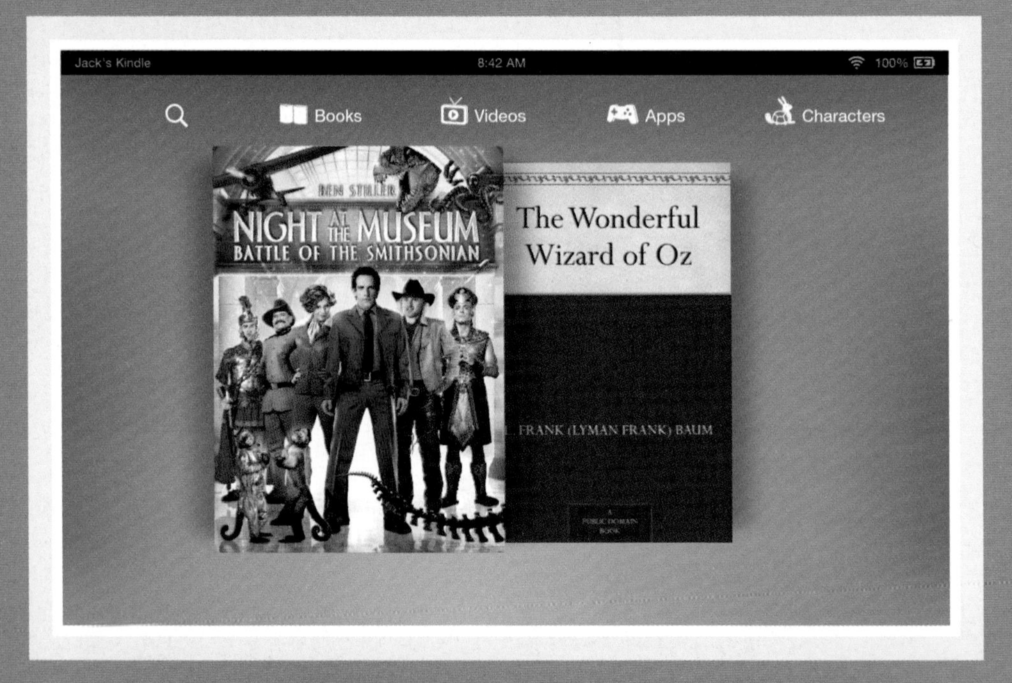

Add an App to Favorites 56
Remove Fire Tablet Content. 57
Install a Printer Plug-In 60
Using Goodreads on the Fire Tablet 62
Set Clocks and Alarms 64
Using Other Clock Features 68
Set Up Kindle FreeTime. 72
Using Kindle FreeTime 78
Explore the IMDb Movies & TV App 80
Find Movie Times and Buy Tickets. 82
Read about Celebrities 84
Examine Yelp. 86

Add an App to Favorites

For easy access, you can add apps and content, such as books, to the Favorites section of the Home screen. When you open an app, it appears in the Home screen Carousel, which is a convenient location from which to reopen the app; this also makes the Carousel a very crowded place. As an alternative, you can add content to the Favorites section on the Home screen, thus making them just as easy to find and open but without all the clutter. You also can remove content from the Favorites section when you no longer need it.

Add an App to Favorites

1. From the Home screen Carousel or from any content library, press and hold an item.
2. Tap **Add to Home**.
3. Tap the **Home** button (🏠).

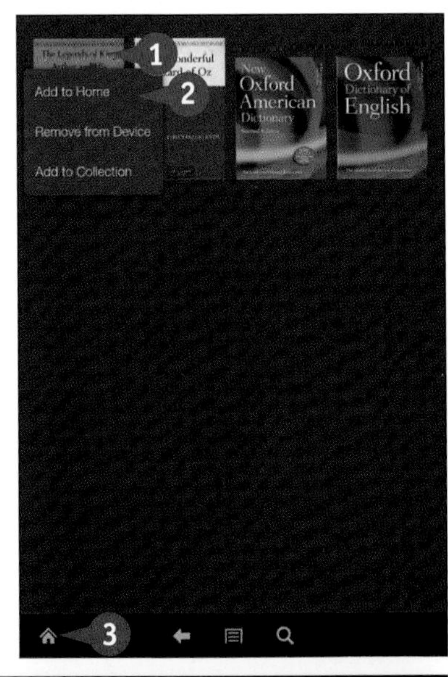

The Home screen appears.

4. Swipe up to scroll down the screen.

Ⓐ The item you selected in step **1** appears in the Favorites section.

Note: To remove an item from the Favorites section, tap and hold it until the item flickers. Then at the top of the screen, tap the **Remove** button.

Remove Fire Tablet Content

You can remove content from your Fire tablet to free up space and keep your device running quickly and smoothly. For example, suppose that you finish reading a book or you decide you no longer want to play a game you downloaded to your Fire tablet. You can remove the book or the game from your device. Any item you remove is still available in your Amazon Cloud account, and you can easily reload that content again if you decide you need it.

You also can delete content from your Amazon Cloud account.

Remove Fire Tablet Content

1. Swipe down from the top of the screen to open Quick Settings.
2. Tap **Settings**.

The Settings screen appears.

3. Tap **Device**.

Note: To permanently remove games from both your Fire tablet and from your Amazon Cloud account, tap the **Games** content library on the Home screen. Then, press and hold the game you want to permanently delete, and tap **Delete from Cloud**.

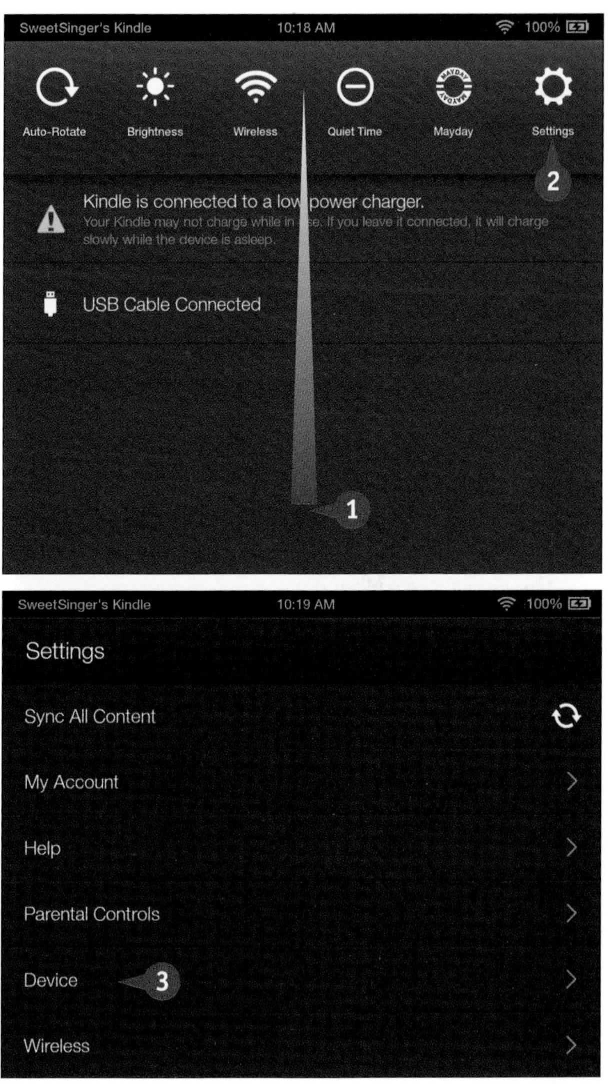

continued ►

Remove Fire Tablet Content (continued)

You can use the *1-Tap Archive* feature, which groups all infrequently used items, to archive items and free up storage space. Alternatively, you can select specific content to remove from your device.

Be aware that removing content from your device may mean the loss of specific settings you established for that content. You may also lose in-app items that came with the content. So before removing content, you may consider checking with the app developer.

Remove Fire Tablet Content (continued)

The Device screen appears.

4. Tap **Storage**.

The Storage screen appears, showing categories that match content libraries.

5. Tap the **1-Tap Archive** ().

The 1-Tap Archive screen appears, showing all items not used recently.

Ⓐ You can tap beside any individual item to deselect it (☑ changes to ■).

Ⓑ You can tap **Archive** to remove all selected items from your device.

6. Tap the **Back** arrow (⬅) to redisplay the Storage screen.

7. Tap any content library to display its items; this example uses **Books**.

Note: You cannot remove items in the System Applications folder or the System folder.

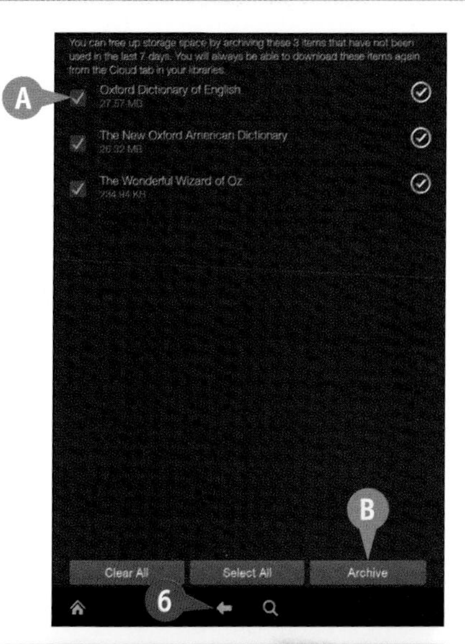

8. Tap beside any item to select it (■ changes to ☑).

9. Tap **Remove**.

The selected content is removed from your device.

You can tap the **Home** button (🏠) to redisplay the Home screen.

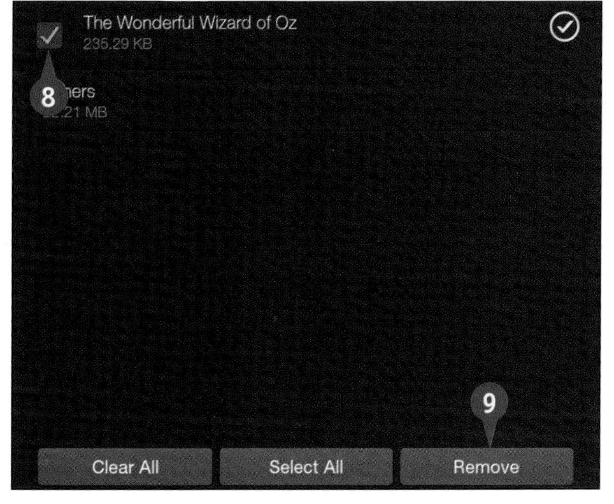

TIP

Can I permanently remove content other than games from my Amazon.com account?

Yes. Open the Silk browser and sign in to your Amazon account. From the Your Account menu, tap **Manage Your Content and Devices**. Select the type of content to delete Ⓐ. Tap the Actions button Ⓑ and tap **Delete** Ⓒ.

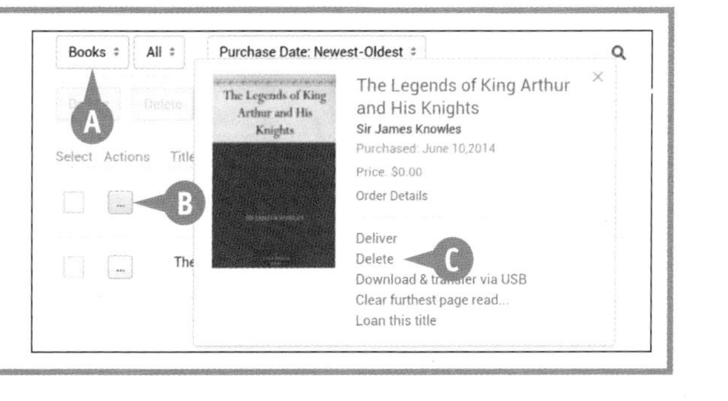

Install a Printer Plug-In

If your printer supports mobile printing — and most modern printers do — you can print documents, photos, web pages, and email stored on your Fire tablet. To do so, you must download a piece of software called a *printer plug-in* to your tablet and install it.

You can print to any printer — those printers connected using Wi-Fi and those printers connected using a cable — as long as the printer is connected to the same network as your Fire tablet.

Install a Printer Plug-In

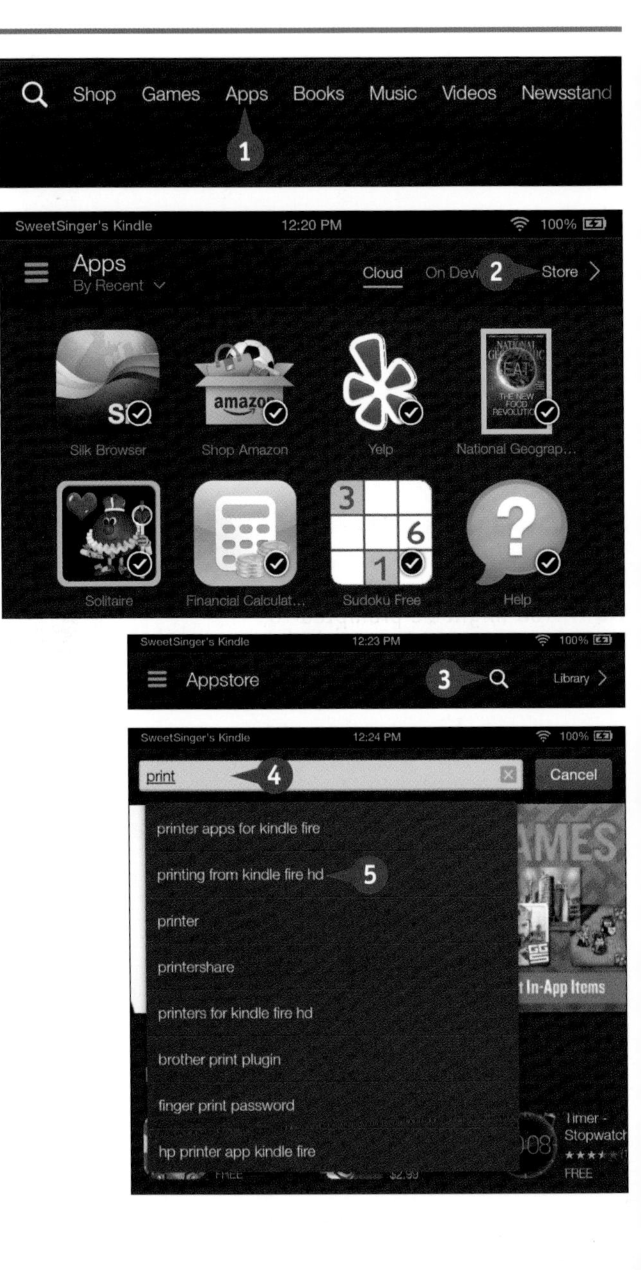

1. From the Home screen, tap **Apps**.

   The Apps content library appears.

2. Tap **Store**.

   The Amazon Appstore for Android appears.

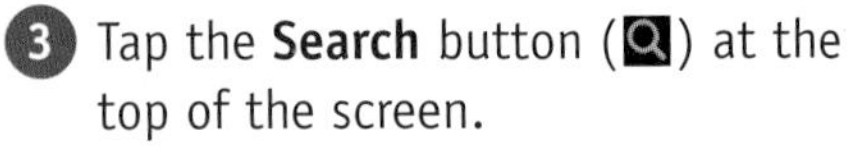

3. Tap the **Search** button (🔍) at the top of the screen.
4. In the text box that appears, type **print**.

Note: For help using the keyboard, see Chapter 1.

5. From the list that appears, tap **printer apps for Fire tablet.**

The search results appear.

6 Tap your printer's plug-in. This example uses the Brother iPrint&Scan app.

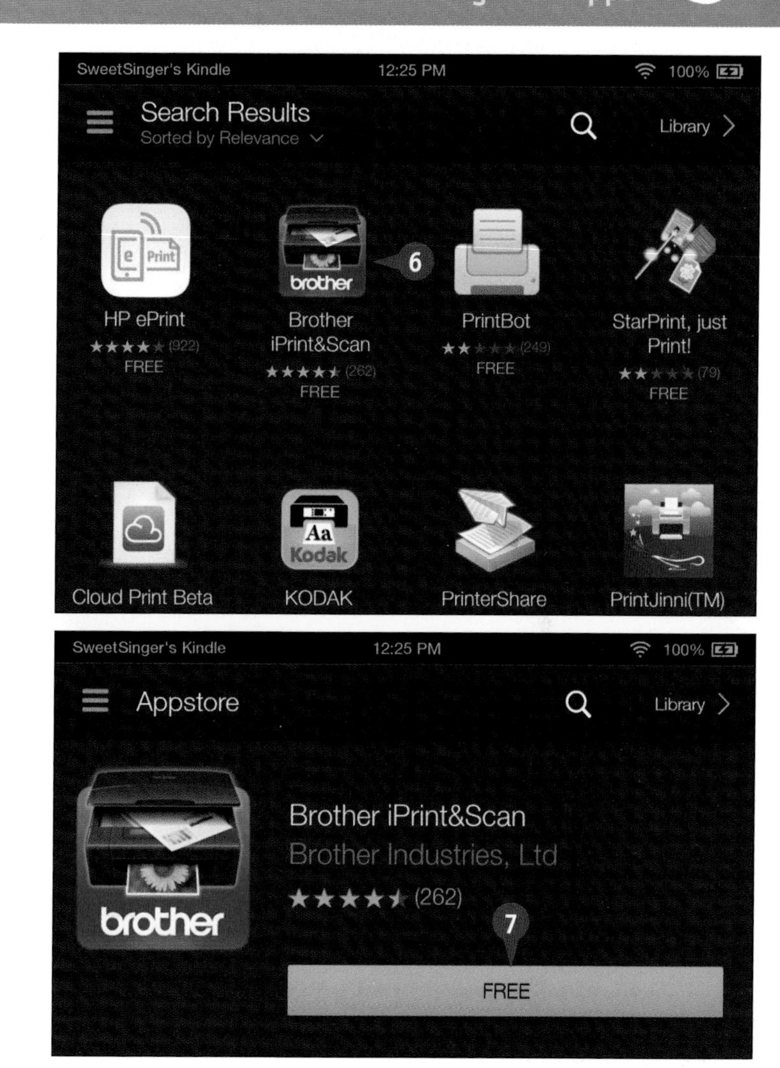

The printer plug-in's product page appears.

7 Tap **Free**.

Note: If prompted, tap **Get App**.

The plug-in downloads and installs.

Note: You might be prompted to agree to an end user licensing agreement.

TIP

How do I print after I have installed the printer plug-in?

The technique varies, depending on your printer. For all printers, make sure your printer is turned on and connected to the network. For any type of printer, you can long-press (press and hold) a photo or a document (A) and, from the menu that appears, tap **Print** (B).

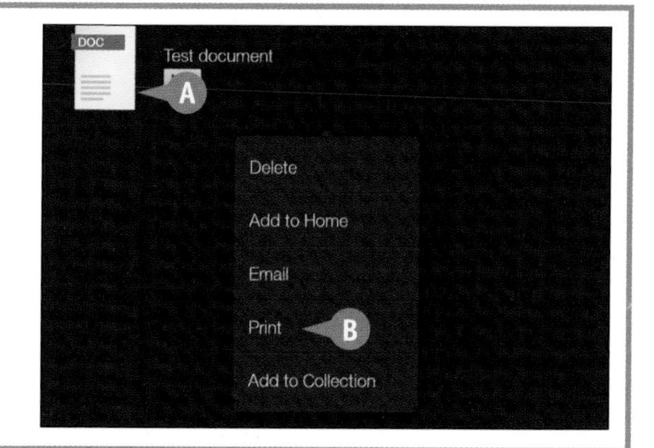

Using Goodreads on the Fire Tablet

Readers in the United States and Canada can use the Goodreads on Kindle app to join a virtual book club. The app requires that you sign in to Goodreads or create an account. If you create an account, follow the on-screen prompts and skip any linking opportunities, including adding books to Goodreads, because you can link later.

With this app, you select books and assign them to a default bookshelf: Read, Currently Reading, or Want to Read. You can follow other readers and favorite authors, and rate books. This section shows you how to add books to a bookshelf and how to rate books.

Using Goodreads on the Fire Tablet

1. From the Home screen, tap **Apps**.
2. In the Apps content library, tap **Goodreads on Kindle**.

Note: The first time you use the app, it might need to download from the Amazon Appstore for Android. Tap again to open the app.

- A You can tap here to add friends from Facebook.
- B Tap the **Close** button (☒) to close this message.
- C You can swipe in this area to find readers to follow; tap a reader to follow that reader.

3. Tap the **Navigation** button (☰) to open the Navigation panel.

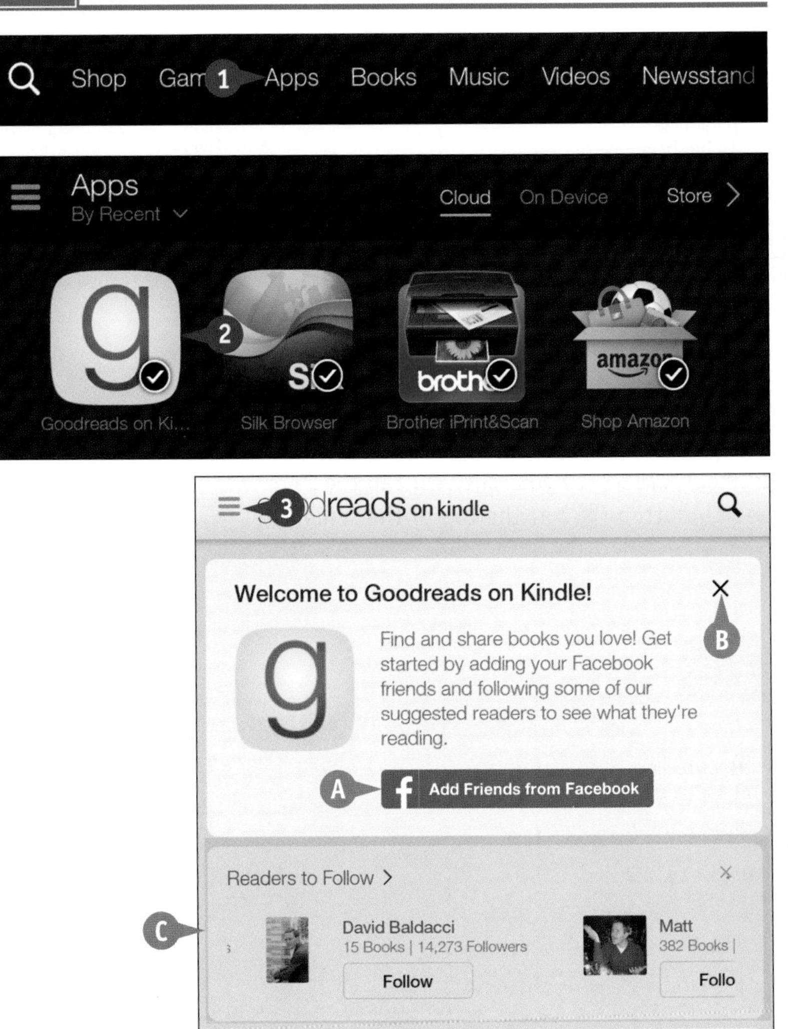

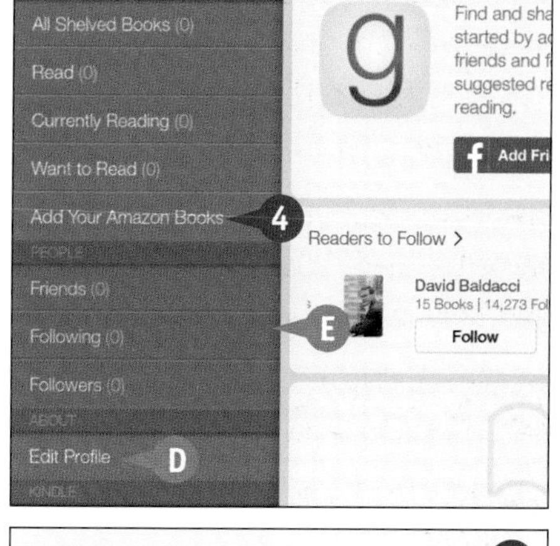

D You can tap **Edit Profile** to change your profile and tell others about yourself.

E You can tap any of the People options to identify other readers, such as your favorite authors and top reviewers, to follow.

4 Tap **Add Your Amazon Books.**

The books in your Amazon Cloud account appear.

5 Tap the **Want to Read** menu button ( ) to display a menu.

6 Tap **Currently Reading**, **Read**, or **Want to Read**.

7 Repeat for each book.

8 When you finish, tap **Done**.

Note: You can add books you did not purchase through Amazon to your shelves. Tap the **Search** button ( ) at the top of the screen to search for them. Then complete steps **5** and **6**.

TIP

How do I rate a book?

Display the book on your Read shelf or search for it by tapping the **Search** button ( ) at the top of the screen. While viewing the book, tap the **My Rating** star ( ) that corresponds to the rating you want to assign **A**. Rating a book automatically adds it to your Read shelf.

Set Clocks and Alarms

You can use the Clock app to set up clocks for as many different cities as you want. You also can set alarms to alert you at a certain time in your default time zone.

You can view clocks individually, or use the All Cities screen to simultaneously view all the clocks you have set up. While working in the Clock app, you can swipe to switch between viewing individual cities or the All Cities view.

Set Clocks and Alarms

Add a City Clock

1. Swipe up to display the Favorites area at the bottom of the Home screen.
2. Tap **Clock**.

The Clock app opens.

3. Tap the Add button (+) to add a city.

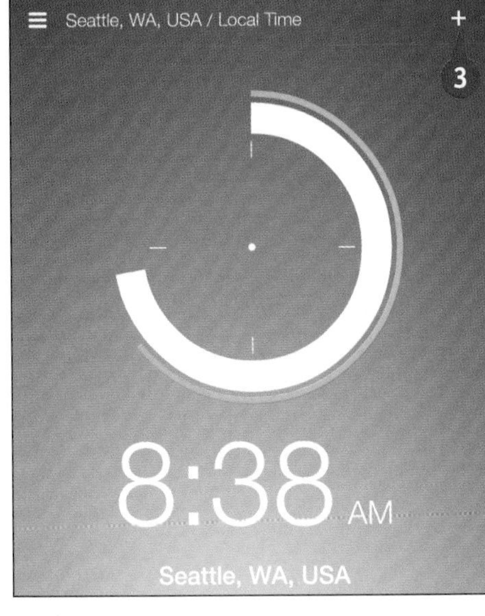

The Add a City screen appears.

4. Type the name of the city.
5. Tap the city in the list of suggestions.

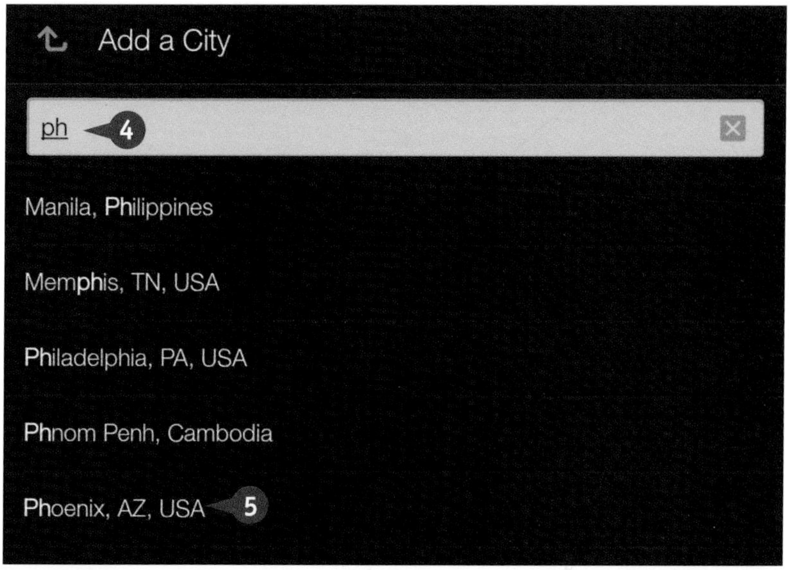

The time for the newly added city appears.

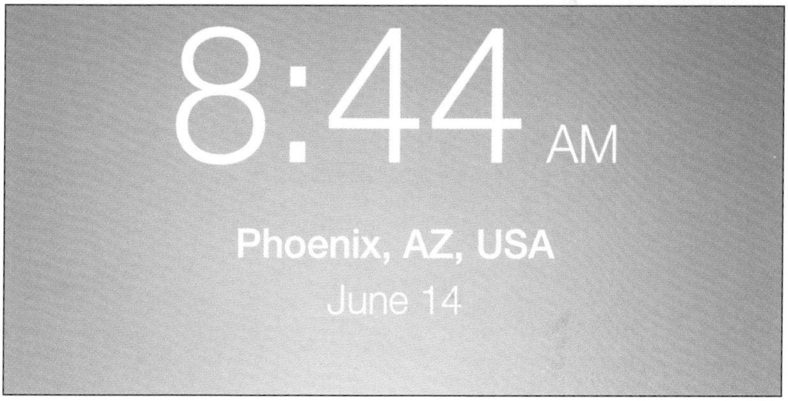

TIPS

How can I display all cities simultaneously?
Tap the **Navigation** button (☰) and, from the Navigation panel, tap **All Cities**. From the All Cities view, you can tap an individual city to select it. You also can cycle through each individual city you have set up and the All Cities view if you swipe from side to side.

Can I delete a city I no longer need?
Yes. In the Navigation panel, tap **All Cities** to display the All Cities view. Then, long-tap (press and hold) the city you want to delete. From the menu that appears, tap **Remove**.

continued ▶

Set Clocks and Alarms (continued)

You can set alarms to notify you when a certain time occurs. You do not need to be viewing the Clock app; alarms will go off regardless of the app you are using or even if your Fire tablet is sleeping. You can set alarms that repeat at an interval you specify — daily, on weekdays, on weekends, or at a customized daily interval that you specify.

The Clock app automatically sets up two default alarms, but they are not enabled; you must turn them on to use them.

Set an Alarm

1 Follow steps **1** to **2** in the subsection "Add a City."

The last view you used in the Clock app appears.

2 Tap ▷.

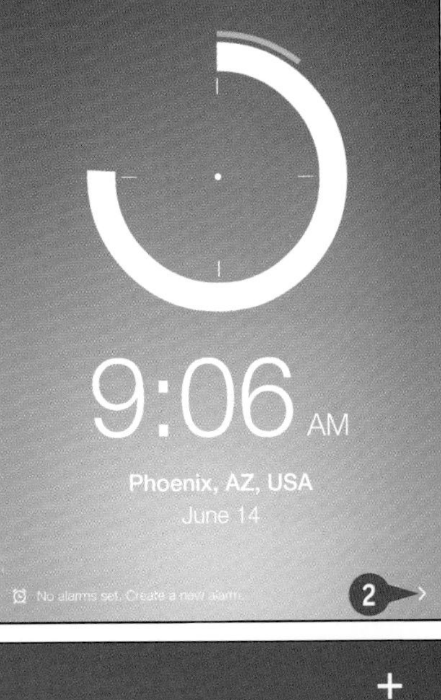

The Alarms screen appears, showing default alarms the app sets.

3 Tap ＋ to create a new alarm.

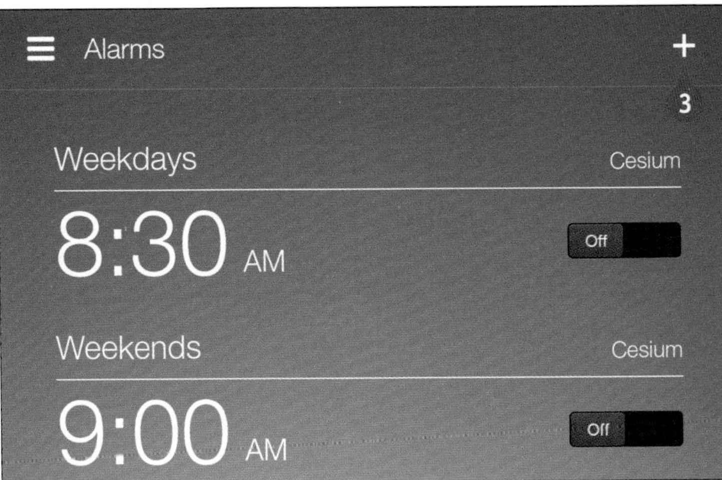

The Add an Alarm screen appears.

4. Tap these numbers to set the alarm time.
5. Tap ▷ to select an option for repeating the alarm.
6. Tap ▷ to select a sound for the alarm.
7. Tap **Set Alarm**.

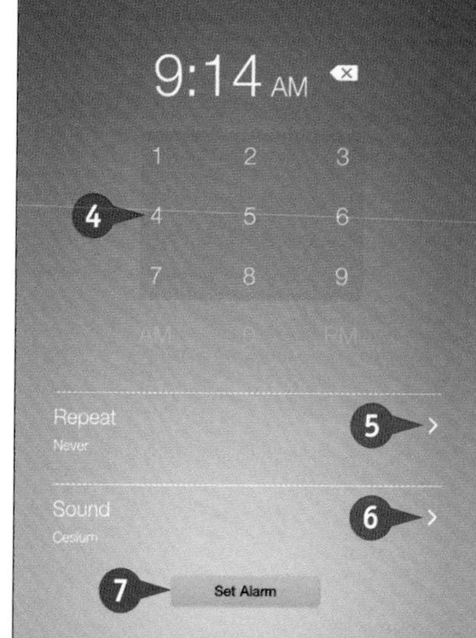

The Alarms screen reappears.

- A The newly created alarm appears, enabled.
- B You can tap **On** or **Off** to enable or disable an alarm.

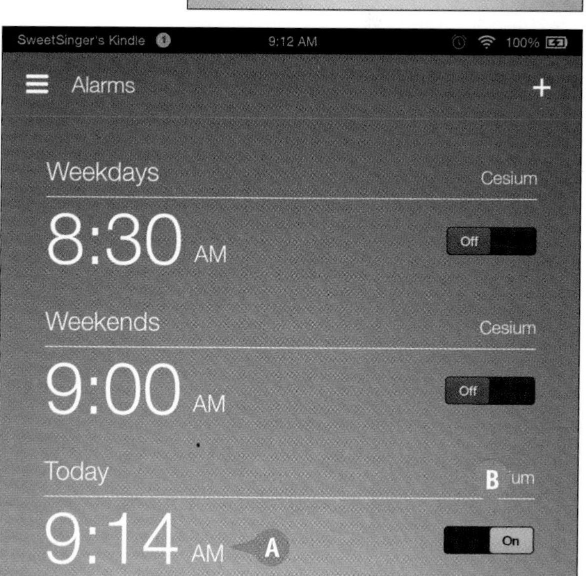

What do I see when an alarm goes off?
A screen like this one appears. You can double-tap the screen to snooze the alarm for 10 minutes, or you can swipe to turn off the alarm.

Hello, it's:
9:14 AM

Using Other Clock Features

In addition to monitoring the time at various locations and setting alarms, the Clock app has other features that let you monitor other time-related activities. You can use the stopwatch to time the length of an event. You also can pause the stopwatch and add time to it as it runs. You can use Nightstand mode to dim the appearance of the clock, keeping the time visible but muted to avoid disturbing sleep. And, the Timer feature counts down an amount of time you specify.

Using Other Clock Features

Using the Stopwatch

1. Follow steps **1** and **2** in the subsection "Add a City" of the section "Set Clocks and Alarms" to open the Clock app.
2. Tap the **Navigation** button (▤) to display the Navigation panel.
3. Tap **Stopwatch**.

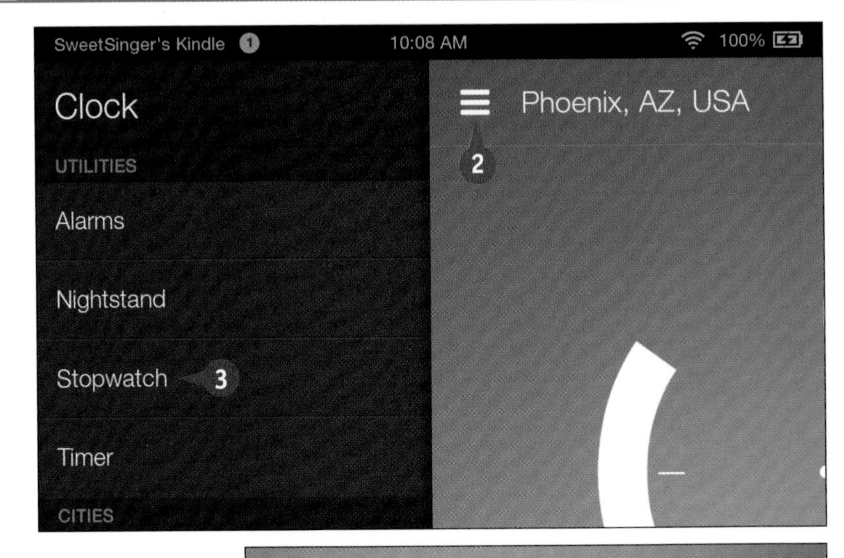

The Stopwatch screen appears.

4. Tap the **Start** button to start the stopwatch (▶ changes to ⏸).

   You can tap the **Pause** button (⏸) to pause the stopwatch.

   A You can tap this button (⊕) to add laps.

   B You can tap here (⟲) to stop and reset the stopwatch.

5. Tap the **Back** arrow (⬅) to redisplay the last view of the Clock app.

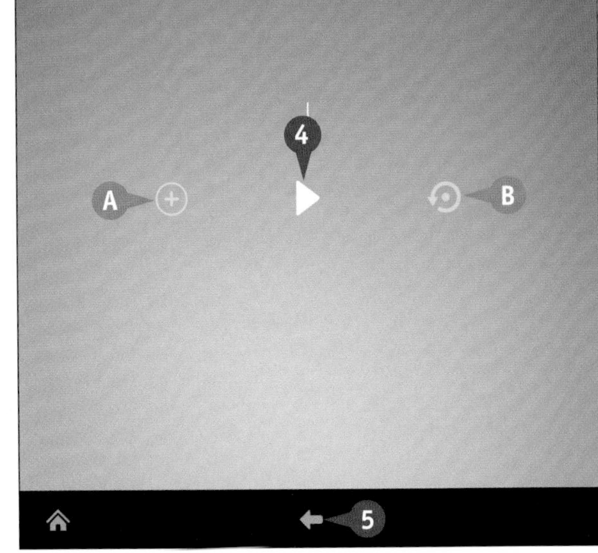

Using Nightstand Mode

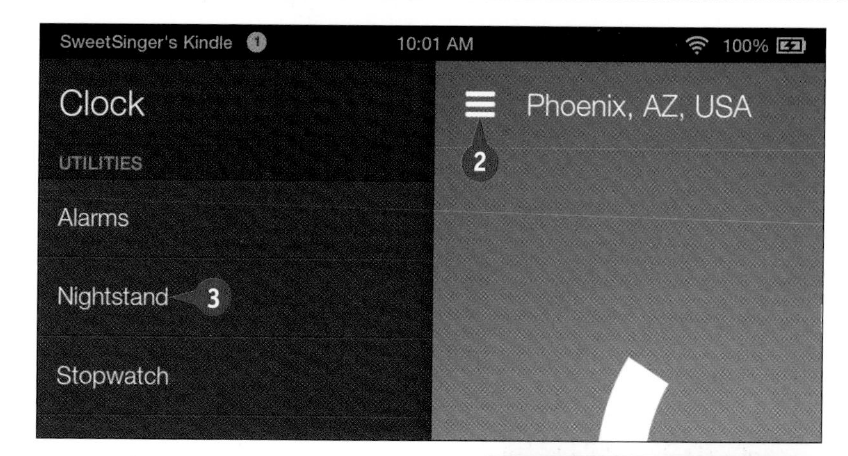

1. Follow steps **1** and **2** in the subsection "Add a City" of the section "Set Clocks and Alarms" to open the Clock app.
2. Tap the **Navigation** button (☰) to display the Navigation panel.
3. Tap **Nightstand.**

   The dimmed Nightstand mode view of the clock appears.

4. Tap ▭ to display the Options bar.

   You can tap the **Back** arrow (⬅) in the Options bar to redisplay the last view of the Clock app.

TIP

What is the difference between the stopwatch and the timer?
The stopwatch measures how much time has elapsed since you started the stopwatch. You can run the stopwatch while you do other tasks on your Fire tablet, and then return to it to determine the time those tasks took you to do. The timer, on the other hand, measures a predetermined amount of time. You can use the timer instead of an alarm as described in the section "Set Clocks and Alarms." Alarms sound at a predetermined time, but timers sound after a predetermined amount of time has elapsed.

continued ▶

Once you start the Timer feature, your Fire tablet can notify you after an amount of time elapses. As the timer runs, you can pause it, add the original amount of time you set to the time remaining, and stop and reset the timer. When the timer reaches the allotted amount of time, a screen appears and an alarm sounds to notify you that time is up.

In addition, you can use the Clock app's settings to control the behavior of alarms.

Using Other Clock Features (continued)

Using the Timer

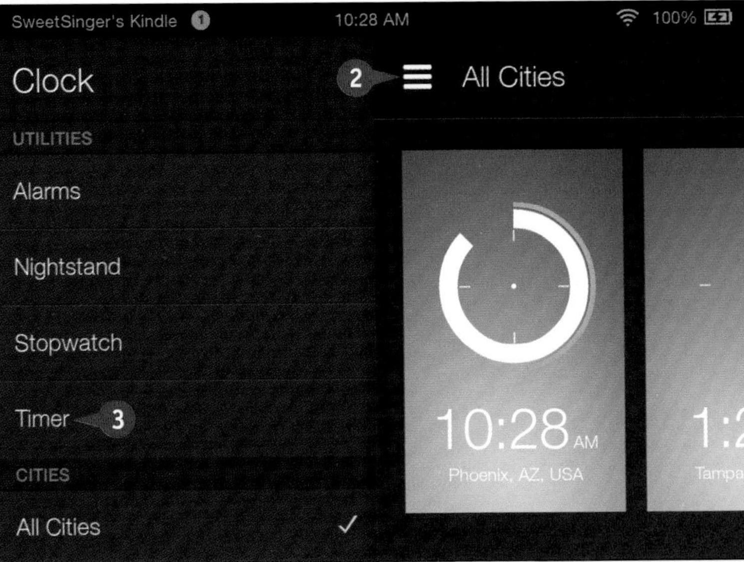

1. Follow steps **1** to **2** in the subsection "Add a City" of the section "Set Clocks and Alarms" to open the Clock app.
2. Tap the **Navigation** button (☰) to display the Navigation panel.
3. Tap **Timer**.

The Add Timer screen appears.

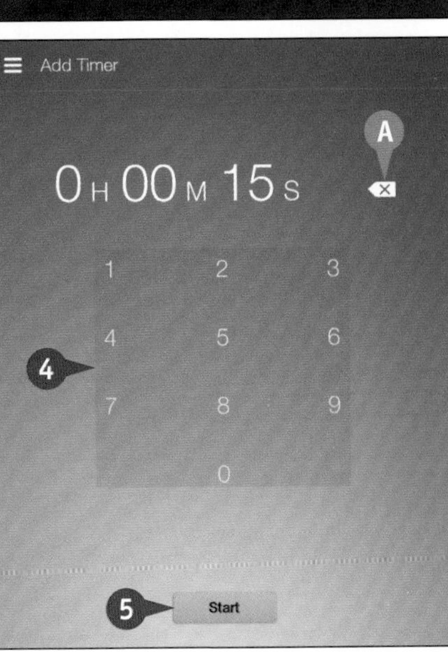

4. Tap numbers to set a timer amount.

A. If you make a mistake while setting the timer amount, tap this button (⌫) to reset the timer.

5. Tap **Start**.

The timer begins.

B You can tap this button (⊕) to add the original timer amount to the remaining time on the timer.

C You can tap the **Pause** button (II) to pause the timer.

D You can tap here (⟲) to stop and reset the timer and redisplay the Add Timer screen.

When the timer finishes, this screen appears, along with an audible beeping alert.

E You can double-tap to restart the timer or swipe to dismiss it.

Note: When you dismiss the timer, the Add Timer screen reappears.

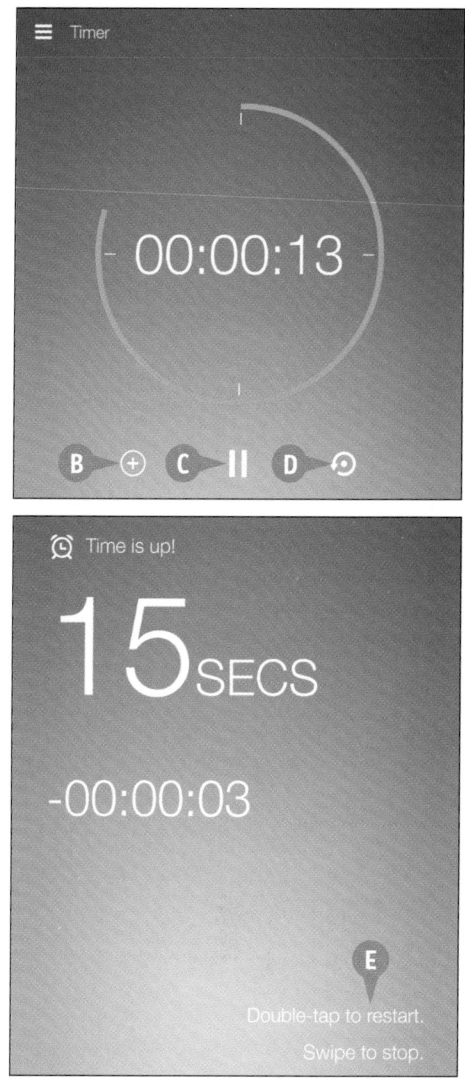

TIP

How can I control the behavior of alarms?

You can set the amount of time before the alarm stops, the length of time to snooze, and the alarm volume via the Clock Settings screen. To get there, tap the **Navigation** button (☰) and, in the Navigation panel, tap **Settings**.

Clock Settings
ALARMS
Silence After
10 minutes
Snooze Length
10 minutes
Alarm Volume

Set Up Kindle FreeTime

Using Kindle FreeTime, you can specify the content on your Fire tablet that your child can use. The Kindle FreeTime app is protected with a *parental controls password* that you, as the parent, set up. You must supply that password each time you want to make changes to the content viewed by your child.

As part of the Kindle FreeTime app, you can subscribe to Kindle FreeTime Unlimited. If you opt to skip the subscription during the setup process but later change your mind, FreeTime app settings allow you to establish a subscription.

Set Up Kindle FreeTime

1. From the Home screen, tap **Apps**.

   The Apps content library appears.

2. Tap **Kindle FreeTime**.

Note: The first time you use the app, it might need to download from the Amazon Appstore for Android. Tap again to open the app.

The setup wizard for Kindle FreeTime begins.

 Tap **Get Started**.

The Parental Controls Password screen appears.

4. Type a password.
5. Retype the password.
6. Tap **Continue**.

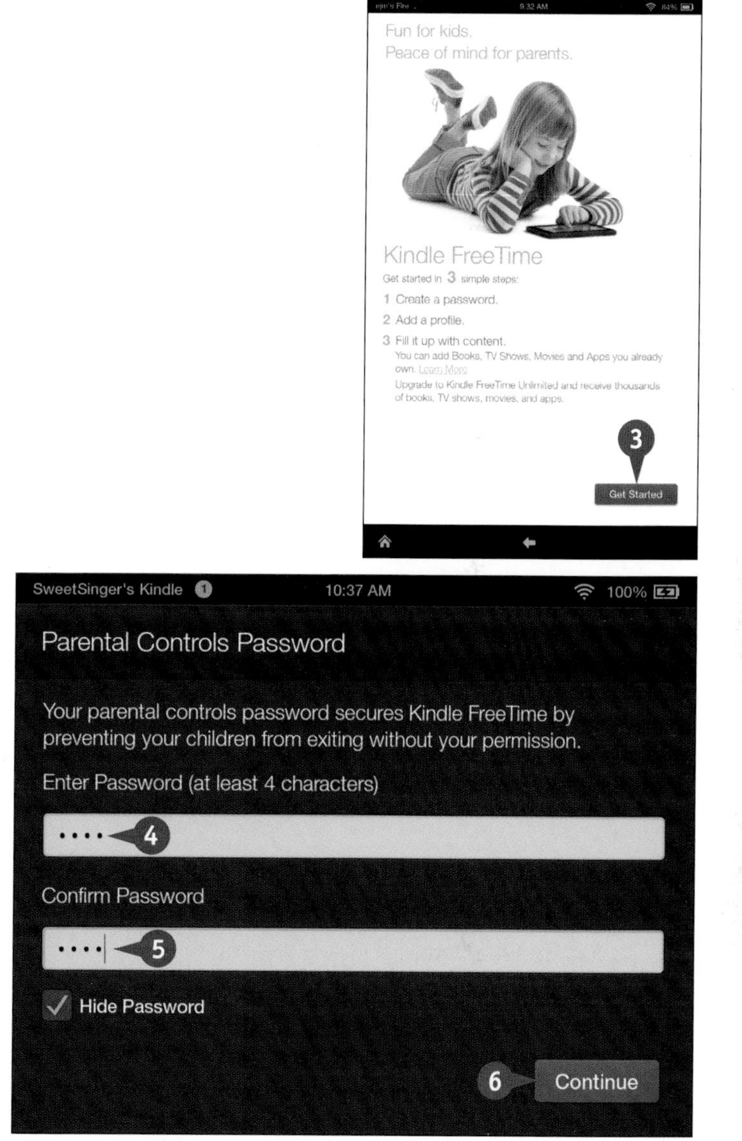

TIP

What is Kindle FreeTime Unlimited?

Kindle FreeTime Unlimited is an optional monthly subscription that offers frequently refreshed content — books, apps, movies, and TV shows — for children ages 3 to 8 years old. The content available through a Kindle FreeTime Unlimited subscription does not display ads, options for in-app purchases, links to websites, or links to social media such as Facebook or Twitter. To subscribe, after the initial FreeTime app setup, tap **Manage Your Content** from the main Kindle FreeTime screen, and then tap **Subscribe to FreeTime Unlimited** and follow the on-screen prompts.

continued ▶

After you create the parental controls password, you then set up a profile for the child who will use your Kindle. In the profile, you identify the child's name, gender, and birthdate; you also can assign an image to help identify the profile. In addition to identification information, you also select content on your Fire tablet for your child to use.

When you use the FreeTime app after the initial setup is complete, you select a profile to provide access to the content for that specific profile. See the section "Using Kindle FreeTime" for more details.

Set Up Kindle FreeTime (continued)

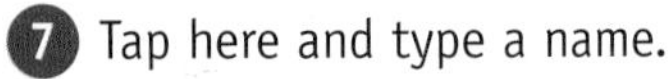

7. Tap here and type a name.
8. Choose a gender.
9. Tap here to supply a birthdate.

The Set Date screen appears.

10. Swipe in the Set Date columns or tap on the calendar to set a birthdate.

11. Tap **Done**.

The Add Child Profile screen reappears.

12 Tap here to set an image.

The Select Photo window appears.

13 Tap a photo.

TIPS

Am I limited to allowing only one child to use my Fire tablet?
No, you can establish individual profiles for each child, which is particularly useful if your children's age differences are significant. Using multiple profiles, you can provide each child with content appropriate to his or her age group.

Can I use a picture of my child for the profile's image?
Not at this time; you are limited to the choices that appear in the Select Photo window.

continued ►

During the final steps of establishing a profile, you identify the content to which you want your child to have access. Although Amazon makes recommendations for appropriate content for your child, you are free to pick and choose from among those recommendations or ignore them altogether.

You also can establish time limits for your child to use Kindle FreeTime. You can set hours that an app is available as well as an amount of time your child can use the app.

Set Up Kindle FreeTime (continued)

The Add Child Profile screen reappears.

(A) If you have another child, you can tap **Add Another Child** and repeat steps **7** to **13**.

14 Tap **Next**.

An advertisement for Kindle FreeTime Unlimited appears.

You can opt to start a free trial and follow the on-screen prompts, or you can tap **No Thanks**.

15 For this example, tap **No Thanks**.

Note: You can opt to subscribe to Kindle FreeTime Unlimited later, if you change your mind.

The Manage Content & Subscription screen appears.

16 In the Share your Content area, tap the button for the child for whom you want to provide content.

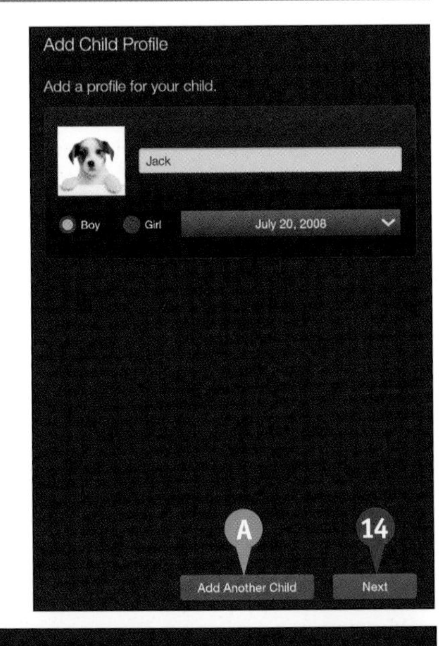

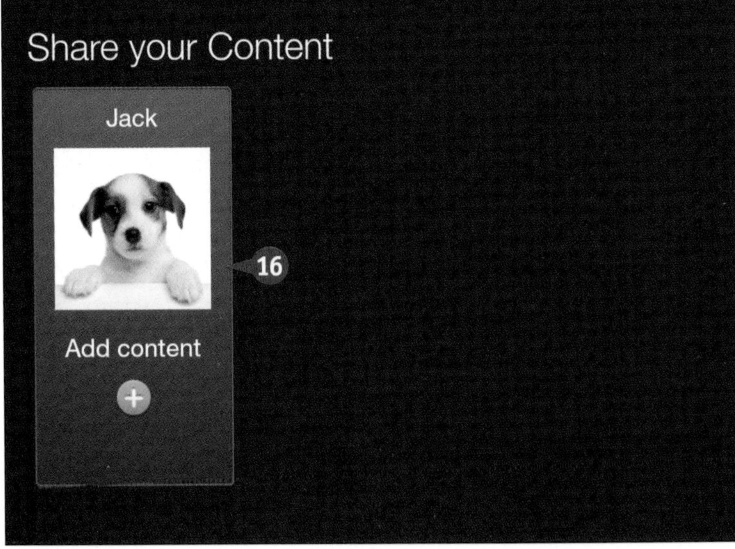

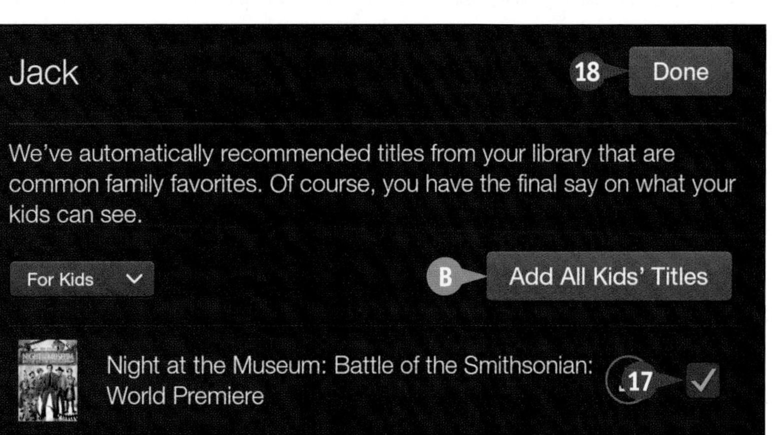

A screen like this one appears, where Amazon displays recommended titles appropriate for children.

17. Tap beside a title to allow the child to see it (■ changes to ☑).

B. You can tap **Add All Kids' Titles** to select all recommended titles.

18. Tap **Done**.

The Manage Content & Subscription page reappears.

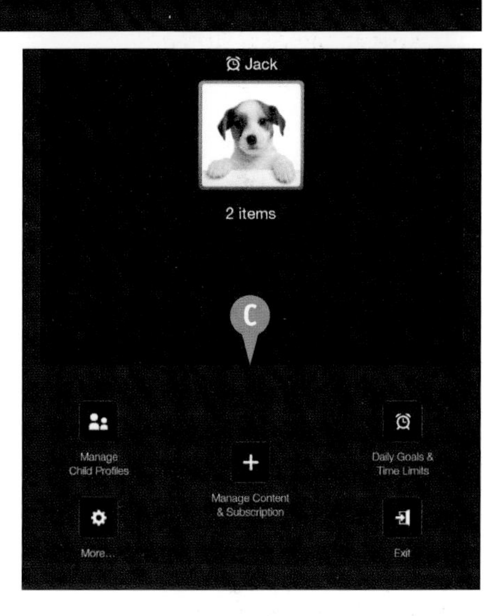

19. Tap **Done** at the top of the screen.

The main page of Kindle FreeTime appears and you see the profiles you set up.

C. You can use these controls to make changes to profiles or their content, to set daily usage limits, and to change the parental password.

TIP

How do I limit the amount of time my child uses my Fire tablet?

On the main Kindle FreeTime screen, tap **Daily Goals & Time Limits**. Supply the parental password, tap a child's profile, and tap the **On** switch (A). The child's profile page appears, and you can set the period and amount of time the child can use the device.

Using Kindle FreeTime

After setting up the Kindle FreeTime app, you can launch it and give your Fire tablet to your child. The app has its own Carousel, like the one on the device's Home screen, where your child views any content to which he or she has access. In addition, the Kindle FreeTime app has its own Navigation bar containing content libraries.

Even if you start the Kindle FreeTime app while holding your Fire tablet in portrait orientation, the device switches to landscape view after you choose a profile.

Using Kindle FreeTime

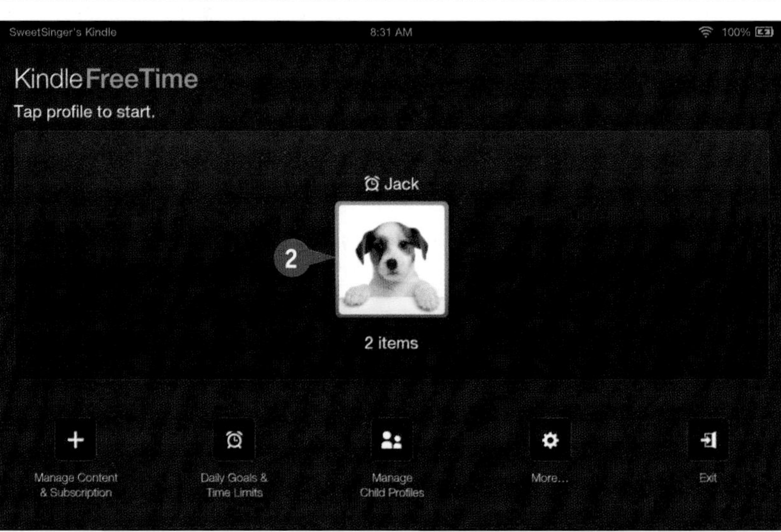

1 Tap **Apps** and then tap **Kindle FreeTime** to open the Kindle FreeTime app. See "Set Up Kindle FreeTime" for details.

2 Tap a profile.

By default, your Fire tablet changes to landscape orientation.

Your child's Carousel appears here, along with any content the child has viewed.

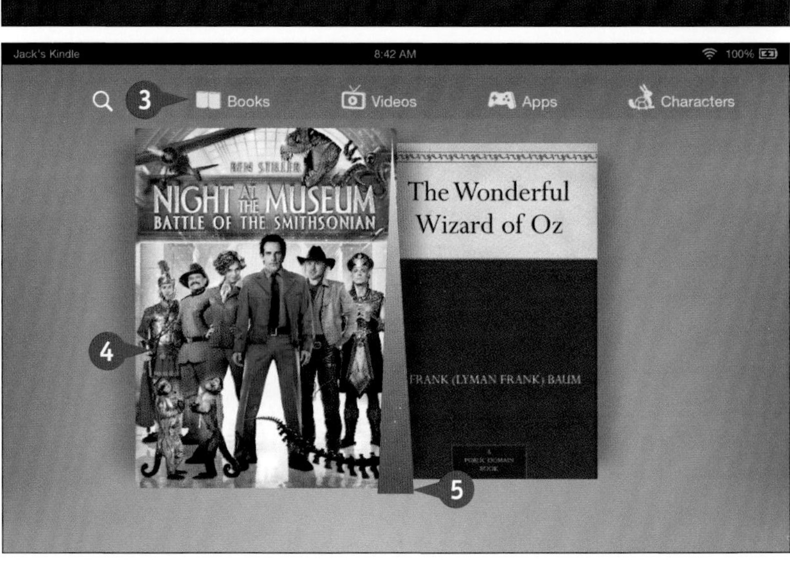

3 Tap one of these content libraries to view the content in that library.

4 Tap any content item to use it.

Note: When your child finishes using Kindle FreeTime, you should exit from the app.

5 Swipe down from the top of the screen.

The Quick Settings appear.

6 Tap **Exit FreeTime**.

You are prompted for your credentials.

7 Type the parental controls password.

8 Tap **Submit**.

You exit FreeTime

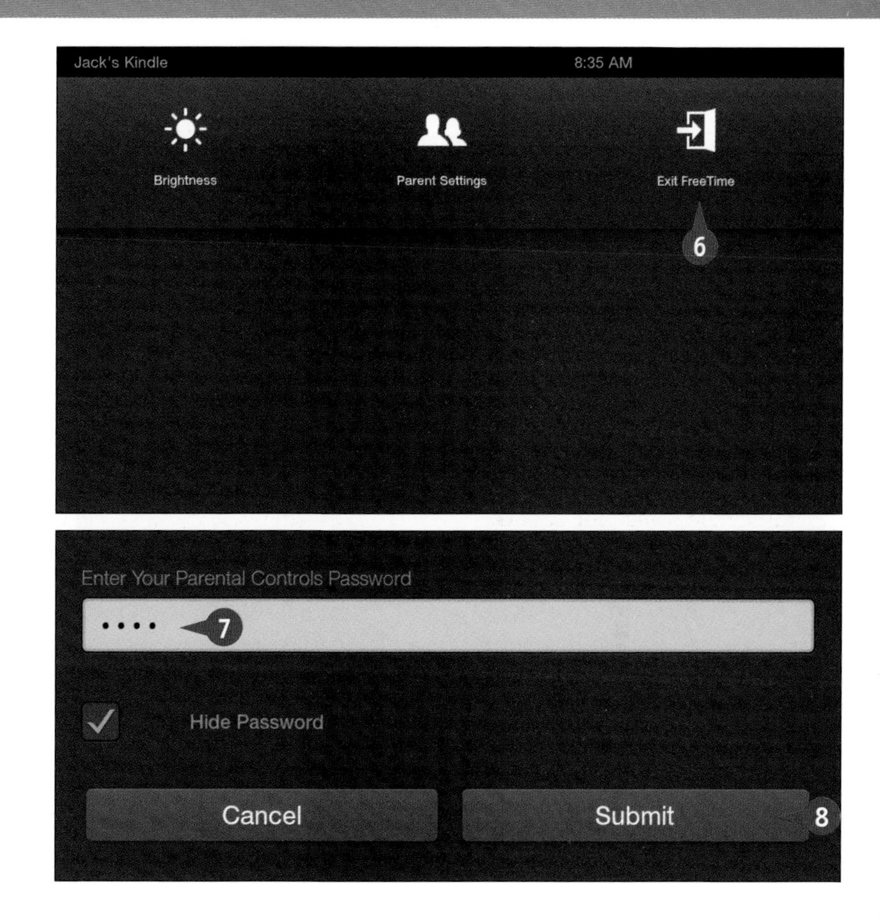

TIP

Why does the Kindle FreeTime app prompt for the parental controls password when you exit from the app?

The Kindle FreeTime app provides a safe and secure environment for your child and limits the content to which he or she has access. If your child could exit from the app without providing the parental controls password, the content to which your child has access would not be limited. Requiring the parental controls password upon exit is one more way in which the Kindle FreeTime app helps you control the content your child can view.

Explore the IMDb Movies & TV App

You can use the IMDb (Internet Movie Database) app to answer questions about movies, TV shows, and Hollywood celebrities. The database is quite complete and contains information about more than 2,000,000 movies and TV shows, and more than 4,000,000 actors, actresses, movie directors, and other crew members.

You also can read reviews of movies and TV shows written both by critics and other users. The IMDb app also keeps track of your queries and saves them so that you can refer back to them at a later date.

Explore the IMDb Movies & TV App

1. From the Home screen, tap **Apps**.

   The Apps content library appears.

2. Tap **IMDb**.

Note: The first time you open the app, it might need to download from the Amazon Appstore for Android. Tap again to open the app. And, you are prompted to use your Amazon account or your IMDb account to sign in; tap the one that applies to you, then tap **Start Using IMDB**.

   The Navigation panel of the IMDb app appears.

3. Tap **Home** to view the IMDb app's Home screen.

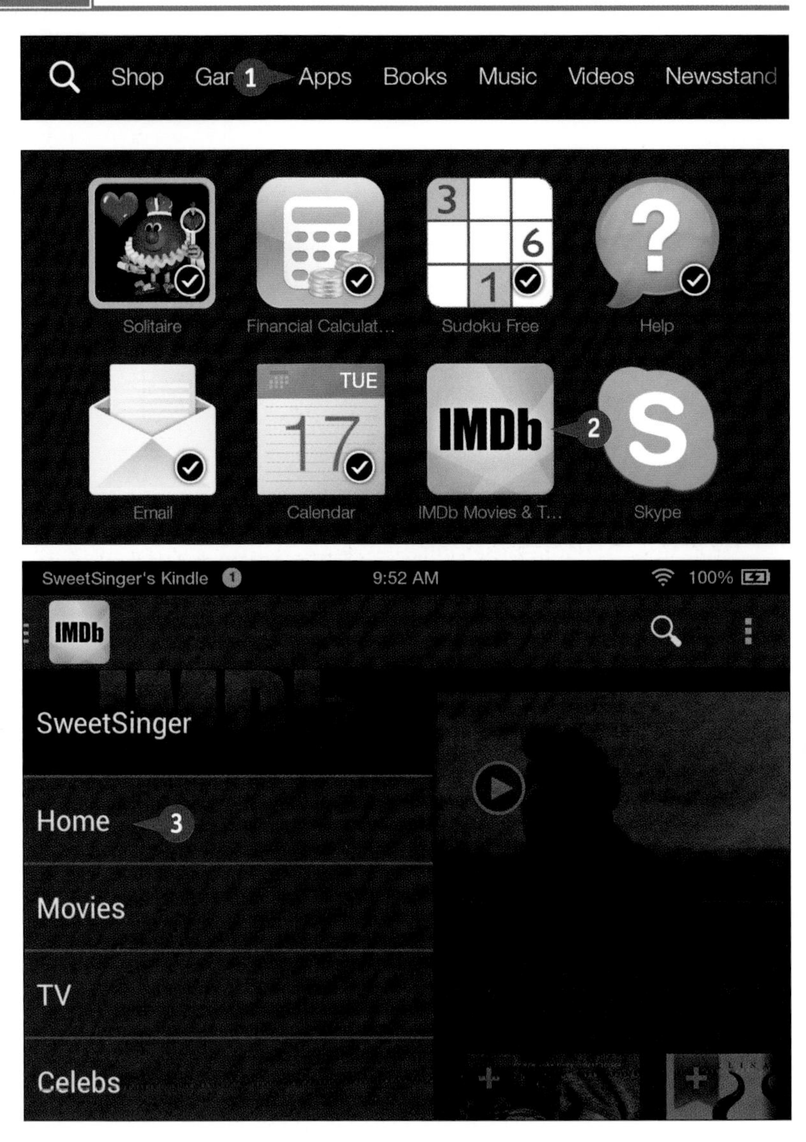

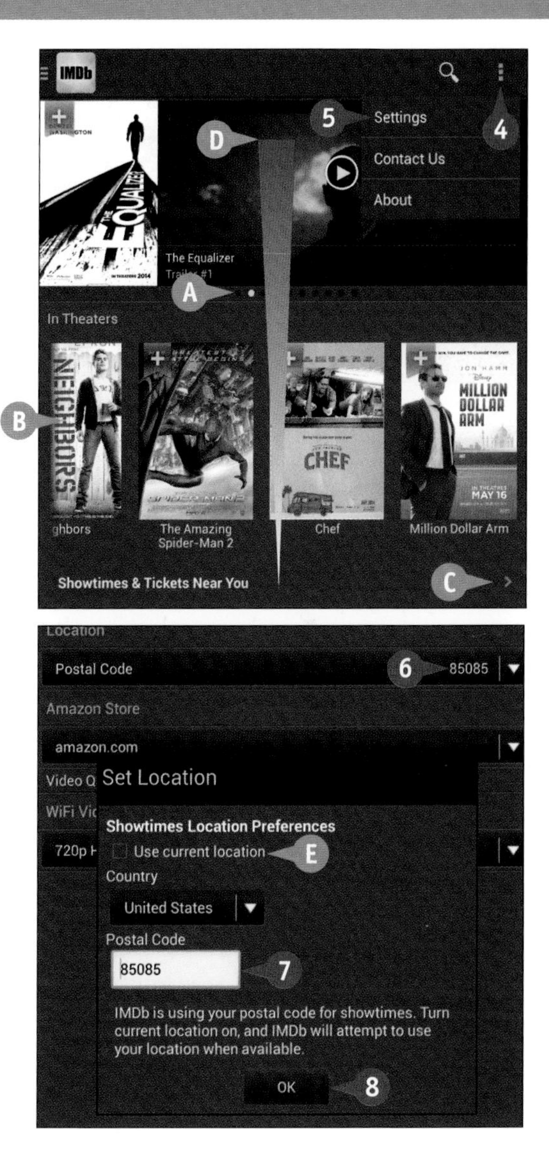

- A Swiping right to left in this section displays available movie trailers; tap any trailer to watch it.
- B Swiping right to left in this section shows recently released and soon-to-be-released movies. Tap any movie to view more information.
- C Tapping ▶ displays showtimes near you.
- D Swiping up displays more information on an item.

4 Tap ⋮ to open the IMDb app's menu.

5 Tap **Settings**.

6 Tap here to set your geographic location.

- E You can tap here to use your GPS location (☐ changes to ☑).

7 Tap here to type and use your postal code.

8 Tap **OK**.

You can tap the **Back** arrow (⬅) to redisplay the IMDb app's Home screen.

TIP

What can I find in the TV section of the IMDb app?

The IMDb Movies & TV app offers trailers for TV shows and provides details on the year a show premiered, the show's length, and the TV rating. You can scroll through TV listings and read recaps of the most recent episodes of various shows, and you can view the TV shows that will air tonight in your local time zone. You can also purchase TV shows released to DVD and Blu-ray.

Find Movie Times and Buy Tickets

You can find the showtime for a particular movie at a theater near you, and, if the theater permits it, purchase tickets for the movie over the Internet. You can find theaters where a particular movie is playing, or view all the movies showing at a particular theater. This section demonstrates how to view all the movies at a particular theater and how to select one to see.

If you view a movie's detail page, you can watch its trailer and read the movie's reviews from both critics and fellow viewers.

Find Movie Times and Buy Tickets

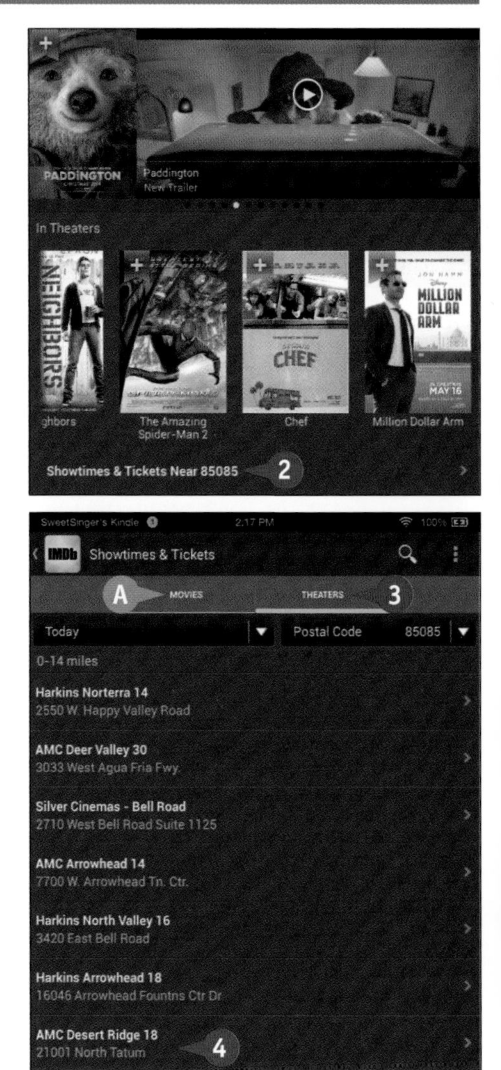

1. Complete steps **1** and **2** in the section "Explore the IMDb Movies & TV App" to open the IMDb app.

2. Tap **Showtimes & Tickets Near *XXXXX***, where *XXXXX* is your ZIP code.

The Showtimes & Tickets screen appears.

A. You can tap **Movies** to search for a movie.

3. Tap **Theaters** to view nearby theaters.

4. Tap a theater.

The movies playing at the theater appear.

Ⓑ The theater's information appears in this area.

The movies currently playing appear in the bottom half of the screen.

Note: You can tap a movie to view its details.

Ⓒ A movie's showtimes appear here.

5 Tap **Tickets**.

Note: Only some theaters sell tickets online.

The Buy Tickets wizard begins.

6 Type in the requested information, swipe up to scroll down, and tap **Next** until you complete your ticket purchase.

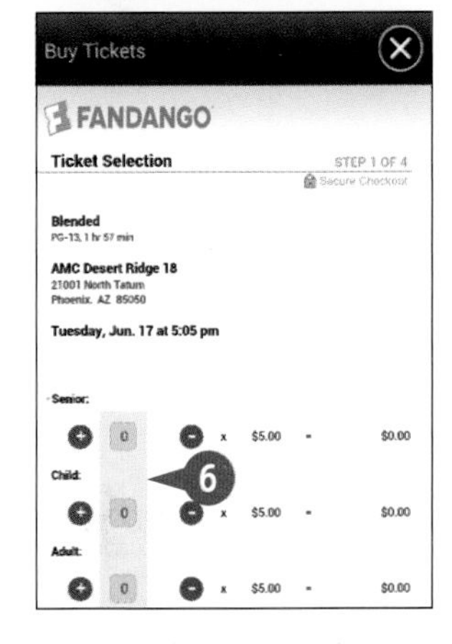

TIP

If the movie is showing at more than one time, how do I select the showing for which I want to purchase tickets?

If the movie is showing at multiple times, the Buy Tickets box is preceded by a box like this one, where you tap the time for which you want to purchase tickets. After you make your choice, the Buy Tickets window appears.

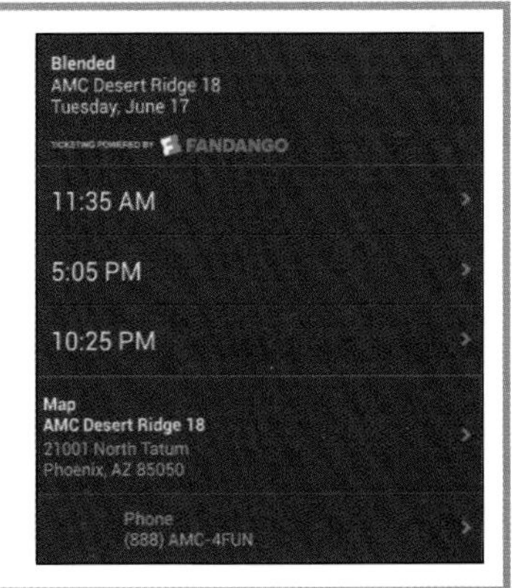

Read about Celebrities

Using the IMDb Movies & TV app, you can view information about various celebrities. You can scroll through a list of celebrities, search for a specific celebrity, or view the celebrities born today. On any selected celebrity's page, you can read the star's biography, including birthdate, hometown, and films for which the celebrity is known. You can browse through photos and read trivia about and quotes from the star. You also can read message boards to see what others are saying about a celebrity as well as news items about the star.

Read about Celebrities

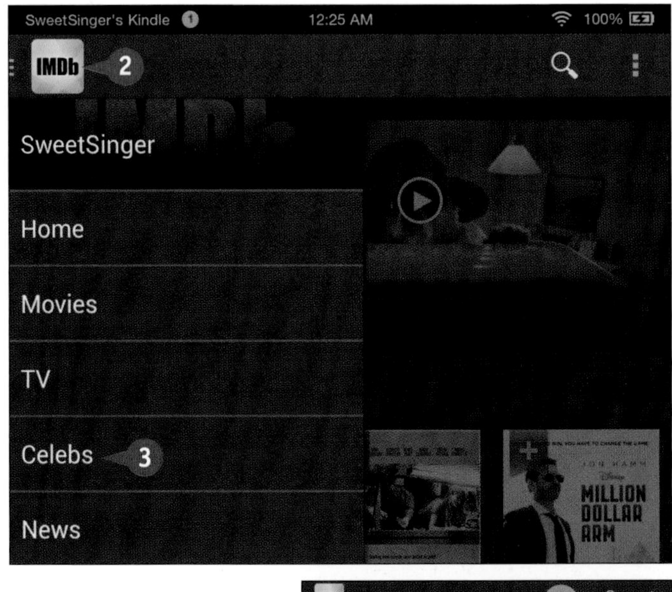

1. Complete steps **1** and **2** in the section "Explore the IMDb Movies & TV App" to open the IMDb app.
2. Tap the **IMDb** logo to open the Navigation panel.
3. Tap **Celebs**.

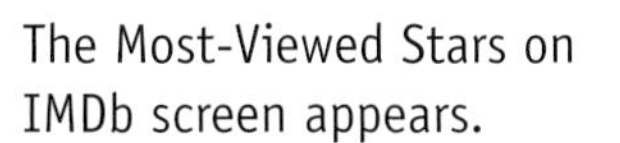

The Most-Viewed Stars on IMDb screen appears.

A. You can swipe up to scroll down and look for a celebrity.

B. You can tap the **Search** button (🔍) to search for a celebrity.

C. You can tap **Born Today** to view celebrities born today.

4. Tap a celebrity.

The celebrity's page appears.

Ⓓ The celebrity's biography appears in this area.

Ⓔ Movies for which the star is known appear in this row.

5 Swipe up to scroll down and view more details.

6 Tap **Trivia**.

Trivia about the star appears.

Ⓕ You can tap the **Back** arrow (⬅) to move back one screen or the **Home** button (🏠) to return to the Fire tablet Home screen.

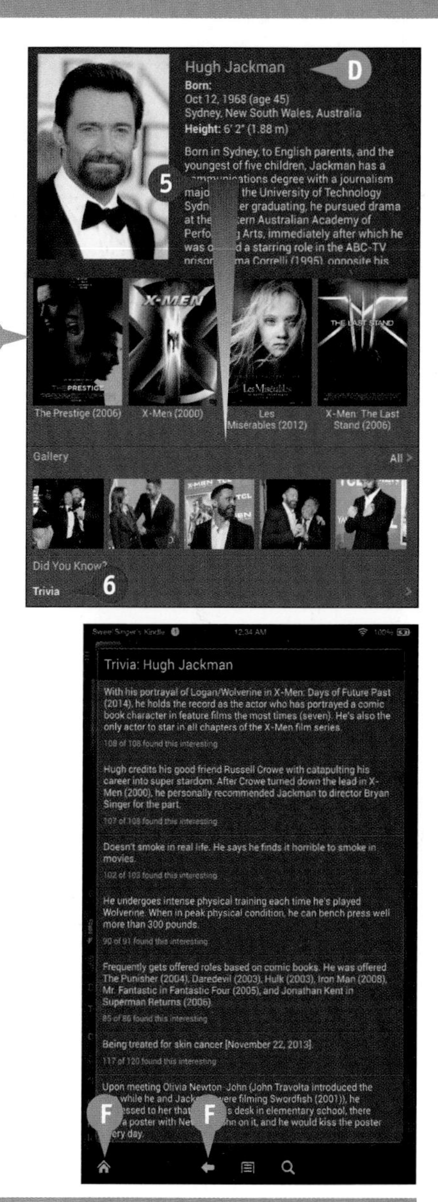

TIP

What happens if I tap View on IMDb.com on a star's page?

The IMDb web page for that star appears, providing biographical information, news, photos, and more.

Hugh Jackman
Actor | Soundtrack | Producer
Born in Sydney, to English parents, and the youngest children, Jackman has a communications degree with journalism major from the University of Technology S After graduating, he pursued drama at the Western Australian Academy of Performing Arts, immediately which he was offered a starring role in the ABC-TV pr drama ... See full bio »
Born: Hugh Michael Jackman
October 12, 1968 in Sydney, New South Wales, Aust

Examine Yelp

You can use the Yelp app to find events and local businesses such as restaurants, dentists, auto mechanics, and hair stylists. Business owners can set up free accounts and post photos and information for their customers. Customers can post reviews and tips, and earn deals from businesses by checking in to those businesses. Yelp makes money by selling ads to local businesses, but advertisers cannot control reviews that customers post.

Not all reviews are posted. Instead, Yelp's software finds the most helpful and reliable reviews by looking at a variety of signals, excluding advertising on Yelp.

Examine Yelp

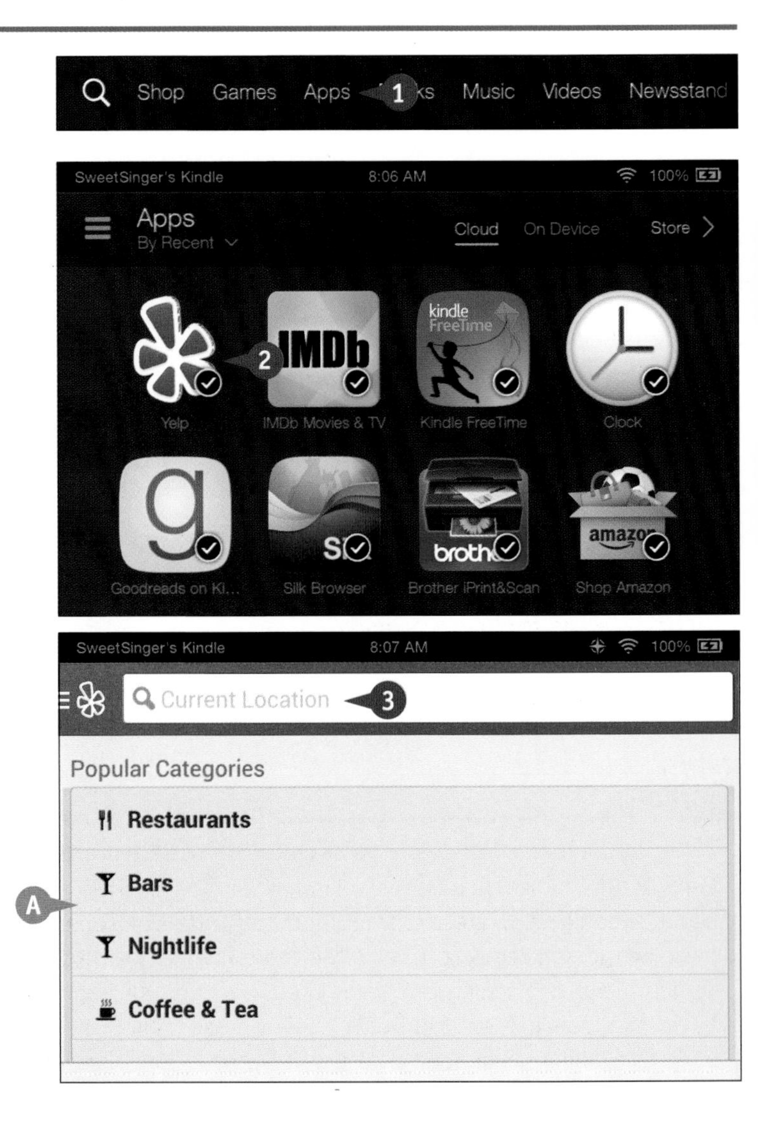

1. From the Home screen, tap **Apps**.

   The Apps content library appears.

2. Tap **Yelp**.

   The Yelp app opens.

   Ⓐ You can tap one of these popular categories to search that category.

3. Tap here to type a search term and tap any **Search** button (🔍) on-screen.

Note: If you type no search term and tap 🔍, Yelp returns a list of all known businesses at your location.

Search results appear in list form and on a map containing a marker for each search result.

B You can tap any marker on the map to determine the search result it represents.

4 Tap a search result.

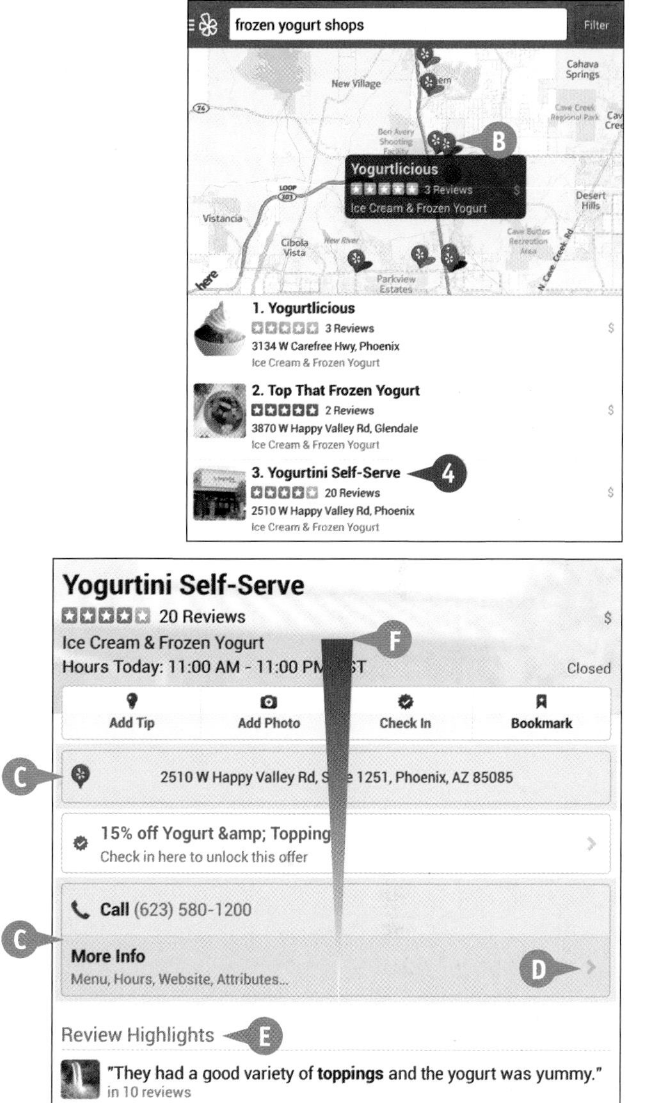

The Yelp page for that search result appears.

C Location and contact information appears here.

D You can tap ▷ to read website details.

E The page contains review highlights and photos.

F You can swipe up to scroll down the page and read reviews and tips and see people who regularly check in to that business.

TIPS

What are Deals and how do I get them?

Deals are discounts that businesses offer to people who check in electronically. You can find deals by tapping the **Yelp** icon in the top-left corner of the Yelp screen to display the Navigation panel. Then, tap **Deals** to view a list of deals available near your location. Tap any deal to view its details.

What are check-ins?

Check-ins are Yelp's method to establish yourself as someone who regularly frequents a business. To achieve the status of a regular at a particular business, you use the Yelp app to check in to that business. The more you check in, the closer you become to being labeled a regular patron. If you stop checking in, you can lose your status.

CHAPTER 4

Playing Games, Music, and Movies

You can play games on your Fire tablet and, using Amazon GameCircle, you can compare your game accomplishments with others. Your Fire tablet also can play music and movies; you buy music and videos from the Amazon Appstore for Android, as described in Chapter 2. You also can copy music from your computer to your Fire tablet.

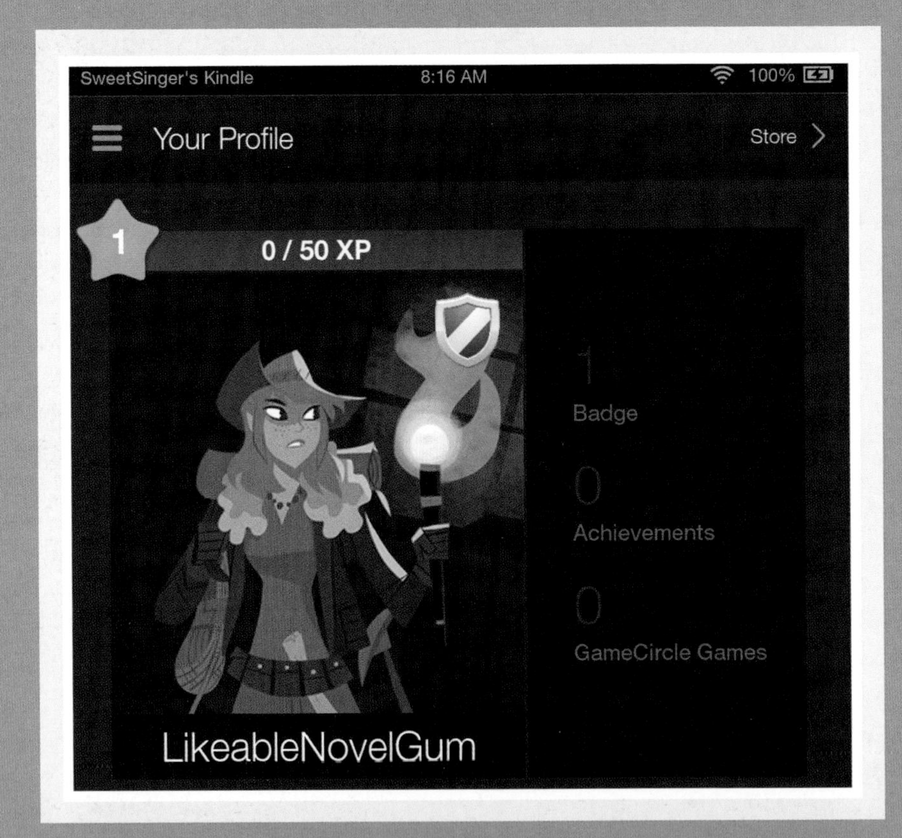

Work with Amazon GameCircle 90
Turn Off In-App Purchasing 92
Listen to Music 94
Transfer Music from Your PC 96
Watch a Movie or a TV Show. 98

Work with Amazon GameCircle

Using Amazon GameCircle, you can view leaderboards and compare your achievements and time played in a game with others. As you play GameCircle-enabled games, your profile gains experience points, levels, and badges. If your game is Whispersync enabled — the Whispersync logo appears when you launch the game — GameCircle syncs your game progress so that you can play on any GameCircle-enabled device.

Amazon automatically creates a public profile for you, with a nickname and profile image, and displays your profile, badges, and high scores in public leaderboards. You can customize your nickname and profile image or hide them from the public.

Work with Amazon GameCircle

1. From the Home screen, tap **Games**.

The Games content library appears.

Ⓐ Your GameCircle avatar appears here.

Ⓑ Your GameCircle nickname appears here.

2. Tap the **Navigation** button (☰).

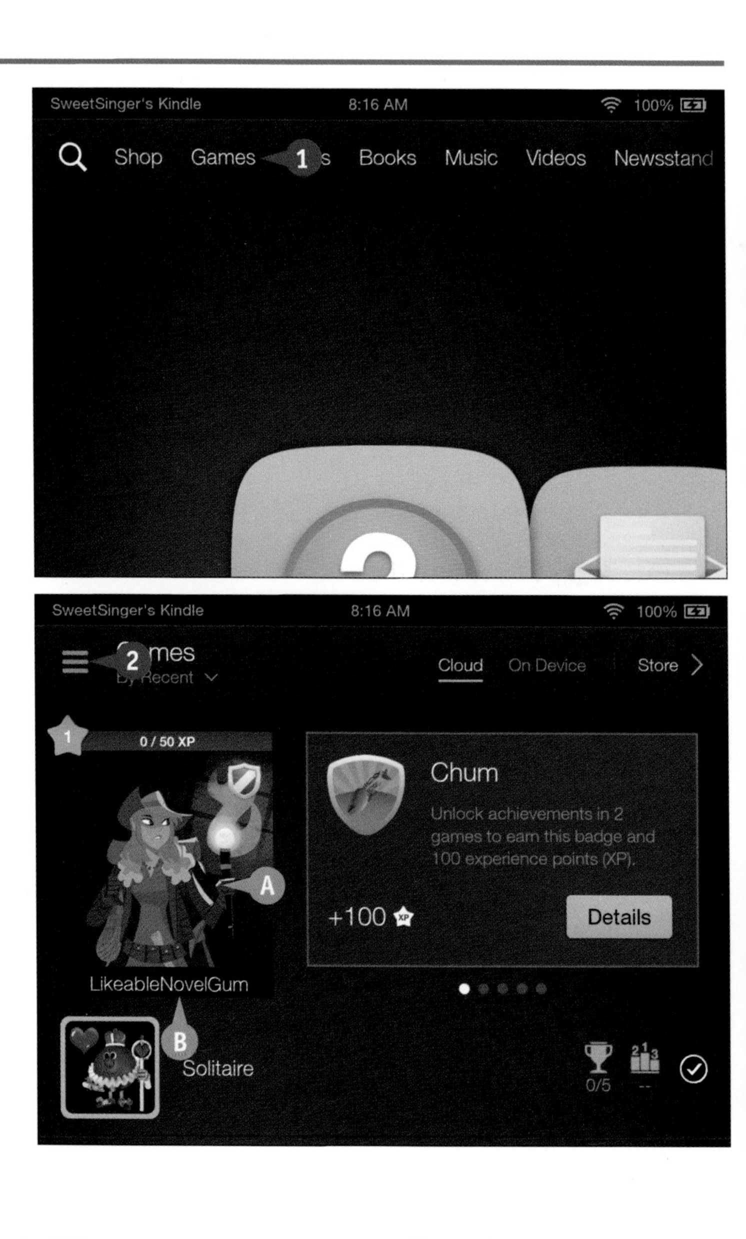

The Navigation panel appears.

3 Tap **Settings**.

The Amazon GameCircle settings page appears.

C You can tap **Show** or **Hide** to reveal or conceal GameCircle information in the Games content library.

D Tapping **Show** or **Hide** reveals or conceals your GameCircle public nickname.

E Tapping **On** or **Off** uploads or disables uploading your game progress to the Amazon Cloud.

At the bottom of the screen, you can tap the **Back** arrow (⬅) to return to the Games content library or the **Home** button (🏠) to return to the Home screen.

TIP

How can I control my GameCircle profile settings?

Tap your avatar in your Games content library. On the Your Profile screen, tap your profile picture A to choose a new one. Tap your name B to change it, tap a badge you have earned C, and tap **Display this Badge** in the menu that appears to display that badge on your profile.

Turn Off In-App Purchasing

You can prevent accidental purchases that some apps and games offer as you use them. In-app purchasing options typically offer some additional functionality for the app or game you are using. For example, a game might offer you the opportunity to purchase in-game currency or new game levels, or it might prompt you to purchase subscriptions.

Because the additional functionality you are offered will cost money, you can prevent in-app purchasing by changing Amazon Appstore for Android settings.

Turn Off In-App Purchasing

1 Swipe down from the top of the Fire tablet.

The Quick Settings screen appears.

2 Tap **Settings**.

The Settings screen appears.

3 Tap **Applications**.

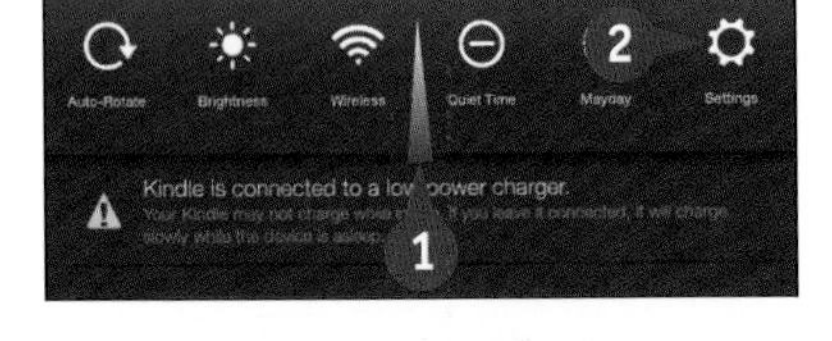

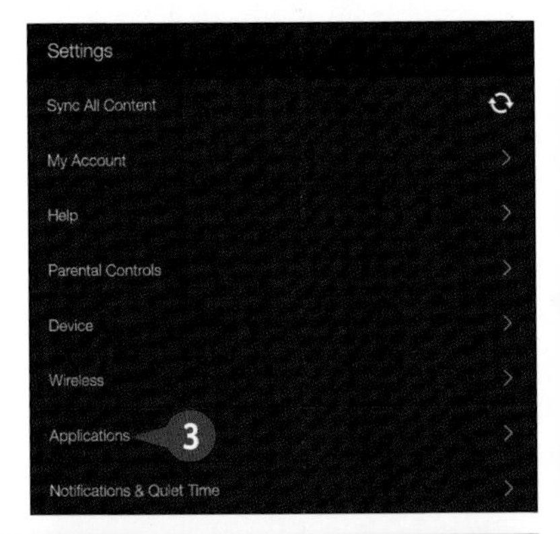

The settings screen for Applications appears.

 Tap **Appstore**.

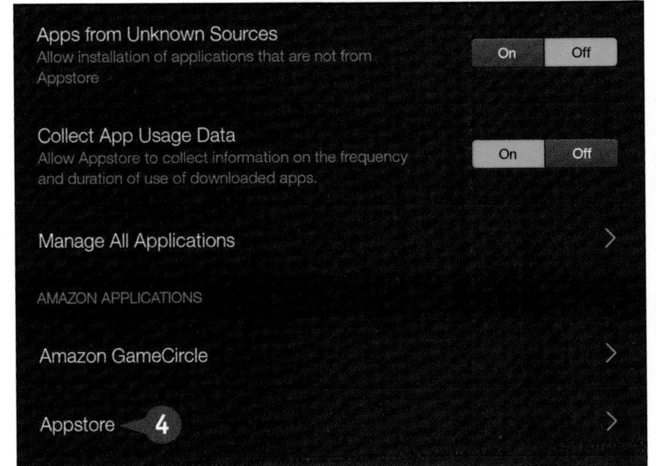

The App Settings screen appears.

5. Tap **In-App Purchasing**.

The In-App Purchasing settings screen appears.

6. Tap **Allow In-App Purchases**.

The Password Required box appears.

7. Type your Amazon account password.

8. Tap **Continue**.

A. You can tap the **Back** arrow (⬅) to back up one level in Settings or the **Home** button (🏠) to return to the Fire tablet Home screen.

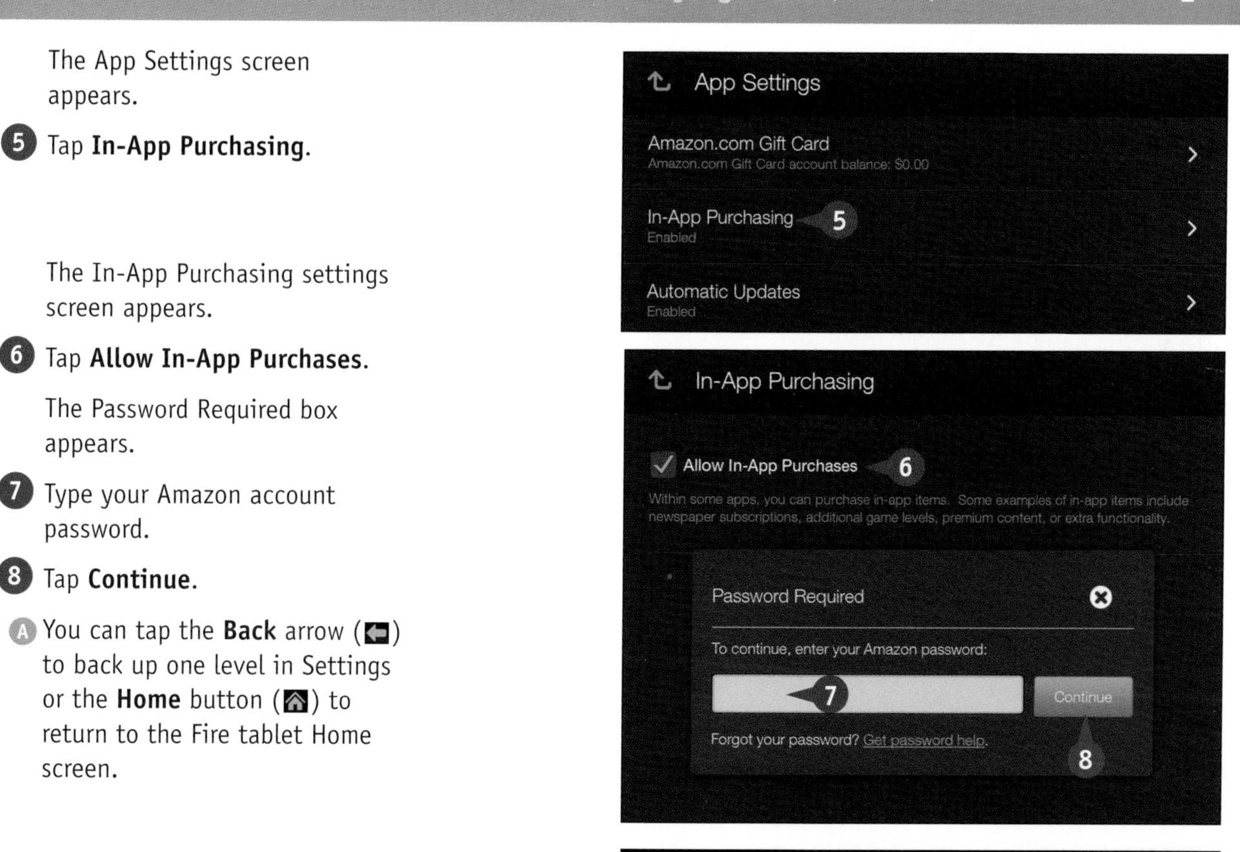

TIPS

What happens if I tap Amazon GameCircle on the Applications settings screen?

You see a settings screen where you can show or hide GameCircle information in the Games content library, show or hide your GameCircle public nickname, and opt to upload your game progress to the Amazon Cloud.

What does the External Market Links setting on the App Settings screen control?

From this screen, you can control how your Fire tablet handles links found in the Amazon Appstore for Android to external markets. You can choose to always open them, never open them, or accept the default option, which displays a prompt that enables you to open the page associated with the external market link.

Listen to Music

You can listen to music stored on your Fire tablet or in the Amazon Cloud. As you listen to a song, you can use playback controls to take charge of your listening experience. If you stream music from the Amazon Cloud, make sure you have a strong wireless connection to avoid pauses while loading or playing music.

Some songs also display and scroll lyrics automatically as the song progresses; these songs take advantage of the X-Ray for Music feature. Lyrics are most visible in landscape orientation. And, you can scroll through lyrics and use them to jump to a different section of the song. Note that you can leave the Music content library and use the tablet for other activities while the music plays.

Listen to Music

1. From the Home screen, tap **Music**.

   The Music content library appears.

   A. You can tap **Store** to visit the Music Store at www.amazon.com.

   B. Songs that use X-Ray for Music display [+Lyrics].

2. Tap the **Navigation** button (☰).

   The Navigation panel appears.

   C. You can use these choices to organize your music in the Music content library.

3. Tap the **Navigation** button (☰) again to redisplay the Music content library.

4. Tap an album or song to display the album's or song's screen and start playing the music.

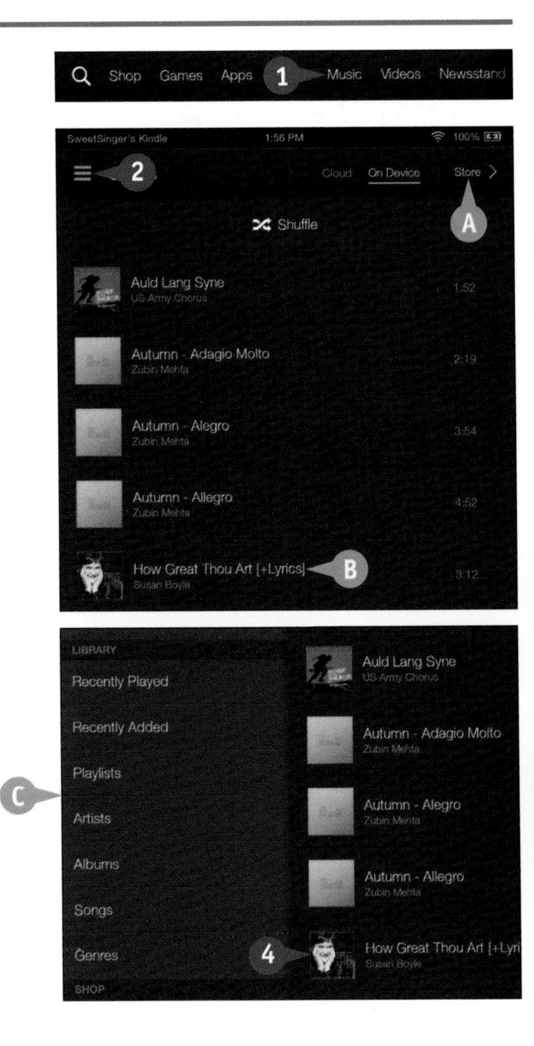

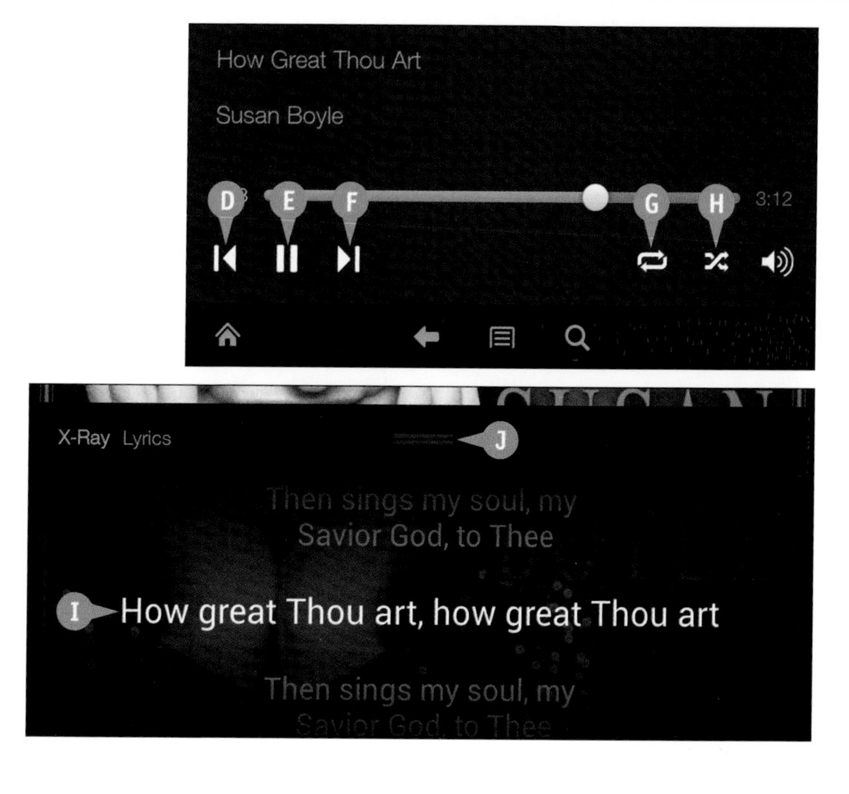

D Tap the **Previous** button (⏮) to skip to the previous track.

E You can tap the **Pause** button (⏸) to pause the music.

F Tap the **Next** button (⏭) to skip to the next track.

G You can tap the **Repeat** button (🔁) once to repeat all songs in the album or playlist. Tap twice to repeat the current song continuously.

H Tap the **Shuffle** button (🔀) to shuffle songs.

I If your song includes X-Ray for Music, lyrics appear on-screen.

Note: You can swipe up or down to scroll through lyrics, and you can tap any line to jump to that line in the song.

J You can tap the gray double line repeatedly to switch between filling the top of the screen with lyrics, hiding lyrics, or displaying lyrics in a window.

TIP

After I finish playing music, the bottom of the screen continues to show the last song played. How do I make that disappear?

Press and hold the song title in the player at the bottom of the screen A; from the menu that appears, tap **Clear Player** B.

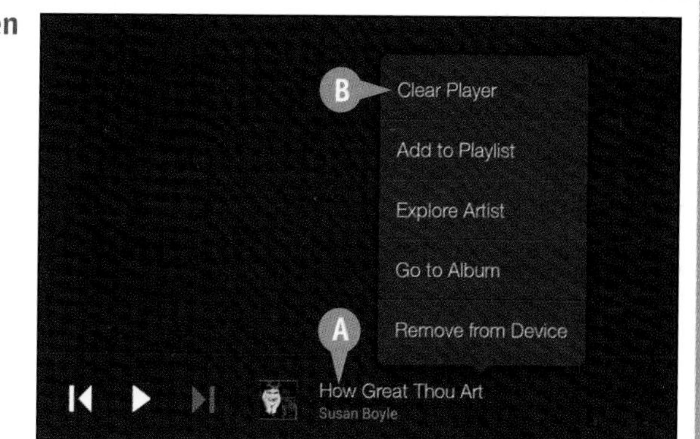

Transfer Music from Your PC

You can copy music from your computer to your Fire tablet by connecting them to each other using the cable that came with your device. You plug the micro-B end of the cable into your Fire tablet as if you were going to charge it. Then, disconnect the standard USB end of the cable from the part that plugs into the wall, and plug that end into an available slot on your computer.

Transfer Music from Your PC

1. Plug one end of your Fire tablet cable into the device.
2. Plug the other end into your computer.

   The AutoPlay window appears.
3. Click **Open device to view files**.

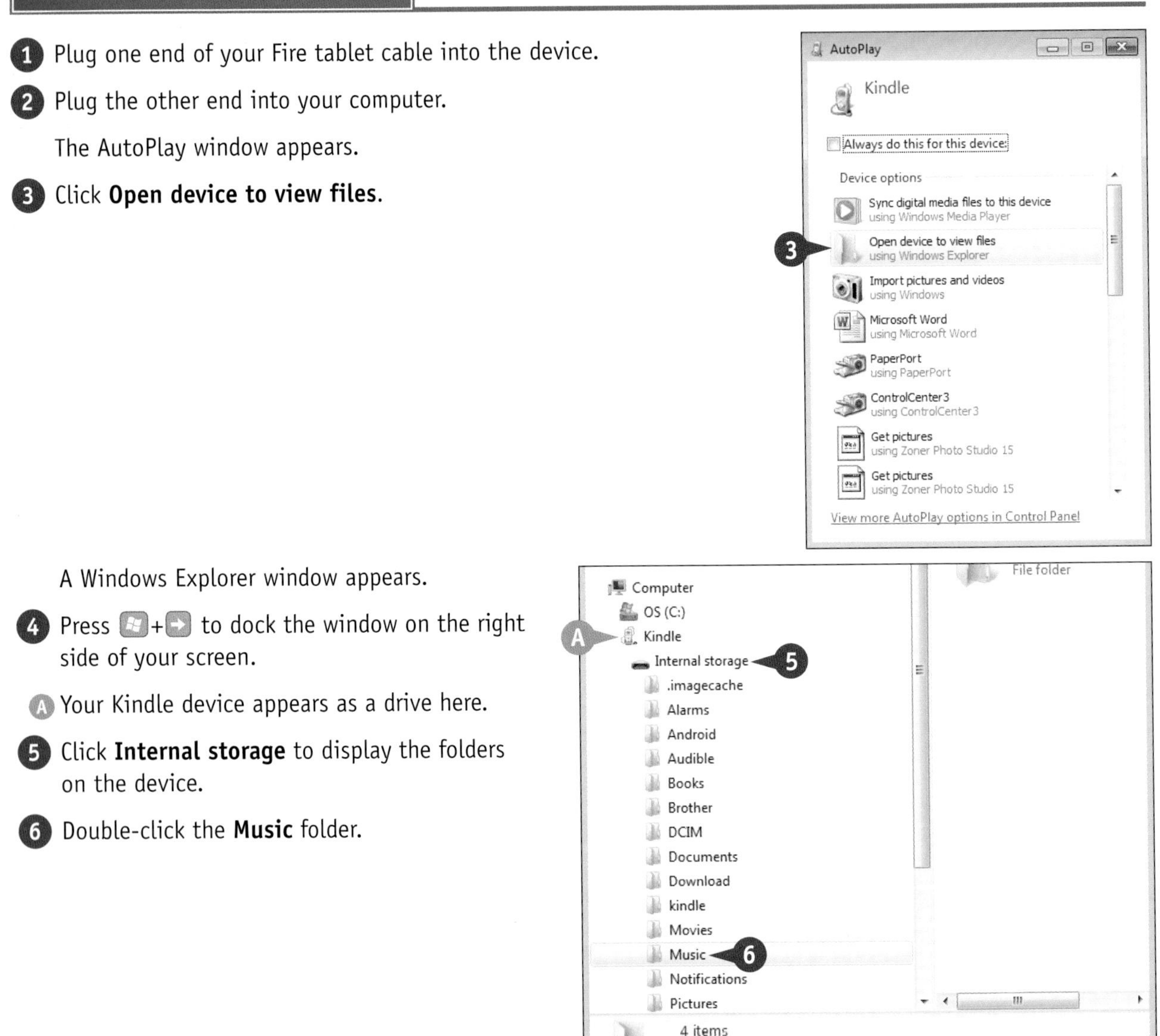

A Windows Explorer window appears.

4. Press ⊞+→ to dock the window on the right side of your screen.

   Ⓐ Your Kindle device appears as a drive here.
5. Click **Internal storage** to display the folders on the device.
6. Double-click the **Music** folder.

7. Press ⊞+E to open another instance of Windows Explorer.
8. Press ⊞+← to dock the window on the left side of your screen.
9. Click the **Music** folder.
10. Right-click a folder.
11. Click **Copy**.

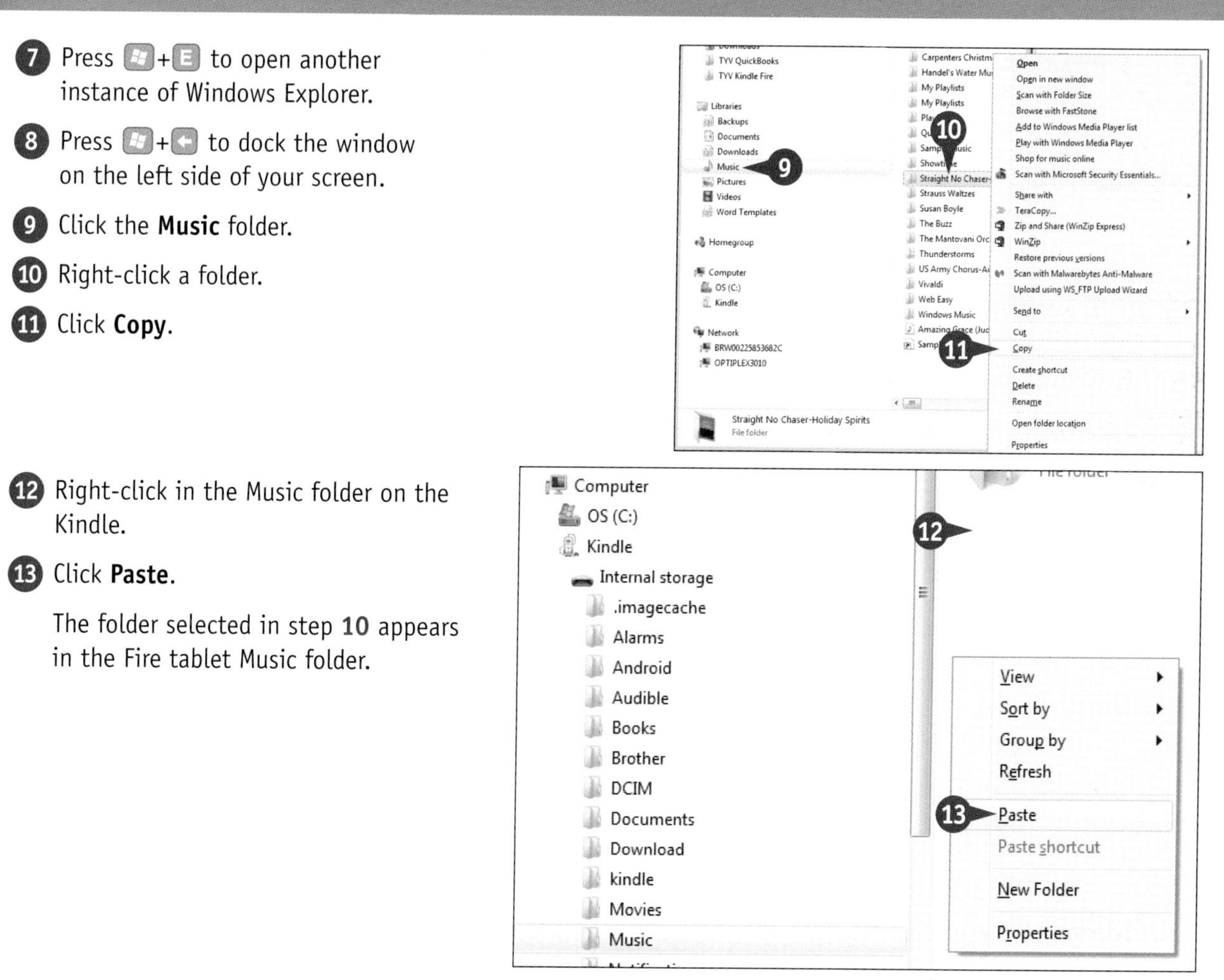

12. Right-click in the Music folder on the Kindle.
13. Click **Paste**.

The folder selected in step **10** appears in the Fire tablet Music folder.

TIP

How do I know how much space I have available on my Fire tablet?

Complete steps **1** to **3**. Your Fire tablet appears selected in the left column of the Windows Explorer window Ⓐ. The amount of free space appears below the Internal Storage bar on the right side of the Windows Explorer window Ⓑ.

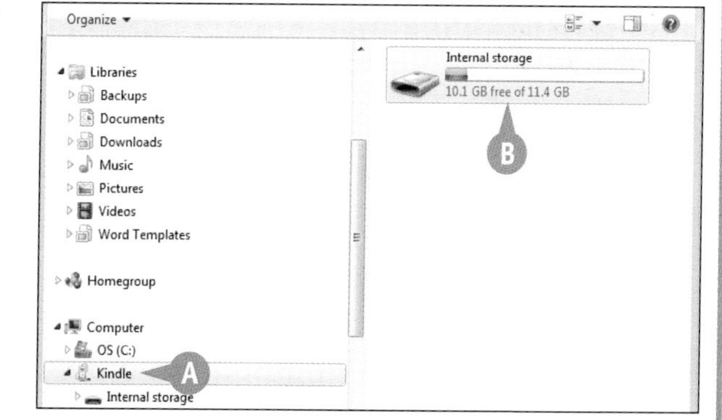

Watch a Movie or a TV Show

You can watch a movie or TV show on your Fire tablet. You can opt to stream the video, or download it to your device and then watch it. To find videos to watch, see Chapter 2. If you are an Amazon Prime member, you can watch Amazon Instant Video titles and Prime Instant Video titles. Note that Prime Instant Video offers more titles to view than Amazon Instant Video.

If you plan to stream a video, make sure you are connected to a wireless network.

Watch a Movie or a TV Show

1. From the Home screen, tap **Videos**.

   The Videos content library appears.

2. Tap the **Navigation** button (☰).

   The Videos content library Navigation panel appears.

3. Tap **Your Video Library** to display your video content library.

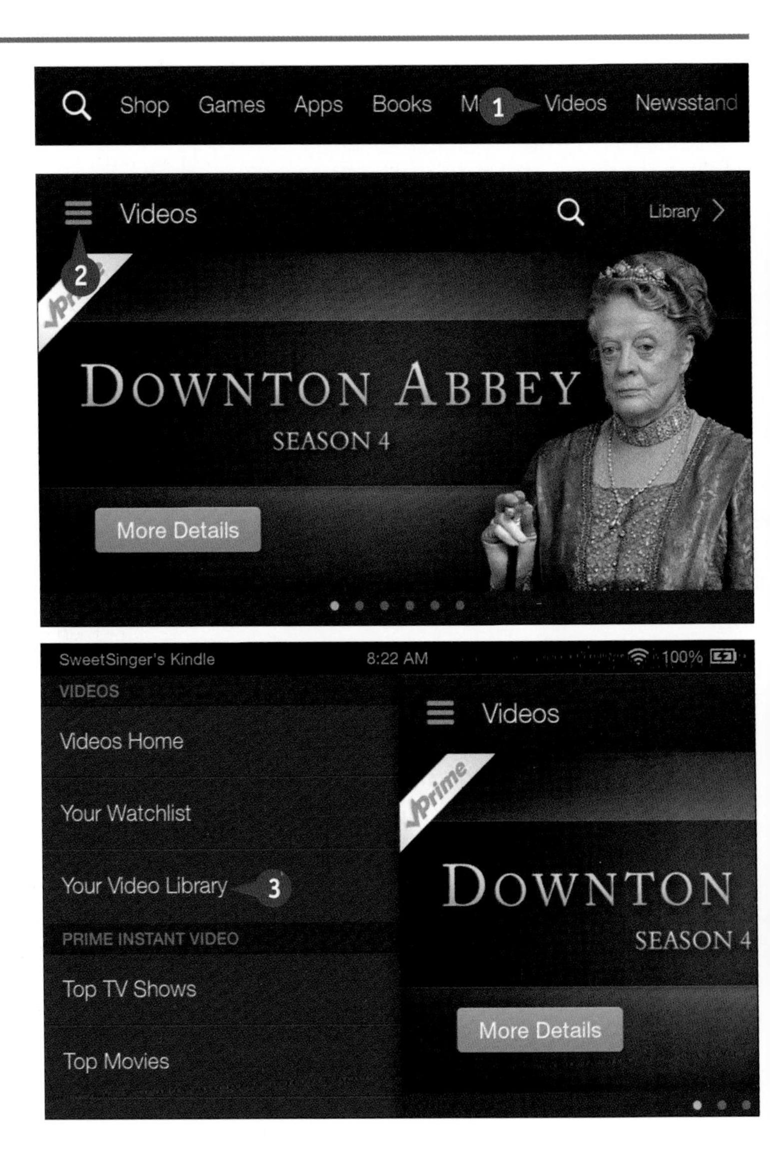

4 Tap **Cloud**.

A You can tap **On Device** to view video content downloaded to your device.

Movies stored in your Amazon Cloud space appear.

B You can tap **TV** to view TV shows stored in your Amazon Cloud space.

5 Tap a title to display its page.

6 To stream content from the cloud to your device, tap **Watch Now**.

The movie streams to your device and starts to play in landscape orientation.

C To download the title to your device, tap **Download**.

The title downloads to your device.

You can tap **Watch Now** or, at a later date, repeat steps **1** to **4** but tap **On Device** rather than **Cloud** in step **4**. Then, complete steps **5** and **6**.

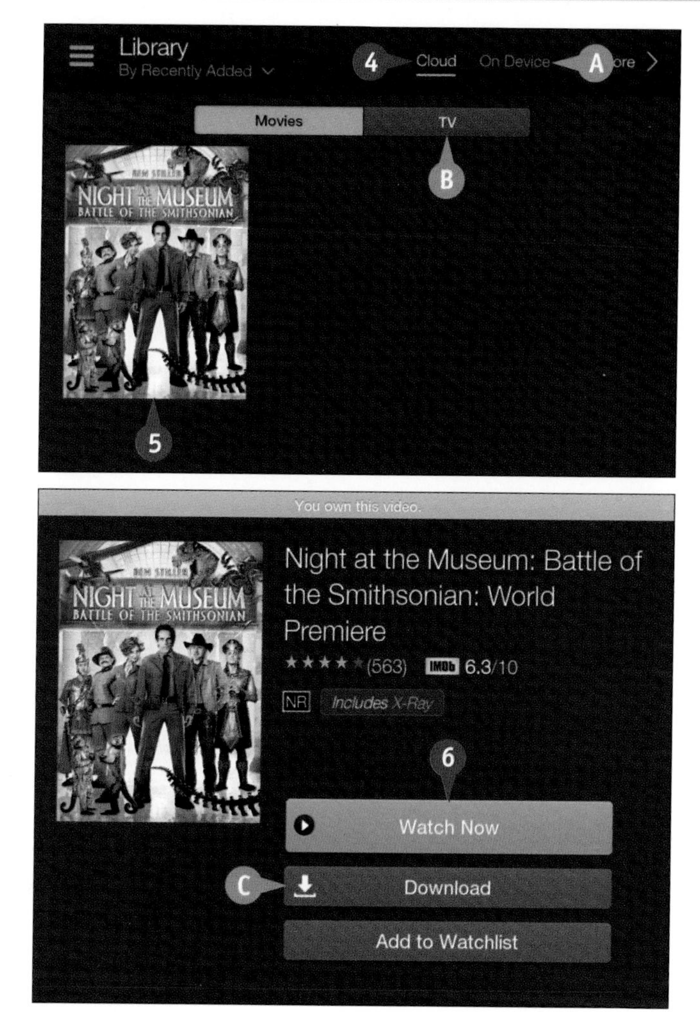

TIP

When should I stream a video, and when should I download (and, if I stream, how do I check my wireless connection)?
Download a video if you will not have access to a wireless network. To check your wireless connection, swipe down from the top of the screen to display Quick Settings. Tap **Wireless**. Make sure that Airplane Mode is off **A** and that you are connected to a wireless network **B**.

SweetSinger's Kindle 9:21 AM 100%
Wireless
Airplane Mode A Off
Wi-Fi
Connected to "mellc" B

CHAPTER 5

Managing Photos and Personal Videos

You can store photos and personal videos on your Fire tablet and on your Amazon Cloud Drive. In this chapter, you learn to transfer photos and videos from your personal computer to your Amazon Cloud Drive and your Fire tablet, and how to work in the Photos content library.

Upload to Cloud Drive via PC 102
Copy Media from Your PC 106
View Photos or Personal Videos 108
Edit Photos 110
Take Pictures or Videos 112
Delete Photos or Videos 114
Share Photos 116

Upload to Cloud Drive via PC

You can upload content such as photos, personal videos under 20 minutes in length, and documents stored on your desktop computer to your Amazon Cloud Drive space. Content stored in your Cloud Drive space is accessible from anywhere you have access to a wireless network. Amazon automatically gives you 5 gigabytes (GB) of cloud storage, and you can purchase more space if needed.

You also can use the appropriate mobile app — Android or iOS — to store content from your mobile device in your Amazon Cloud Drive space; download the app from the appropriate app store.

Upload to Cloud Drive via PC

1. On your desktop computer, open your web browser and navigate to www.amazon.com.
2. On the Amazon Home page, click **Sign in**.

The Amazon Sign In screen appears.

3. Type your Amazon email address.
4. Type your Amazon password.
5. Click **Sign in using our secure server**.

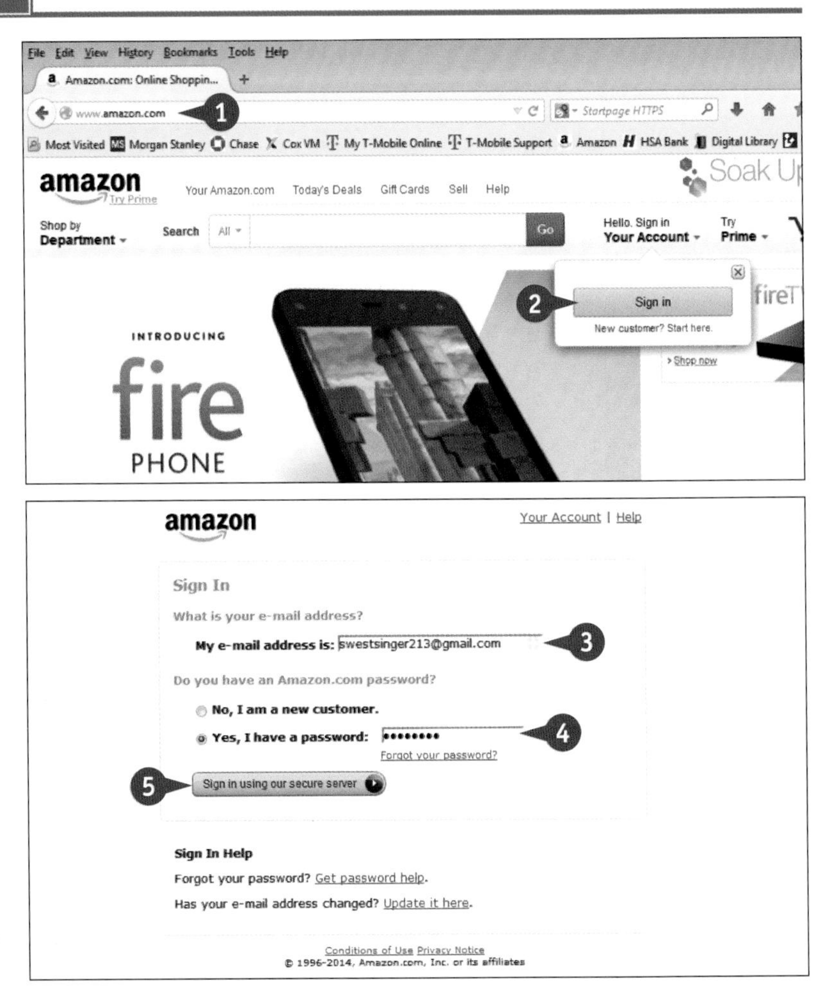

The Amazon home page reappears.

6. Position the mouse pointer over your Amazon name.

7. In the menu that appears, click **Your Cloud Drive**.

Note: The first time you select **Your Cloud Drive**, Amazon displays this page.

8. Click **Your Cloud Drive**.

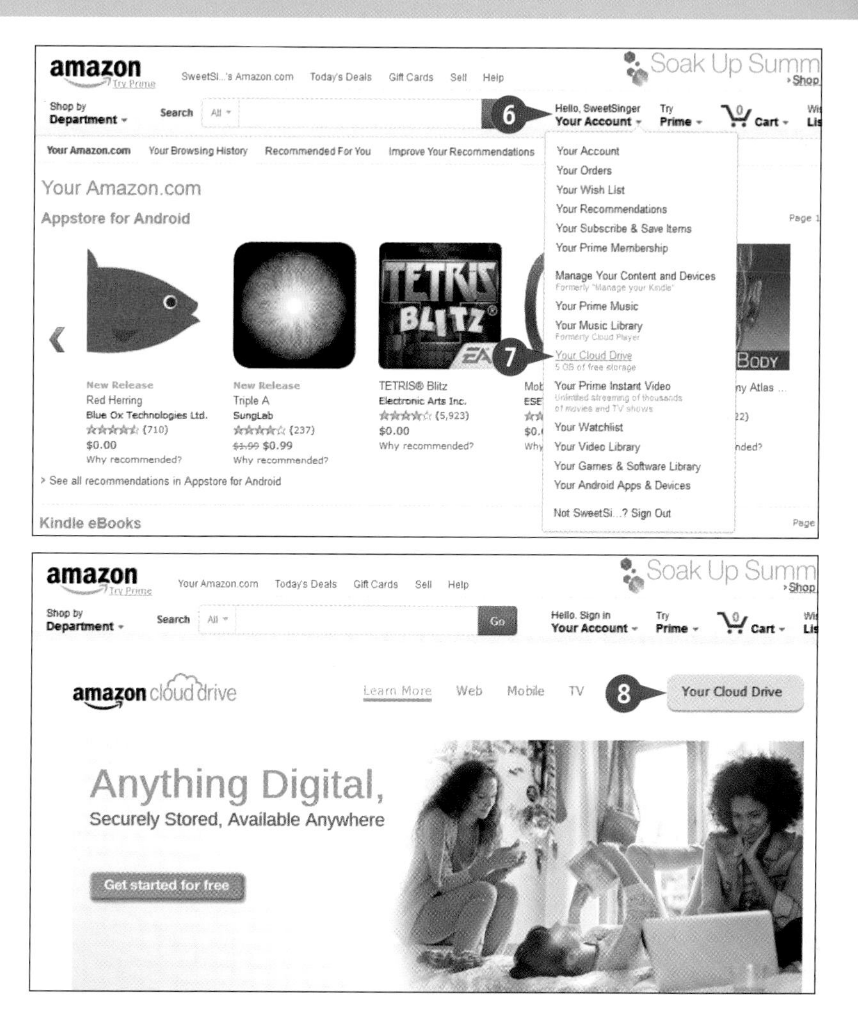

TIP

Does my Cloud Drive content appear on my Fire tablet?

Once you connect your Fire tablet to a wireless network, a Cloud Drive option appears on the Navigation panel of the corresponding content library. To download Cloud Drive content to your device, display the appropriate content library's Navigation panel and tap **Cloud Drive** (A). Then, tap an item to download it (B).

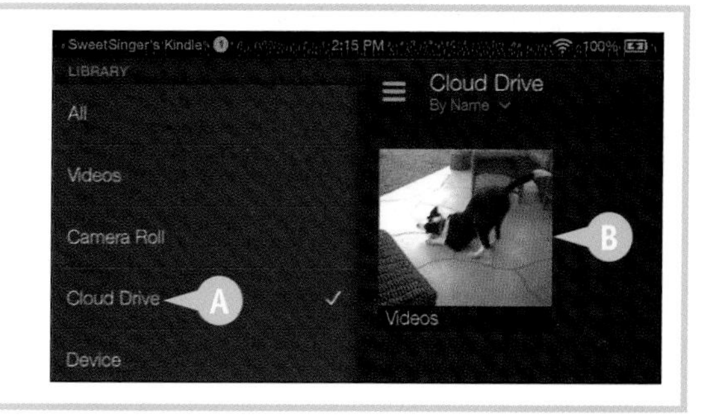

continued

By default, Amazon sets up three folders on your Cloud Drive to help you organize content: a Documents folder, a Pictures folder, and a Videos folder. When you upload content, you choose a folder for the content you intend to upload, and then select the content from your computer's hard drive.

When you connect your Fire tablet to a wireless network after uploading content, the uploaded content appears in the corresponding content library on your Fire tablet. For example, videos and pictures appear in the Photos content library.

Upload to Cloud Drive via PC (continued)

The Cloud Drive page appears.

A Folders automatically created for you appear here.

B You can create a new folder by clicking here.

9 Click a destination folder for the file you want to upload.

10 Click **Add Files**.

The Upload Files to Your Cloud Drive window appears.

11 Click **Select files to upload**.

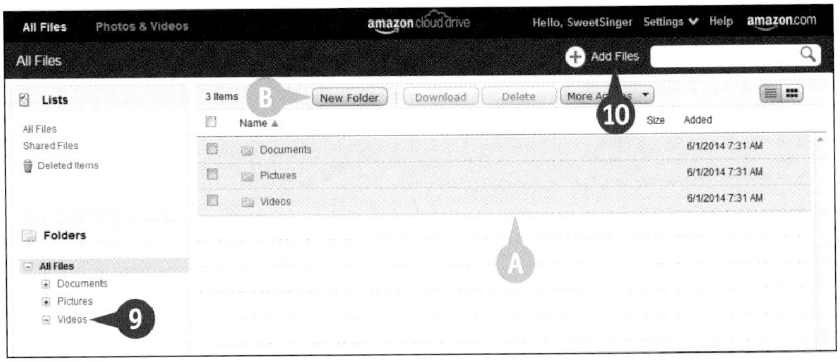

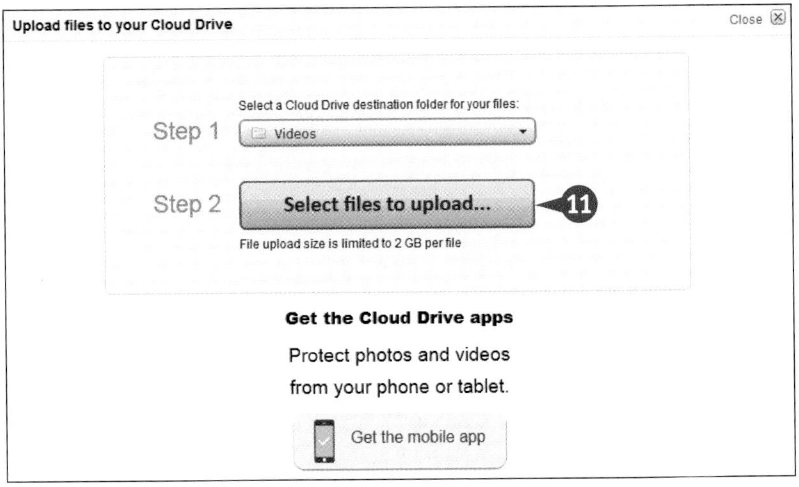

The Open window appears.

12. Navigate to the folder containing the file you want to upload.
13. Click the file.
14. Click **Open**.

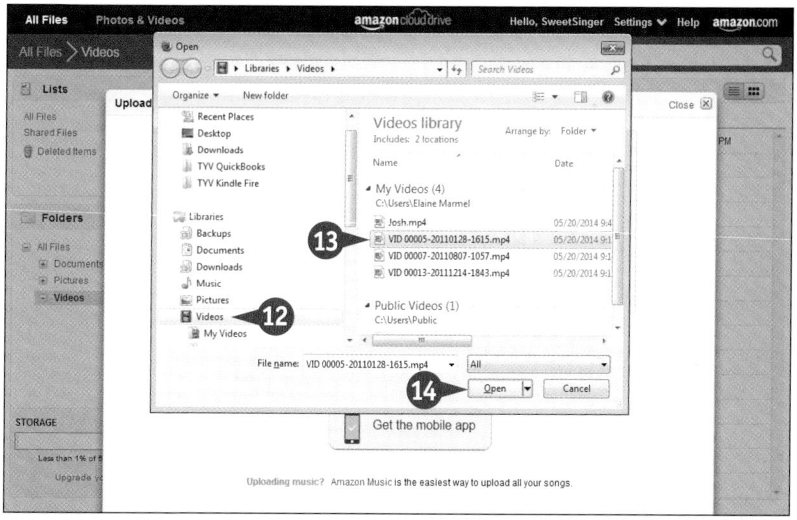

All Files
Photos & Videos
amazon cloud drive
Hello, SweetSinger
Settings
Help
amazon.com
All Files > Videos
Lists
All Files
Shared Files
Deleted Items
Upload
Open
Libraries ▸ Videos ▸
Search Videos
Organize ▾
New folder
Recent Places
Desktop
Downloads
TYV QuickBooks
TYV Kindle Fire
Libraries
Backups
Documents
Downloads
Music
Pictures
Videos
My Videos
Videos library
Includes: 2 locations
Arrange by: Folder ▾
Name
Date
My Videos (4)
C:\Users\Elaine Marmel
Josh.mp4 05/20/2014 9:4
VID 00005-20110128-1615.mp4 05/20/2014 9:1
VID 00007-20110807-1057.mp4 05/20/2014 9:1
VID 00013-20111214-1843.mp4 05/20/2014 9:1
Public Videos (1)
C:\Users\Public
File name: VID 00005-20110128-1615.mp4
All
Open
Cancel
Close
Folders
All Files
Documents
Pictures
Videos
STORAGE
Get the mobile app
Uploading music? Amazon Music is the easiest way to upload all your songs.

Your file uploads.

C. A progress bar appears near the top of the Cloud Drive window.

D. When the file finishes uploading, it appears here.

All Files
Photos & Videos
amazon cloud drive
Hello, SweetSinger
Settings
Help
amazon.com
All Files > Videos
Add Files
Lists
Uploading file: 1 of 1
(5.0 MB / less than 1 min remaining)
› See upload details
All Files
Shared Files
Deleted Items
1 Item
New Folder
Download
Delete
More Actions ▾
Name ▲
Size
Added
Josh.mp4
47.0 MB
6/25/2014 1:36 PM
Folders
All Files
Documents
Pictures
Videos
STORAGE
Less than 1% of 5.00 GB in use
Upgrade your plan
We're Hiring
Send Us Feedback
© 2014, Amazon.com, Inc. or its affiliates

TIP

What happens if I do not select any destination folder in step 9?

Your files are uploaded to the root folder of your Cloud Drive on your desktop computer and appear in the Carousel on your Fire tablet. When you tap the appropriate content library on the Fire tablet, your file appears on the Cloud Drive page of the content library. You can move a file after uploading it; click the check box that appears beside it to select it (☐ changes to ☑). Then, click the **More Actions** button above the list of files and click **Move.** In the window that appears, click a destination folder location and click the **Move** button.

Copy Media from Your PC

You can copy pictures and personal videos stored on your computer to your Fire tablet Photos content library, which supports the JPEG, PNG, GIG, BMP, and MP4 file types. To do so, use the USB cable that came with your Fire tablet to connect the device to your computer. Disconnect the standard USB end of the cable from the wall plug, and plug that end of the cable into an available slot on your computer.

The example in this section shows how to copy pictures from the Pictures folder on your desktop computer to your Fire tablet.

Copy Media from Your PC

1. Plug one end of your Fire tablet cable into the device.
2. Plug the other end into your computer.

   The AutoPlay window appears.
3. Click **Open device to view files**.

   A Windows Explorer window appears.
4. Press ⊞+→ to dock the window on the right side of your screen.

   (A) Your Kindle device appears as a drive here.
5. Double-click **Internal storage** to display the folders on the device.
6. Double-click **Pictures**.

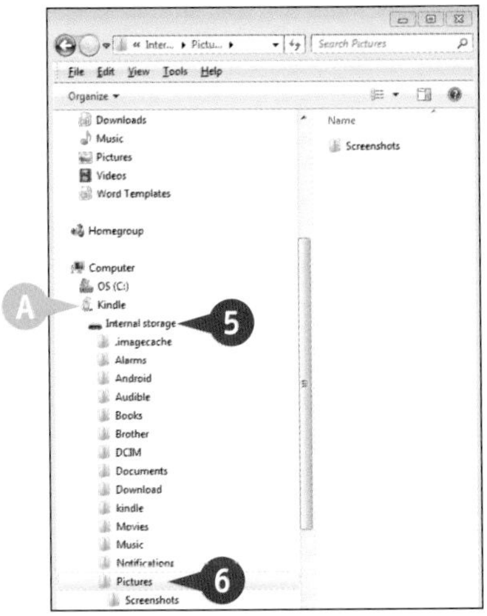

7. Press ⊞+E to open another instance of Windows Explorer, and press ⊞+← to dock the window on the left side of your screen.

8. Click **Pictures**.

B. If pictures are stored in folders on your computer, double-click the folder to view them.

9. Right-click the picture(s).

Note: To select contiguous picture files, click the first file, press and hold Shift, and click the last file. To select noncontiguous files, press and hold Ctrl and click each picture. Then, right-click one of them.

10. Click **Copy**.

11. Right-click in the Pictures folder area on the Kindle.

12. Click **Paste**.

The picture(s) selected in step **9** appears in the Fire tablet Picture folder.

TIP

What do you mean by "personal videos," and how do I copy them to my Fire tablet?

Personal videos are ones you shot with a digital camera instead of videos you purchased. To copy them to your Kindle, complete the steps in this section with these changes: In step **6**, double-click the **Movies** folder (if no Movies folder appears, double-click the **Pictures** folder). In step **8**, click the folder on your computer where you stored your personal videos. After step **12**, if a message appears saying you might not be able to view your videos on your Fire tablet, paste them anyway. Chances are good they will play.

View Photos or Personal Videos

In the Photos library, you can view photos and personal videos you upload to your Amazon Cloud Drive, transfer to your Fire tablet with a micro-USB cable, import from Facebook, take with the Fire tablet camera, or download from the Internet or from email attachments.

When you view all items in the Photos library in portrait orientation, the content appears organized by date. In landscape mode, images appear as a mosaic. While viewing a photo, you can use two fingers to drag or pinch in or out to enlarge or reduce the image's appearance.

View Photos or Personal Videos

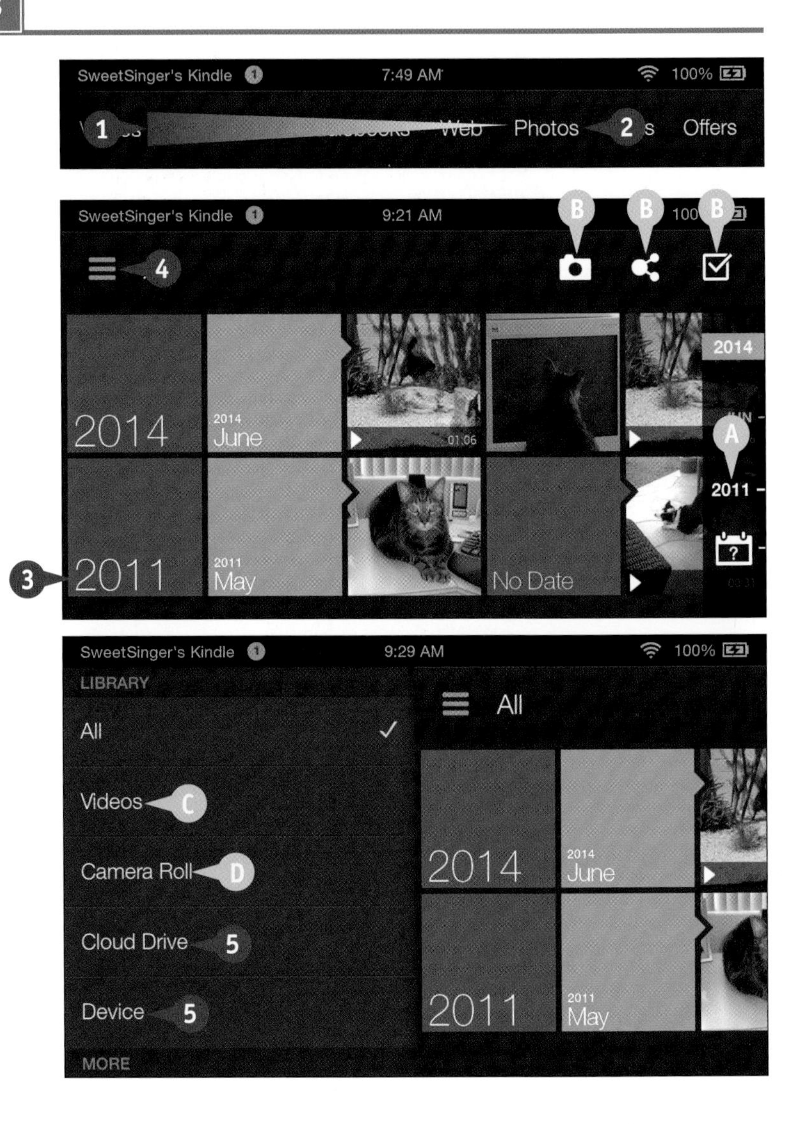

1. From the Home screen, swipe the Navigation bar from right to left.
2. Tap **Photos**.
3. In the Photos content library, tap a date.

   A. In the timeline bar that appears on the right, you can tap a date to jump to items in that timeframe.

   B. You can tap the **Camera** button (▣) to display the camera, the **Share** button (◪) to share an image, or click the **Check Box** button (☑) to select photos to print or delete.

4. Tap the **Navigation** button (☰) to display the Navigation panel.

   C. You can tap **Videos** to view only personal videos.

   D. You can tap **Camera Roll** to view photos and videos taken with the camera.

5. Tap **Cloud Drive** or **Device** to view content in the associated location. For this example, tap **Device**.

Images stored on your device appear, organized into folders, such as Pictures and Movies.

6 Tap a folder to view images in it; for this example, tap **Pictures**.

Images in the Pictures folder appear.

7 Tap a photo to view it full screen.

You can use two fingers to drag out to enlarge a photo or pinch in to reduce the size of the photo.

You can tap the **Back** arrow (◼) or the **Home** button (◼) at the bottom of the screen when you finish viewing the photo.

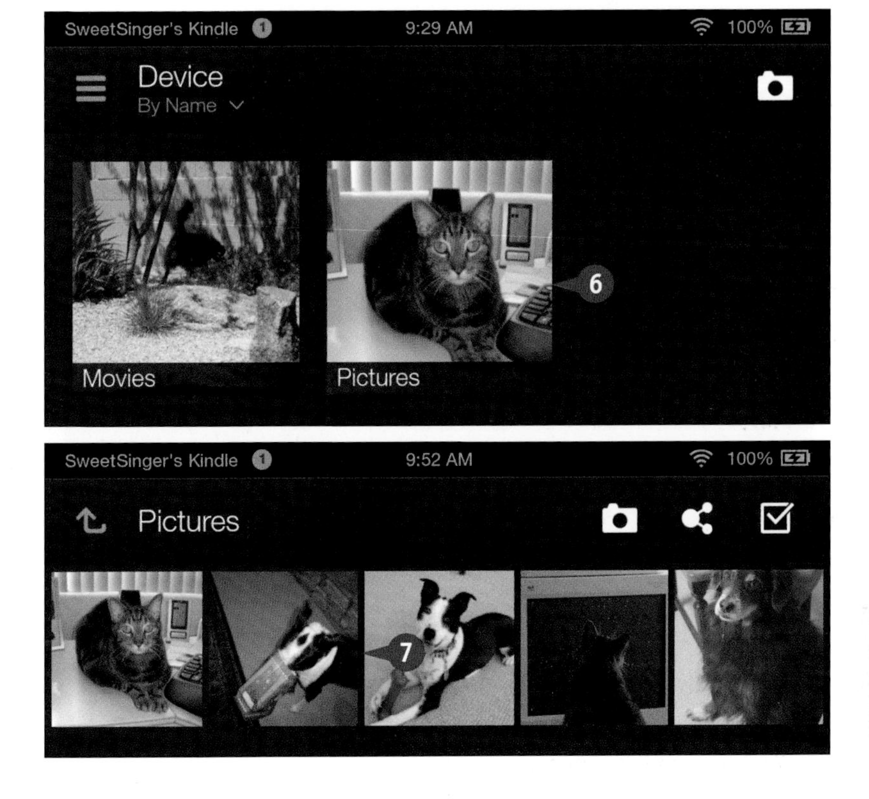

TIP

What do you mean when you say photos appear in a mosaic?
In landscape orientation, items are not organized by date; instead, you see thumbnails of all images on the device. You can swipe from right to left to scroll through images and tap any image to display it alone.

Edit Photos

You can edit photos to change their appearance. For example, you can rotate or crop a photo; remove red eye; adjust its brightness, contrast, saturation, sharpness, and focus; or add text or stickers to it.

When you make changes to a photo, your Fire tablet does not replace your original photo with the edited one; instead, you will find two copies of the photo in the Photos content library — one before and one after editing. You can delete either copy as an extra that you do not need; see the section "Delete Photos or Videos" for details.

Edit Photos

1 From the Home screen, swipe the Navigation bar from right to left.

2 Tap **Photos**.

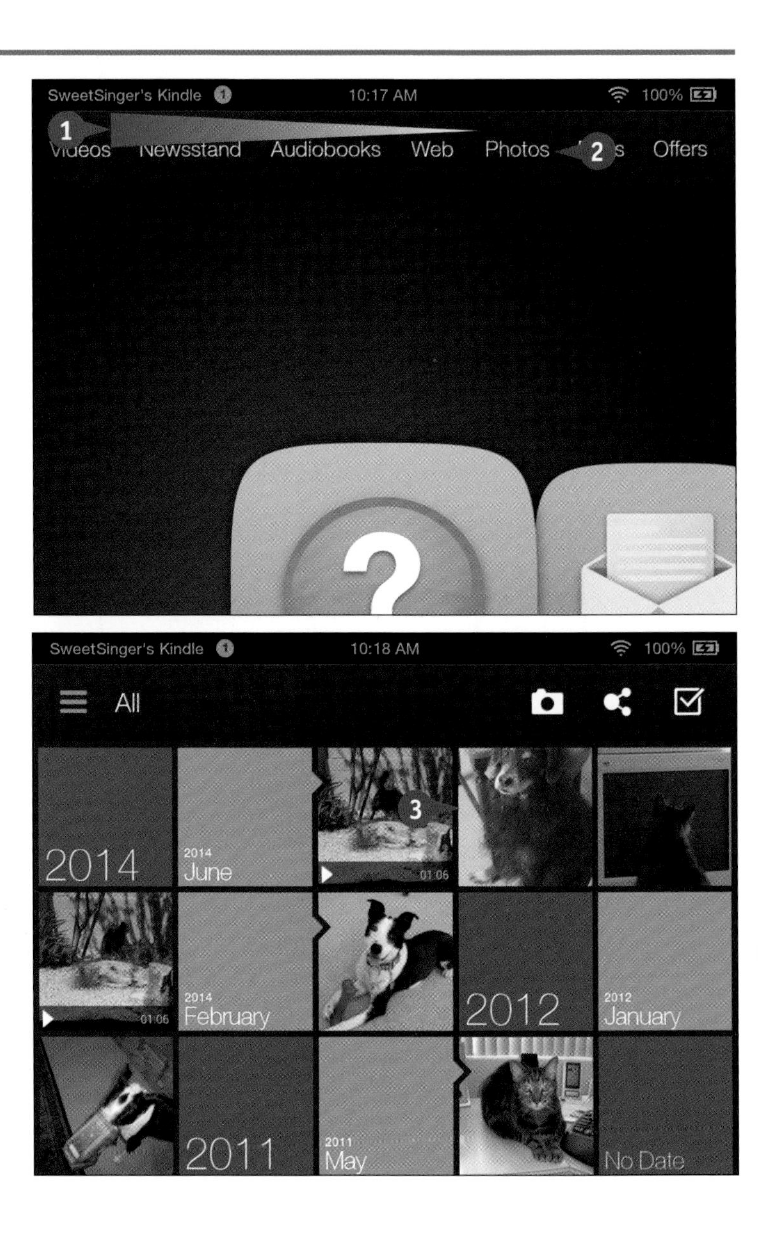

The Photos content library appears.

Note: To find the photo you want to edit, work in portrait orientation and tap a date to narrow the search.

 Tap a photo.

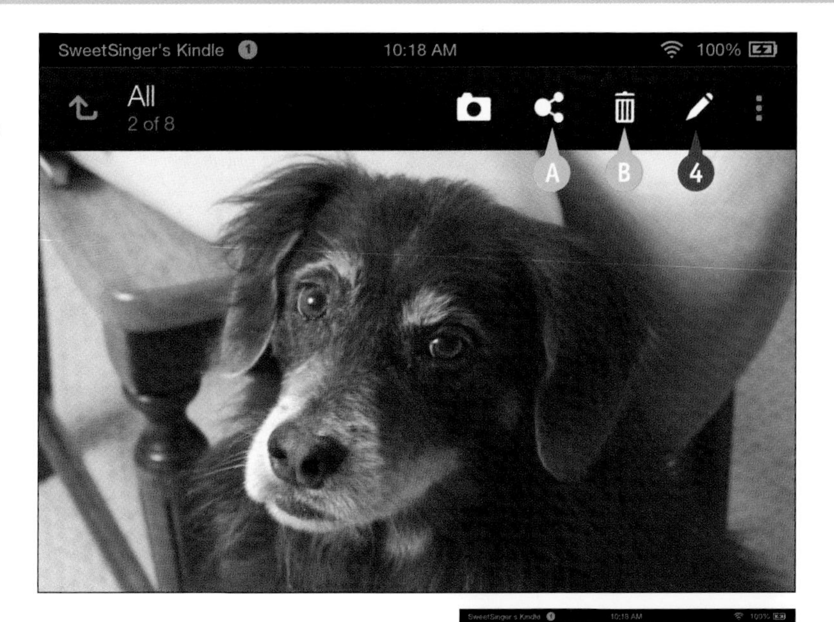

The photo appears and fills the Fire tablet screen.

Ⓐ You can tap the **Share** button ( ) to share the photo via Facebook, Twitter, or email.

Ⓑ You can tap the **Delete** button ( ) to delete the photo.

4 Tap the **Edit** button ( ) to edit the photo.

The Fire tablet displays the photo and editing tools for making changes to the photo.

5 Swipe the toolbar from right to left to view additional editing tools.

6 Tap a tool to use it.

Note: You can test each tool; if you do not like its effect, tap the **Back** arrow ( ) to return to the original image without changing it.

7 When you finish making changes to your photo, tap the **Done** button ( ).

TIP

How do I include a change I made with an editing tool?

When you select an editing tool, the **Done** button ( ) changes to Apply Ⓐ. Tap **Apply** to keep your changes.

Take Pictures or Videos

You can take pictures and videos with your Fire tablet. By default, all versions of the Fire tablet give you a front-facing camera. The Fire tablet 8.9-inch model also has a rear-facing camera. You can set the focal point for the photo or video, and you can zoom as you shoot. As you take pictures and videos, you can preview them.

All pictures and videos you take are uploaded by default to the Amazon Cloud Drive, but you can change that setting.

Take Pictures or Videos

Display the Camera

1. From the Home screen, swipe the Navigation bar from right to left.

2. Tap **Photos**.

A. If you prefer, you can tap the Camera app in the Favorites section of the Home screen.

The Photos content library appears.

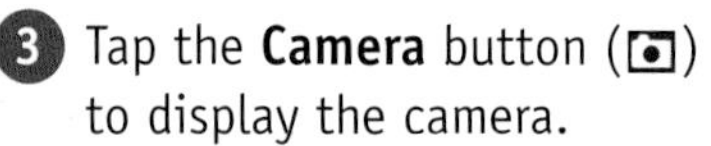

3. Tap the **Camera** button ( ) to display the camera.

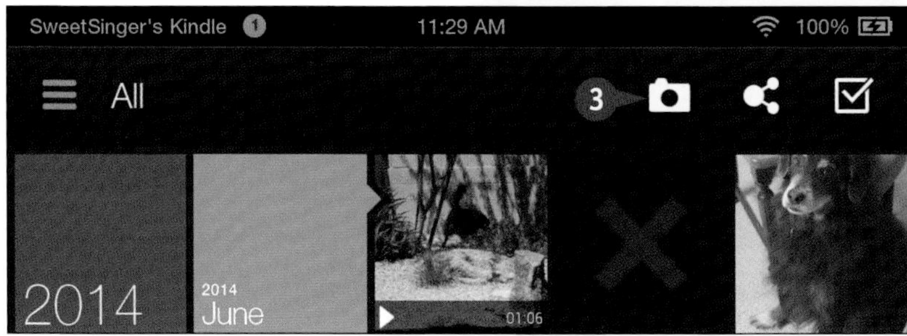

Take Still Pictures

1. Tap the **Shutter** button (⊛).

   You hear a camera shutter sound as the photo is taken.

B Review your photo by tapping the thumbnail to the right of ⊛.

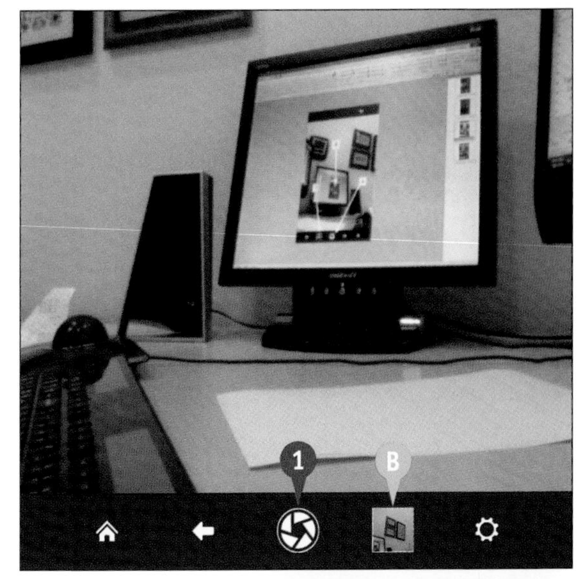

Take Personal Videos

1. Complete the steps in the subsection "Display the Camera."

2. Tap ▣ (▣ changes to ▣) and the camera switches to video mode.

3. Tap the red **Record** button (●) to start recording your video; ● is replaced by a Stop Recording button.

Note: A counter appears, showing the recording time.

4. When you finish recording the video, tap the Stop Recording button.

C You can tap here to review your video.

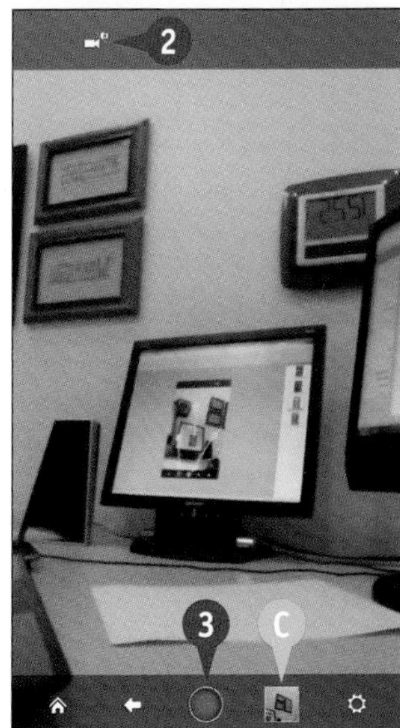

TIPS

How do I set the focal point and zoom in and out?
To set the focal point for a photo or a video, tap the Fire tablet screen at the location where you want to set the focal point. To zoom in and out, use the volume buttons on the back of your device.

How do I stop the Fire tablet from automatically uploading photos and videos to the cloud?
In the Photos content library, tap the **Navigation** button (☰) to display the Navigation panel. Then, tap **Settings** and tap **Off** beside the Auto-Save option.

Delete Photos or Videos

Using your Fire tablet, you can delete photos you no longer want to store on your device or in the Amazon Cloud Drive. You can delete photos individually, or you can delete multiple photos or videos simultaneously.

To specifically work with items on your device or on your Amazon Cloud Drive, display the Navigation panel and opt to view either your device or your Cloud Drive. The example in this section shows items in both locations rather than in only one location or the other.

Delete Photos or Videos

Delete Individual Items

1. From the Home screen, swipe the Navigation bar from right to left.
2. Tap **Photos.**

   The Photos content library appears.
3. Tap and hold the photo or video you want to delete.
4. From the menu that appears, tap **Delete.**

   A message appears, asking you to confirm the deletion.
5. Tap **Delete.**

   The Fire tablet deletes the photo or video.

Delete Multiple Items

1. Tap ☑.

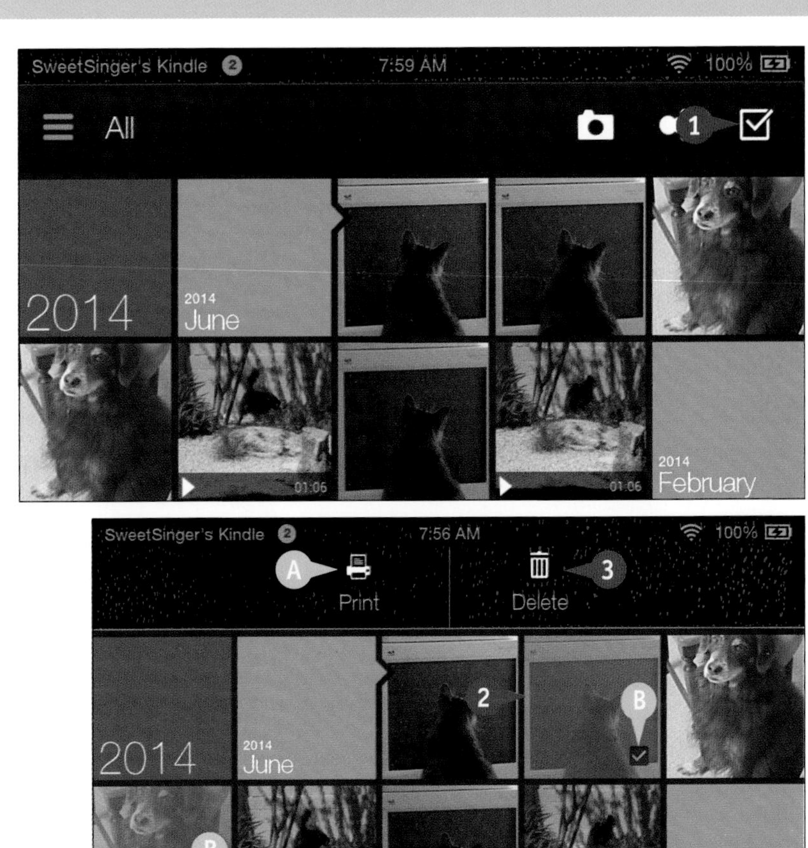

Ⓐ The top of the screen displays options for printing or deleting.

2. Tap photos or videos you want to delete.

Ⓑ A check mark (☑) appears in the lower right corner of each selected item.

3. Tap the **Delete** button (🗑).

   As shown in the subsection "Delete Individual Items," a message asks you to confirm the deletion appears.

4. Tap **Delete**.

   The Fire tablet deletes the selected photos or videos.

TIPS

How do I limit the items I see to only those on my device?
Complete step **1** in the subsection "Delete Individual Items" to display the Photos content library. Then, tap the **Navigation** button (☰) to display the Navigation panel and tap **Device** to view photos and videos stored on your device. To view photos and videos stored on your Amazon Cloud Drive, tap **Cloud Drive**.

What should I do differently if I want to print photos?
Make sure you have installed a printer plug-in app as described in Chapter 3. Then, follow steps **1** and **2** in either subsection, depending on whether you want to print an individual photo or multiple photos. In step **3**, tap **Print**.

Share Photos

You can use your Fire tablet to share photos and videos stored in your Photos content library. You can share items stored on the device or on your Amazon Cloud Drive. You can also share via email or by posting photos or videos to your Facebook and Twitter accounts.

While selecting items to share, you can limit the items displayed in the Photos content library to those stored on your device, or those stored on your Amazon Cloud Drive. Limiting the items you see can help you more easily find them.

Share Photos

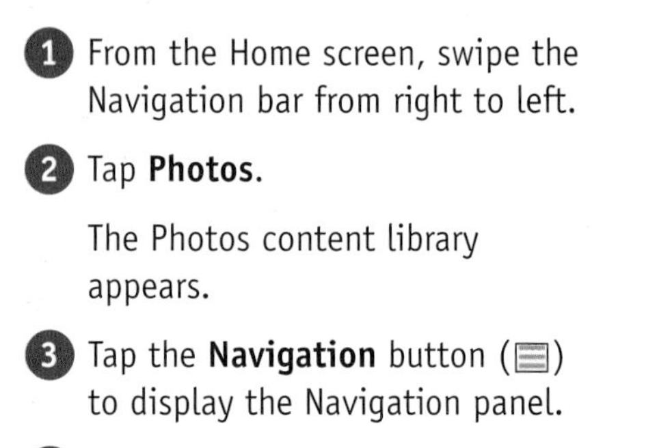

1. From the Home screen, swipe the Navigation bar from right to left.
2. Tap **Photos**.

   The Photos content library appears.
3. Tap the **Navigation** button (☰) to display the Navigation panel.
4. Tap **Cloud Drive** or **Device** to narrow the choices displayed on the Fire tablet screen and to help you find the photo or video.
5. Tap the folder containing the item you want to share.

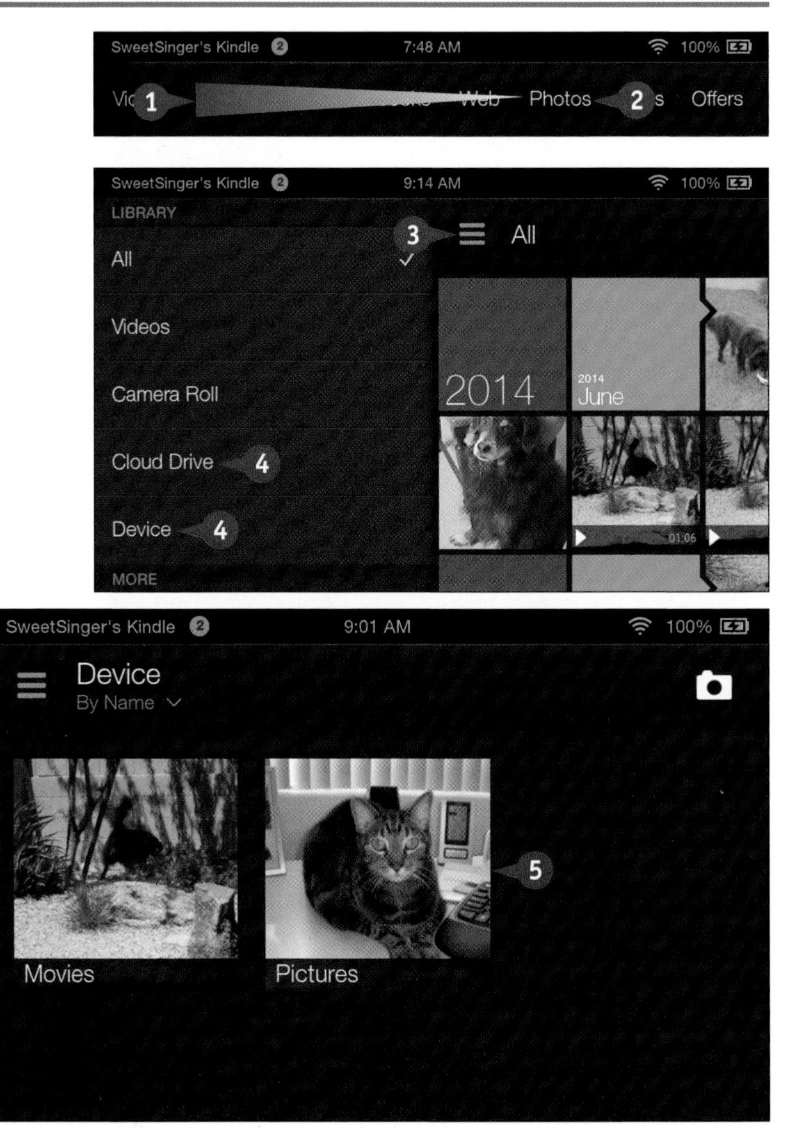

(A) Thumbnails of the items in that folder appear.

6 Tap and hold the photo or video you want to share.

7 From the menu that appears, tap **Share**.

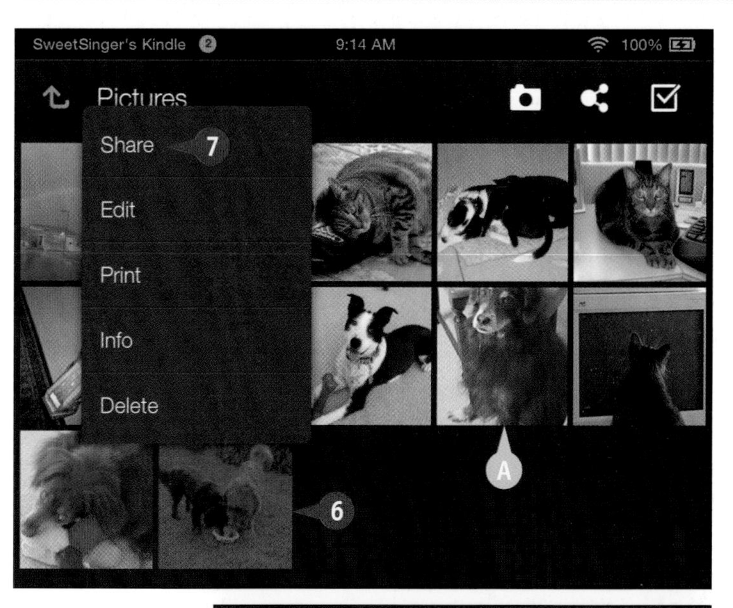

The Share To menu appears.

8 Tap the method you want to use to share.

(B) If you tap **Email**, the Fire tablet Email app opens.

(C) If you tap **Facebook**, you can tag people, add your location, and choose the audience for your photo or video before you share it.

(D) You can tap **Twitter** to post a photo or video; your tweet must be no more than 140 characters.

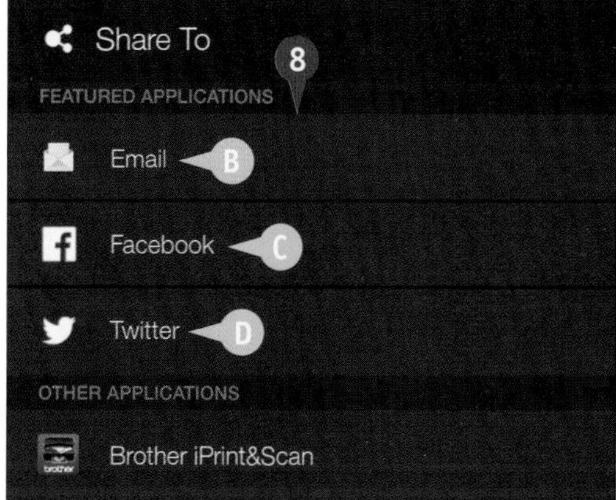

TIP

Can I share multiple items?

Yes. Complete steps **1** to **4** in this section. While viewing all the items in a particular folder, tap the **Share** button (). Then, tap the items you want to share; a check mark appears in the lower-right corner of each item (A). Then, tap a method of sharing (B).

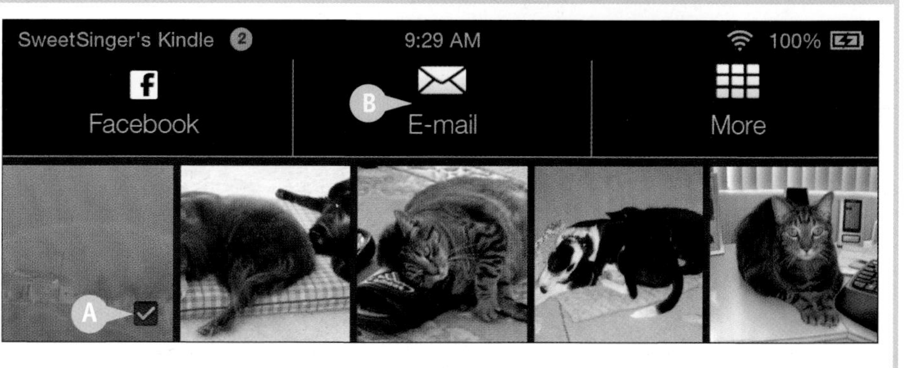

CHAPTER 6

Reading Books

As you read a book, you can control its appearance by changing the font and increasing its size. You also can look up information as you read, highlight passages, make notes, include bookmarks, and listen as a narrator reads the book. You can also borrow books and organize books in the Amazon Cloud.

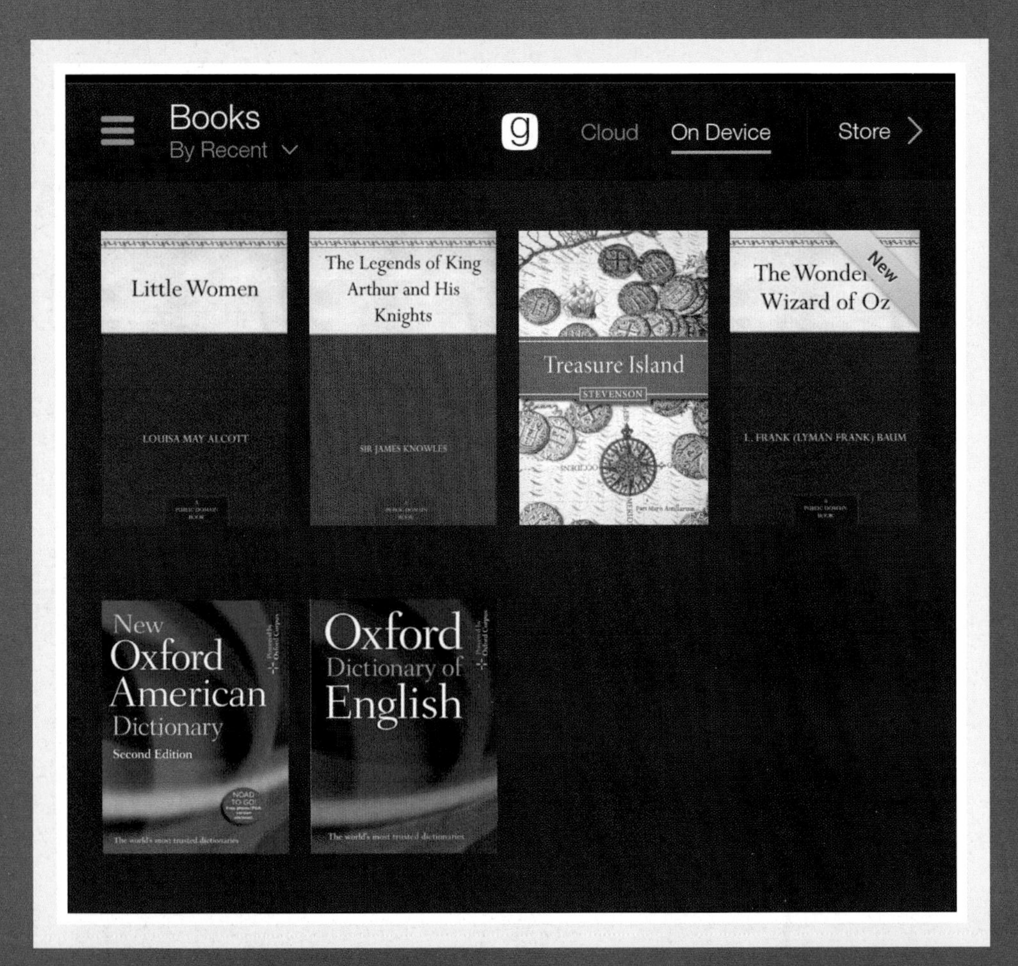

Read a Book 120
Change the Reading View 124
Listen to Books with Text-to-Speech 128
Experience Immersion Reading 131
Using X-Ray to Explore a Book 134
Look Up Information While Reading. 136
Add, Edit, or Remove Highlights 138
Add, Edit, or Remove Notes 140
Add or Remove Bookmarks 142
Read without Buying 143
Work with Cloud Collections 144

Read a Book

You can use your Fire tablet to read ebooks. You can purchase ebooks, or borrow them as discussed in the section "Read without Buying." Books you purchase are stored in the Amazon Cloud and are available to download to your Fire tablet at any time. In fact, you can delete a book from your device and later reread it by downloading it again.

As you read, you can determine where you are in the book and how much time you need to finish both the current chapter and the rest of the book.

Read a Book

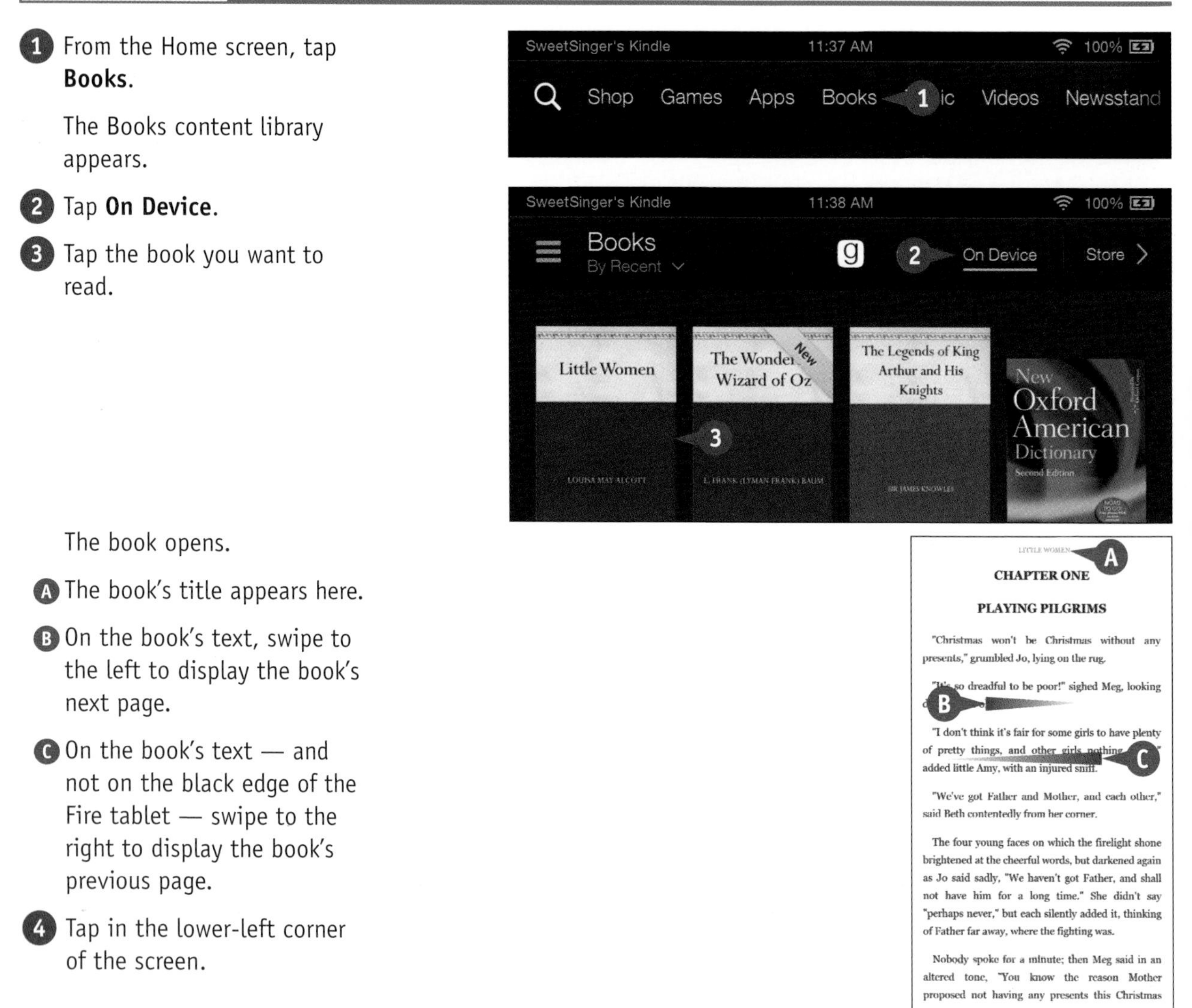

1. From the Home screen, tap **Books**.

   The Books content library appears.

2. Tap **On Device**.

3. Tap the book you want to read.

   The book opens.

   A The book's title appears here.

   B On the book's text, swipe to the left to display the book's next page.

   C On the book's text — and not on the black edge of the Fire tablet — swipe to the right to display the book's previous page.

4. Tap in the lower-left corner of the screen.

D The location number appears.

E This percentage represents your progress in the book.

5 Tap the lower-left corner again.

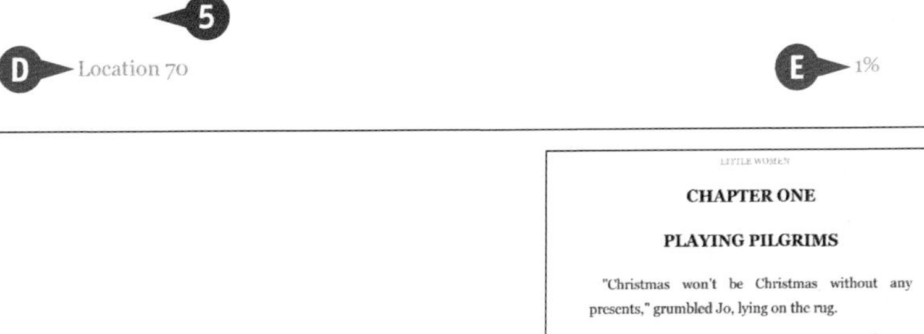
as Jo said sadly, "We haven't got Father, and shall not have him for a long time." She didn't say "perhaps never," but each silently added it, thinking of Father far away, where the fighting was.

Nobody spoke for a minute; then Meg said in an altered tone, "You know the reason Mother proposed not having any presents this Christmas

F The location number changes to the amount of time you need to finish the chapter.

Note: You can tap the lower-left corner repeatedly to cycle through viewing the location number, the time to finish the current chapter, the time to finish the book, the current page number, and then no information at all.

6 Tap the center of the screen.

CHAPTER ONE

PLAYING PILGRIMS

"Christmas won't be Christmas without any presents," grumbled Jo, lying on the rug.

"It's so dreadful to be poor!" sighed Meg, looking down at her old dress.

"I don't think it's fair for some girls to have plenty of pretty things, and other girls nothing at all," added little Amy, with an injured sniff.

"We've got Father and Mother, and each other," said Beth contentedly from her corner.

The four young faces on which the firelight shone brightened at the cheerful words, but darkened again as Jo said sadly, "We haven't got Father, and shall not have him for a long time." She didn't say "perhaps never," but each silently added it, thinking of Father far away, where the fighting was.

Nobody spoke for a minute; then Meg said in an altered tone, "You know the reason Mother proposed not having any presents this Christmas

TIP

What should I do if the book I purchased and want to read does not appear on my Fire tablet?

To read a book you purchased, you download it to your Fire tablet. In step **2**, make sure your Fire tablet has a wireless connection and then tap **Cloud**. When you tap the book, it downloads after a brief moment. Tap the book cover again to open it. In the future, the book appears on the On Device screen.

continued ►

As you read, you can view location numbers and page numbers, but not all Kindle books include page numbers. You also can control on-screen elements, as described in "Change the Reading View." If your Fire tablet is connected to a network, closing your book automatically syncs the furthest page you read to the Amazon Cloud.

Your Fire tablet uses your reading speed to let you know how much time you need to finish the current chapter and the rest of the book. Your reading speed is stored only on your Fire tablet and not on any Amazon servers.

Read a Book (continued)

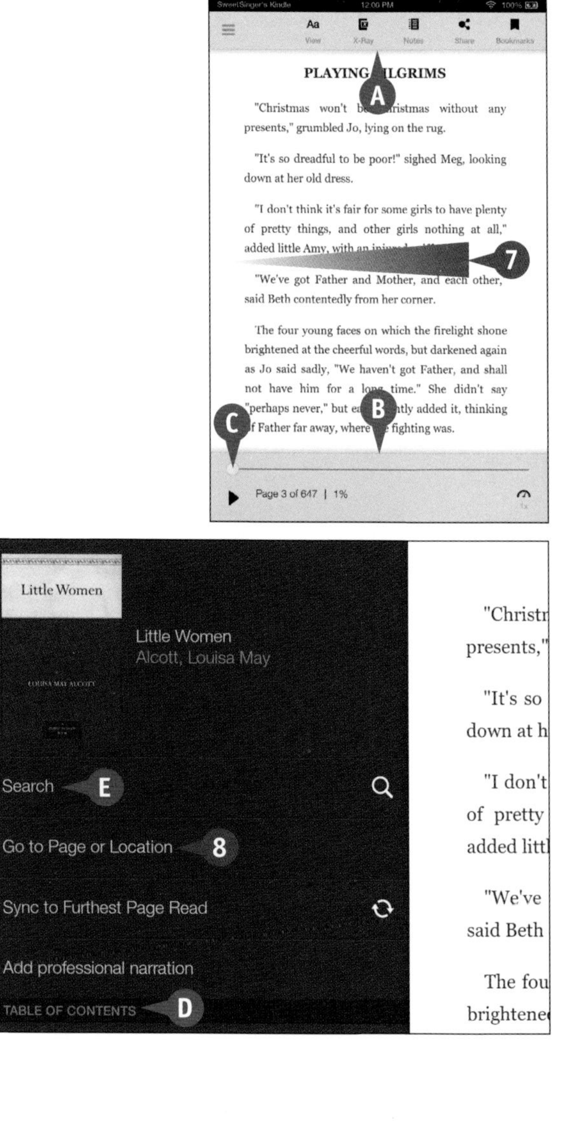

A The Reading toolbar appears at the top of the screen.

B The Progress toolbar appears at the bottom of the screen.

C You can drag this circle to scroll forward or backward in the book.

7 Placing your finger in the black portion of the Fire tablet on the left side (and not on the book's text), swipe right.

The Navigation panel appears.

D You can tap an entry in the table of contents to go to that location.

E You can tap here to search the book for specific text.

8 Tap **Go to Page or Location**.

The Enter Page Number or Location dialog box appears.

9 Type a page number or location; this example uses a page number.

10 Tap **Page** or **Location**, depending on the type of number you entered in step **9**.

F The page or location you entered appears on-screen.

To close your book, you can tap the center of the screen and then, in the Options bar at the bottom of the screen, tap the **Home** button (🏠) or the **Back** arrow (⬅).

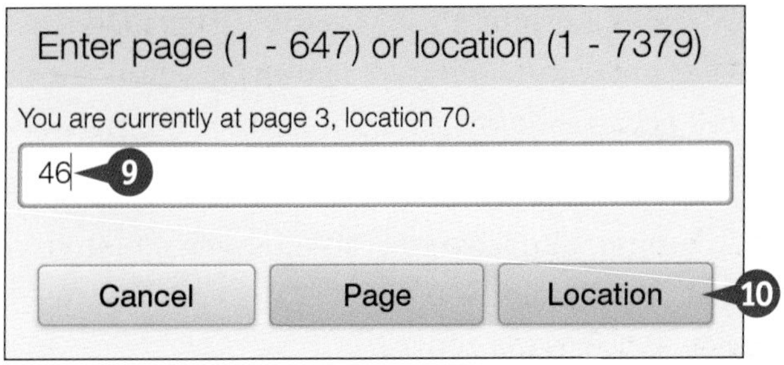

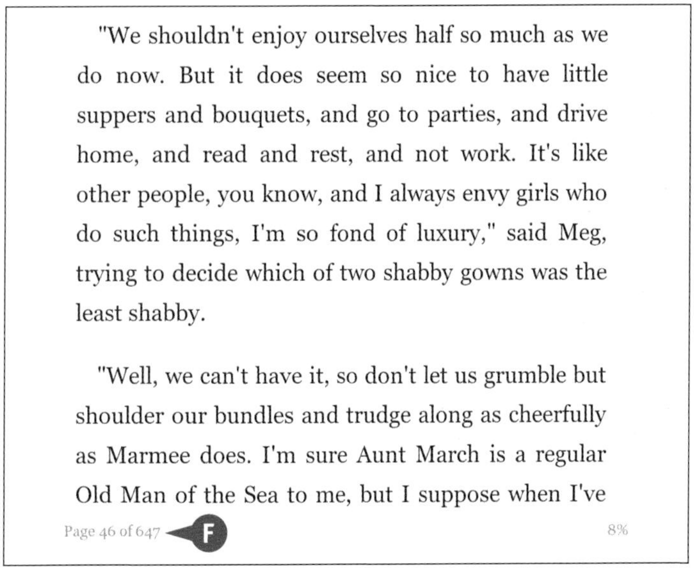

Enter page (1 - 647) or location (1 - 7379)

You are currently at page 3, location 70.

46

Cancel | Page | Location

"We shouldn't enjoy ourselves half so much as we do now. But it does seem so nice to have little suppers and bouquets, and go to parties, and drive home, and read and rest, and not work. It's like other people, you know, and I always envy girls who do such things, I'm so fond of luxury," said Meg, trying to decide which of two shabby gowns was the least shabby.

"Well, we can't have it, so don't let us grumble but shoulder our bundles and trudge along as cheerfully as Marmee does. I'm sure Aunt March is a regular Old Man of the Sea to me, but I suppose when I've

Page 46 of 647 — 8%

TIP

What is a location?

Location numbers are the Amazon Kindle's digital equivalent of physical page numbers; you can use them the same way you use page numbers — to easily find a place in your reading material. The location number is not dependent on the font size you use while reading. Be aware that the location number does not translate to the page number of the printed book or other electronic versions of the book.

Change the Reading View

You can control the appearance of the page in your book. For example, you can control the size and the appearance of the font, the background color of the book's page, the amount of space allotted to the book's margins, and the amount of space between lines on the page. You should make changes to these settings to make reading easier on your eyes.

The changes you make affect each book you open; if you do not like a particular setting, you can always change it again.

Change the Reading View

1. Open a book as described in the section "Read a Book."
2. Tap in the center of the screen.

   A. The Reading toolbar appears.
3. Tap **Aa View**.

   This menu appears.
4. Tap the **Increase Font Size** button.

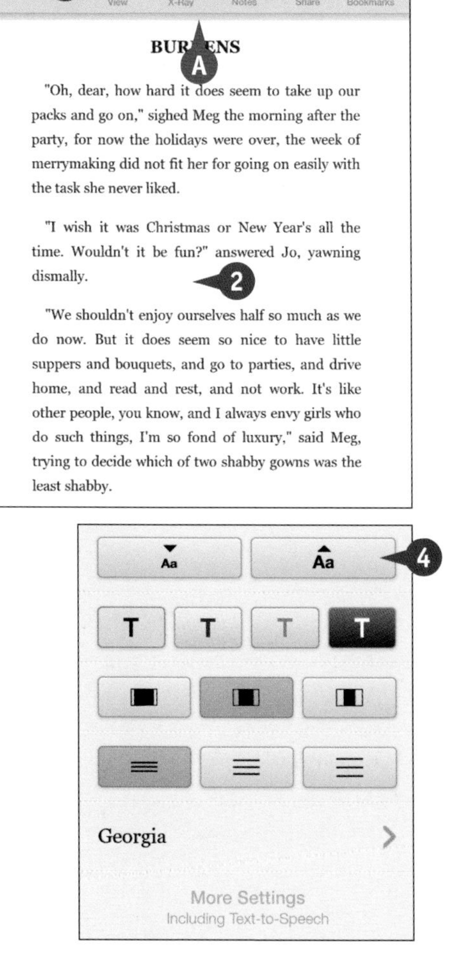

B The font size increases.

C You can tap the **Decrease Font** button to decrease the font size.

5 Tap one of these buttons to change the background color of the book.

D This example illustrates using the sepia background color.

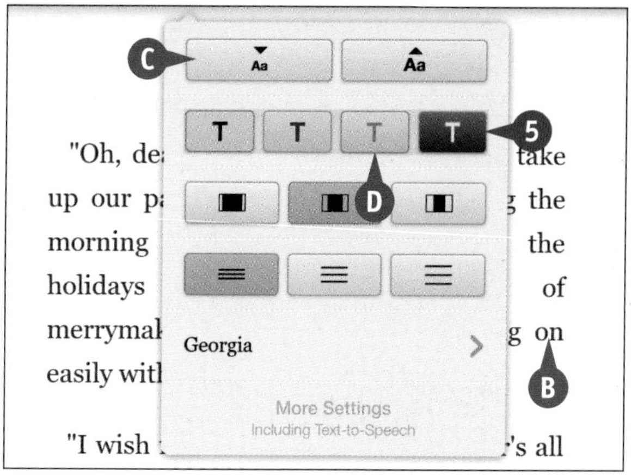

E Your book display uses the new background color.

6 Tap one of these buttons to change the space allotted to the book's margins.

F This example illustrates using the Wide Margin button.

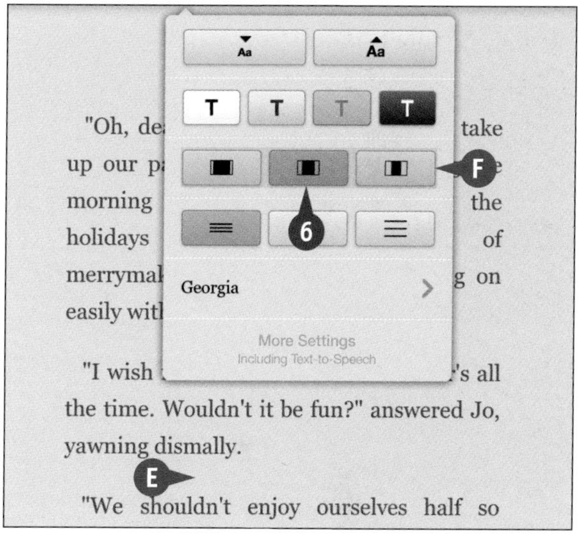

TIP

Are there other settings I can control?

Yes. Using Reader Settings for books, you can opt to hide popular highlights made and shared by others, and you can opt to use Text-to-Speech when available. See the sections "Add, Edit, or Remove Highlights" and "Listen to Books with Text-to-Speech" for more information.

continued ►

Although you can control the way your book looks as you read it, you cannot control the settings precisely. For example, you can opt to view narrow, wide, or normal margins on the page. Similarly, you can set the spacing between lines to narrow, wide, or normal. You can set the book's background to sepia, soft green, white, or black; when you choose black, the text changes to white.

You can choose from a wide variety of font sizes, but you are limited in the font faces you can use.

Change the Reading View (continued)

Ⓐ The space allotted to the book's margins changes.

7 Tap one of these buttons to control the space between the lines on the page.

Ⓑ For this example, tap the Increased Spacing button.

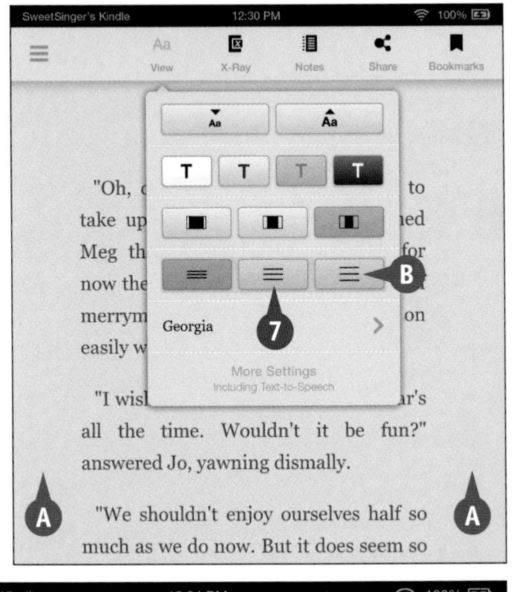

Ⓒ The space between the lines on the page changes.

8 Tap ⟩ to change the reading font.

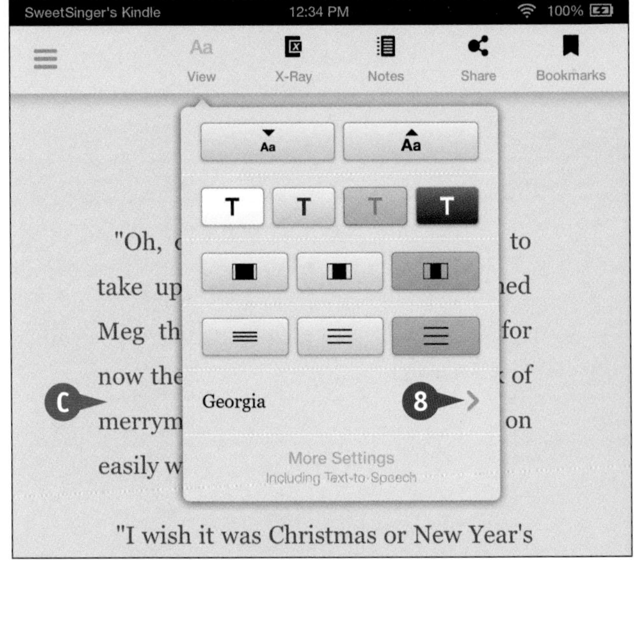

The list of available fonts appears.

D You can swipe down the list to view additional fonts.

9 Tap a font (◯ changes to ◉).

E The Fire tablet applies the new font to the book.

10 Tap anywhere on the manuscript to hide the Reading toolbar and resume reading your book.

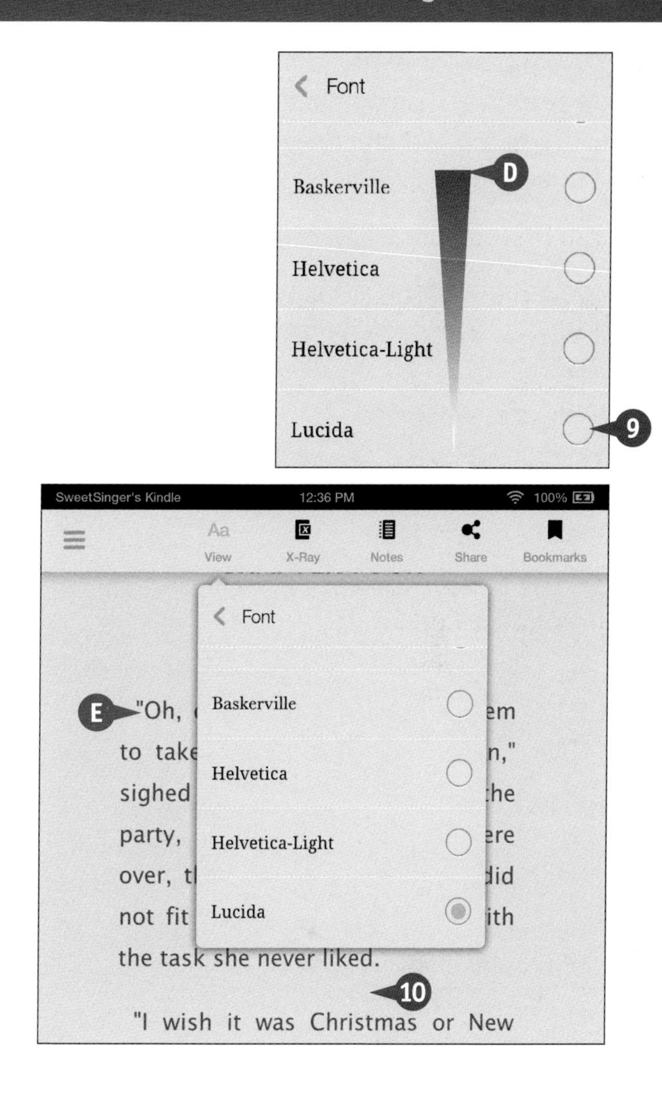

TIPS

What does the Bookmarks button on the Reader toolbar do?
The Bookmarks button places an electronic bookmark on the page, much in the same way you might use a physical bookmark in a hardback or paperback book. See "Add or Remove Bookmarks" for details.

What does the X-Ray button do?
For electronic books that utilize the X-Ray feature, you can get detailed information about characters. See "Using X-Ray to Explore a Book" for more information.

Listen to Books with Text-to-Speech

If the book's rights holder permits the *Text-to-Speech* feature, you can use it to listen to most books, newspapers, magazines, and even personal documents. You can tell if your book takes advantage of this feature when you purchase the book by looking at its product details page, where you should see the words "Text-to-Speech: Enabled." This feature, if the book uses it, is available only for books written in English.

You can listen to books either using the Fire tablet's external speakers or by plugging earphones into the Fire tablet's headphone jack.

Listen to Books with Text-to-Speech

Turn On Text-to-Speech

1. In the Books content library, tap to open the book you want to read that uses Text-to-Speech.

Note: See steps **1** to **3** in the section "Read a Book" for details on opening a book.

2. Tap the center of the screen.

- A The Reading toolbar appears at the top of the screen.
- B The Progress bar appears at the bottom of the screen.

3. Tap the **Aa View** button.

4. On the menu that appears, tap **More Settings**.

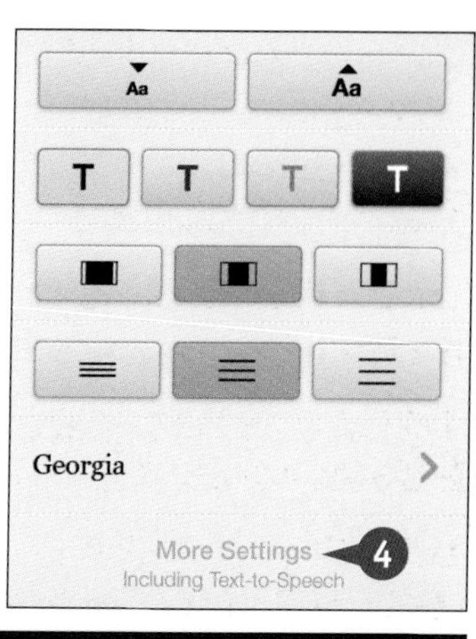

The Reader Settings page appears.

5. Tap the Text-to-Speech **On** button to enable the feature.
6. Tap the **Back** arrow (⬅) to redisplay the book.

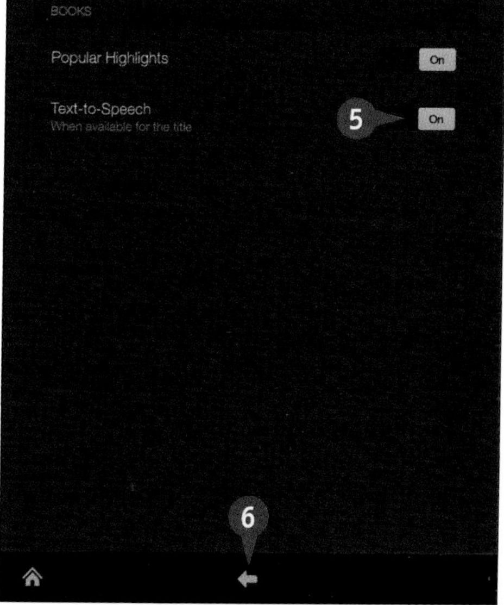

TIP

Can I control the speed with which the narrator reads?

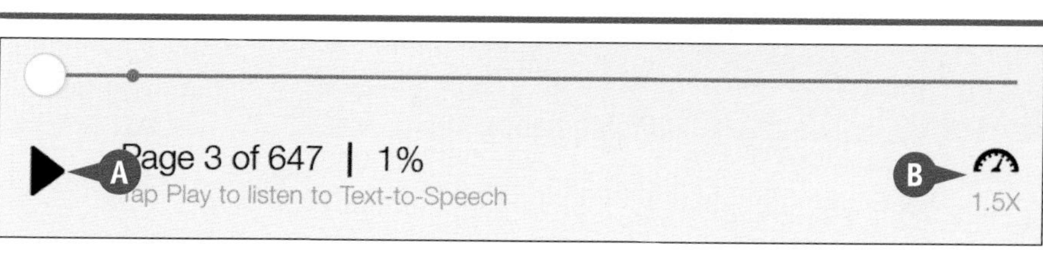

Yes. With the book open, tap the center of the screen to display the Reading toolbar and the Progress bar. Tap the **Play** button (▶) in the Progress bar **A** and then repeatedly tap the **Narration Speed** button (⏲) **B** to increase the speed up to four times normal or to decrease speed to 7/10 of normal.

continued ▶

Listen to Books with Text-to-Speech (continued)

You only need to enable the Text-to-Speech feature once — that is, you only need to complete the steps in the subsection "Turn On Text-to-Speech" once — to be able to listen to any book that uses the feature.

As you listen to the narrator read the book, you can pause the narration, and you can control the speed with which the narrator reads. Normal speed is listed below the Narration Speed button as 1X. You can increase the speed up to 4X, or four times normal speed, and you can decrease the speed down to 7/10 of normal speed.

Listen to Books with Text-to-Speech (continued)

Listen and Read

1. Tap the center of the screen to display the Reading toolbar at the top of the screen and the Progress bar at the bottom of the screen.
2. Tap the **Play** button, which turns into a Pause button (▶ changes to ⏸).

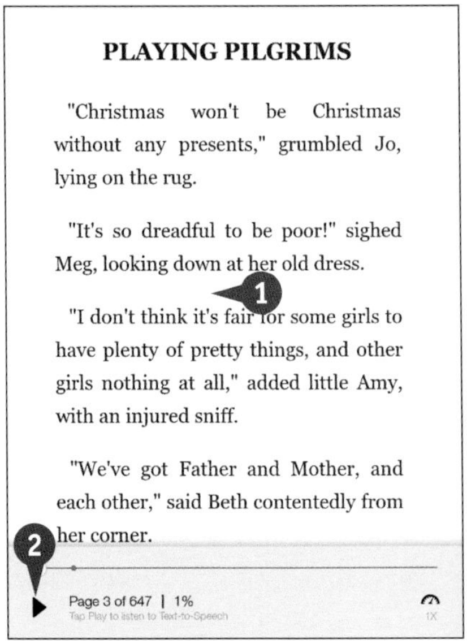

PLAYING PILGRIMS

"Christmas won't be Christmas without any presents," grumbled Jo, lying on the rug.

"It's so dreadful to be poor!" sighed Meg, looking down at her old dress.

"I don't think it's fair for some girls to have plenty of pretty things, and other girls nothing at all," added little Amy, with an injured sniff.

"We've got Father and Mother, and each other," said Beth contentedly from her corner.

Page 3 of 647 | 1%
Tap Play to listen to Text-to-Speech
1X

After a short pause, the Reading toolbar and the Progress bar disappear from view and you hear the book being read.

The page turns when the reader reaches the end of the page.

A. To stop the narration, tap the center of the screen and then, in the Progress bar, tap the **Pause** button (⏸).

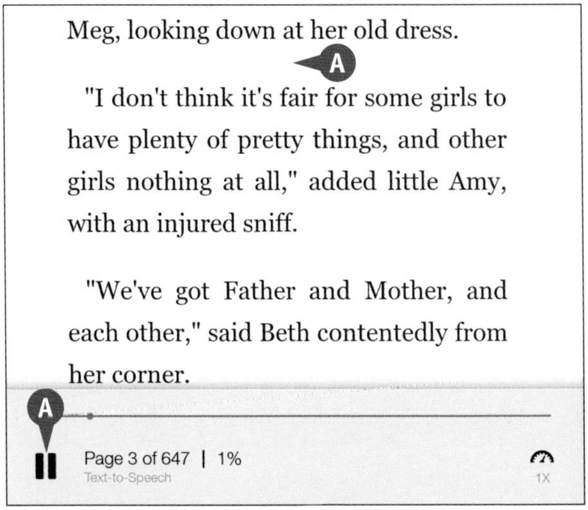

Meg, looking down at her old dress.

"I don't think it's fair for some girls to have plenty of pretty things, and other girls nothing at all," added little Amy, with an injured sniff.

"We've got Father and Mother, and each other," said Beth contentedly from her corner.

Page 3 of 647 | 1%
Text-to-Speech
1X

CHAPTER 6

Experience Immersion Reading

In addition to the Text-to-Speech feature described in the section "Listen to Books with Text-to-Speech," you can take advantage of the Immersion Reading feature if you own or buy books that are labeled "Whispersync for Voice-ready."

The *Immersion Reading* feature is similar to the Text-to-Speech feature in that a narrator reads the book aloud, and the book's pages advance as the narrator finishes a page. It differs in that a professional narrator reads the ebook, and each word the narrator reads is highlighted as it is read.

Experience Immersion Reading

1. From the Home screen, tap **Books** to display the Books content library.
2. Tap the **Navigation** button (☰) to display the Navigation panel.
3. Tap **Immersion Reading**.
4. Find a book and tap it.

continued ►

Experience Immersion Reading (continued)

To use the Immersion Reading feature, you essentially purchase two copies of the book: one that you read, and the other a corresponding audiobook version of the title — typically supplied by www.audible.com, the audiobook seller that has partnered with Amazon to offer the Immersion Reading feature.

The Immersion Reading feature costs extra money, and the amount varies from book to book. You can use the Books content library's Navigation panel to find books that use the Immersion Reading feature. You also can add professional narration to any title you own if that title offers professional narration.

Experience Immersion Reading (continued)

Ⓐ You can search for a book by tapping the **Search** button (🔍) and typing a book title.

The book's product details page appears.

Ⓑ To ensure you can use the Immersion Reading feature, look for a phrase like this or "Whispersync for Voice-ready."

5. Tap **Buy** or **Buy for Free**.

The book downloads to your Fire tablet, and the book's product details page reappears containing new choices.

6. Tap **Add Narration**.

Note: The cost of the narration appears in the Add Narration button.

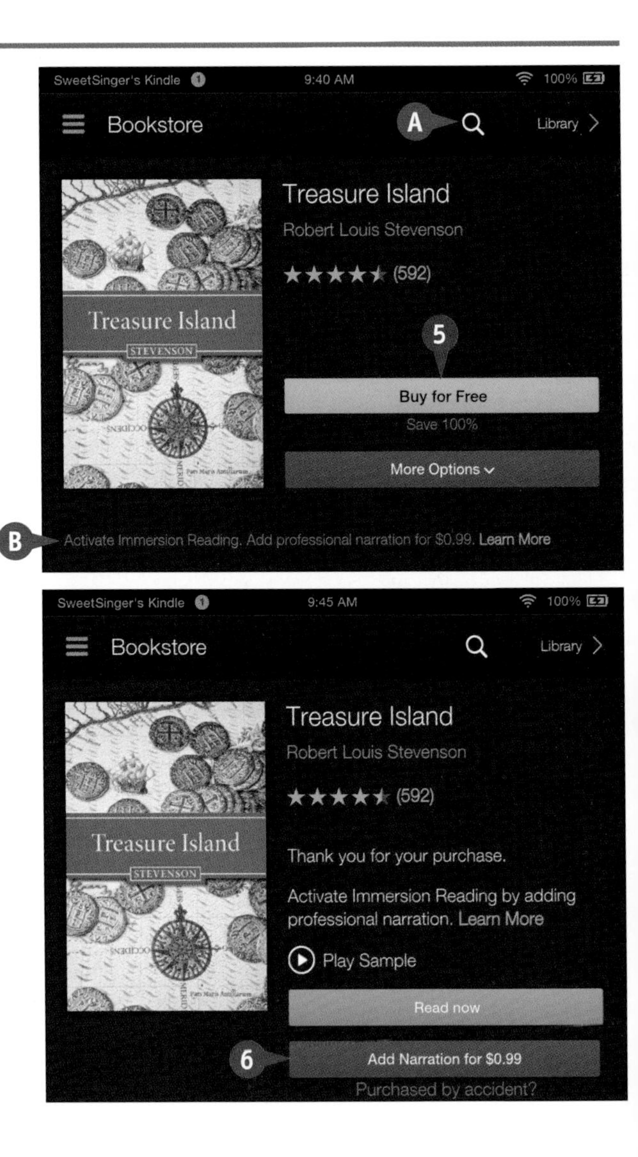

Amazon processes your purchase and redisplays the book's product details page.

 Tap **Read and Listen Now**.

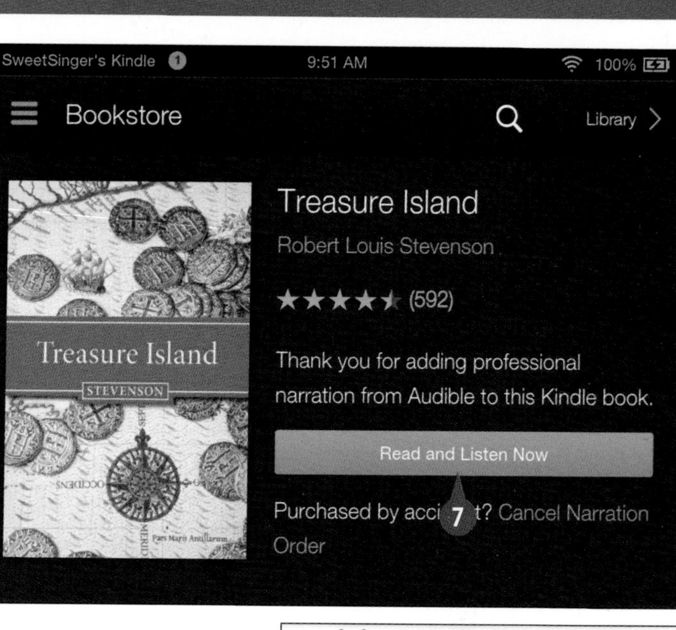

The book opens.

8. Tap the center of the screen to display the Reading toolbar at the top of the screen and the Progress bar at the bottom of the screen.

9. In the Progress bar, tap the **Play** button, which changes to a Pause button (▶ changes to ⏸).

C. As the narrator reads, the words are highlighted on the page.

asked me to write down the whole particulars abo C Treasure Island, from the beginning to the end, keeping nothing back but the bearings of the island, and that only because there is still treasure not yet lifted, I take up my pen in the year of grace 17__ and go back to the time when my father kept the Admiral Benbow inn and the brown old seaman with the sabre cut first took up his lodging under our roof.

I remember him as if it were yesterday, as he came plodding to the inn door, his sea-chest following behind him in a hand-barrow—a tall, strong, heavy, nut-brown man, his tarry pigtail

Page 1 of 174 | 6:42:18 to end of narration

TIP

If I already own a book, how do I add professional narration to use the Immersion Reading feature?
In the upper-right corner of the Books content library, tap **Store**. Then tap the **Search** button (🔍) at the top of the screen and search for the title you already own. When you find it, tap it to display its product details page. Look for the **Add Narration** button, tap it, and then complete steps **7** to **9**.

Using X-Ray to Explore a Book

If your book supports the *X-Ray* feature, you can use it to explore descriptions of each character and important terms in the book. You also can browse a list of pages on which the character or term appears with excerpts from those pages. You can easily tap an entry to go to that page in the book.

You can sort X-Ray entries alphabetically, by relevance in the book, or in order of appearance. You also can filter the list to view all entries, only characters, or only terms.

Using X-Ray to Explore a Book

1. Open a book as described in the section "Read a Book."
2. Tap in the center of the screen.
3. In the Reading toolbar that appears, tap **X-Ray**.

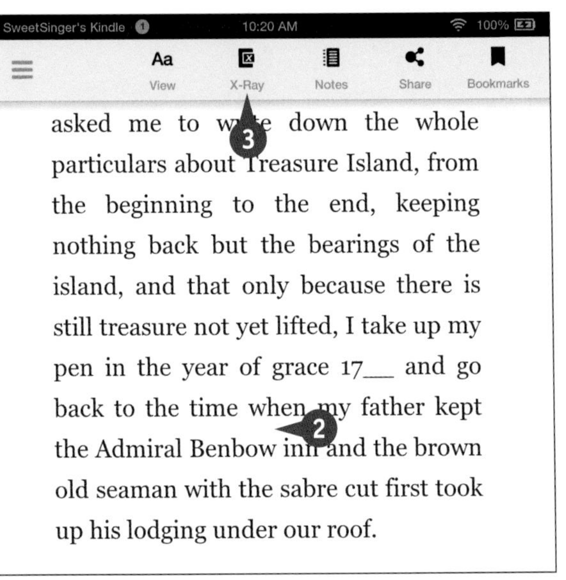

The X-Ray screen appears.

A. You can swipe up to scroll down the list.

4. Tap **X-Ray**.

B. The Sort menu appears, giving you choices for sorting X-Ray entries.

5 Tap this area to filter the X-Ray list by People, Terms, or All (displays both).

Note: The numbers beside each filter represent the number of entries, characters, and terms listed in X-Ray.

C The bars represent the various locations where a character or term is mentioned.

6 Tap a character or term.

A list of the pages containing that character's name or that term appears.

D If more information is available on the Internet, you can tap a link to view that information.

E The page number appears below the entry.

Note: You can tap an entry to display that page in the book.

TIP

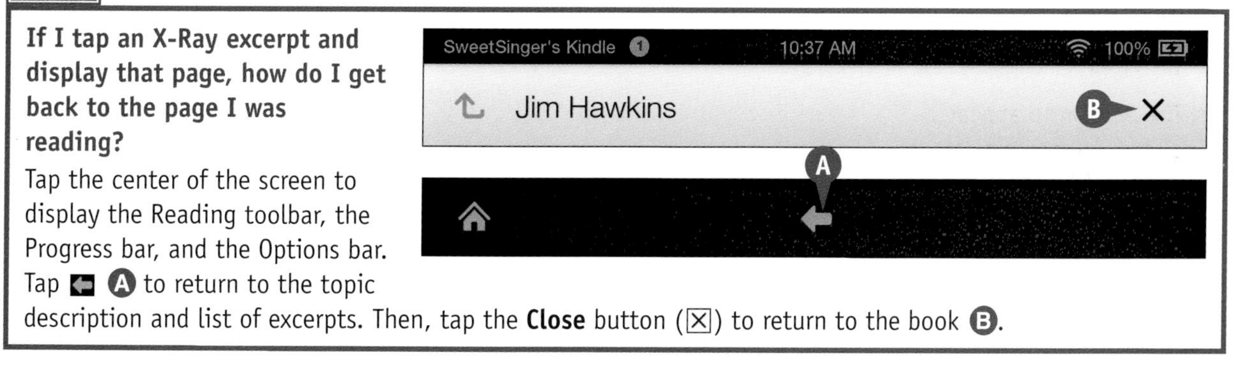

If I tap an X-Ray excerpt and display that page, how do I get back to the page I was reading?

Tap the center of the screen to display the Reading toolbar, the Progress bar, and the Options bar. Tap the back button (A) to return to the topic description and list of excerpts. Then, tap the **Close** button (☒) to return to the book (B).

Look Up Information While Reading

While reading, you can look up information using the built-in dictionaries or online sources such as Wikipedia and the Bing Translator. To use online sources, your Fire tablet must be connected to a network.

When you look up information, the Smart Lookup feature displays cards, which provide information about the word you select. For any given word, you might see an X-Ray card if your book is X-Ray-enabled, a Wikipedia card, a Dictionary card, and a Translation card. You see only those cards relevant to the term you look up.

Look Up Information While Reading

1. Open a book as described in the section "Read a Book."
2. Press and hold a word you want to know more about.

   A. The word appears highlighted and a Smart Lookup card appears.

   Note: If you chose a character or a term in an X-Ray-supported book, an X-Ray Smart Lookup card appears.

   B. These dots represent the number of Smart Lookup cards available for the character or term.

3. After reading the information, swipe the Smart Lookup card to the left.

   C. A Dictionary Smart Lookup card appears.

4. After reading the information, swipe the Smart Lookup card to the left.

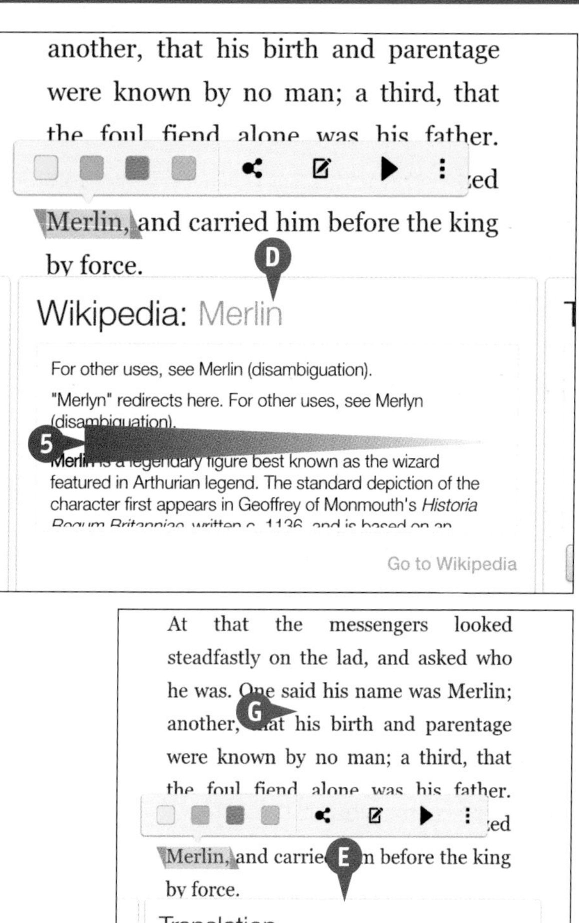

D If information is available on Wikipedia, a Wikipedia Smart Lookup card appears.

5 After reading the information, swipe the Smart Lookup card to the left.

E A Translation Smart Lookup card appears.

F You can tap these buttons to select translation languages; when you tap the second button and make a selection, the Bing Translator provides the translation.

G You can tap anywhere on the book to hide the Smart Lookup cards and return to reading.

TIPS

When I am on the X-Ray card, what happens if I tap Go to X-Ray?
The X-Ray page appears; you can read more about X-Ray in the section "Using X-Ray to Explore a Book." To return to your book and continue reading, tap the **Close** button (☒) in the upper-right corner of the X-Ray screen.

When I am on the Wikipedia card, what happens if I tap Go to Wikipedia?
The Silk browser on your Fire tablet opens and displays the Wikipedia page related to the word you selected. To return to your book and continue reading, tap the **Back** arrow (⬅). To read more about the Silk browser, see Chapter 11.

Add, Edit, or Remove Highlights

You can use the *Highlight* feature to mark passages in a book that you deem important. This feature is like using a marker as you read a book — without the permanent consequence. When you highlight a word or passage, you add a color to it that appears in the manuscript. You can add highlighting in yellow, blue, magenta, or orange.

Unlike using highlighters on a print book, in a digital book, you can remove the highlighting if you later change your mind about having marked a passage.

Add, Edit, or Remove Highlights

Add a Highlight

1. Open a book as described in the section "Read a Book."
2. Press and hold a word to highlight it, or drag to select a phrase.
   - A. As you drag, blue shading appears over selected text and a rectangle appears, magnifying the text beneath it.
3. When you finish selecting, lift your finger.

Note: You highlight a phrase that continues onto another page by dragging to the lower-right corner of the screen. Without lifting your finger, continue selecting text after the page automatically changes.

The Highlighting toolbar appears.

4. Tap a color to apply it to the selected text.

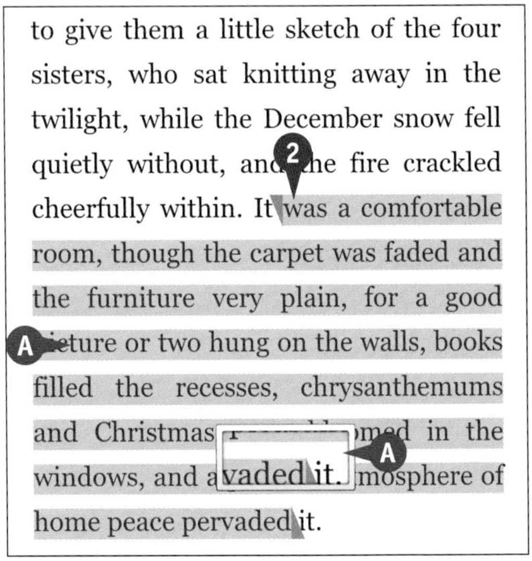

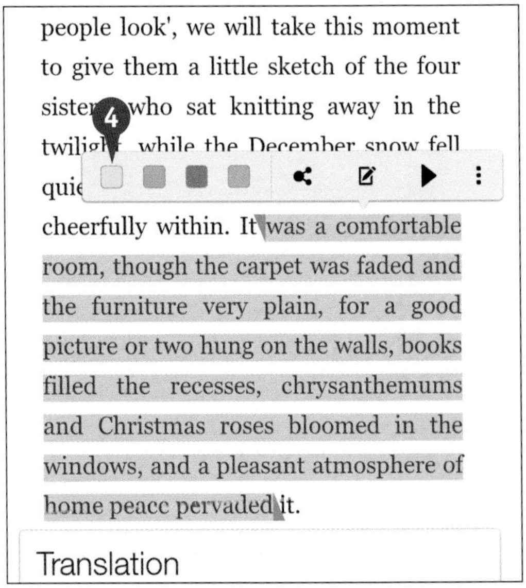

Ⓑ The color appears on the selected text.

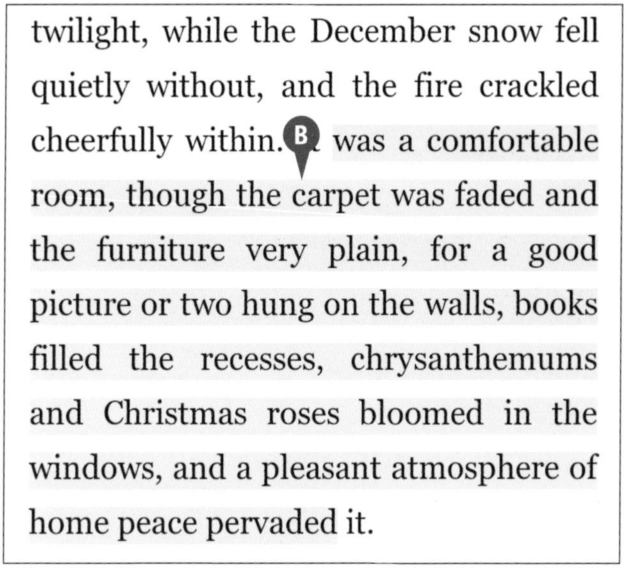

Remove Highlighting

1. Press and hold a word in the highlighted text.

   A Smart Lookup card and the Highlighting toolbar appear.

2. Tap the color containing the X.

Ⓒ You can change the highlight color by simply tapping another color.

The highlighting disappears from all the text surrounding the word you selected in step **1**.

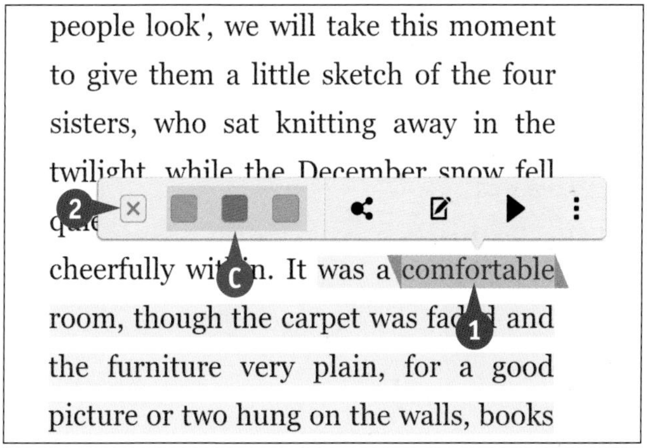

TIP

What are the dotted lines I see below certain phrases?

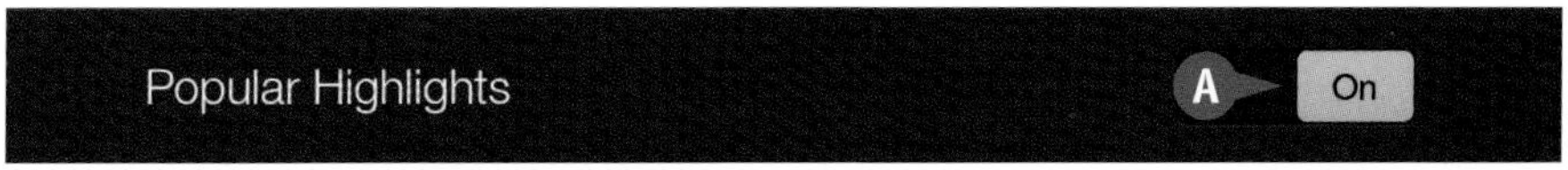

The *Popular Highlights* feature is turned on; under these circumstances, your book displays phrases that have been highlighted by many readers; the number of readers appears at the beginning of the line. You can turn off the Popular Highlights feature: Tap the center of the screen, tap the **Aa View** button, and then tap **More Settings.** On the Reader Settings screen, tap to turn off **Popular Highlights** Ⓐ.

Add, Edit, or Remove Notes

As you read a book, you can add notes to it that you can later review. When you add a note, you select text to annotate, and the Fire tablet automatically adds highlighting and lets you type a note.

Using the Share button on the Highlighting toolbar, you can share your notes and highlights from your Fire tablet to Facebook, Twitter, or Goodreads. By default, notes are automatically shared with Goodreads if you have linked your Fire tablet to your Goodreads account.

Add, Edit, or Remove Notes

Add a Note

1. Press and hold a word or press and drag to select text.

   Selected text appears shaded in blue.

2. Lift your finger.

   The Highlighting toolbar appears.

3. Tap the **Note** button (📝).

   The Note card appears.

   Ⓐ The page number where you are placing the note appears here.

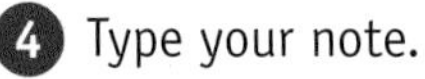

4. Type your note.
5. Tap **Save**.

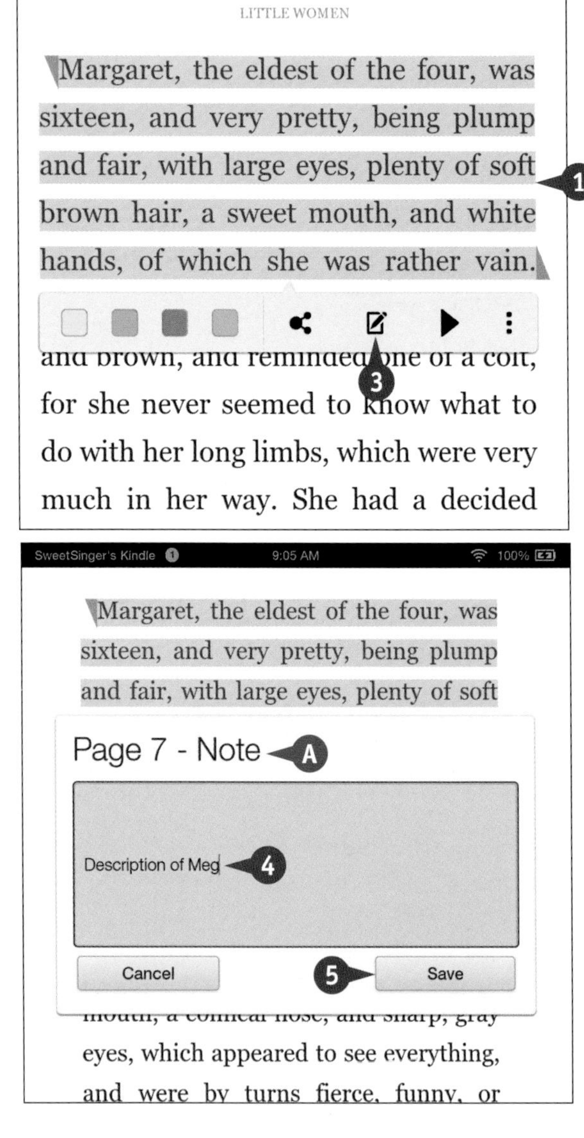

LITTLE WOMEN
Margaret, the eldest of the four, was sixteen, and very pretty, being plump and fair, with large eyes, plenty of soft brown hair, a sweet mouth, and white hands, of which she was rather vain.
and brown, and reminded one of a colt, for she never seemed to know what to do with her long limbs, which were very much in her way. She had a decided
SweetSinger's Kindle
9:05 AM
100%
Margaret, the eldest of the four, was sixteen, and very pretty, being plump and fair, with large eyes, plenty of soft
Page 7 - Note
Description of Meg
Cancel
Save
eyes, which appeared to see everything,

B The selected text appears highlighted.

C A **Note** icon (▤) appears beside the highlighted text.

Edit or Remove a Note

1. Tap ▤ in the text.

   The Note card appears.

2. Make changes and tap **Save** or tap **Delete** to remove the note and its associated highlighting.

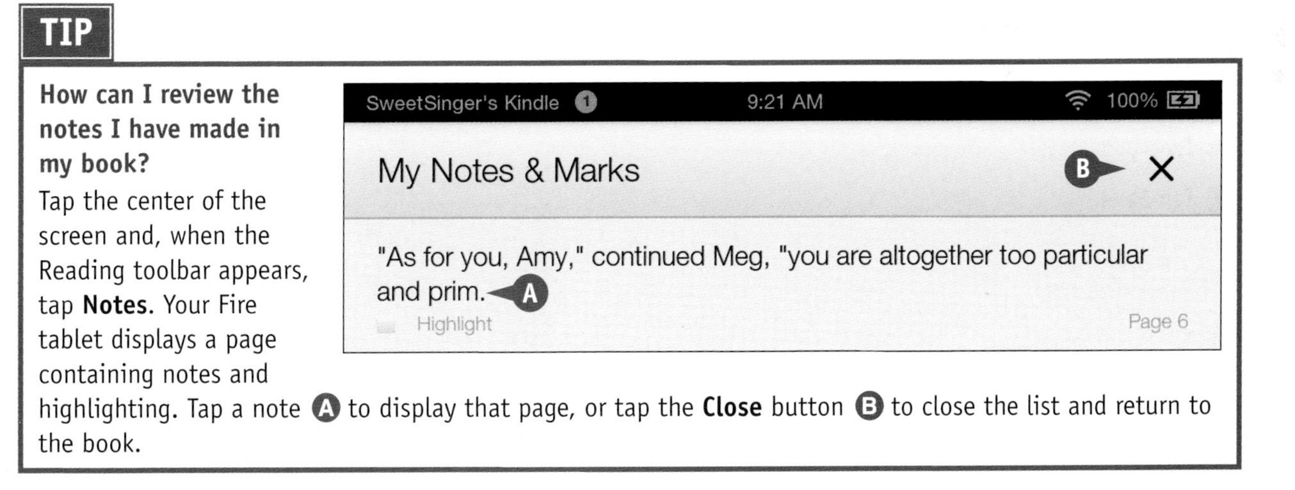
SweetSinger's Kindle
9:21 AM
100%
My Notes & Marks
"As for you, Amy," continued Meg, "you are altogether too particular and prim.
Highlight
Page 6

TIP

How can I review the notes I have made in my book?

Tap the center of the screen and, when the Reading toolbar appears, tap **Notes**. Your Fire tablet displays a page containing notes and highlighting. Tap a note **A** to display that page, or tap the **Close** button **B** to close the list and return to the book.

Add or Remove Bookmarks

You can add or remove bookmarks at any location in a Kindle book. You can use bookmarks in your digital book the same way you would use a physical bookmark in a print book. That is, bookmarks help you mark your place.

You can add bookmarks to as many pages in a digital book as you want. You can use digital bookmarks to navigate in your book because all bookmarks appear on a Bookmark list, along with the page number containing each bookmark. You can use the list to return to a bookmarked page at a later point in time.

Add or Remove Bookmarks

Add a Bookmark

1. Open a book as described in the section "Read a Book."
2. Navigate to the page that you want to bookmark.
3. Tap the top-right corner of the screen.

   A bookmark appears.

Note: To remove a bookmark, repeat steps **1** to **3**.

LITTLE WOMEN

3

sit looking at me while I opened the bundles," said Beth, who was toasting her face and the bread for tea at the same time.

"Let Marmee think we are getting things for ourselves, and then surprise her. We must go shopping tomorrow afternoon, Meg. There is so much to do about the play for Christmas night," said Jo, marching up and down, with her hands behind her back, and her nose in the air.

Navigate Using Bookmarks

1. In an open book, tap the center of the screen to display the Reading toolbar.
2. Tap **Bookmarks**.

   A list of bookmarks in the book appears.

3. Tap a bookmark.

   The page containing the bookmark appears. You can tap the **Back** arrow (⬅) in the Options bar to return to the page you were reading.

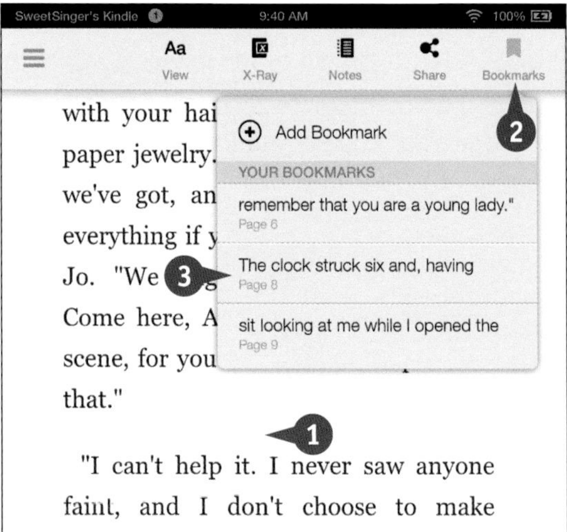

Read Without Buying

Instead of buying books for your Fire tablet, you can borrow books from the Kindle Owners' Lending Library, from a public library, or from a friend.

Borrow Using Amazon Prime

Amazon Prime members can borrow one book each month from the Kindle Owners' Lending Library, which contains over 500,000 titles. There are no due dates, but you must return one book before borrowing another. In the Books content library, open the Kindle Store and search for ***prime books***. Titles you can borrow have the Amazon Prime logo. On the book's product page, tap the **Borrow for Free** button.

Borrow from a Public Library

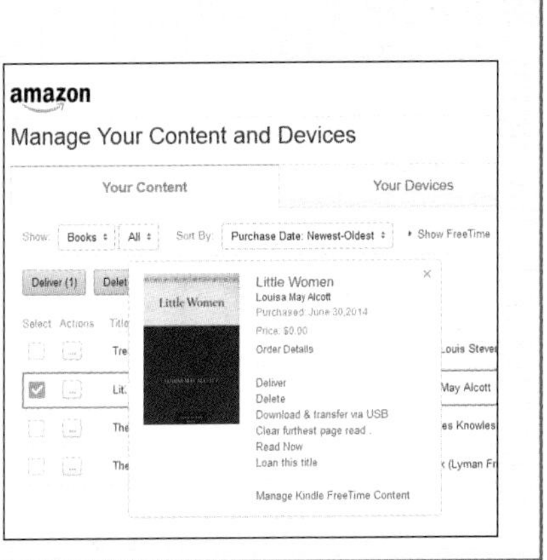

Many U.S. public libraries participate in the *OverDrive* service, which lets you to check out books to your Kindle. If you have a library card and your library participates, you can check out ebooks via your library's website using a Wi-Fi connection. You then sign in to your Amazon account and select your Kindle as the device that should receive the book to have it automatically download. When your library sends a due date reminder email, simply sign in to your Amazon account and, from the main menu, select **Manage Your Content and Devices**. Tap beside the book to select it, tap the **Actions** button (...), and from the Actions menu, tap **Return This Book.**

Lend a Book to a Friend

Depending on copyrights, you can lend some purchased books to friends. In your Amazon account, select **Manage Your Content and Devices** from the main menu. Tap beside the title you want to lend to select it and tap the **Actions** button. Then, tap the **Loan this title** option.

Work with Cloud Collections

You can use *Cloud Collections* to organize the books you have purchased or borrowed. You can think of Cloud Collections as bookshelves, which most people use to organize their book collections so they can easily find a particular title.

Some people organize books by book type, such as mystery or self-help, and others organize them by author. Still others order books by the date they read them. You can organize your books in any way you want, and you can use multiple organization methods — the equivalent of placing a book on two different bookshelves.

Work with Cloud Collections

Create a Collection

1. From the Home screen, tap **Books**.

   The Books content library appears.

2. Tap the **Navigation** button (☰).

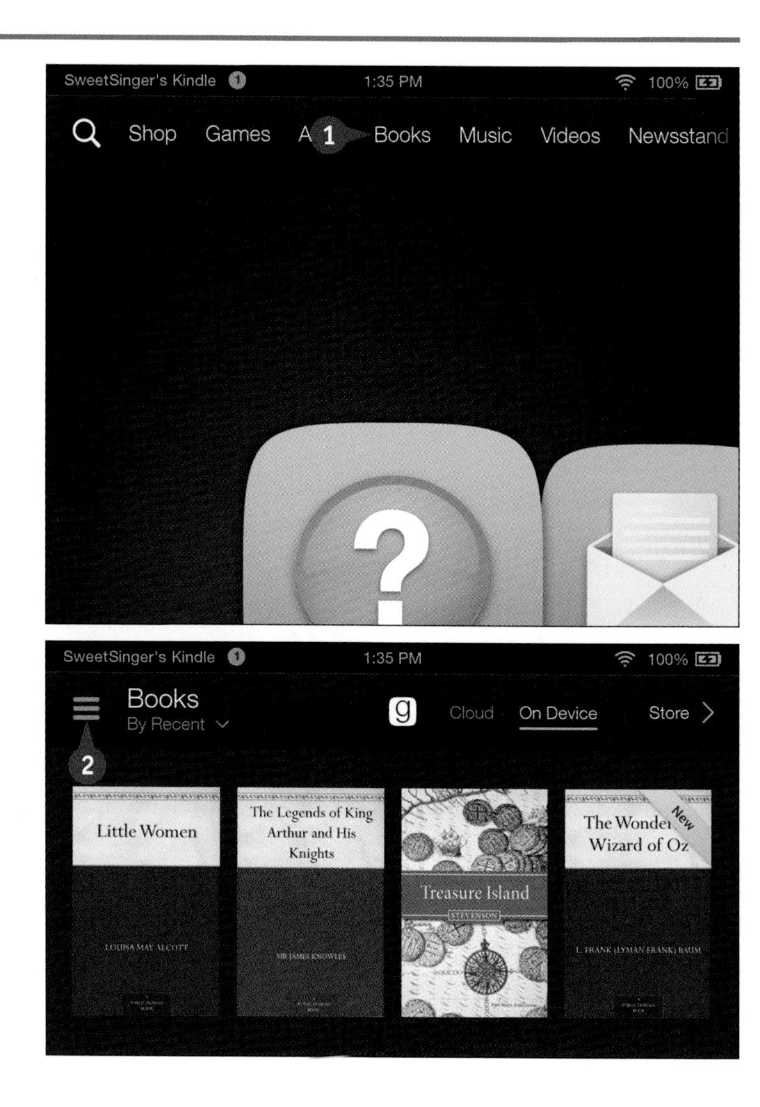

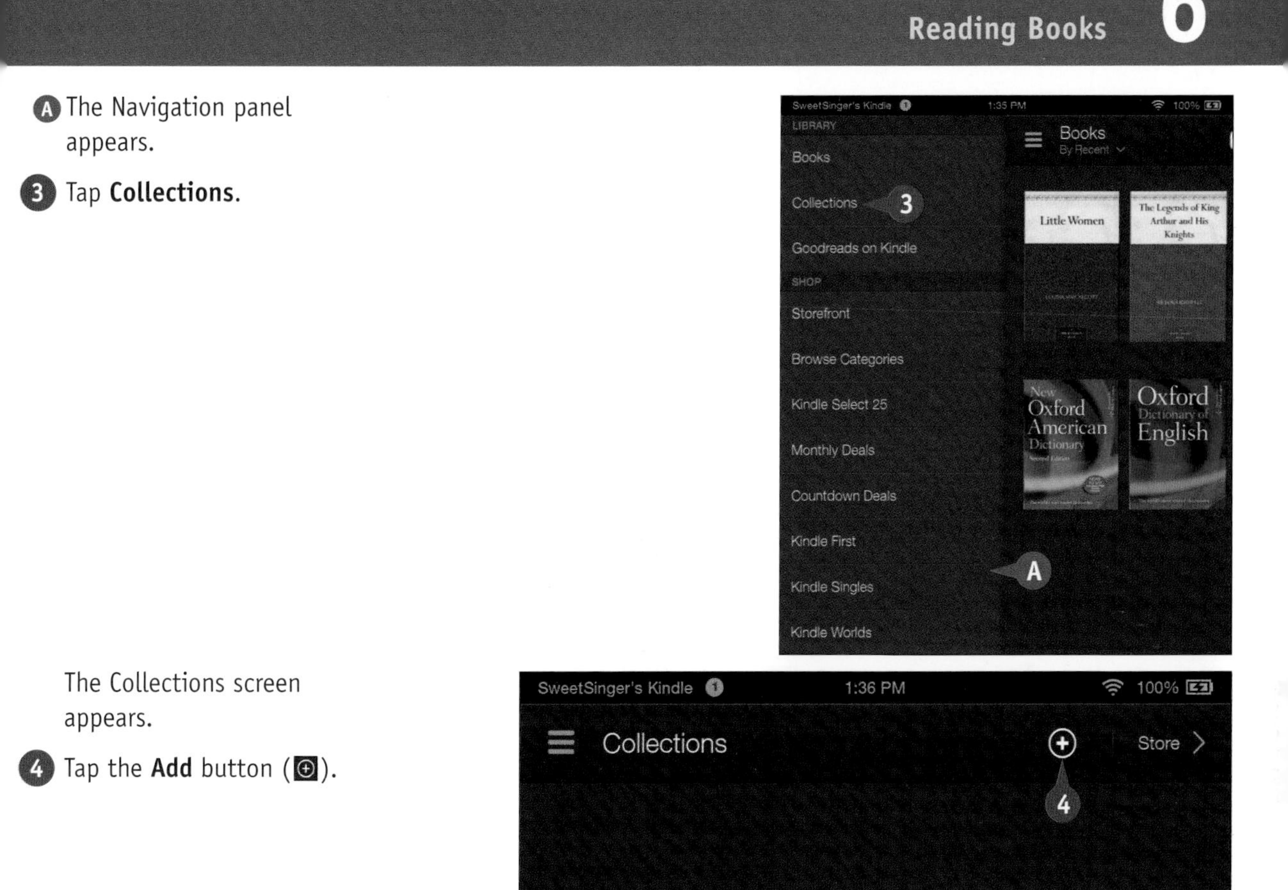

Ⓐ The Navigation panel appears.

3 Tap **Collections**.

The Collections screen appears.

4 Tap the **Add** button (⊕).

TIP

How can I edit a collection to remove a book?
Complete steps **1** to **3** in the subsection "Create a Collection" to display the Collections screen. Tap a collection to open it Ⓐ. Then, press and hold the book you want to remove from the collection and drag it outside the collection Ⓑ.

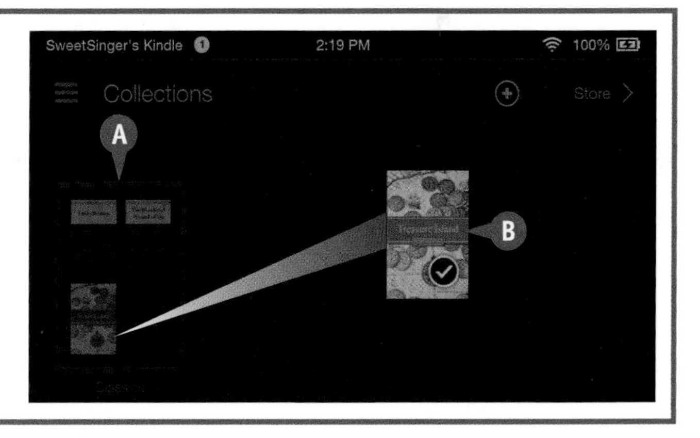

continued ►

Work with Cloud Collections (continued)

You can include the same book in as many collections as you want. You can also update a collection with additional books at any time, and the collection becomes available and visible on all Kindle devices you own.

When it comes time to delete a Cloud Collection, remember that doing so does not delete the books in the collection; the books remain available to you in your Amazon Cloud account. If you own more than one Kindle device that supports collections, deleting the collection on one device deletes it on all devices.

Work with Cloud Collections (continued)

The Create Collection dialog box appears.

5 Type a name for the collection.

6 Tap **Add**.

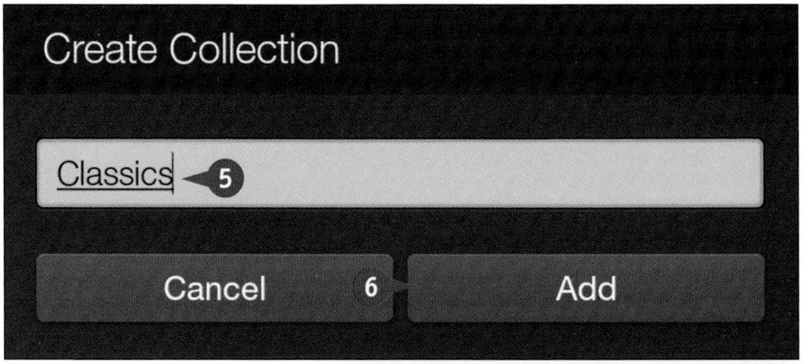

Create Collection

Classics 5

Cancel 6 Add

A list of books in your Books content library appears.

7 Scroll through the list and tap ■ beside each book you want to include in the collection (■ changes to ☑).

8 Tap **Add**.

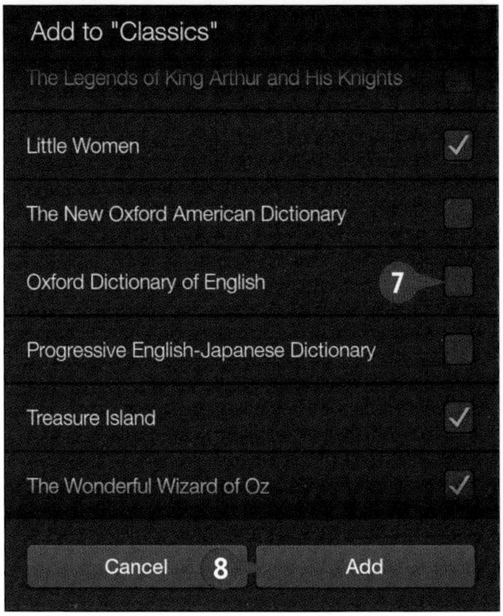

Add to "Classics"

The Legends of King Arthur and His Knights

Little Women

The New Oxford American Dictionary

Oxford Dictionary of English 7

Progressive English-Japanese Dictionary

Treasure Island

The Wonderful Wizard of Oz

Cancel 8 Add

Ⓐ The Collections screen reappears, showing the newly added collection.

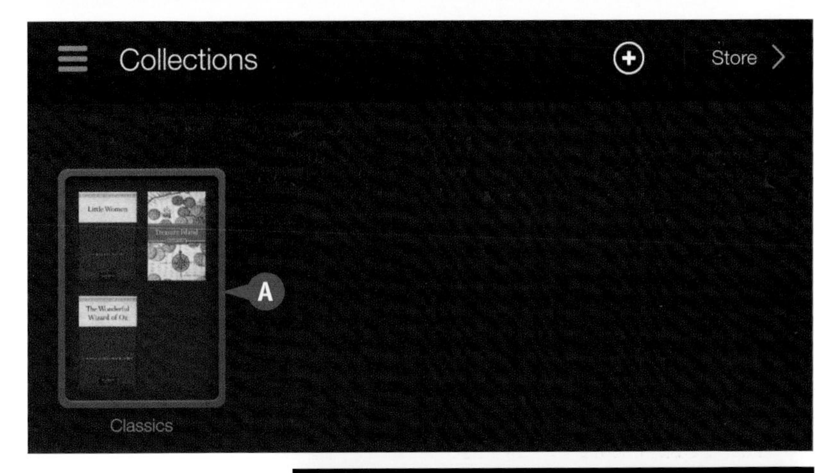

Add to a Collection

1. Complete steps **1** to **3** in the subsection "Create a Collection" to display the Collections screen.
2. Tap the collection to which you want to add a book.

   The Add to Collection window appears.

Note: You can change a collection's name by tapping the name in this window.

3. Tap the **Add** button (⊕)

   The list of books in your Books content library appears.

4. Repeat steps **7** and **8** in the subsection "Create a Collection."

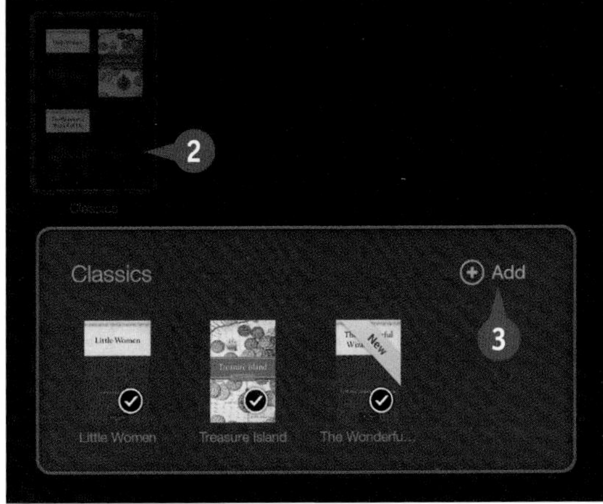

TIP

How do I delete a Cloud Collection?
In the Books content library, display the Collections screen by completing steps **1** to **3** in the subsection "Create a Collection." Tap and hold the collection you want to delete; from the menu that appears, tap **Delete Collection** Ⓐ.

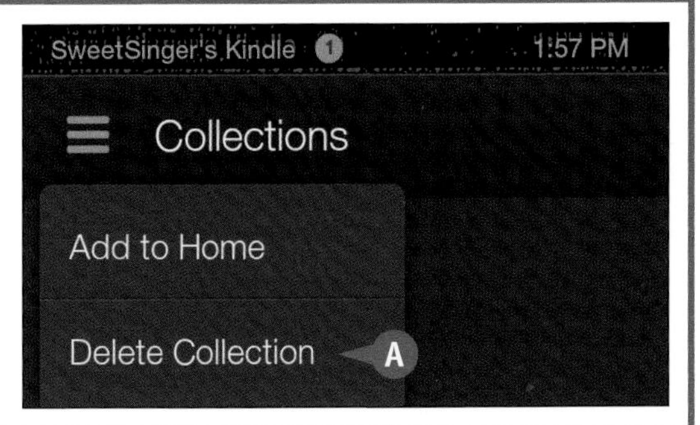

CHAPTER 7

Reading Magazines and Newspapers

You can purchase single issues or subscribe to and read magazines and newspapers on your Fire tablet. Whereas you read a newspaper or magazine the same way you read a book on your Fire tablet, subscriptions behave differently from books. This chapter shows you how to manage subscriptions.

Learn about Subscriptions 150
Manage Magazine or Newspaper Subscriptions 152
Change Privacy Settings for Subscriptions 154
Keep an Issue on Your Device 155

Learn about Subscriptions

You can buy single issues or subscribe to magazines and newspapers and read them on your Fire tablet. The techniques for reading magazines or newspapers are the same as those you use to read books; see Chapter 6 for details.

Subscription Frequency and Free Periods

The subscription's product page shows you delivery frequency, and all subscriptions include, at a minimum, a 14-day free period, during which you can cancel without being charged (A). To automatically receive the latest issue of your subscription, which appears at the front of your Carousel, your device must be connected to a wireless network.

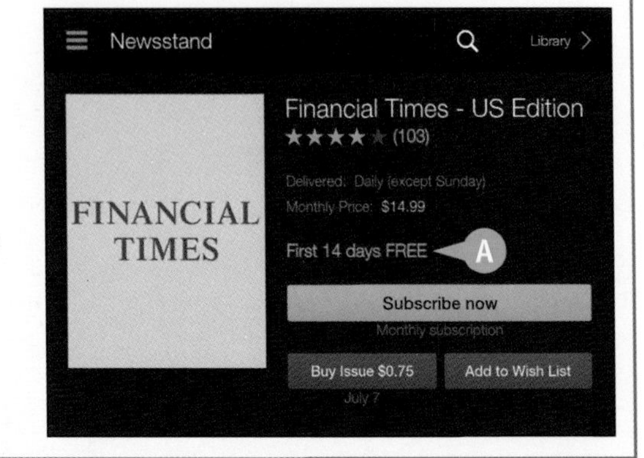

Magazines and Newspapers Apps

Some newspaper and magazine titles in the Newsstand, such as *The Wall Street Journal* and *National Geographic*, deliver content to subscribers through an app. All current and past issues are accessible from the app.

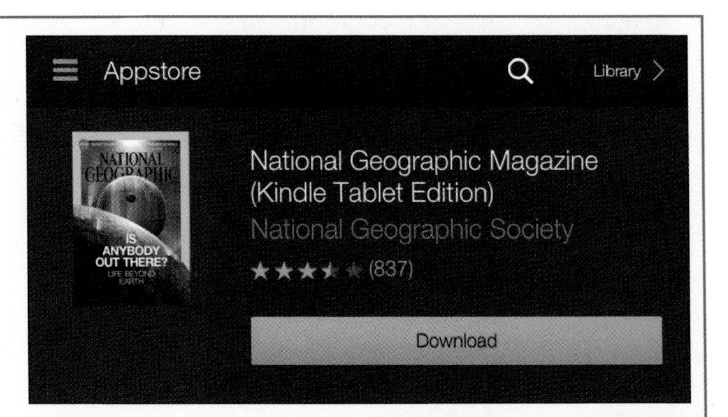

Page View and Text View

Most magazines display in page view and look just like the pages of the printed edition of the magazine; you can flip through the magazine in either portrait or landscape mode. Most Kindle subscriptions are available in text view, where you can navigate and read articles using the techniques used to read a Kindle book.

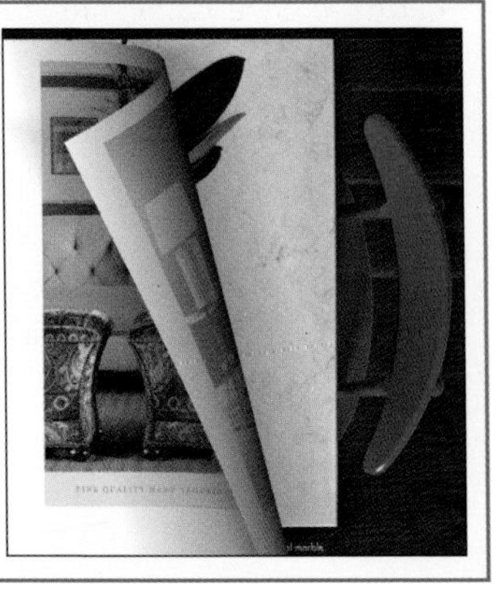

Subscriptions Lengths

Subscriptions are either annual or monthly. At the end of the subscription period, annual subscriptions auto-renew at the lowest price available in the Kindle Store or at the renewal price indicated on the product details page, unless you cancel or change your auto-renewal preferences as described in the section "Manage Magazine or Newspaper Subscriptions."

Monthly subscriptions auto-renew at the end of every month until you cancel. Unlike annual subscriptions, there are no auto-renewal settings for monthly subscriptions.

Link to an Existing Magazine Subscription

If you already have a subscription, some magazines offer you the option to receive the Kindle edition at no extra cost. On the product page for eligible magazines, you find a line you can tap to verify your existing subscription A. You can verify an existing subscription using your account number, mailing address, or login information.

Past Issues and Additional Subscription Features

Past issues of magazine and newspaper subscriptions are stored in your Amazon Cloud account, and the length of time issues are stored in the Cloud at Amazon depends on the device you own. Fire tablet owners have access to all issues of a magazine or newspaper subscription. You can download past issues from the Amazon Cloud, even if you cancel your subscription.

Some magazines, such as *Bon Appétit* magazine, are interactive and contain elements such as video, audio, and slide shows; an "Interactive Magazine" designation appears below the title on the product details page. *The New York Times*, *The New Yorker*, and *The Wall Street Journal* offer subscribers additional features, such as the ability to view the publisher's online archive.

Manage Magazine or Newspaper Subscriptions

Your Fire tablet enables you to change magazine and newspaper subscription settings to suit your particular needs. For example, you can opt to wirelessly deliver past issues of a subscription to your device. Or, you can download and transfer past issues to your computer and then copy them to your device the same way you transfer photos stored on your PC; see Chapter 5 for details.

You also can cancel a subscription and, if appropriate, reactivate an inactive subscription. And, because most subscriptions automatically renew, you can control automatic renewal settings.

Manage Magazine or Newspaper Subscriptions

1. Open your browser and navigate to www.amazon.com.
2. Click or tap the **Hello. Sign in Your Account** button.
3. Click or tap **Sign in**.

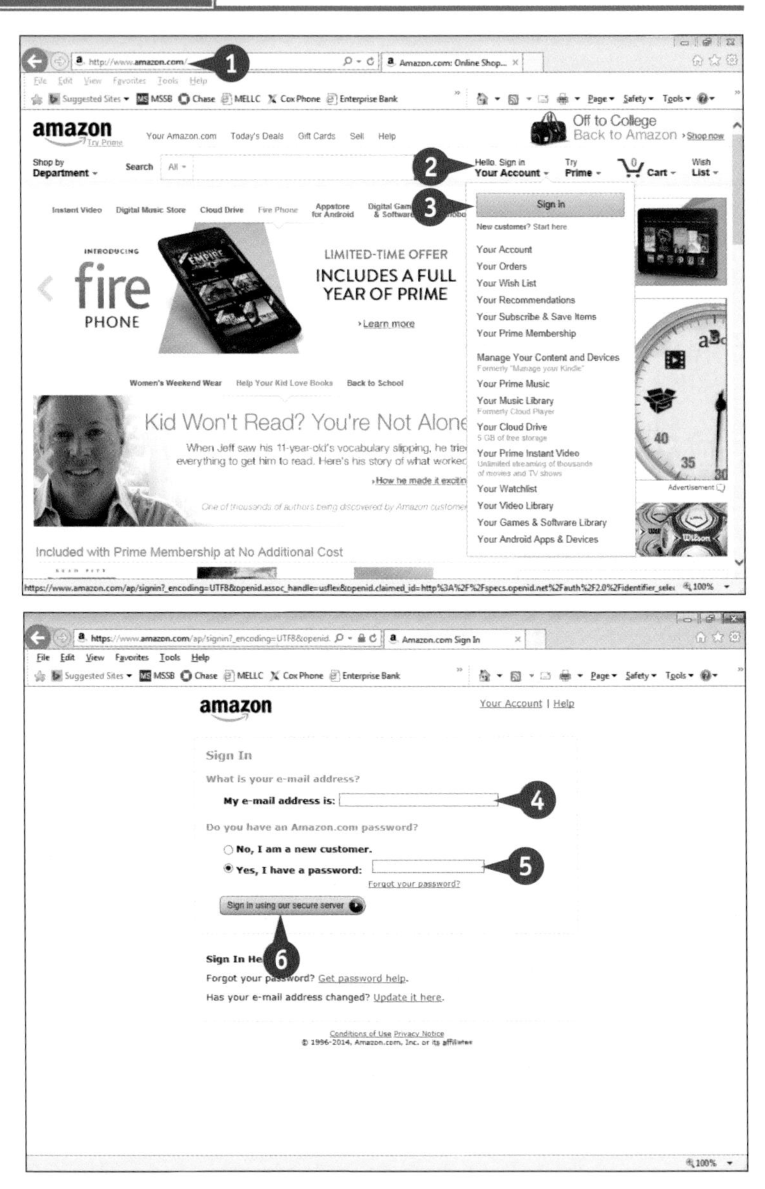

The Amazon Sign In page appears.

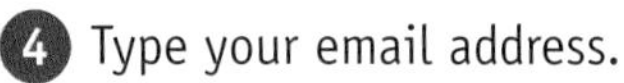

4. Type your email address.
5. Type your password.
6. Click or tap **Sign in using our secure server**.

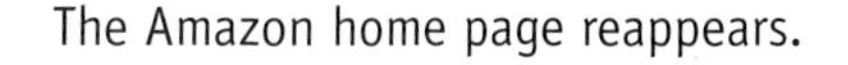

The Amazon home page reappears.

7. Click or tap your sign-in name.
8. Click or tap **Manage Your Content and Devices**.

The Manage Your Content and Devices page appears.

9. Click or tap the drop-down list to filter for magazines or newspapers.

Note: This example filters for magazines. To reactivate a cancelled subscription, choose **View inactive subscriptions**.

10. Click or tap the **Actions** button (…) to view subscription management choices.
11. Click or tap a choice.
12. When you finish working in your Amazon account, sign out.

TIP

How can I manage auto-renewal settings?

Complete steps **1** to **10**. Then, click or tap **Newsstand Subscription Settings**. On the page that appears, click or tap **Actions** (A) and click or tap **Turn off auto-renewal** (B).

Change Privacy Settings for Subscriptions

You can change the privacy settings associated with any newspaper or magazine subscription. When you subscribe to a newspaper or magazine, the publisher asks permission to use your email address for marketing purposes. Amazon shares your name, billing address, and order information with your newspaper or magazine publisher but does not share your credit card information. If you change your mind about sharing your email address, or if you do not want the publisher to share your name and billing address, you can change privacy settings at any time.

Change Privacy Settings for Subscriptions

1. Complete steps **1** to **10** in the section "Manage Magazine or Newspaper Subscriptions."
2. Click or tap **Newsstand Subscription Settings**.

The Newsstand Subscription Settings page appears.

3. Click or tap **Edit** to open the Privacy Settings box.
4. Make changes as appropriate.
5. Click or tap **Update**.

After you subscribe to a newspaper or magazine, you can download and read the newspaper or magazine and then remove it from the device. For Fire tablet users, past issues of magazines and newspapers that you receive as part of your subscription are stored in your Amazon Cloud account, and you can download those issues, even if you cancel your subscription.

Sometimes, you may want to keep an issue on your Fire tablet; to do so, follow the steps in this section.

Keep an Issue on Your Device

1. From the Home screen, tap **Newsstand**.

The Newsstand content library appears.

2. Press and hold the issue you want to keep on the device.
3. From the menu that appears, tap **Keep**.

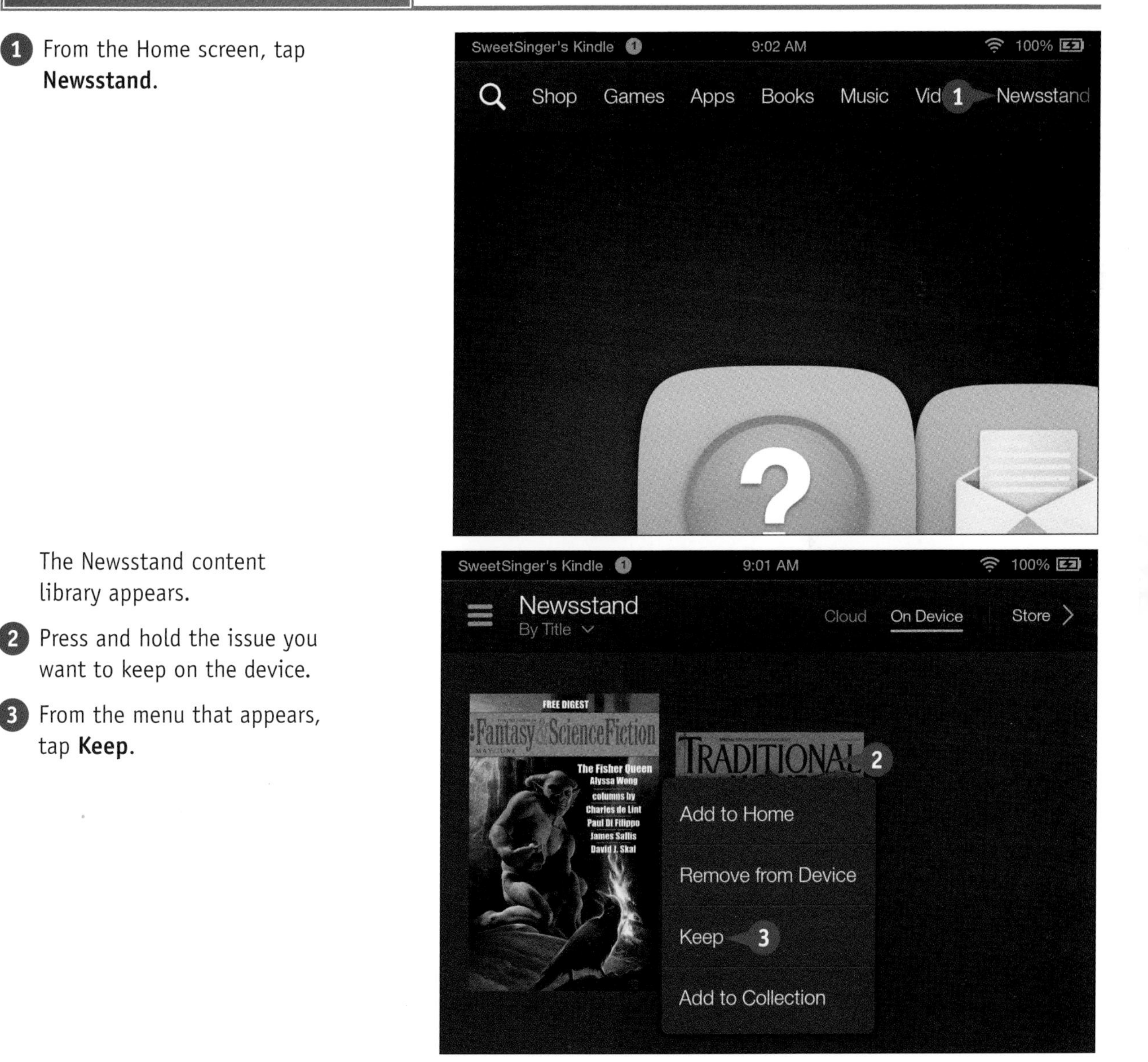

CHAPTER 8

Working with Email

You can send and receive email on your Fire tablet; setting it up to collect email is typically a very simple process. You can receive attachments via email and, if you need, you can collect email for multiple email addresses.

SweetSinger's Kindle 9:46 AM 100%

Google

Sign in with your Google Account

swestsinger213@gmail.com

••••••••••

Sign in

Need help?

Create an account

One Google Account for everything Google

Set Up an Email Account 158
Set Up an Email Account Manually 160
Explore the Email app 162
Work with Multiple Email Accounts 164
Read a Message 166
Delete Messages 167
Move a Message to Another Folder 168
Search for an Email. 170
Manage Messages from the Inbox 171
Create and Send an Email Message 172
Check for New Messages 174
Forward an Email Message 175
Add an Attachment to an Email 176
Reply to an Email 178
Open an Email Attachment 180
Receive Documents via Email 182
Review General Email Settings 184
Review Settings for Specific Accounts 186

Set Up an Email Account

Before you can use the Email app, you need to set up an account, which is what the Fire tablet prompts you to do the first time you open the app.

Setting up an email account is, typically, easy; the Fire tablet recognizes common email domain names, such as Gmail, Hotmail, Yahoo!, and Outlook, as well as other, not-quite-so-common email domain names. If your Fire tablet does not recognize your email address and set things up for you, see the section "Set Up an Email Account Manually."

Set Up an Email Account

1. On the Home screen, swipe up to display the Favorites area.
2. Tap **Email**.

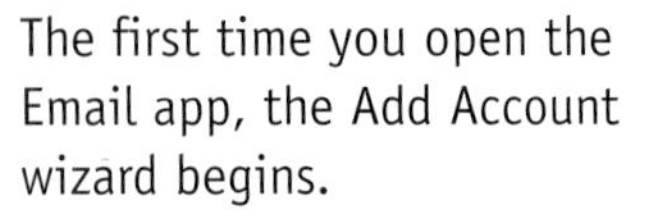

The first time you open the Email app, the Add Account wizard begins.

3. Type your email address.
4. Tap **Next**.

For most common email providers, the sign-in screen appears.

Note: For less common email providers, a screen appears where you can type your email password.

5 Type your email password.

6 Tap **Sign in** or **Next**.

A screen displaying privacy information might appear; if so, tap **Accept**.

The Fire tablet connects, looks for common email provider settings and, if it finds them, displays the Setup Complete! screen.

7 Tap **Go to Inbox**.

If you prefer, you can tap the **Home** button (🏠) in the bottom-left corner to redisplay the Home screen.

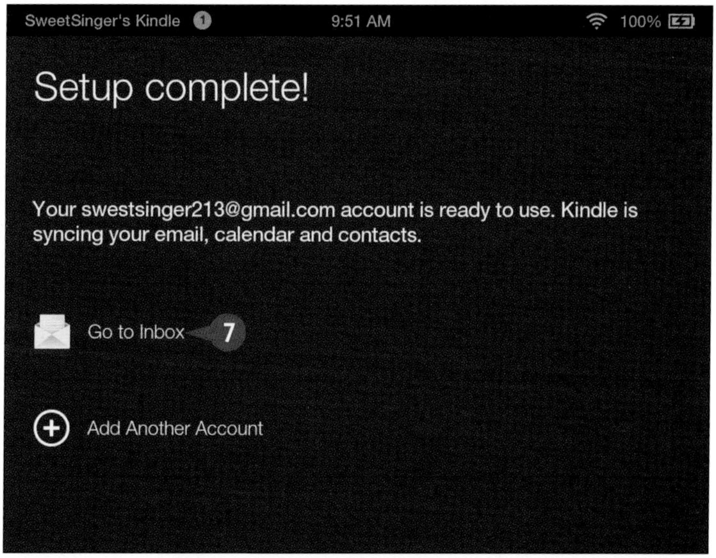

TIP

If I am setting up an email account that is not commonly recognized, what would I do differently?
After you type your email address, a screen like this one appears, prompting you for your email password. Your Fire tablet might still recognize your email provider and set up your account.

Set Up an Email Account Manually

If your Fire tablet does not recognize your email address, you can set up the account manually. Or, you might have multiple email accounts and the tablet might recognize one but not another. Your Fire tablet can recognize POP3, IMAP, and Exchange Server email accounts.

This section shows how to set up a second POP3 email account that the Fire tablet does not recognize; the steps would be almost the same even if you were setting up the account as your first account.

Set Up an Email Account Manually

1. Complete steps **1** and **2** in the section "Set Up an Email Account."

   The Inbox for the first account you set up appears.

2. Tap the **Navigation** button (▤) to display the Navigation panel.

3. Tap **Settings**.

   The Email, Contacts, Calendars settings screen appears.

4. Tap **Add Account**.

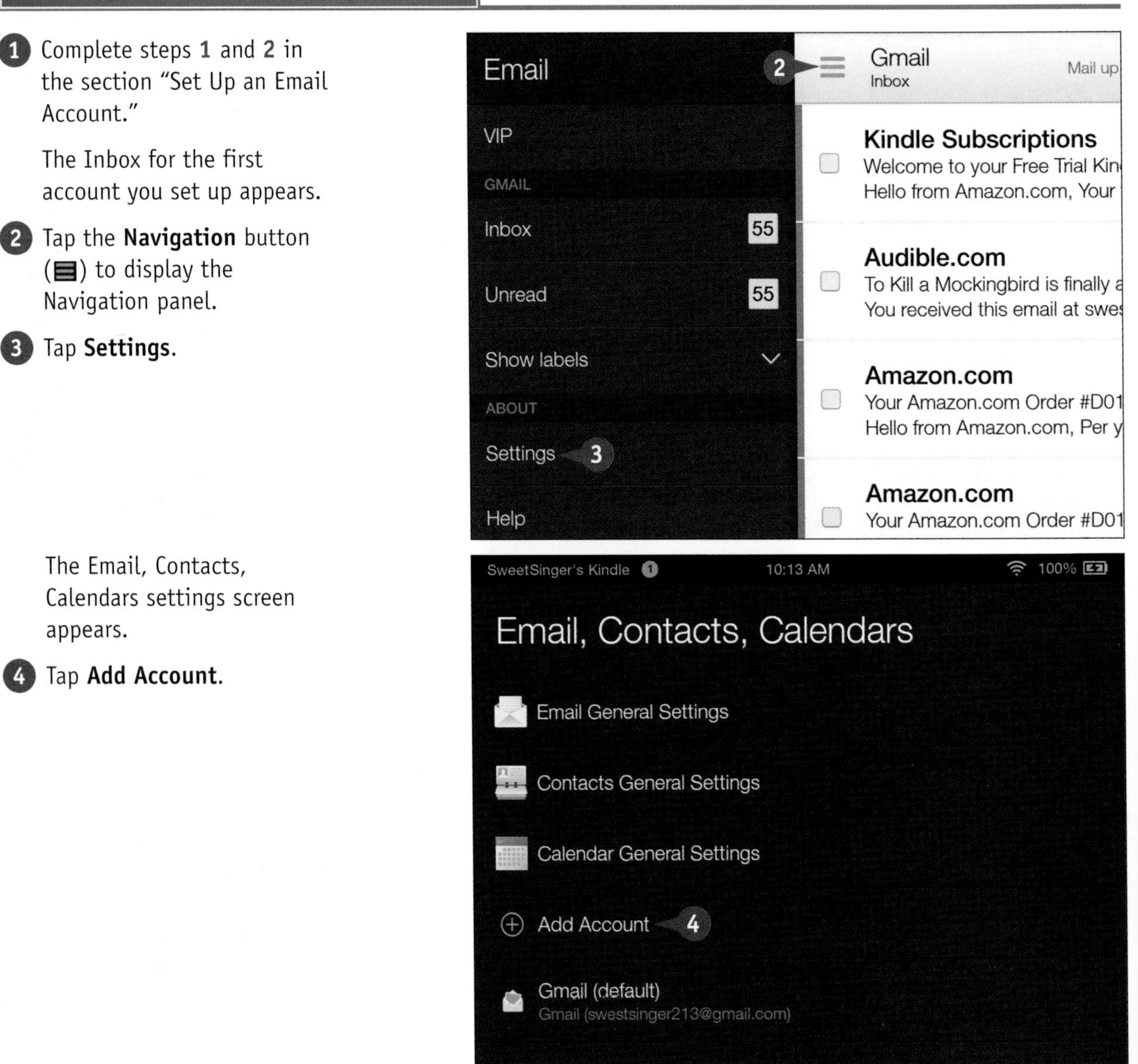

The Add Account wizard begins.

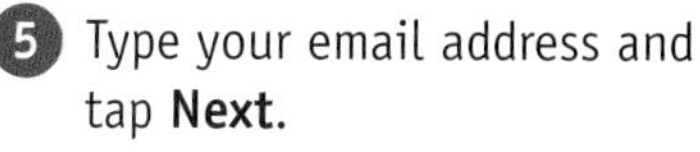

5. Type your email address and tap **Next**.
6. When the wizard prompts for an account type, tap **POP3**.
7. Type the POP3 server.

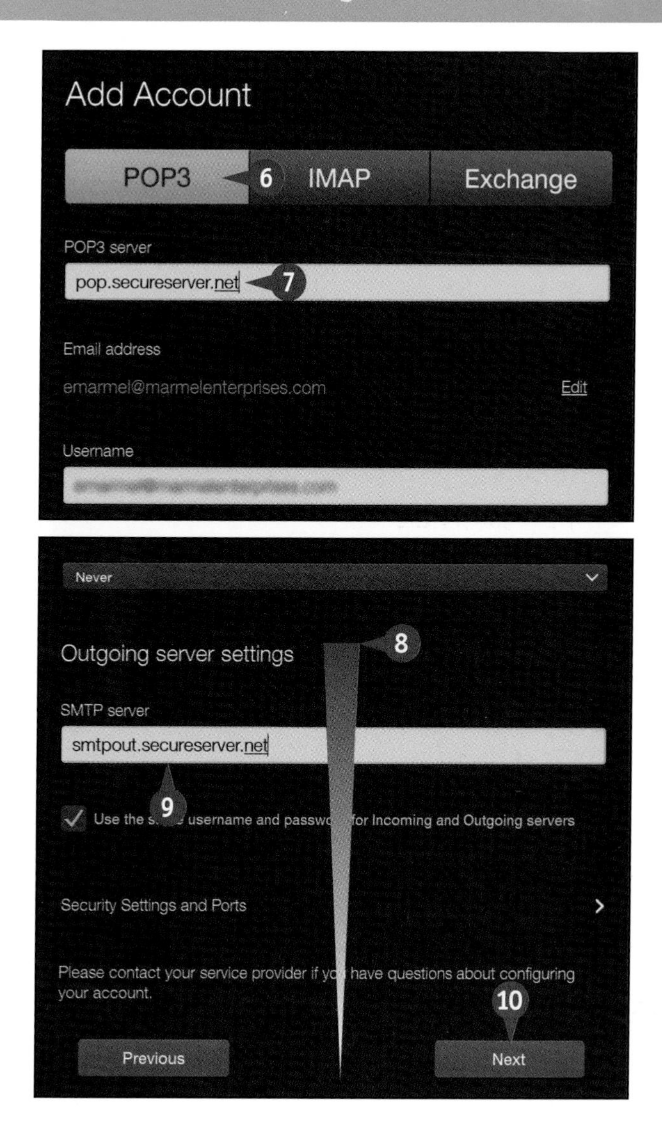

8. Swipe up to scroll down.
9. Type the SMTP server.
10. Tap **Next**.

The Fire tablet connects, looks for settings and displays the Setup Complete! screen.

You can tap **Go to Inbox**, or you can tap the **Home** button (🏠) to redisplay the Home screen.

TIPS

How do I know if my account is a POP3 account?
Check your email provider's website; you will most likely find directions there to set up email on mobile phones and tablets. Typically, personal email accounts are POP3 or IMAP, whereas Exchange accounts are used by large corporations.

What would I do differently if the Fire tablet does not recognize my first email account?
Complete steps **1** to **6** in the section "Set Up an Email Account." When the Fire tablet does not recognize your email address and password, the Add Account wizard begins, prompting you to choose a POP3, IMAP, or Exchange account type. Then, complete steps **6** to **10** in this section.

Explore the Email app

Once you set up an email account, you can use the Email app to receive, read, respond to, forward, compose and send, and manage your email, as described in the rest of the sections in this chapter.

In this section, you see how to navigate around the Email app, how to select messages, and how to look through the various email folders. You also learn a little about the VIP folder and how to use it to organize emails. This section helps you understand the general behavior of the Email app.

Explore the Email app

1. From the Home screen, swipe up to display Favorites section.
2. Tap **Email**.

The Inbox of your default email account appears.

A. Messages you have received appear listed latest to earliest.

B. You can tap a check box (☐ changes to ☑) to select a message.

Note: You take actions on selected messages, such as moving them to another folder as described in the section "Move a Message to Another Folder," or delete them, as described in the section "Delete Messages."

3. Tap the **Navigation** button (☰).

The Navigation panel opens and Email accounts you have set up appear there.

Ⓒ For each email account you establish, you see, by default, its Inbox folder and the Unread messages folder.

Ⓓ The number of unread messages appears beside each folder.

4 Tap **Show labels** or **Show folders**.

The folders for the email account appear in the Navigation panel on the left-hand side of the screen, enabling you to organize your messages easily.

You can tap any folder to view its content.

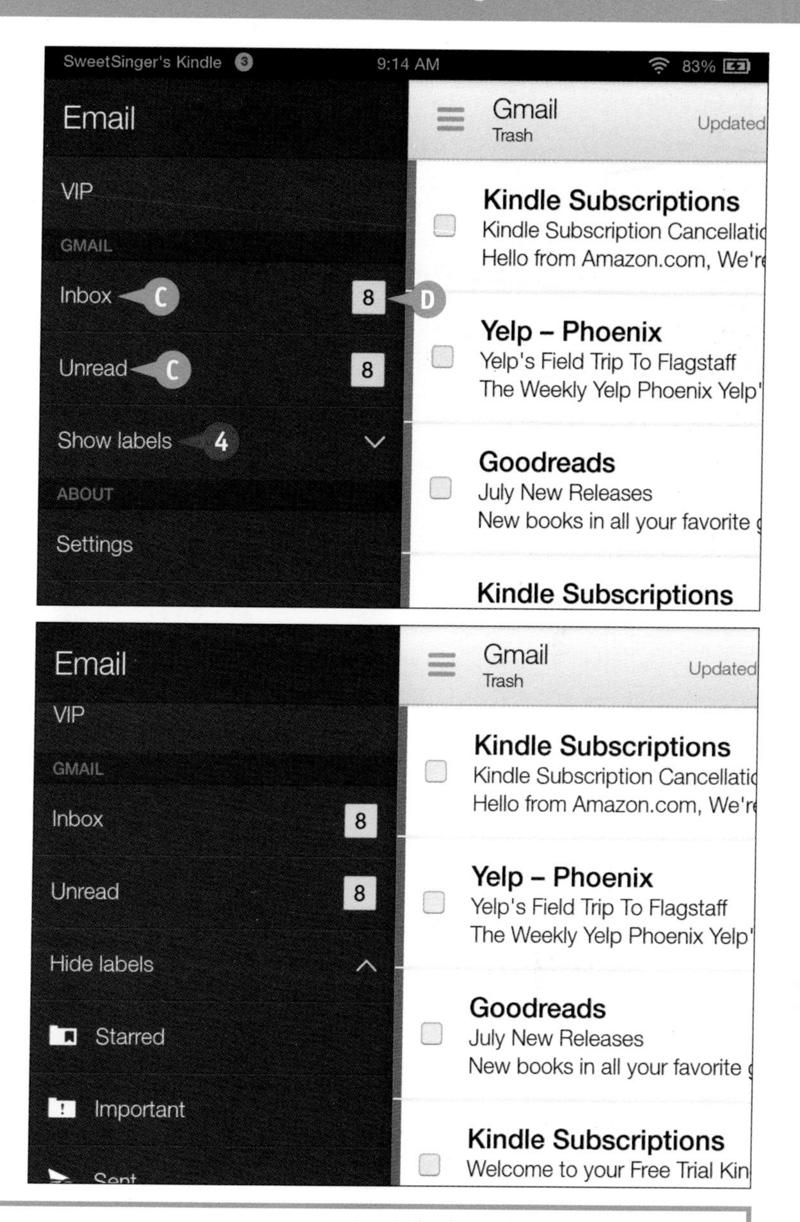

TIP

What is VIP?

The VIP folder displays messages from contacts you designate as VIPs; you can use this folder as a way to automatically segregate messages you receive from contacts you deem important. To mark a contact as a VIP, open the message as described in the section "Read a Message." Then, tap the contact's picture or the avatar representing the contact Ⓐ and tap **Set as VIP** Ⓑ.

Work with Multiple Email Accounts

You can set up your Fire tablet to work with email from multiple email accounts. The first part of this section shows you how to set up an additional email account after you have established your first email account. You can use the steps in this section to set up as many email accounts as you want.

The second part focuses on showing you how to manage email when you have set up multiple email accounts on your Fire tablet.

Work with Multiple Email Accounts

Add a Second Account

1. Complete steps **1** to **3** in the section "Explore the Email app."
2. Tap **Settings**.

   The Email, Contacts, Calendars settings page appears.
3. Tap **Add Account**.

   The Add Account wizard begins; to complete the process, refer to the sections "Set Up an Email Account" or "Set Up an Email Account Manually" as appropriate for the email account you are setting up.

Note: When the wizard finishes, you can tap **Go to Inbox**.

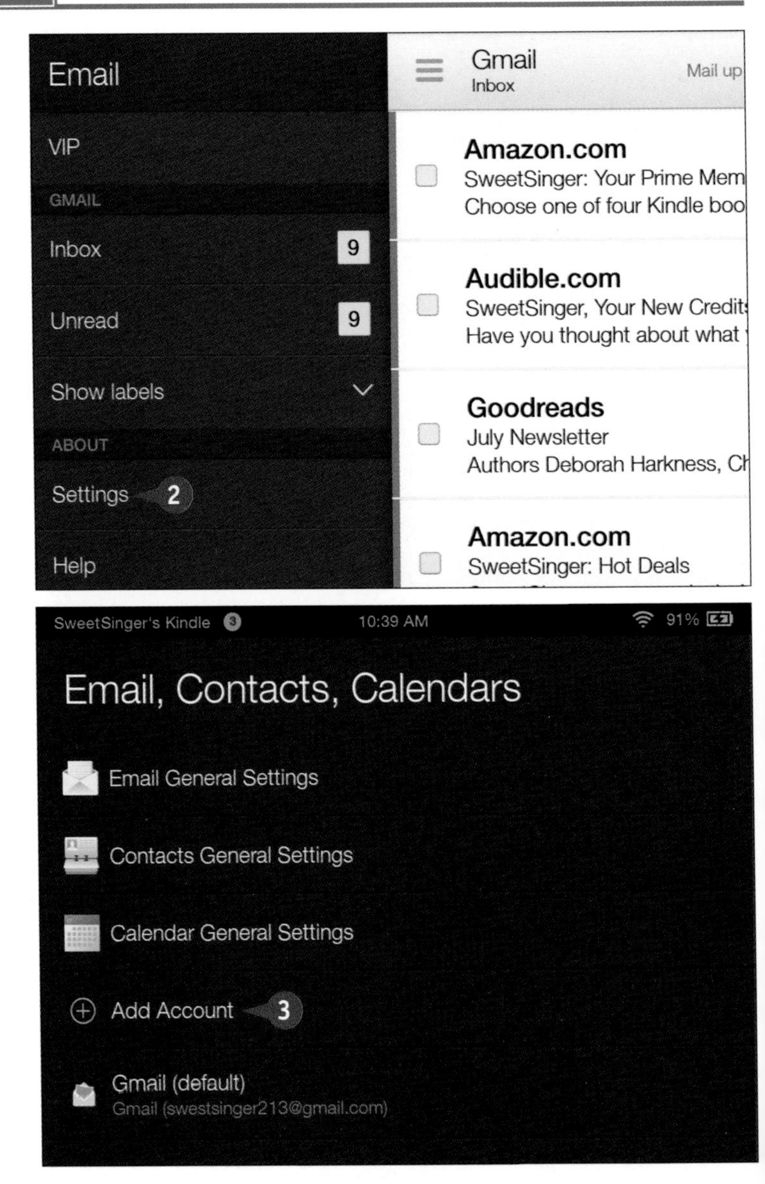

Switch between Accounts

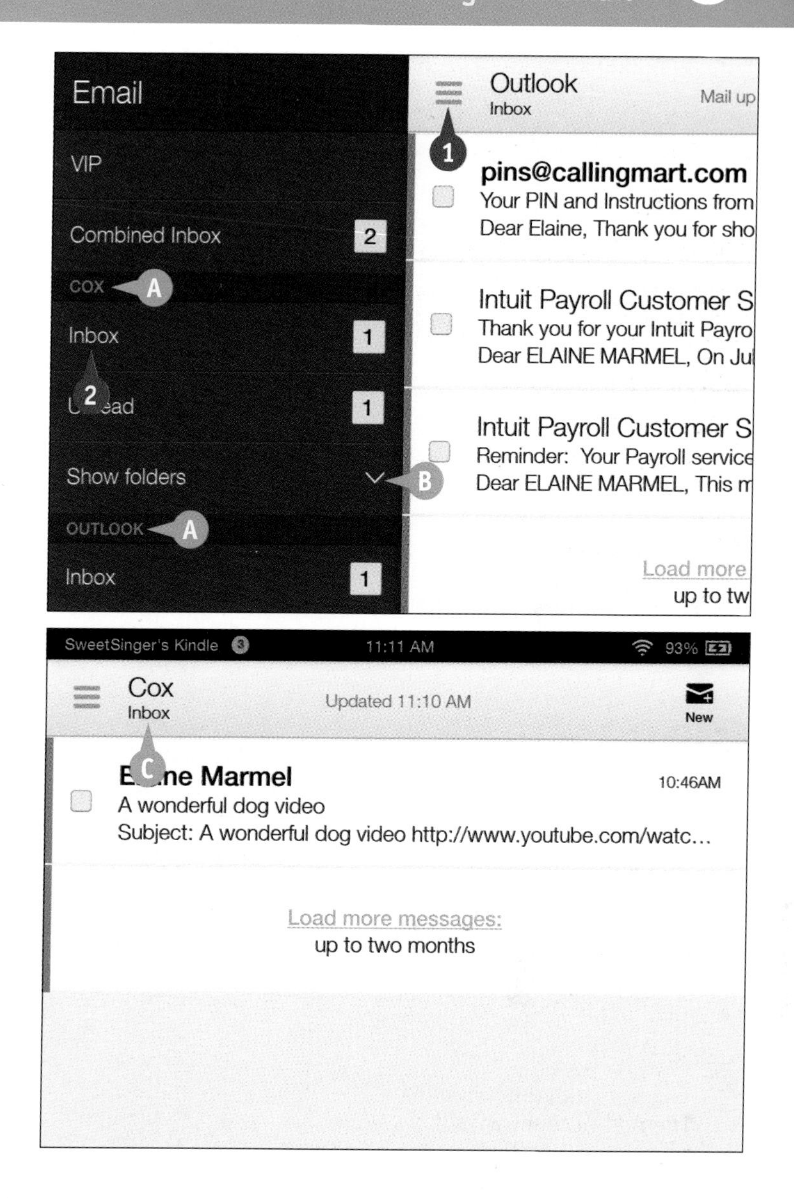

1. In the Email app, tap the **Navigation** button (☰) to display the Navigation panel.

   Ⓐ Each email account you have set up appears in its own section.

   Ⓑ You can tap the **Show folders** arrow (⌄) to view the folders for that account.

2. Tap an **Inbox** for any account to view the messages in that account's Inbox.

   Ⓒ The Fire tablet displays messages in that Inbox.

TIP

Can I view all my messages at the same time, regardless of the Inbox in which they reside?

Yes. Tap the **Navigation** button (☰) to display the Navigation panel and tap **Combined Inbox**. You can identify the Inbox you are viewing by its name Ⓐ.

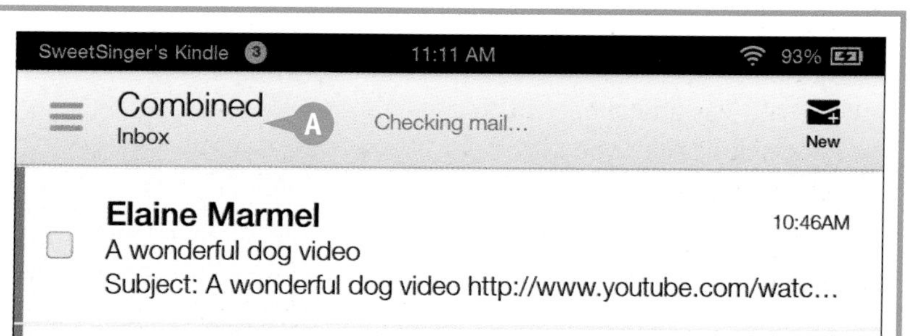

Read a Message

Your Inbox displays the general subject of a message, but to actually read it, you have to open it. If your Inbox contains more than one message, you do not need to redisplay the Inbox list of emails to open and read another message. Your tablet's Email app contains buttons that enable you to view additional messages based on whether they are newer or older than the one you are currently viewing.

Read a Message

1. Complete steps **1** and **2** in the section "Explore the Email App" to open the Email app and display messages in an inbox.

   A. The sender's name appears in boldface type if you have not opened the message.

   B. The sender appears in regular type if you have already opened the message.

2. Tap any message.

Note: Opening a message automatically marks the message as read.

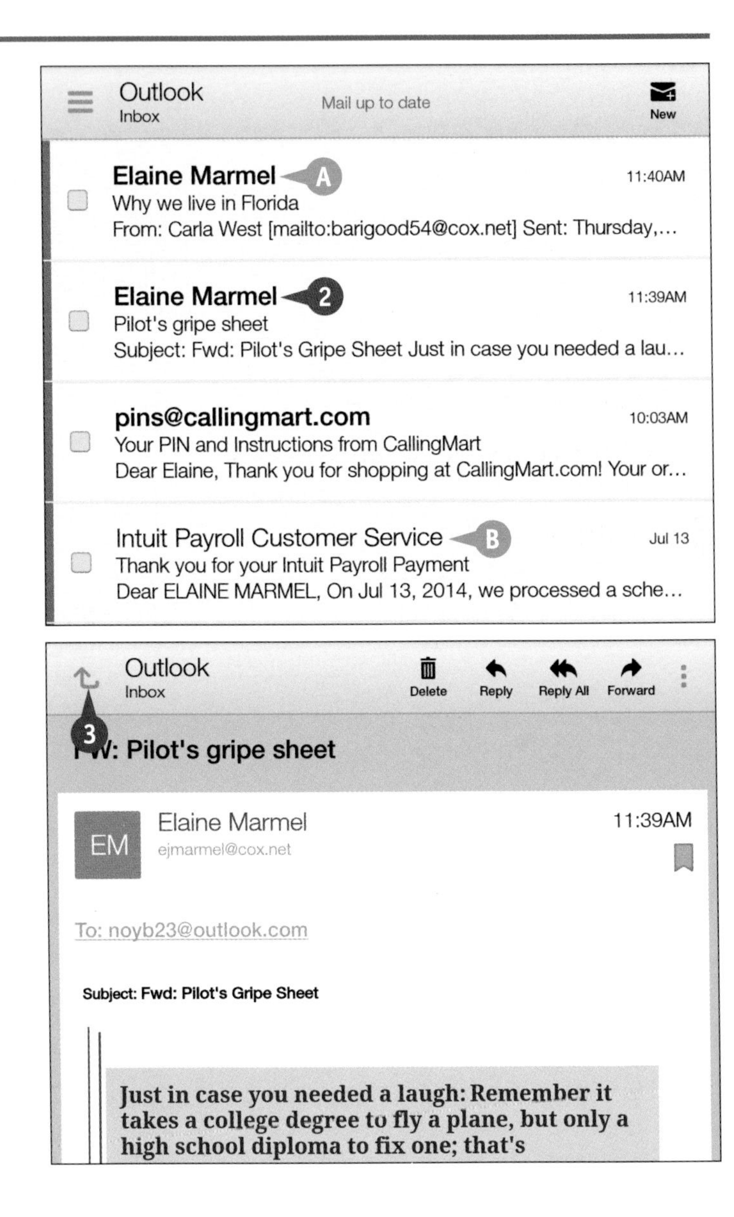

The message's content appears.

If multiple messages appear in your Inbox, you can tap either **Newer** or **Older** at the bottom of the screen to read the next newer or older messages.

3. To redisplay the Inbox, tap this arrow (↰).

Delete Messages

You can mark messages for deletion as you read them or using the list of messages that appears in the Inbox and in each folder. To mark messages for deletion from a folder other than the Inbox, display the Navigation panel and show folders for the account. Then select the folder containing the messages you want to delete.

When you mark a message for deletion, it does not disappear from your Fire tablet; instead, the Email app places messages you mark in the Trash folder. To permanently delete a message, you must empty the Trash folder.

Delete Messages

Delete While Reading

1. Complete steps **1** and **2** in the section "Explore the Email App" to open the Email app and display messages in an Inbox, tapping a message to open and read it.
2. Tap **Delete** to delete the message.

   The Email app moves the message to the Trash folder.
3. To redisplay the Inbox, tap ⮤.

Delete from the Inbox

1. Complete steps **1** and **2** in the section "Explore the Email App" to open the Email app and display messages in an Inbox.
2. Tap the check box (☐) beside a message to select it for deletion (☐ changes to ☑).
3. Tap **Delete.**

   The Email app moves the message to the Trash folder.

Note: To delete messages in the Trash folder, you do not need to select them. Instead, display the folder, tap ⋮, and tap **Empty Trash**.

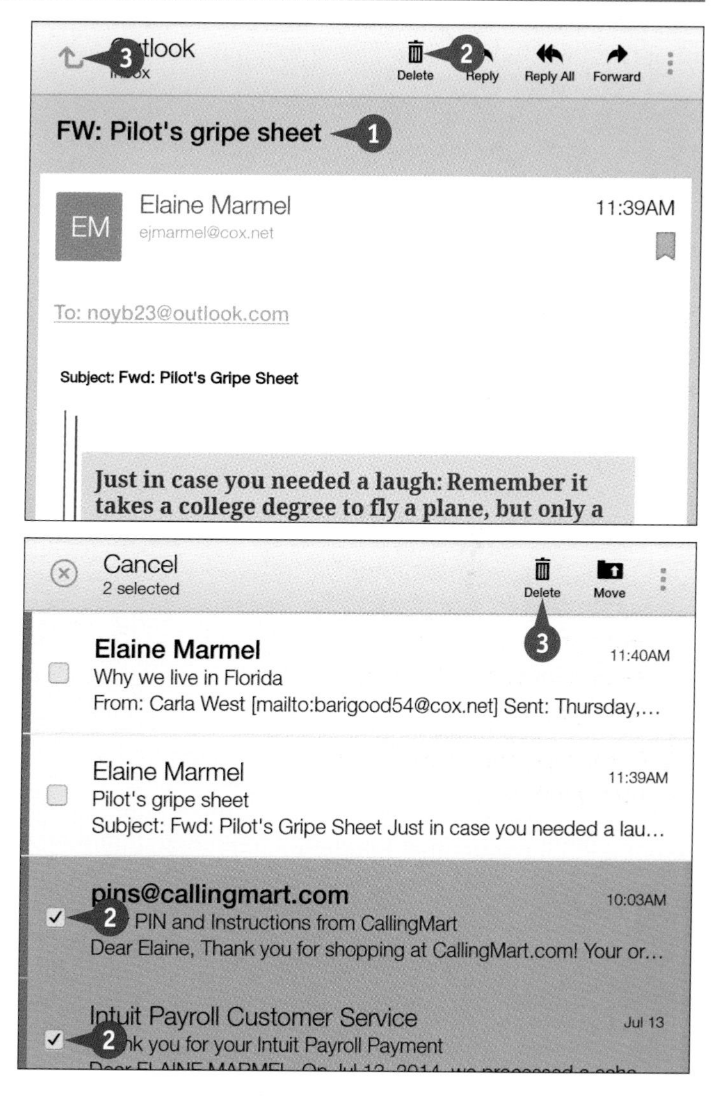

Move a Message to Another Folder

You can move messages from your Inbox to other folders in that email account, based on the settings established by your email provider. For example, you can move messages in a www.outlook.com Inbox to the Junk folder. Be aware that your ability to move messages depends entirely on your email provider.

If your email provider lets you move messages from the Inbox to another folder, then you also can move messages from other folders to the Inbox. For example, if you accidentally delete a message, you can move it from the Trash folder to the Inbox.

Move a Message to Another Folder

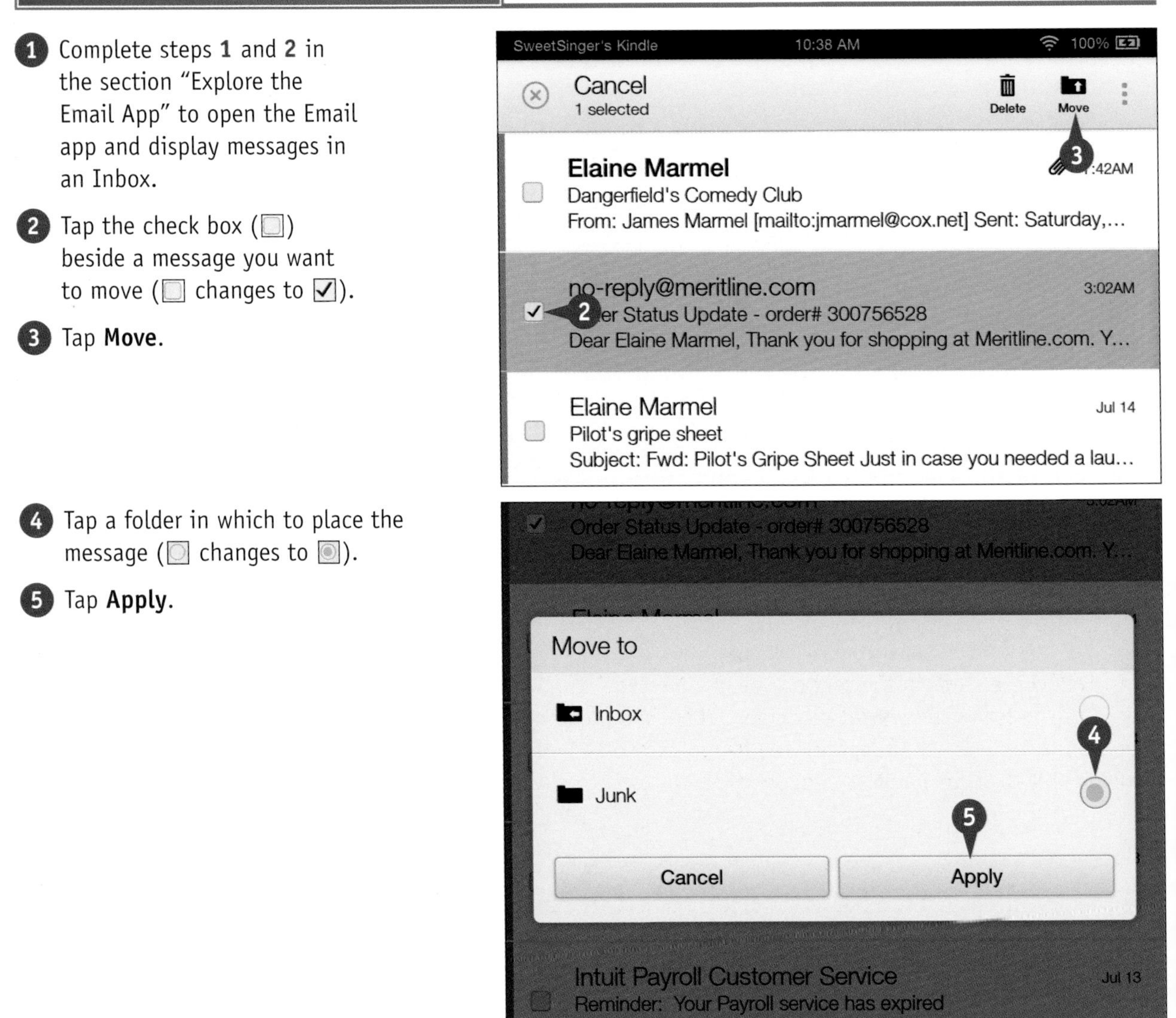

1. Complete steps **1** and **2** in the section "Explore the Email App" to open the Email app and display messages in an Inbox.
2. Tap the check box (☐) beside a message you want to move (☐ changes to ☑).
3. Tap **Move**.
4. Tap a folder in which to place the message (◯ changes to ◉).
5. Tap **Apply**.

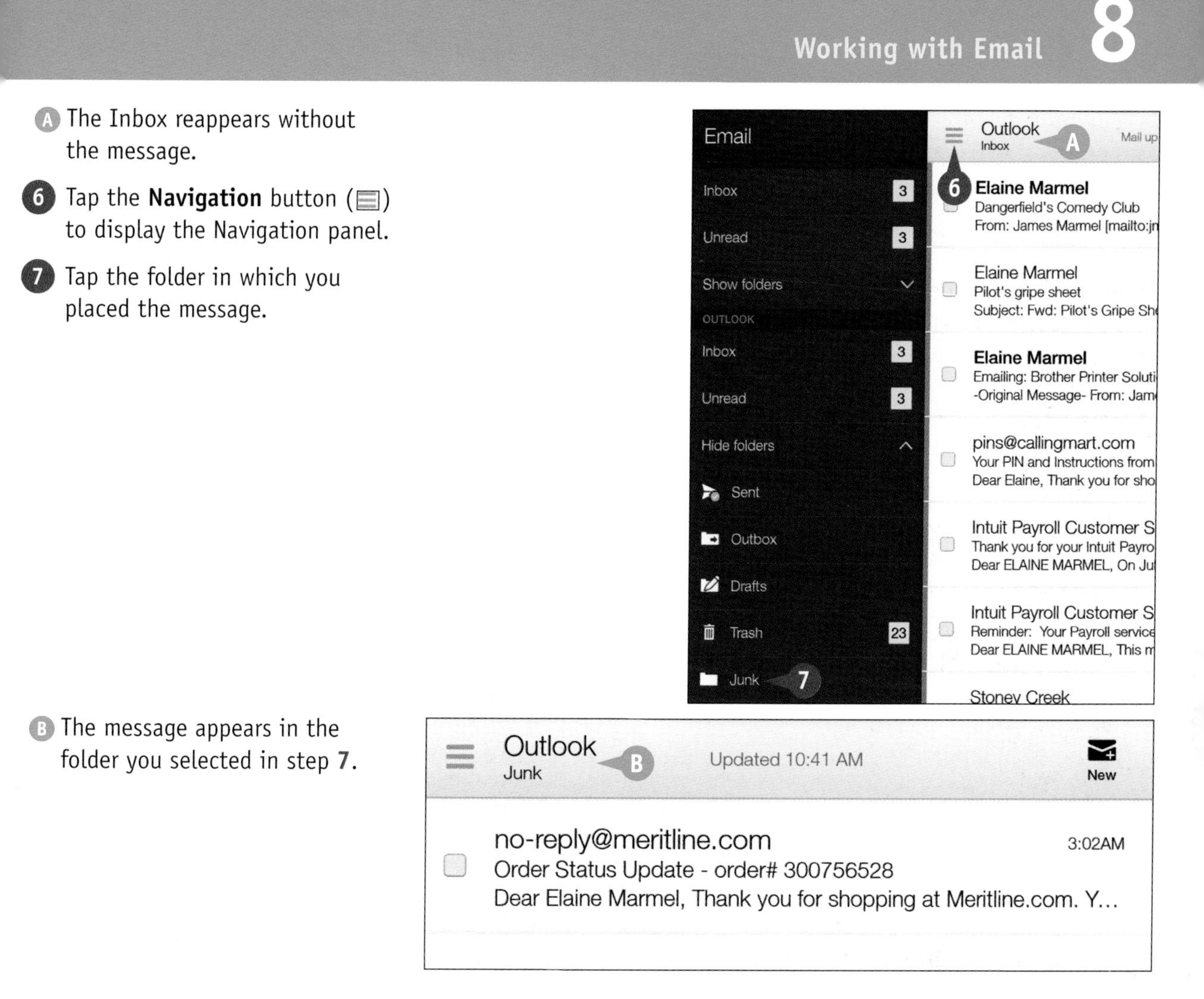

Ⓐ The Inbox reappears without the message.

6. Tap the **Navigation** button (☰) to display the Navigation panel.

7. Tap the folder in which you placed the message.

Ⓑ The message appears in the folder you selected in step **7**.

TIP

Can I move a message while I view it?

Yes. Follow the steps in the section "Read a Message" to open the message and view it on-screen. Then, tap ⋮ Ⓐ and, from the menu that appears, tap **Move** Ⓑ. Then, complete steps **4** to **7** in this section.

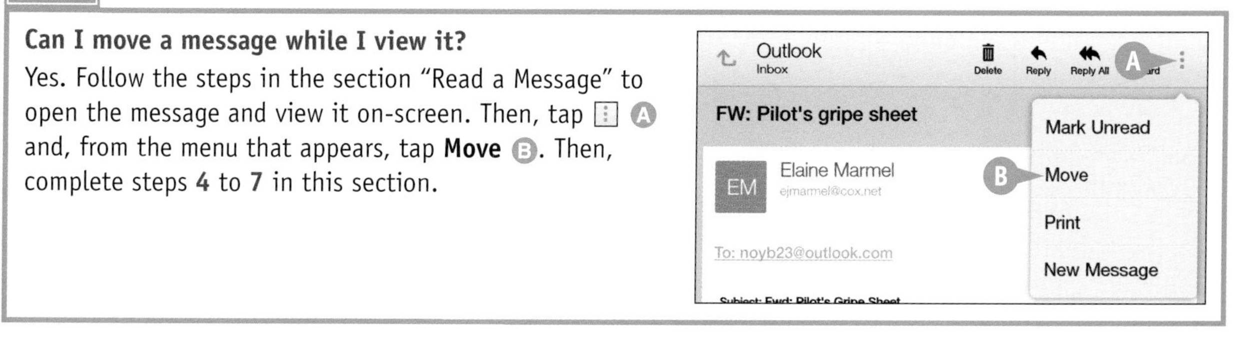

Search for an Email

Your Inbox can become a crowded place if you do not regularly delete messages. The Fire tablet makes navigating cluttered Inboxes easier by enabling you to search for messages in your Inbox or any other folder. When you search for messages, you specify whether to search the message's From field, To field, Subject field, or all three fields. You then supply a search term, and your Fire tablet displays messages that match the search criteria.

You also can search from another folder; display that folder before starting the steps in this section.

Search for an Email

1. Complete steps **1** and **2** in the section "Explore the Email App" to open the Email app and display messages in an Inbox.
2. Tap the **Search** button (🔍).

The Search text box and on-screen keyboard (not shown) appear.

- A You can tap **From** to specify the part of the email message to search.

3. Type your search term.

- B Messages that match what you type appear.

Note: You can tap any message to open it.

- C You can tap ⊗ to delete your search term.
- D You can tap **Cancel** to cancel the search and redisplay the contents of the Inbox.

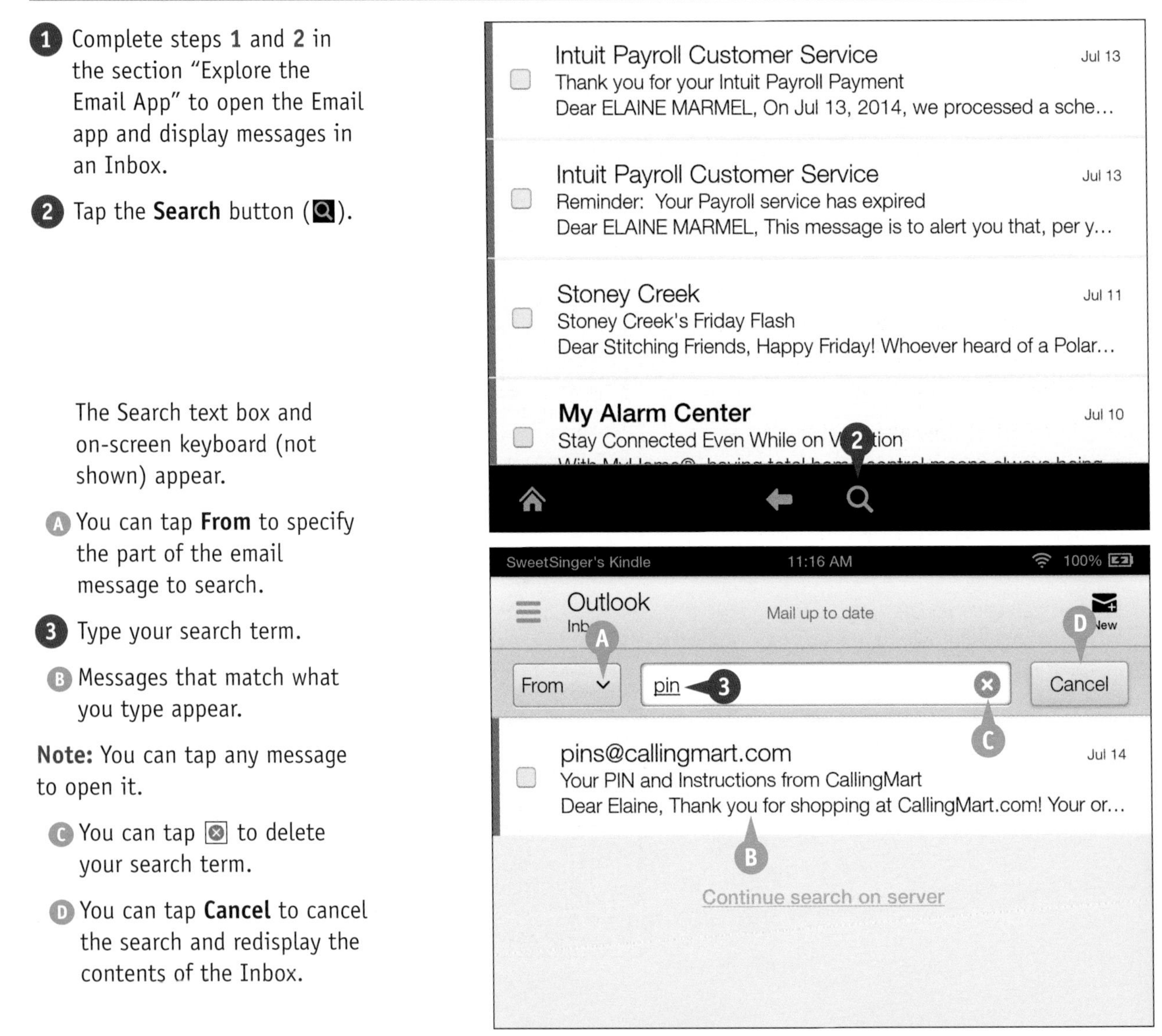

Manage Messages from the Inbox

You can manage messages in your Inbox; you can delete them, as described in the section "Delete Messages," and you can move them to another folder if your email provider offers that choice, as described in the section "Move a Message to Another Folder."

In addition, you can change the status of a message from "Read" to "Unread" and, as shown in this section, you can flag a message to indicate visually that the message is important to you.

Manage Messages from the Inbox

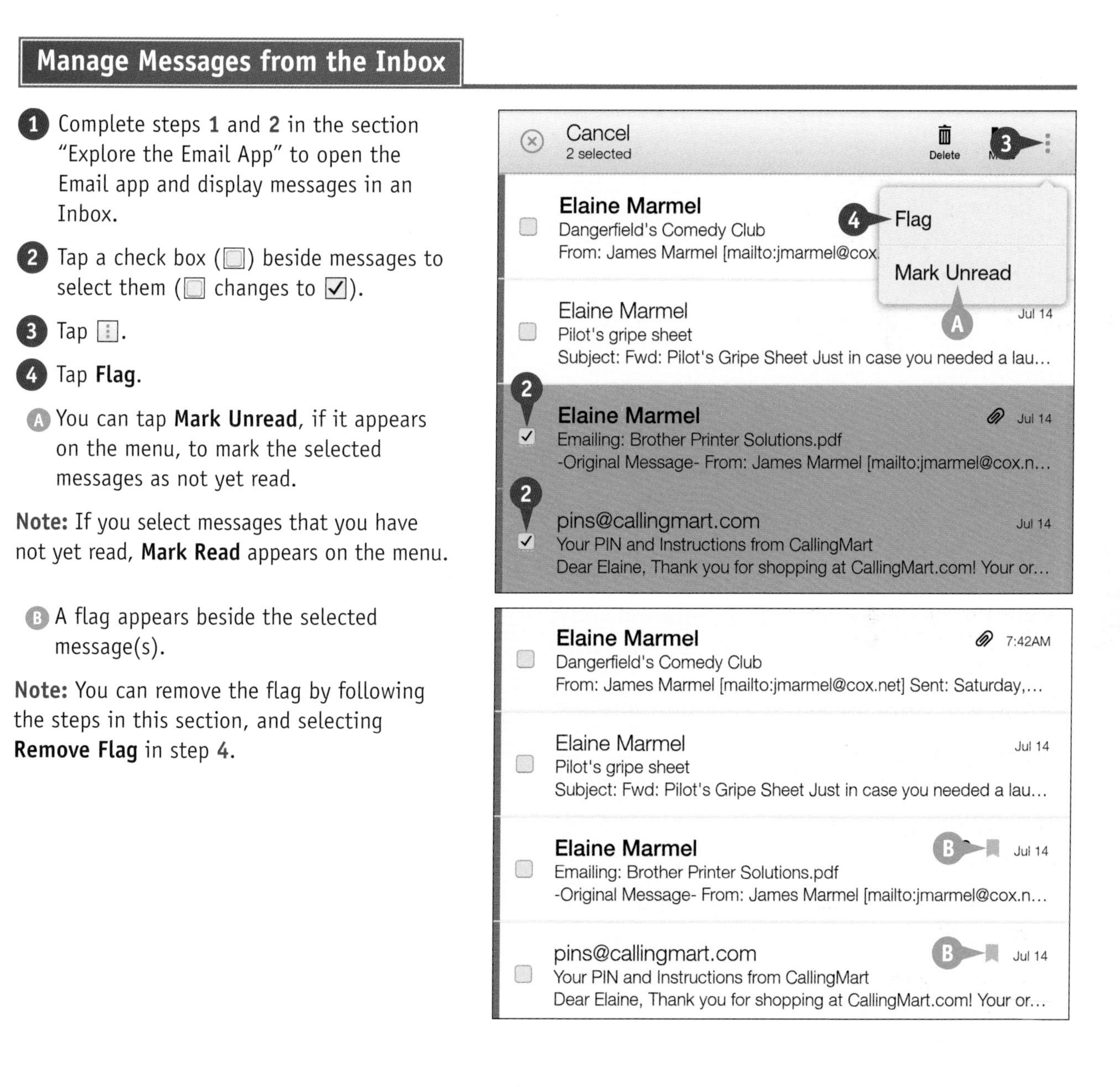

1. Complete steps **1** and **2** in the section "Explore the Email App" to open the Email app and display messages in an Inbox.
2. Tap a check box (☐) beside messages to select them (☐ changes to ☑).
3. Tap ⋮.
4. Tap **Flag**.

A. You can tap **Mark Unread**, if it appears on the menu, to mark the selected messages as not yet read.

Note: If you select messages that you have not yet read, **Mark Read** appears on the menu.

B. A flag appears beside the selected message(s).

Note: You can remove the flag by following the steps in this section, and selecting **Remove Flag** in step **4**.

Create and Send an Email Message

You can create and send email messages using the Email app on your Fire tablet. Creating an email message using the Email app is similar to creating email messages using the software of many email providers: You identify the recipients of the message and any people to whom you want to send copies or blind copies. You supply a subject for the message, and then you type the text to include in the message.

Create and Send an Email Message

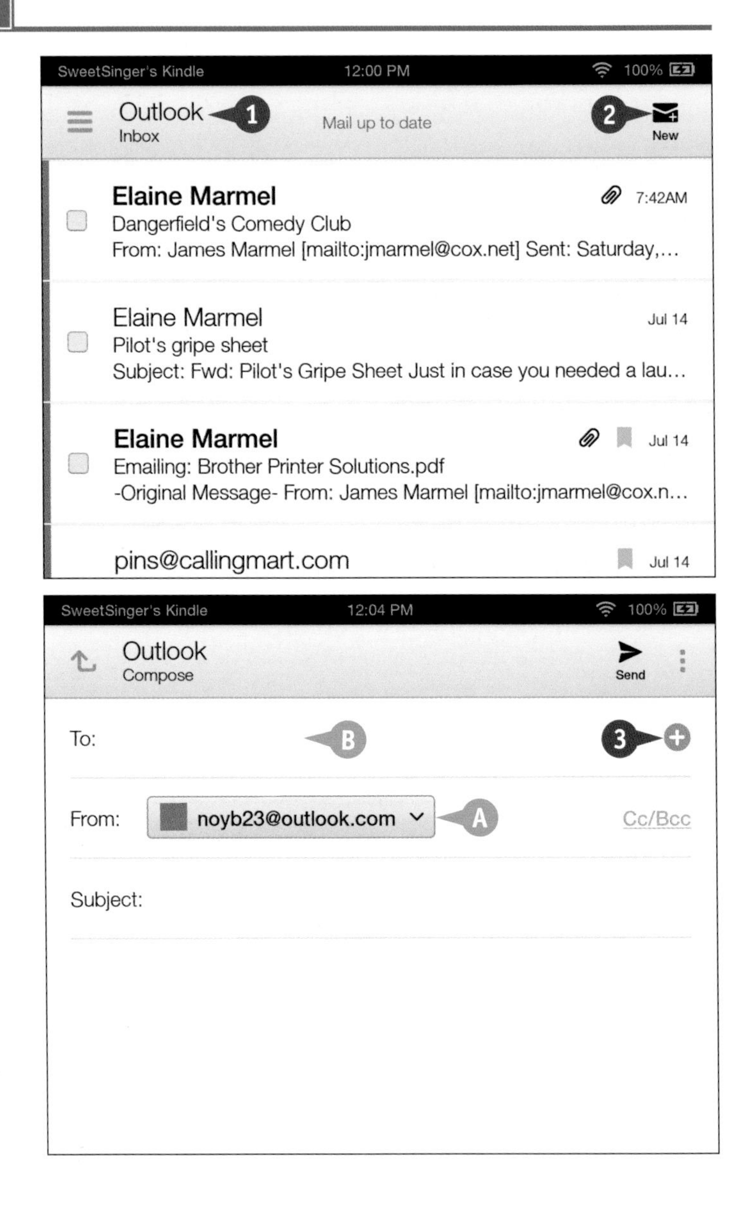

1. Complete steps **1** and **2** in the section "Explore the Email App" to open the Email app and display the Inbox of the account you want to use to send your message.

2. Tap **New**.

A new email message window appears.

A. If appropriate, you can tap here to select a different account to use to send the message.

3. Tap ⊕ to search your contacts for the email recipient.

Note: Chapter 9 covers storing contacts on your Fire tablet.

B. You also can type a recipient's email address.

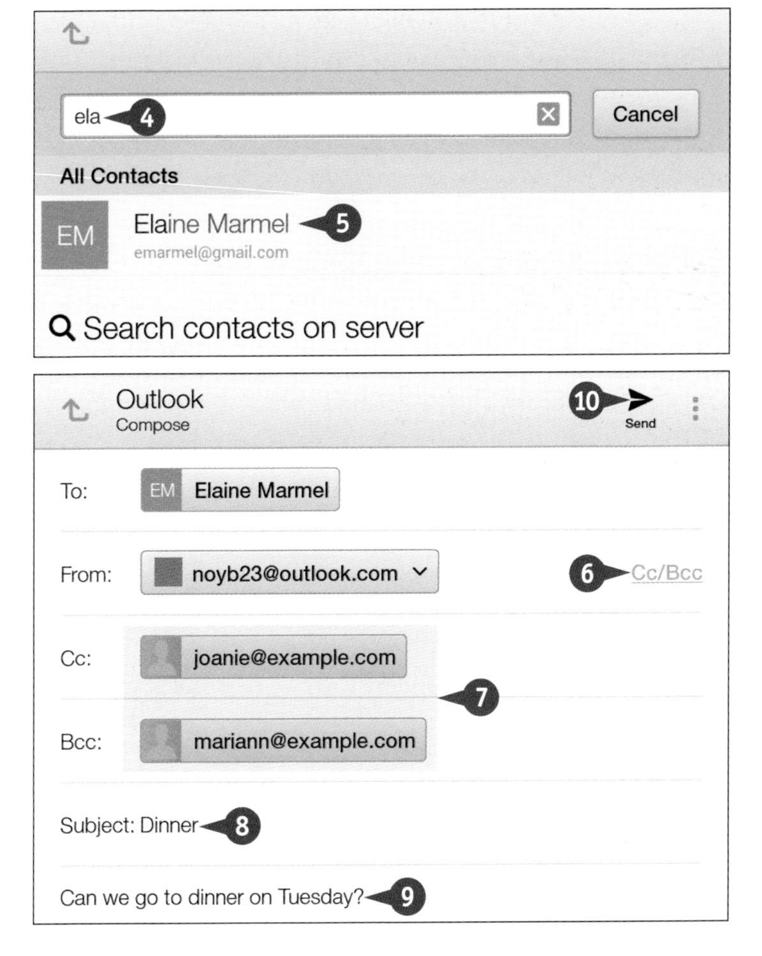

4. To search for a contact, type some letters of the contact's name here.
5. Tap the contact.

   The Compose window reappears.

6. Tap **Cc/Bcc**.
7. Repeat steps **4** and **5** to add recipients to the email.

Note: Use **Bcc** to send your message to recipients without displaying them to other recipients of the email.

8. Type a subject.
9. Type the message here.
10. Tap **Send**.

    The Email app sends your message. You can find a copy in the Sent folder for the account you used to send the message.

TIP

What happens if I decide I do not want to send the message?

Tap the **Back** arrow (⬅) in the Options bar. The Email app places your message in the Drafts folder. You can tap the **Navigation** button (☰) to display the Navigation panel and switch to the Drafts folder (A), where you can delete the email or finish and send it.

Check for New Messages

By default, the Email app checks for messages at a predetermined interval, which you can change; see "Review Settings for a Specific Email Account" for details. However, sometimes you may not want to wait for the predetermined interval to occur and would rather check for new messages on your own. For example, a friend might have let you know that you will receive a particular email. Your Fire tablet enables you to manually check for new email messages whenever you want.

Check for New Messages

1. Complete steps **1** and **2** in the section "Explore the Email App" to open the Email app and display messages in an Inbox.
2. Place your finger on any message in the list.
3. Swipe down.

Note: Make sure you swipe in the message list and not at the top of the Email app.

A. As you swipe down, this arrow appears.

4. Lift your finger.

B. At the top of the app, a message appears, indicating that the Email app is checking for new mail.

C. This symbol also appears.

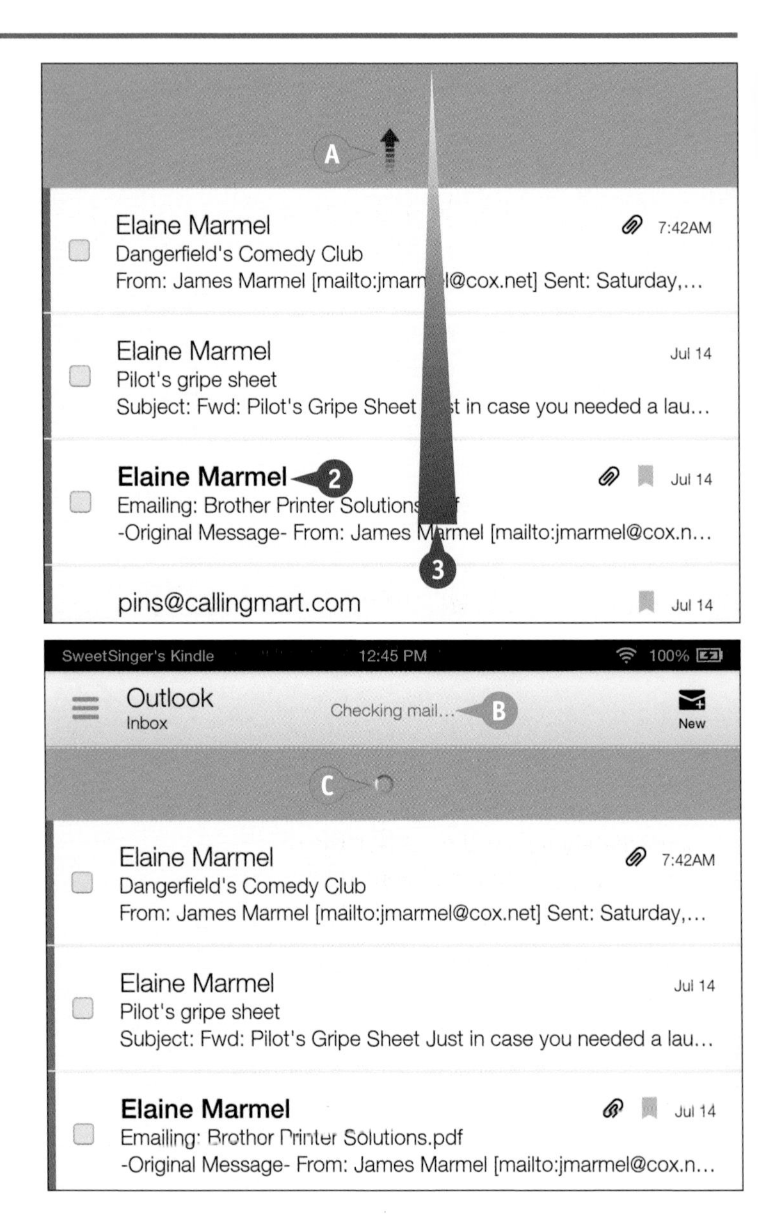

Forwarding an email message is the technique you use to share an email you receive from one person with another person. You can forward any message you want, and you can forward a message to one person or to multiple people. You also can change the subject line and modify the text of the message you forward.

Although you can designate many recipients, be aware that some email providers might view large numbers of recipients as spam and refuse to send your message. If this is the case, the message appears in your Inbox, typically without explanation.

Forward an Email Message

1. Complete steps **1** and **2** in the section "Explore the Email App" to open the Email app and display messages in an Inbox.
2. Tap the message you want to share to open it.
3. Tap **Forward**.
4. In the Compose window, supply recipients and, if appropriate, copy and blind copy recipients.

Note: See "Create and Send an Email Message" for details.

A. Messages you forward display Fwd: immediately before the subject they had when they arrived in your Inbox, and, you can change the subject.

B. You can tap here and type your own message.

5. Tap **Send**.

The Email app sends the message.

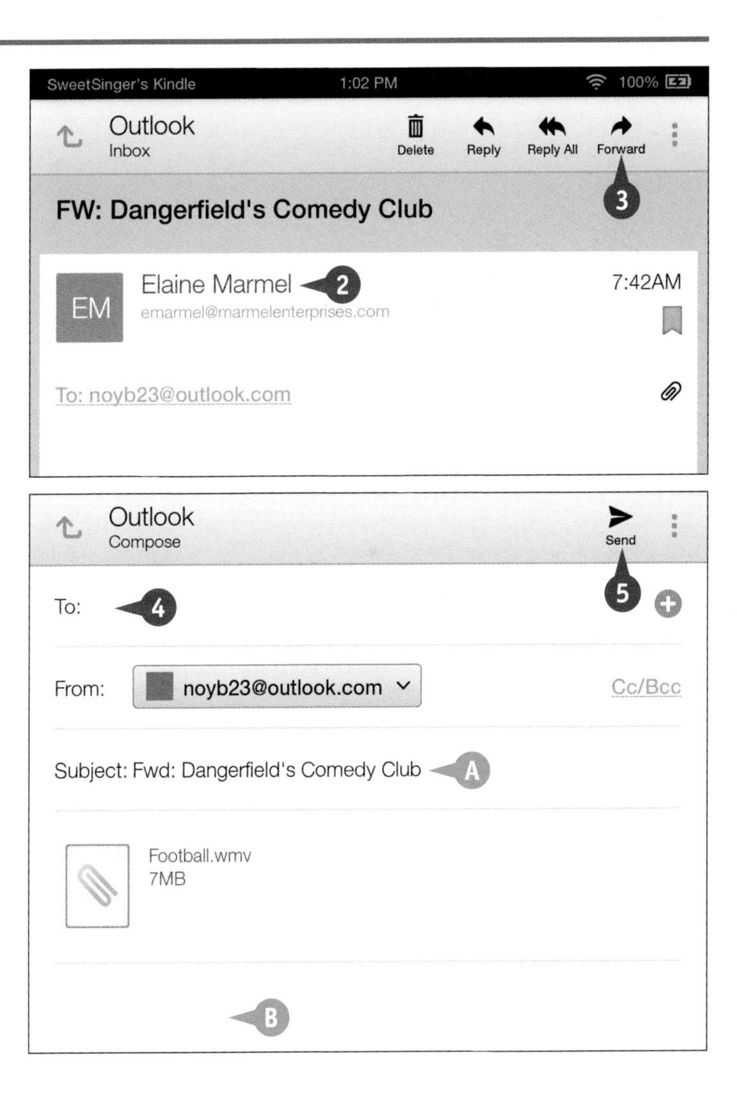

Add an Attachment to an Email

You can attach photos or documents stored on your Fire tablet to an email message to share with the recipient of your message. The basic process involves setting up an email message — either a new message or a reply — and then adding the attachment. For details on setting up an email message, see the section "Create and Send an Email Message."

This section demonstrates how to attach a photo to an email message, but the steps are the same to attach any type of file.

Add an Attachment to an Email

1. Complete steps **1** and **2** in the section "Create and Send an Email Message" to start a new message.
2. Supply a recipient's email address.

Note: You can type an email address or select one from your contacts; Chapter 9 covers storing contacts on your Fire tablet.

A. You can tap **Cc/Bcc** and provide email addresses to send copies and blind copies of the message to additional recipients.

3. Type a subject.
4. Type the message here.
5. Tap ⋮.
6. Tap **Attach Photo**.

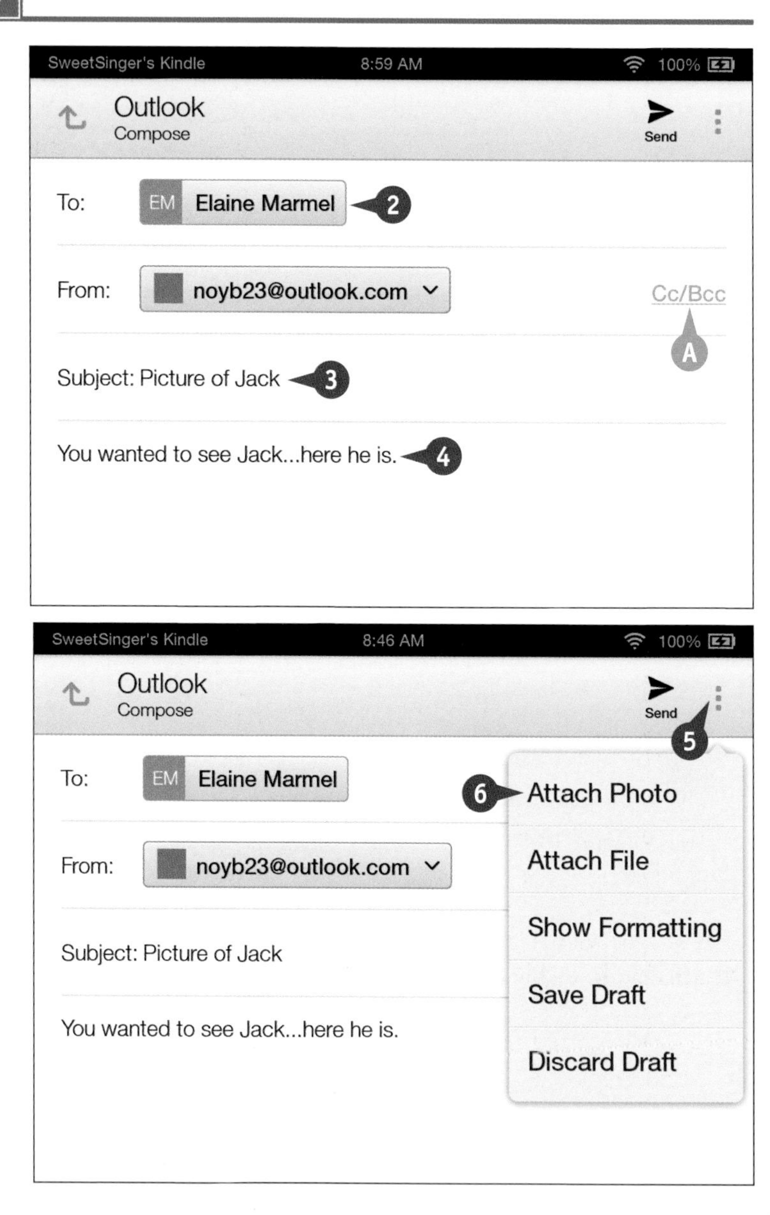

The photos stored on your Fire tablet appear.

7. Tap the photo you want to attach.

B. The photo you selected in step **7** appears in the email message.

8. Tap **Send** to send the message.

TIP

What should I do if I accidentally select the wrong photo?

You can remove the attachment by tapping ⊗ beside the attachment A. To select a different photo, complete steps **5** to **8** in this section.

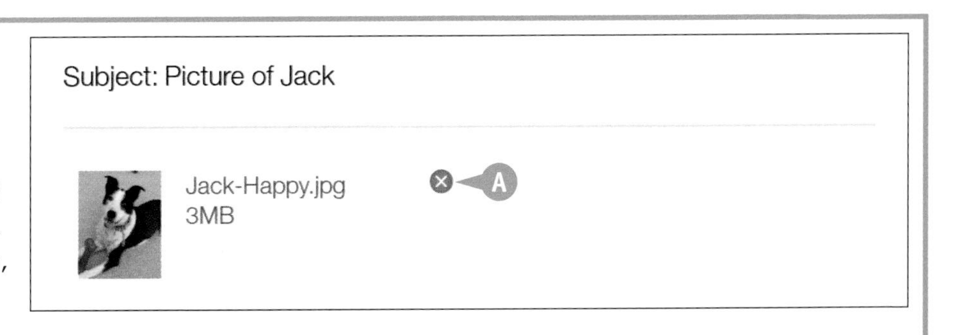

Reply to an Email

You might want to respond to some email messages you receive; you reply to a message from the same screen you use to read the message. You can reply to the message sender or to the sender and all recipients.

You can include formatting in any message you send — both replies to messages and new messages you create. You can add boldface, italics, and underlining to text, and you can change the font and the font color. You also can apply a highlight color to text in your message.

Reply to an Email

1. Complete steps **1** and **2** in the section "Explore the Email App" to open the Email app and display messages in an Inbox.
2. Tap a message.

The message opens.

3. Read the message.

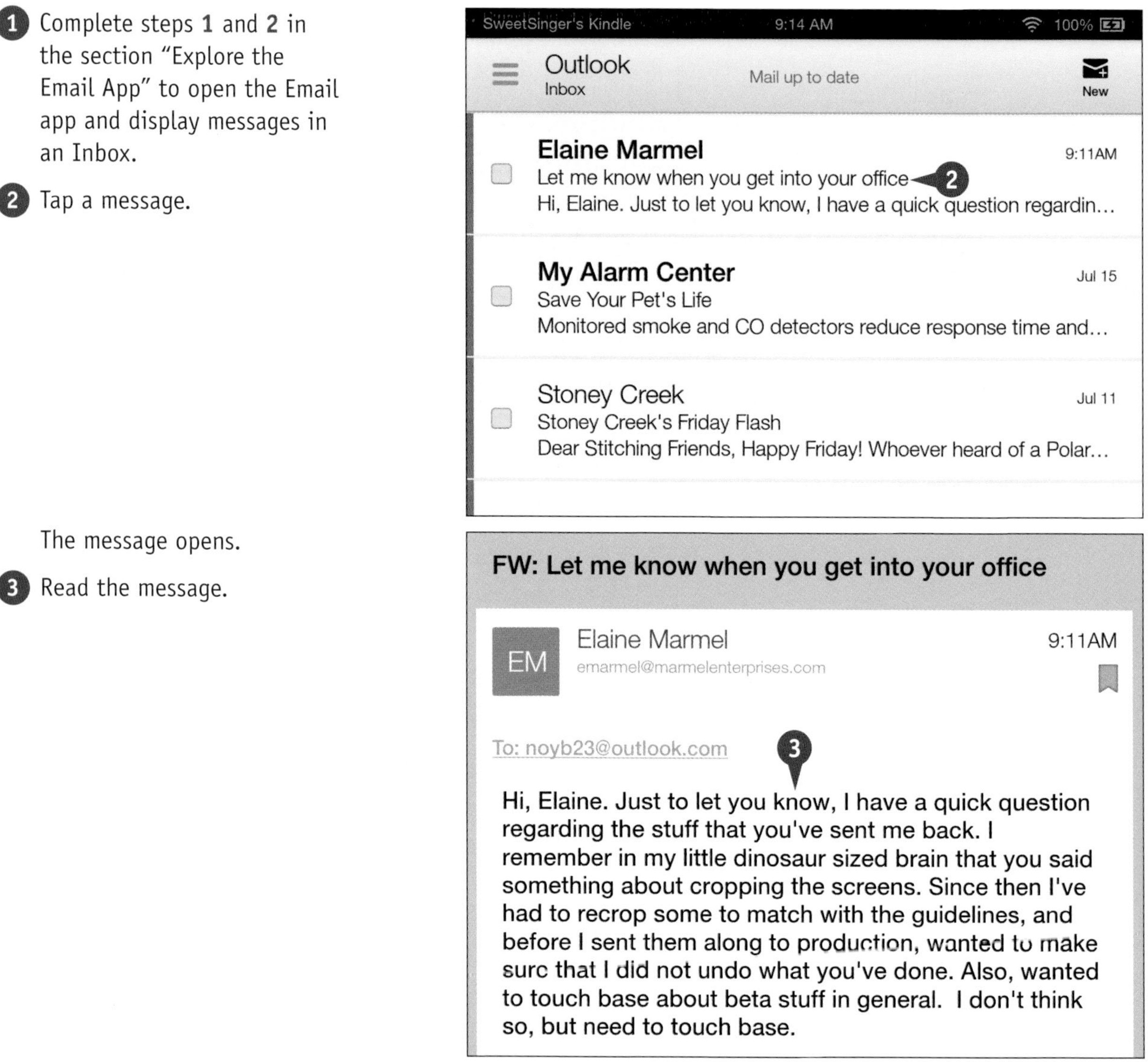

4 Tap **Reply**.

A You can tap **Reply All** to send your response to everyone who originally received the message.

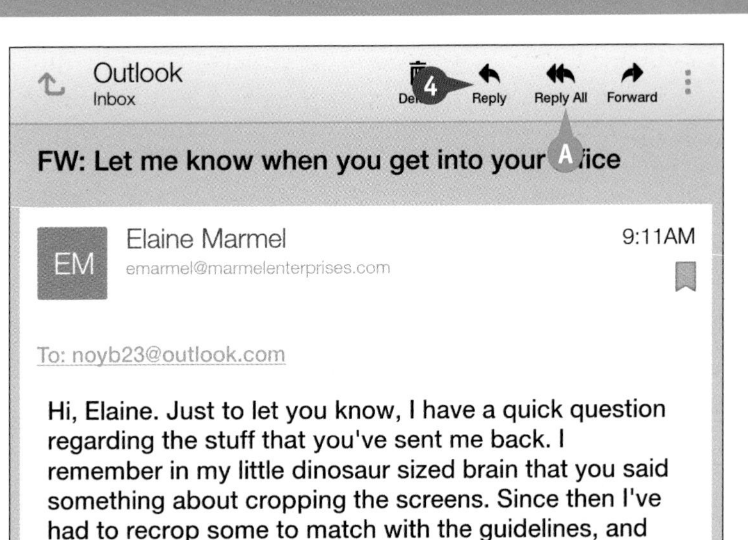

B The Compose window appears.

5 Type your reply.

6 Tap **Send**.

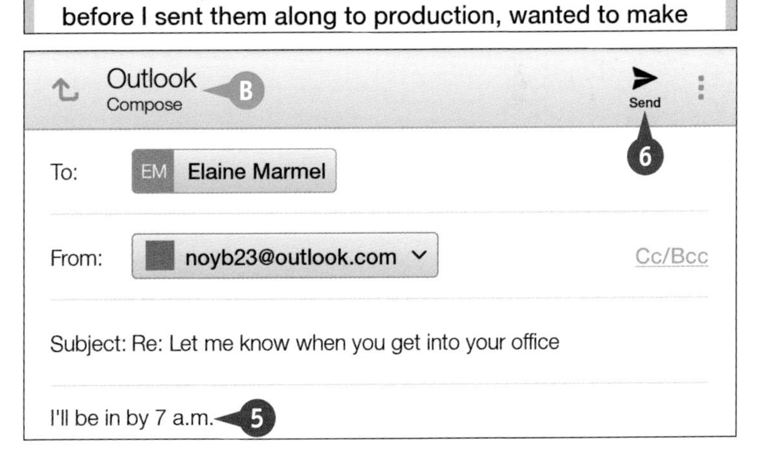

TIP

Can I include formatting when I respond to or create a message?

Yes. While viewing the message, tap ⋮ (A) and, from the menu that appears, tap **Show Formatting** to display the Formatting bar. Tap Aa (B) to change the font, **B** (C) to apply boldface, *I* (D) to apply italics, U (E) to underline, A (F) to change the font color, and A (G) to apply highlighting.

Open an Email Attachment

When you receive an attachment in an email, you can open and view the attachment and, if you want, you can save the attachment to your Fire tablet.

To save time delivering email and to help you avoid viruses that attachments might contain, your Fire tablet does not automatically download attachments. Instead, messages containing attachments display a paperclip icon. You then can choose to download or ignore the attachment. And, even after you download an attachment, your tablet does not automatically open the attachment; you must open it manually.

Open an Email Attachment

1. Complete steps **1** and **2** in the section "Explore the Email App" to open the Email app and display messages in an Inbox.
2. Tap a message containing an attachment.

   A. Messages containing attachments display a paperclip ( ).

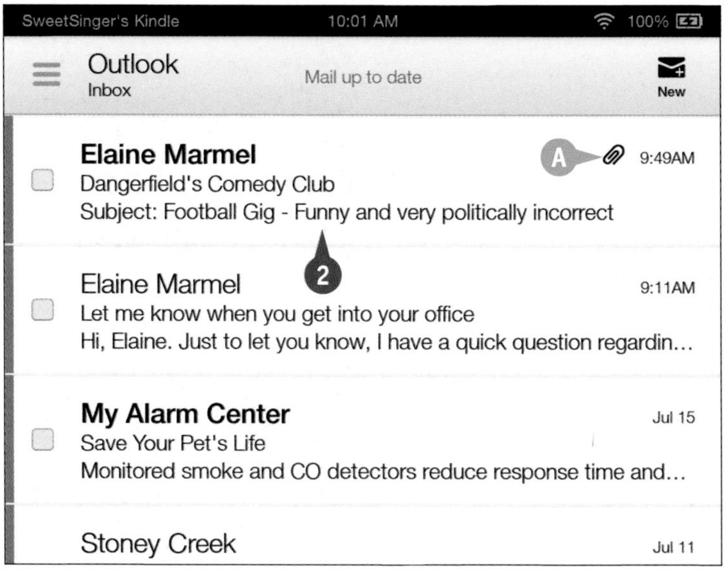

   The message appears.
3. Tap the attachment.

   B. The attachment downloads to your Fire tablet.

   C. You can tap ( ) to cancel the download.

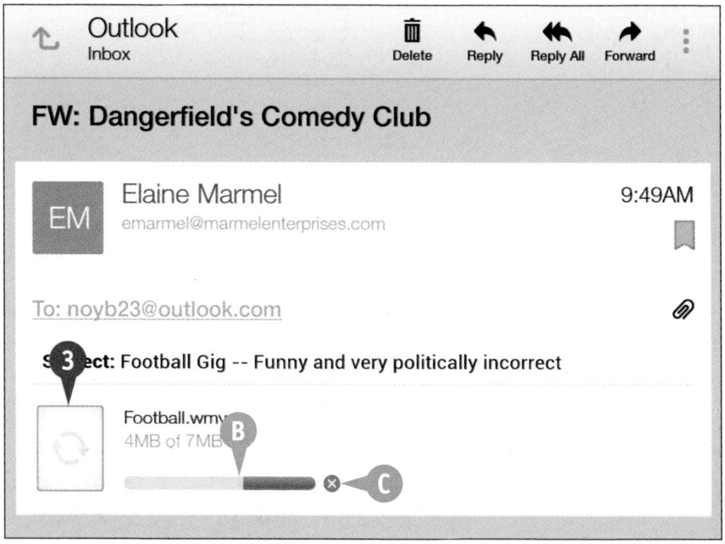

SweetSinger's Kindle 10:01 AM 100%
Outlook
Inbox
Mail up to date
New
Elaine Marmel 9:49AM
Dangerfield's Comedy Club
Subject: Football Gig - Funny and very politically incorrect
Elaine Marmel 9:11AM
Let me know when you get into your office
Hi, Elaine. Just to let you know, I have a quick question regardin...
My Alarm Center Jul 15
Save Your Pet's Life
Monitored smoke and CO detectors reduce response time and...
Stoney Creek Jul 11

Outlook
Inbox
Delete Reply Reply All Forward
FW: Dangerfield's Comedy Club
Elaine Marmel 9:49AM
EM
emarmel@marmelenterprises.com
To: noyb23@outlook.com
Subject: Football Gig -- Funny and very politically incorrect
Football.wmv
4MB of 7MB

D When the attachment finishes downloading to your Fire tablet, a filled-in check box (☑) appears in the corner of the attachment.

4 Tap the attachment again.

Note: You might be prompted to choose an app to use to open the attachment. If so, tap the app you want to use and tap **Just once**.

The attachment opens.

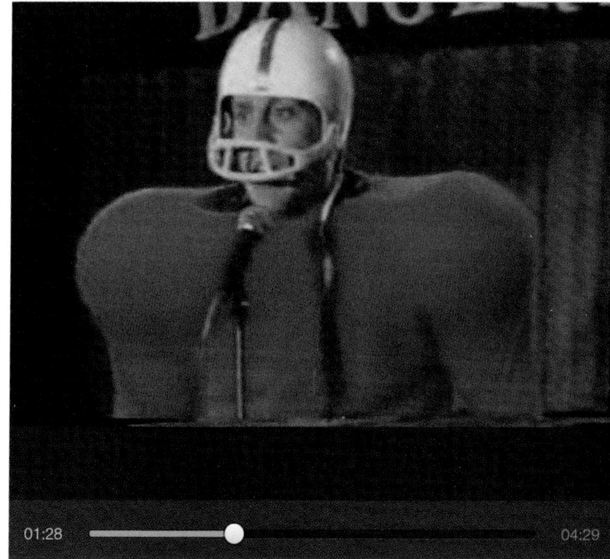

TIPS

Can I save an attachment to my Fire tablet?
Yes. Tap and hold the attachment in the email message. From the menu that appears, tap **Save**. Your Fire tablet places the attachment in the appropriate content library; for example, photos and videos appear in the Photos content library.

If the Fire tablet prompts me to choose an app to open the attachment, how do I choose?
Choose the one that seems most logical to you, and tap **Just once**. That way, if you make a mistake, you can try using a different app to open the attachment. Tap **Always** only when you know you always want to use a particular app to open an attachment.

Receive Documents via Email

When you set up and register your Fire tablet, Amazon automatically assigns you a Send-To-Kindle email address. You can use that address to receive documents after completing the steps in this section to approve the email address of the person sending you the document.

If you receive a document from an unapproved sender, you receive a notification so that you can approve the sender. Documents from approved senders appear on your Carousel and in the Docs content library. They do not appear in the Email app.

Receive Documents via Email

1. Open your browser and navigate to www.amazon.com.
2. Tap or click **Sign in** to display the Amazon Sign In screen.
3. Type your email address.
4. Type your password.
5. Tap or click **Sign in using our secure server.**

6. Tap or position the mouse pointer over the **Your Account** menu.
7. Tap or click **Manage Your Content and Devices.**

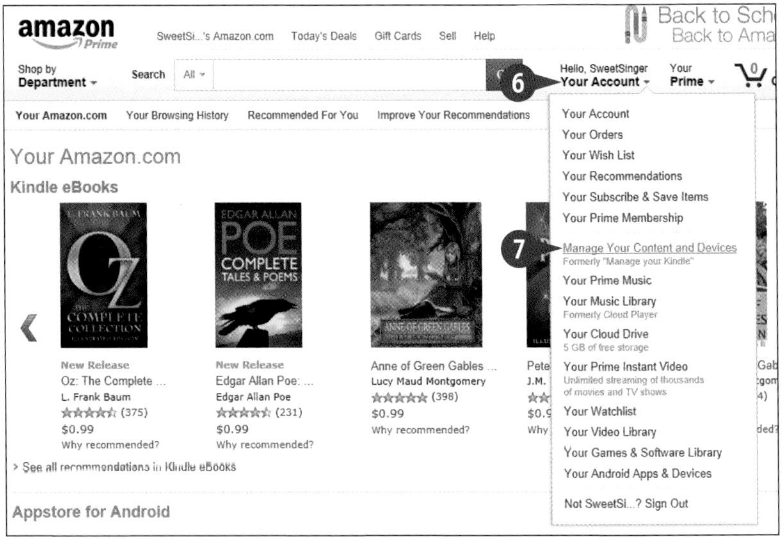

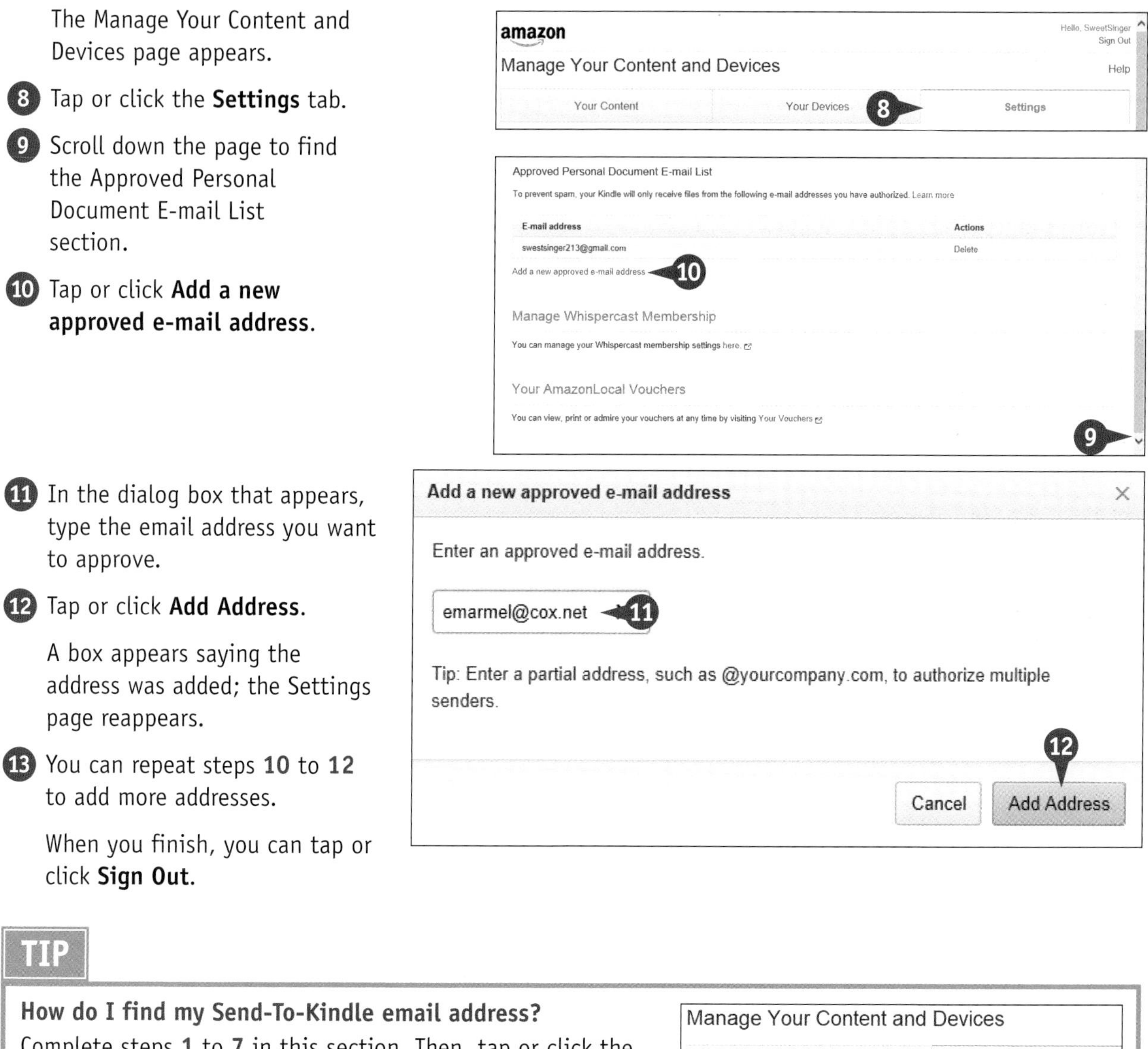

The Manage Your Content and Devices page appears.

8. Tap or click the **Settings** tab.
9. Scroll down the page to find the Approved Personal Document E-mail List section.
10. Tap or click **Add a new approved e-mail address.**
11. In the dialog box that appears, type the email address you want to approve.
12. Tap or click **Add Address.**

    A box appears saying the address was added; the Settings page reappears.

13. You can repeat steps **10** to **12** to add more addresses.

    When you finish, you can tap or click **Sign Out.**

TIP

How do I find my Send-To-Kindle email address?

Complete steps **1** to **7** in this section. Then, tap or click the **Your Devices** tab (A). Your Send-To-Kindle email address appears (B).

Review General Email Settings

You can control many aspects of the Email app's behavior. For example, you can make the size of message text larger or smaller, and you can hide the embedded images that come in many emails. You also can change the Email app's default behavior and opt to automatically download attachments. In email replies, you can exclude original text, and you can choose to view only the latest message in an email exchange.

When you delete a message you are currently viewing, you can specify whether the Email app displays the next newer message, the next older message, or the message list.

Review General Email Settings

1. Complete steps **1** and **2** in the section "Explore the Email App" to open the Email app and display messages in an Inbox.
2. Tap the **Navigation** button (☰).

The Navigation panel appears.

3. Tap **Settings**.

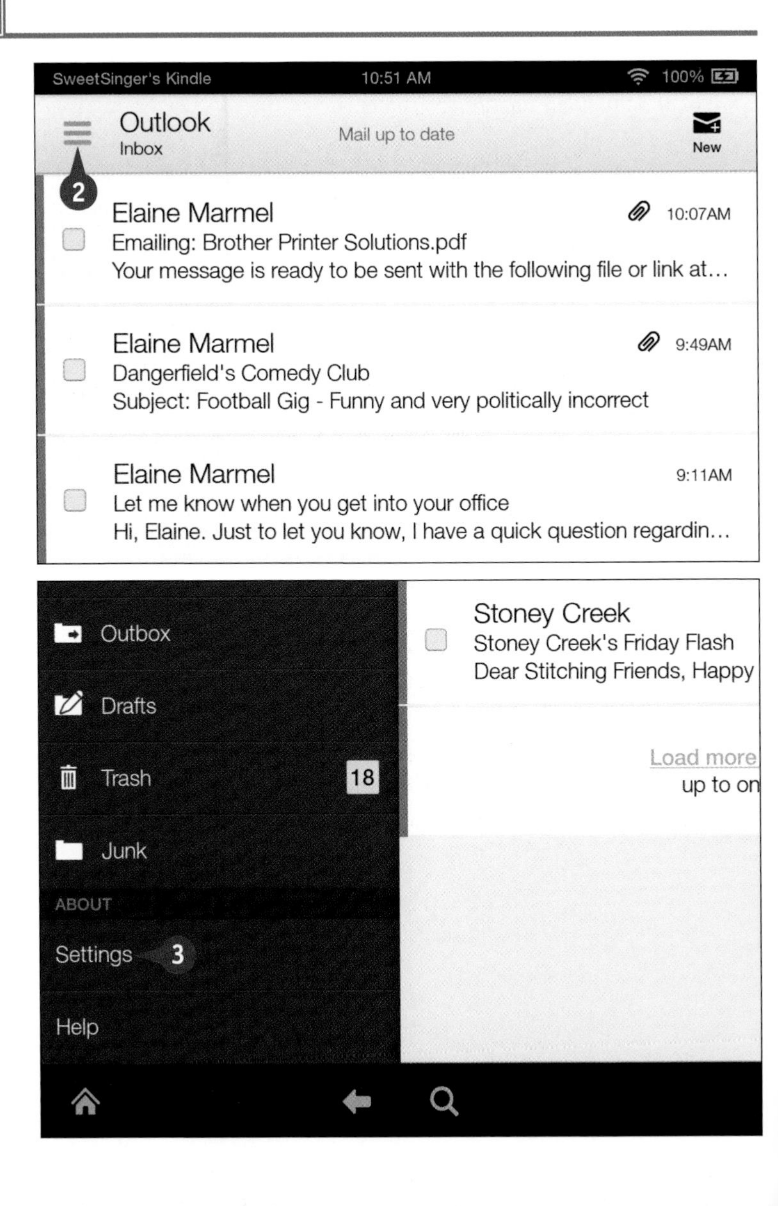

The Email, Contacts, Calendars screen appears.

4 Tap **Email General Settings**.

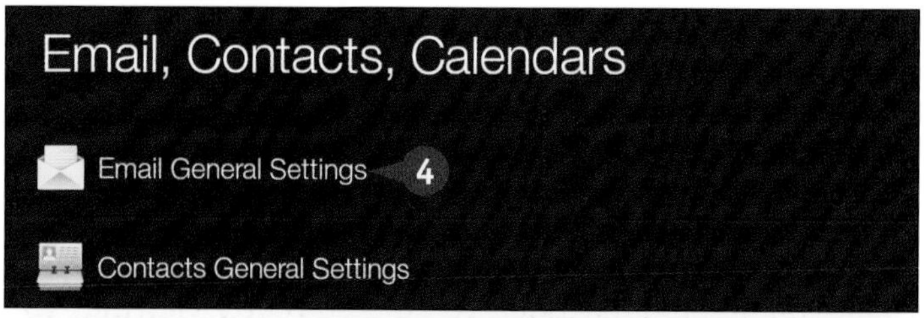

A You can tap any icon in this row to change the size of message text.

You can toggle any of the following settings On or Off:

B Show embedded images in emails.

C Automatically download attachments.

D Include original text when you reply to a message.

E Hide all but the latest message in an email exchange.

F Determine whether the Email app displays the next newer message, the next older message, or the message list when you delete the message you are currently viewing.

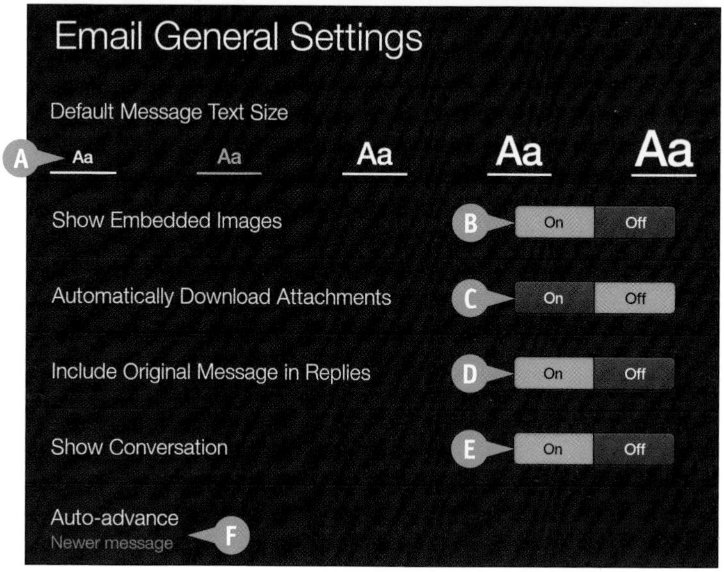

TIP

If I choose to show email conversations, how does that change my screen?

When you show email conversations, your screen might look like this one. If you hide email conversations, your screen shows only the white part of the message; the gray ones do not appear.

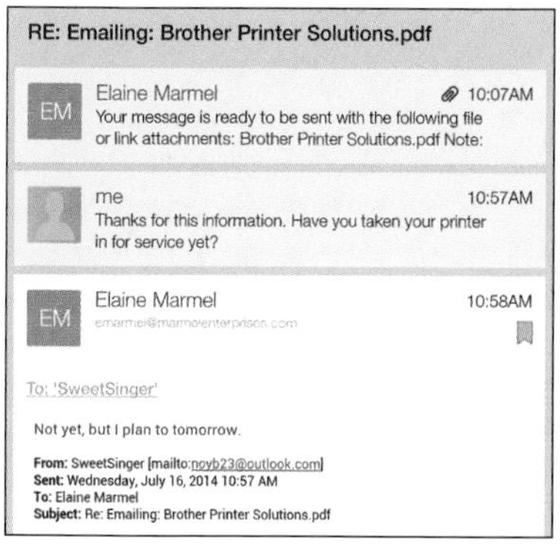

Review Settings for Specific Accounts

You can control many settings for each email account you set up on your Fire tablet. For example, you can control how often the Fire tablet checks for email for each account as well as how long the Email app stores email messages.

You also can set up a signature line that the Email app appends to each message you send; and, if you collect email for more than one account, you can select the account you want the Email app to use as the default.

Review Settings for Specific Accounts

1. Complete steps **1** and **2** in the section "Explore the Email App" to open the Email app and display messages in an Inbox.
2. Tap the **Navigation** button (▤) at the top of the screen to display the Navigation panel.
3. Tap **Settings**.

The Email, Contacts, Calendars screen appears.

4. Tap the email account you want to review.

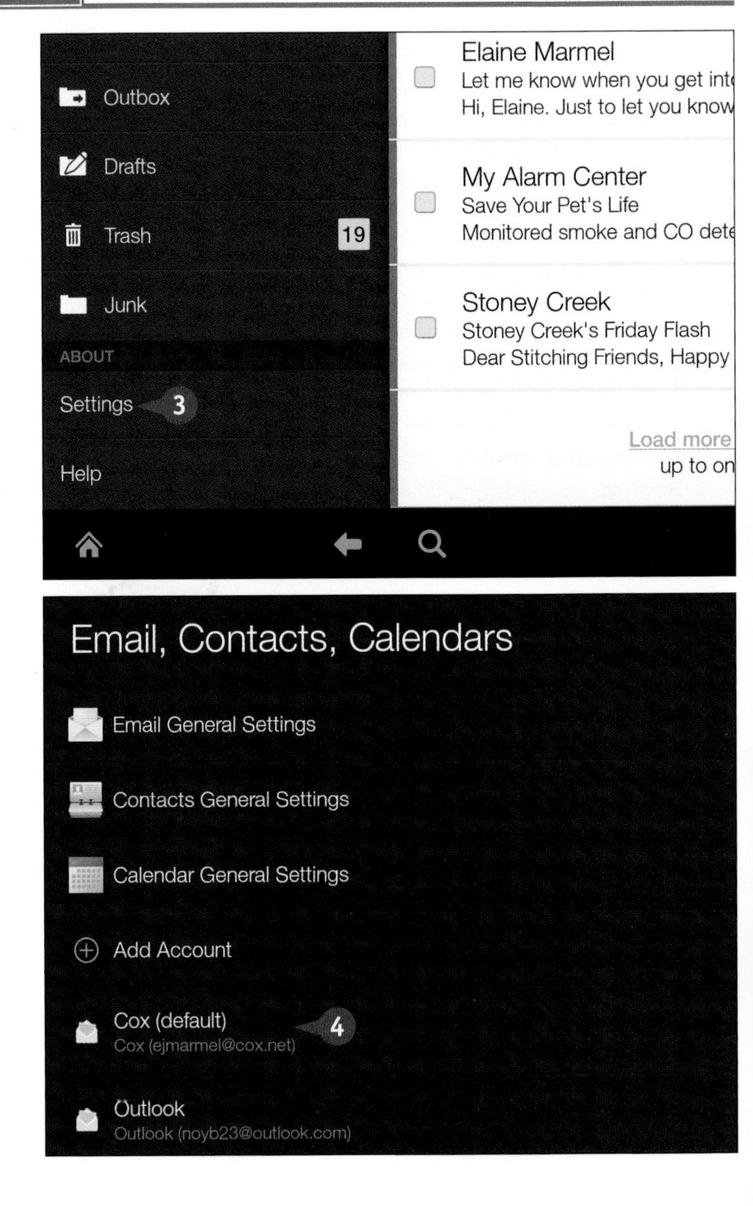

The settings for the selected email account appear.

A You can tap the check box (■ changes to ☑) to make this email account the default one you use to send email.

B You can tap this area to control how long messages are stored on your Fire tablet.

C You can tap this area to provide a signature for each email you send.

5 Tap **Inbox check frequency**.

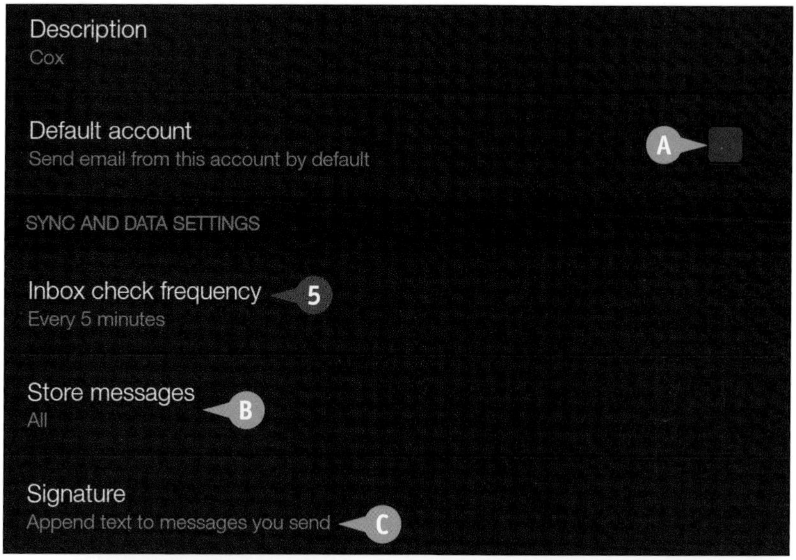

The Inbox check frequency dialog box appears.

6 Tap a frequency that the Email app should use to check for new email (■ changes to ◘).

You can tap the **Back** arrow (⬅) to return to the Inbox or the **Home** button (🏠) to redisplay the Home screen.

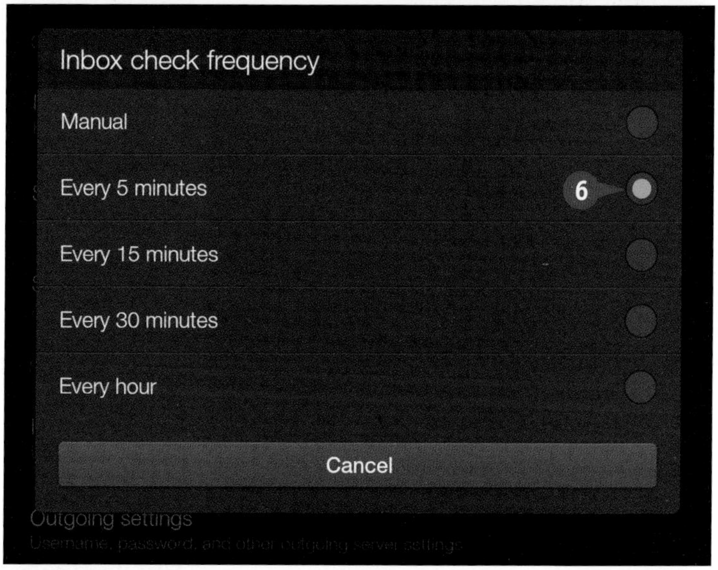

TIP

Is there a way to control synchronization settings?

Yes. By default, synchronization is on for accounts that offer synchronization. But, from the account's Settings page, you can turn off synchronization for email, calendar, and contacts.

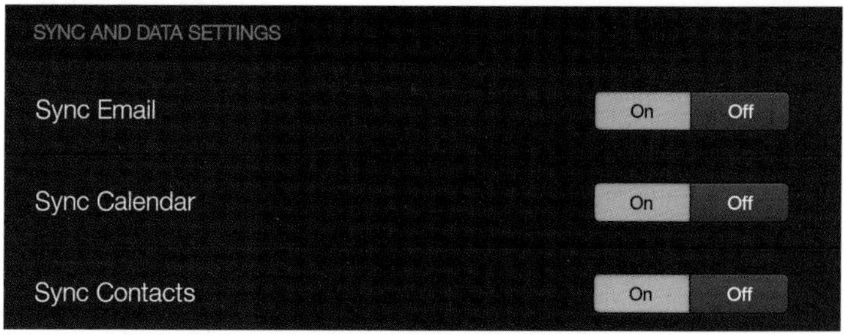

CHAPTER 9

Maintaining Contacts

The Contacts app that comes with your Fire tablet enables you to store basic information about contacts, such as name, multiple street and email addresses, and phone numbers. You also can store birthdays and anniversaries and notes about each contact. You can even use stored contact information to address emails.

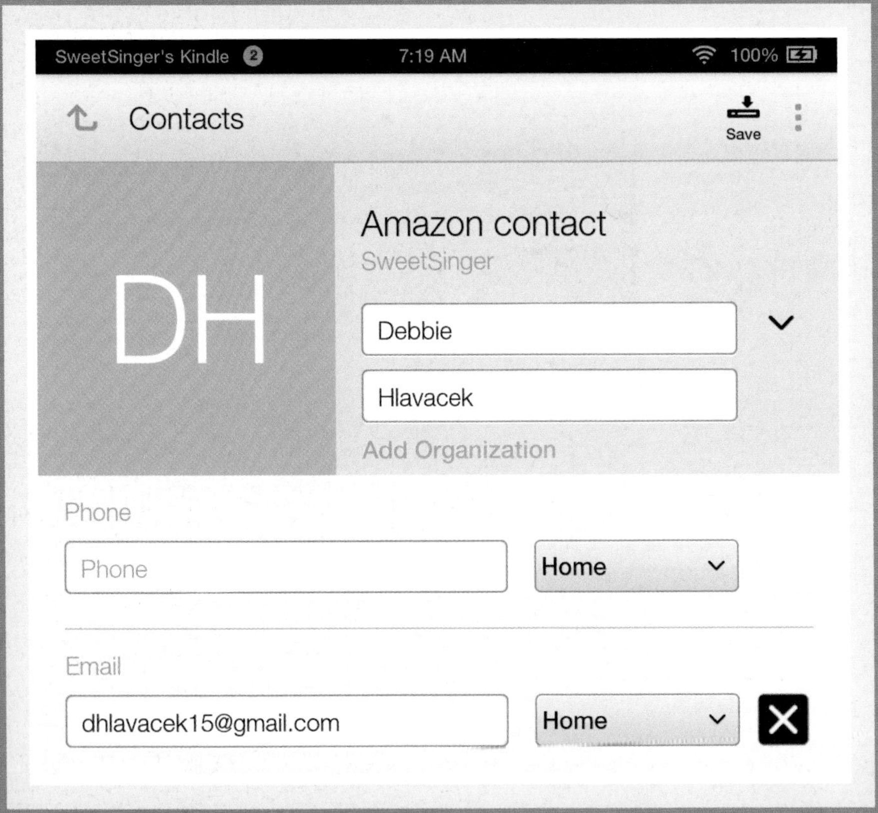

SweetSinger's Kindle 2 7:19 AM 100%

Contacts Save

Amazon contact
SweetSinger

DH

Debbie

Hlavacek

Add Organization

Phone

Phone Home

Email

dhlavacek15@gmail.com Home

Open the Contacts App 190
Set Up Your Contact Profile 192
Add a Contact 194
Add a Contact from an Email Message 196
Import Contacts 198
Edit or Delete a Contact 200
Combine Contacts 202
Search for a Contact 205
Establish Settings for Contacts 206

Open the Contacts App

You can use the Contacts app to store contact information for people you email or phone. You cannot use the Contacts app until you have set up an email address, as described in Chapter 8. When you set up a web-based email account such as a Gmail or Hotmail account on your Fire tablet, contacts associated with that email address are automatically imported into the Contacts app. You can then use those contacts in other apps and services on your tablet, such as the Email app or Skype.

Open the Contacts App

1. From the Home screen, tap **Apps**.

   The Apps content library appears.

2. Tap **Contacts**.

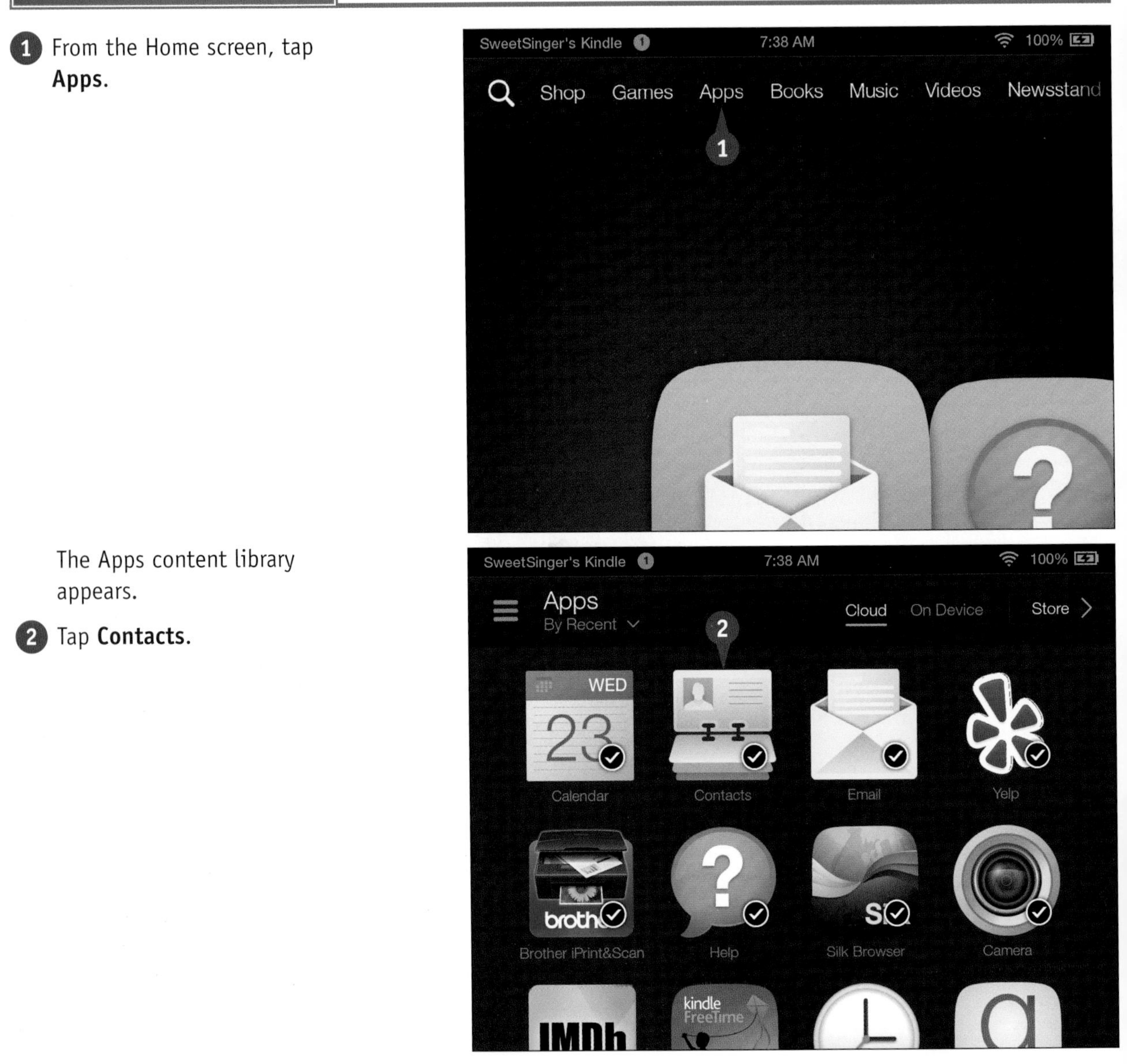

The Contacts app opens.

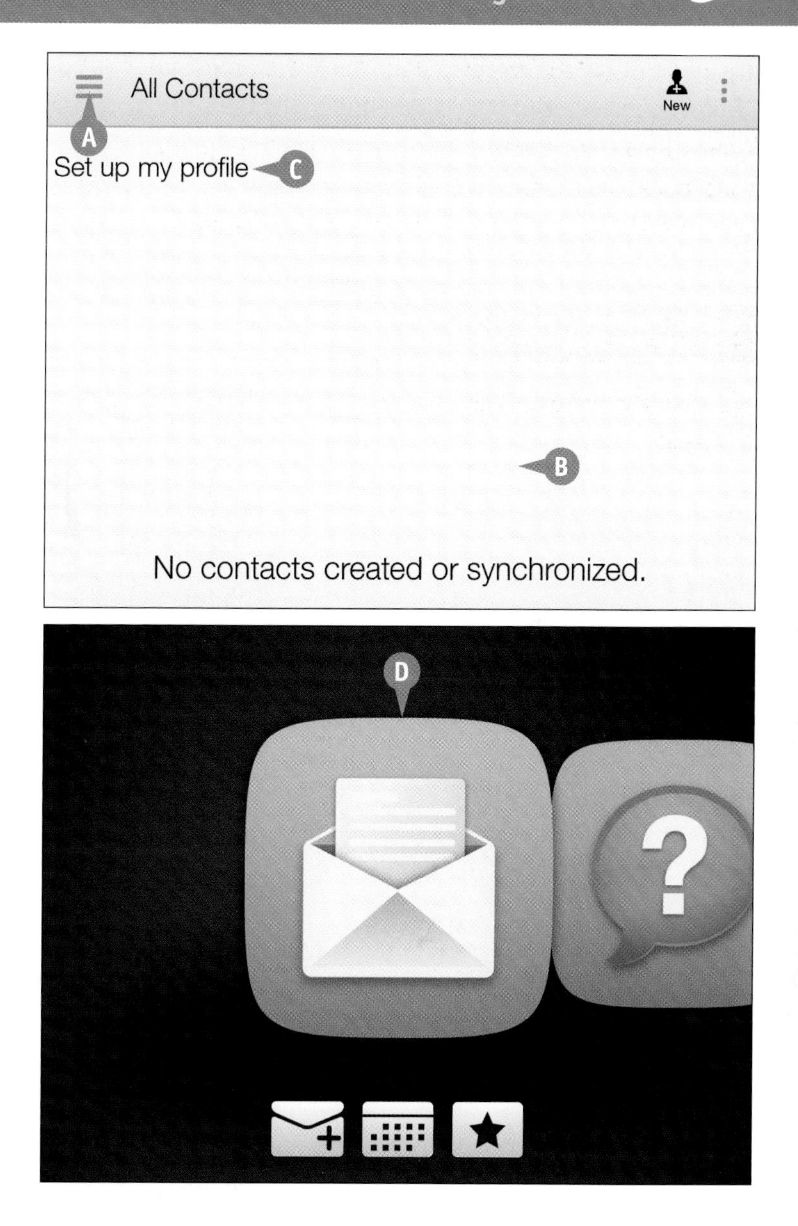

A You can tap the **Navigation** button (☰) to open the Navigation panel.

B After you create contacts, they appear in this area, alphabetized.

C You tap here to set up your profile, as described in the next section.

3 Tap the **Home** button (⌂) in the bottom-left corner of the screen.

The Home screen appears.

D The Contacts app appears in the Carousel.

TIP

Does adding a contact to my Fire tablet affect my Gmail contacts?

Adding and deleting contacts is account-dependent, not device-dependent. By default, your Fire tablet synchronizes Gmail contacts, email, and calendars with those on your Fire tablet. If you set up your Gmail account on your Fire tablet as described in Chapter 8, and you add or delete a contact using your devise's Contacts app, that contact automatically appears or disappears in your Gmail contacts when you open Gmail in your browser. Similarly, adding a contact to your Gmail account using your browser adds the contact in the Contacts app.

Set Up Your Contact Profile

You can set up and store your information using your Contact Profile. Your profile includes your first, middle, and last name along with an appropriate prefix and suffix. You also can provide the name of the company for which you work and your job title. You can store several phone numbers, such as your home phone number, your cell phone number, your work number, and more.

Other details you can add are your various email addresses, your street address, your nickname, your website address, your birthday and anniversary, and any notes.

Set Up Your Contact Profile

1. Follow steps **1** and **2** in the section "Open the Contacts App."
2. Tap **Set up my profile**.

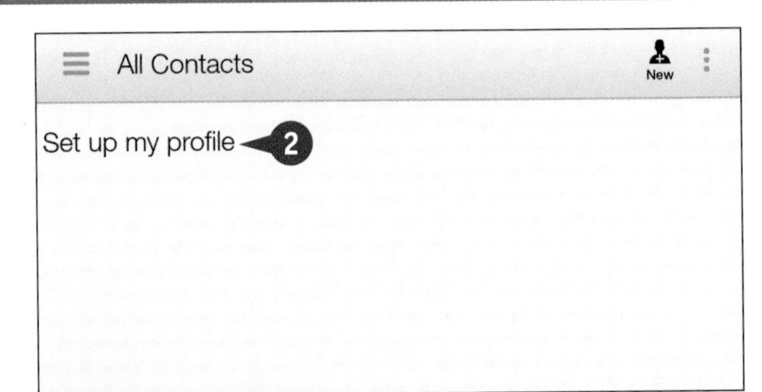

The My Local Profile screen appears.

3. Fill in your first and last name.

A. You can tap ☐ to display fields to enter a prefix, middle name, and suffix.

4. Tap the **Add Organization** link below your last name to display new fields on-screen.
5. Type your company's name and your title.

B. You can supply a phone number.

6. Type your email address.

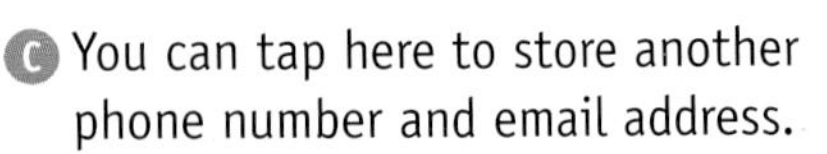

C. You can tap here to store another phone number and email address.

7. Swipe up.

D You can type your address here.

E You can tap here to identify the type of address: Work, Home, or Other.

8 Tap **Add More Fields**.

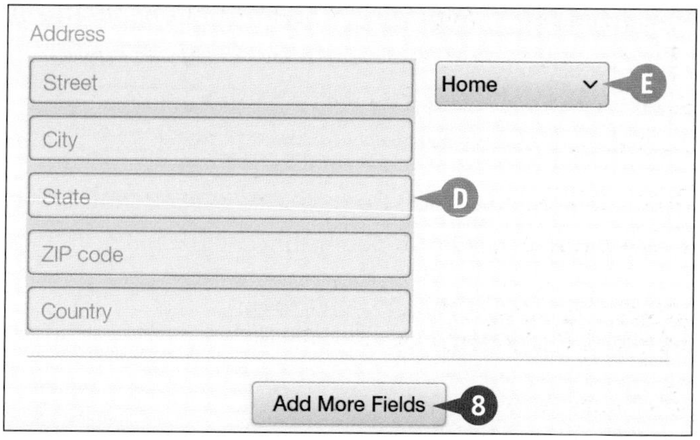

F You can supply a nickname here.

G You can type your website address here.

H You can supply a birthday or anniversary date and tap **Add New** to define another type of date.

I You can type notes here.

9 Tap the **Save** button () in the upper-right area of the Contacts app screen.

The Contacts app saves your profile and displays it.

You can tap the **Back** arrow () to redisplay the All Contacts screen.

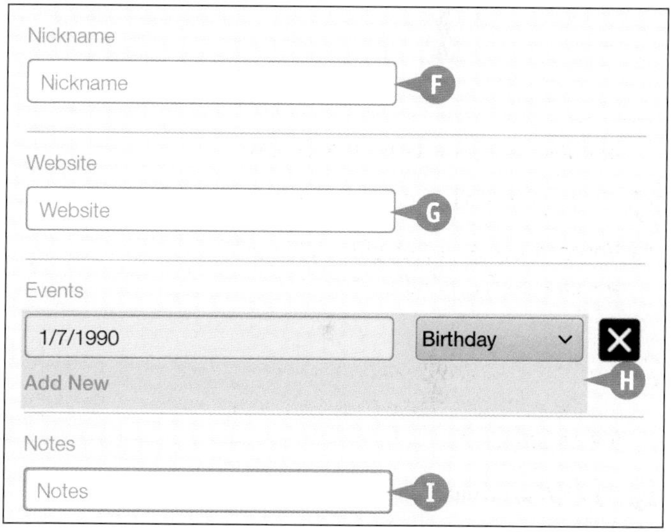

Address
Street
Home
City
State
ZIP code
Country
Add More Fields

SweetSinger's Kindle 2 12:18 PM 100%
Contacts
Save

Nickname
Nickname
Website
Website
Events
1/7/1990
Birthday
Add New
Notes
Notes

TIP

How do I add a photo to my profile contact?

During profile setup, tap the avatar that appears beside your name and tap **Add Photo**. In the Complete Action Using dialog box, tap Photos and then **Just once**. In the **Photos** content library, tap a photo for your profile. To add the picture after setup, edit your profile as described in the section "Edit or Delete a Contact." Tap your initials, which appear instead of the avatar, and follow the procedure outlined at the beginning of this Tip.

Add a Contact

You add contacts to the Contacts app in much the same way you set up your profile. You can store basic contact management information about each contact, including name, street address, email address, multiple phone numbers, and more.

The Contacts app synchronizes contacts with email addresses you establish on your Fire tablet. If you have set up multiple email addresses, the Contacts app asks you to select an account to use when synchronizing contact information. That way, setting up, changing, or deleting a contact on your Fire tablet also occurs for the selected email account.

Add a Contact

1. Follow steps **1** and **2** in the section "Open the Contacts App."
2. Tap **New**.

The Contacts window appears.

3. Tap the email account with which you want to synchronize the contact's information.

Note: This example uses the Amazon email account.

Note: A message appears, explaining that Amazon contacts are synchronized across Amazon devices; tap **OK**.

4. Fill in the contact's information including name, organization, contact information, and address; you can also add an IM address, website URL, nickname, and other information.

Note: See the section "Set Up Your Contact Profile" for details of the various fields available.

5. Tap the **Save** button (Save icon) in the upper-right area of the Contacts app screen.

The contact's basic information appears.

A. You can tap the **Back** arrow (Back icon) to display contacts in list format.

TIP

How do I view contacts associated with a particular email address?

From the All Contacts screen, tap the **Navigation** button (Navigation icon) A to display the Navigation panel. Then, tap the account for which you want to view contacts B.

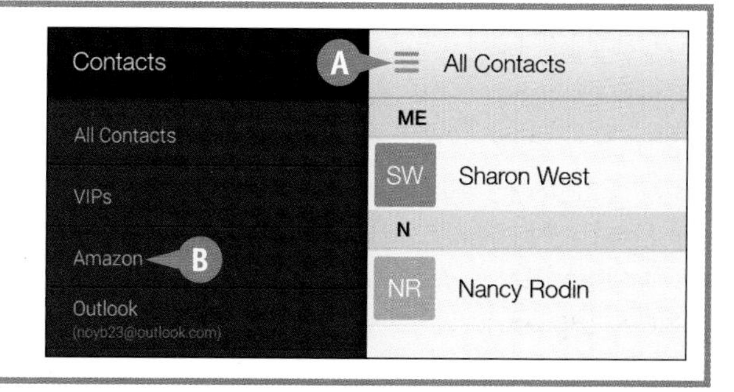

Add a Contact from an Email Message

You can add the sender of an email message to your contacts and save the time you would spend typing to set up the contact. By default, when you add the sender of an email message as a contact, the Contacts app copies the email sender's name and email address into the Contact record.

You start in the Email app and, from the list of messages in your Inbox, select the message whose sender you want to set up as a contact.

Add a Contact from an Email Message

1. From the Home screen, swipe up to display the Favorites section.

2. Tap **Email**.
3. (Not shown) Tap the message containing the contact you want to add.

   The Email app opens the message.
4. Tap the message sender's initials.

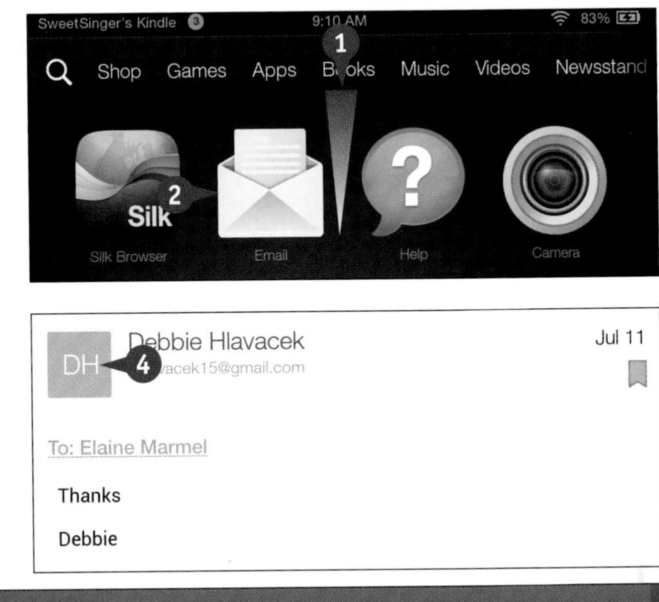

   The Add Contact window appears.
5. Tap **Add to Contacts**.

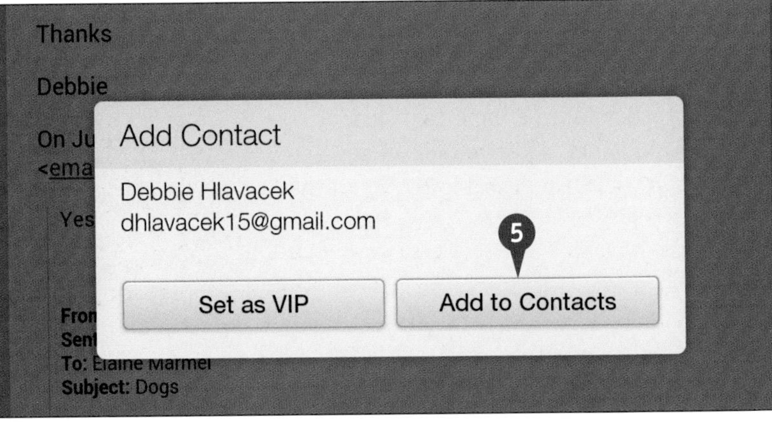

6. Tap **Create New Contact.**

   The Contacts window appears.

7. (Not shown) Tap the account you want to use to synchronize the contact; see "Add a Contact" for details.

   The Contacts window appears with the contact's name and email address filled in.

8. Fill in any other fields you want to save.

9. Tap the **Save** button (Save icon).

   Your contact's information is saved.

TIP

What happens if, in step 5, I tap Set as VIP?

VIP contacts might be important and/or favorites of yours. After you designate a contact as a VIP, you can tap ☰ (A) in the Contacts app to open the Navigation panel and then tap **VIPs** (B) to view a list of VIP contacts.

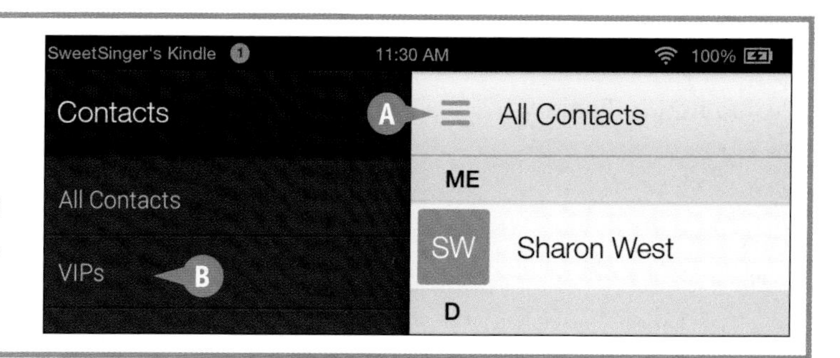

Import Contacts

By default, when you set up a web-based email account such as Gmail or Outlook.com, your Fire tablet automatically imports contacts established in those accounts. If, however, you are using a desktop-based email program, such as Microsoft Outlook or Eudora, you can import your contacts manually.

You create electronic business cards (vCards) for your contacts, and the technique you use depends on your desktop program. This section assumes you have created vCards on your desktop PC.

Import Contacts

1. Connect your Fire tablet to your desktop PC using a USB cable.
2. Copy your vCard files from your desktop PC to the Documents folder on your Fire tablet. See Chapters 4 and 5 for details on transferring files.

Note: As you copy vCards to your Fire tablet, you might see a message warning about files not being usable; click **Yes** to copy the files anyway.

3. Follow steps **1** and **2** in the section "Open the Contacts App."
4. Tap .
5. Tap **Import/Export**.

   The Import/Export Contacts menu appears.
6. Tap **Import from storage**.

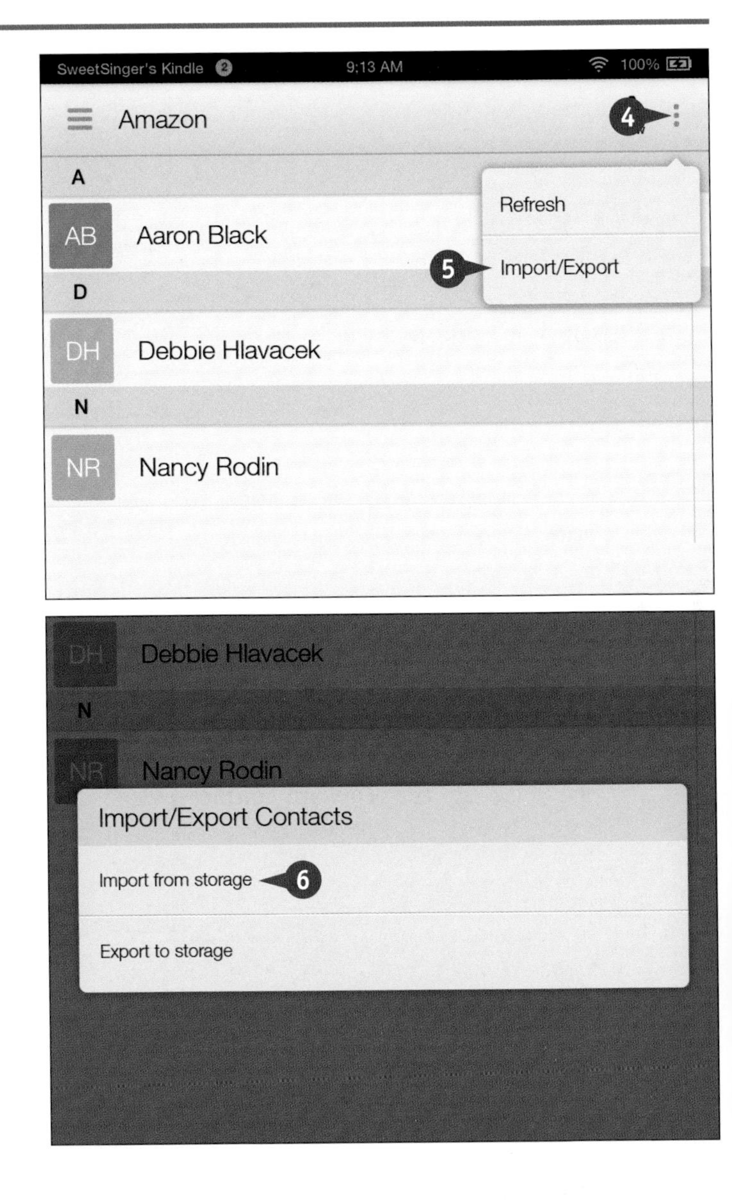

If you have multiple email accounts set up on your Fire tablet, the Create Contact Under Account menu appears.

7 Tap an account. This example uses the Amazon account.

Note: If you import multiple vCards, the tablet displays a menu asking if you want to import one vCard or all vCards; tap **All vCards**.

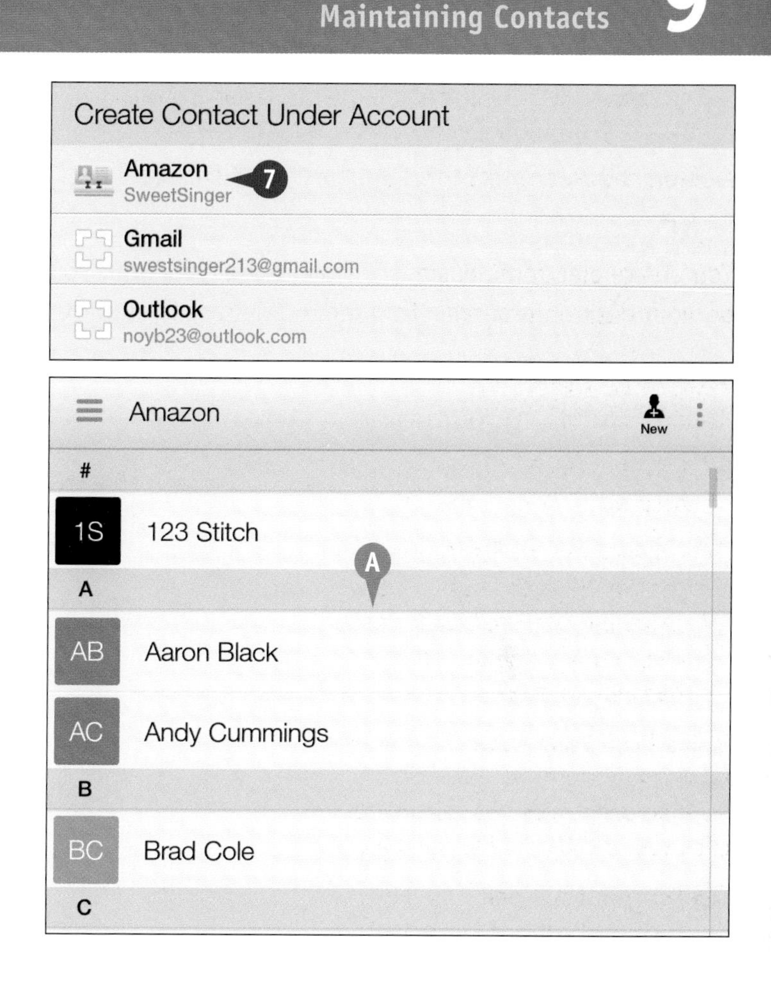

Ⓐ The Fire tablet imports the vCards and displays them in the account you selected in step **7**.

TIP

How do I create vCards in the desktop version of Microsoft Outlook?

In Outlook 2010, click the Contacts folder (in Outlook 2010, click the People folder) and select the contacts. Next, on the Home tab, click **Forward Contact** Ⓐ and then click **As a Business Card** Ⓑ. Outlook opens an email with the .vcf cards attached. Click any attached vCard and then press Ctrl+A to select all of them. Right-click and choose **Copy**; you can then close the email message. Paste the vCards into the Documents folder on your Fire tablet.

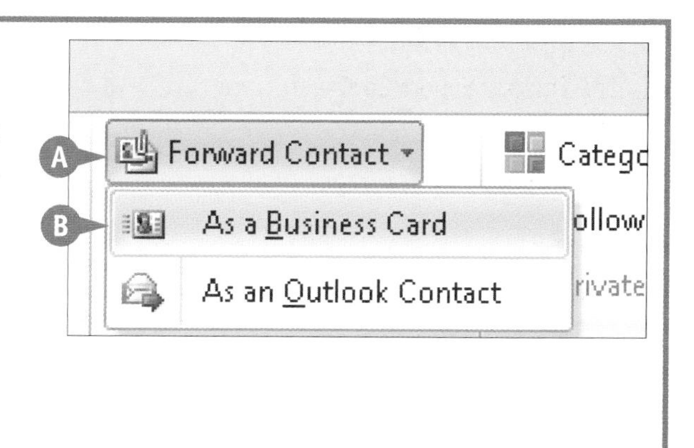

Edit or Delete a Contact

You can make changes to any contact you set up, and you can delete a contact. When you edit a contact, you use a screen that closely resembles the one you used to create the contact; see the section "Add a Contact" for details.

When you delete a contact, you remove it from your Fire tablet and, after the device synchronizes, from the email account to which the contact was connected. That is, deleting a contact associated with your Amazon.com email address removes the contact from both your Fire tablet and your Amazon Cloud account.

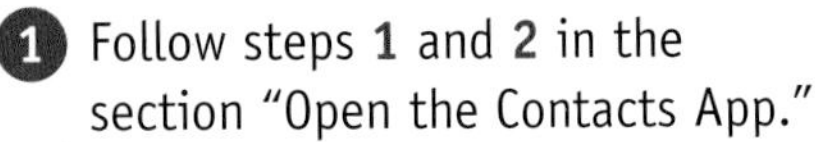

Edit or Delete a Contact

Edit a Contact

1. Follow steps **1** and **2** in the section "Open the Contacts App."
2. Tap and hold a contact.

A menu of options appears.

3. Tap **Edit**.

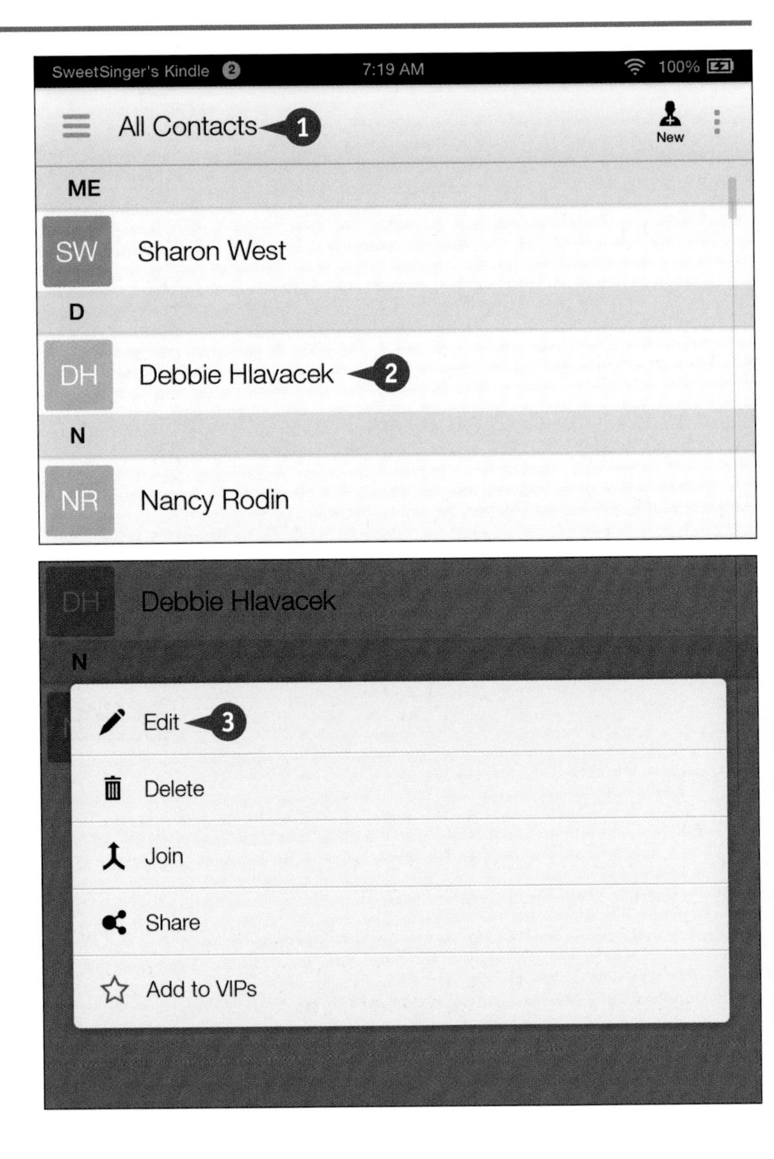

The contact's information appears.

4. Make changes as needed; see the section "Add a Contact" for details.
5. Tap the **Save** button ().

The Contacts app saves your changes and redisplays the list of contacts.

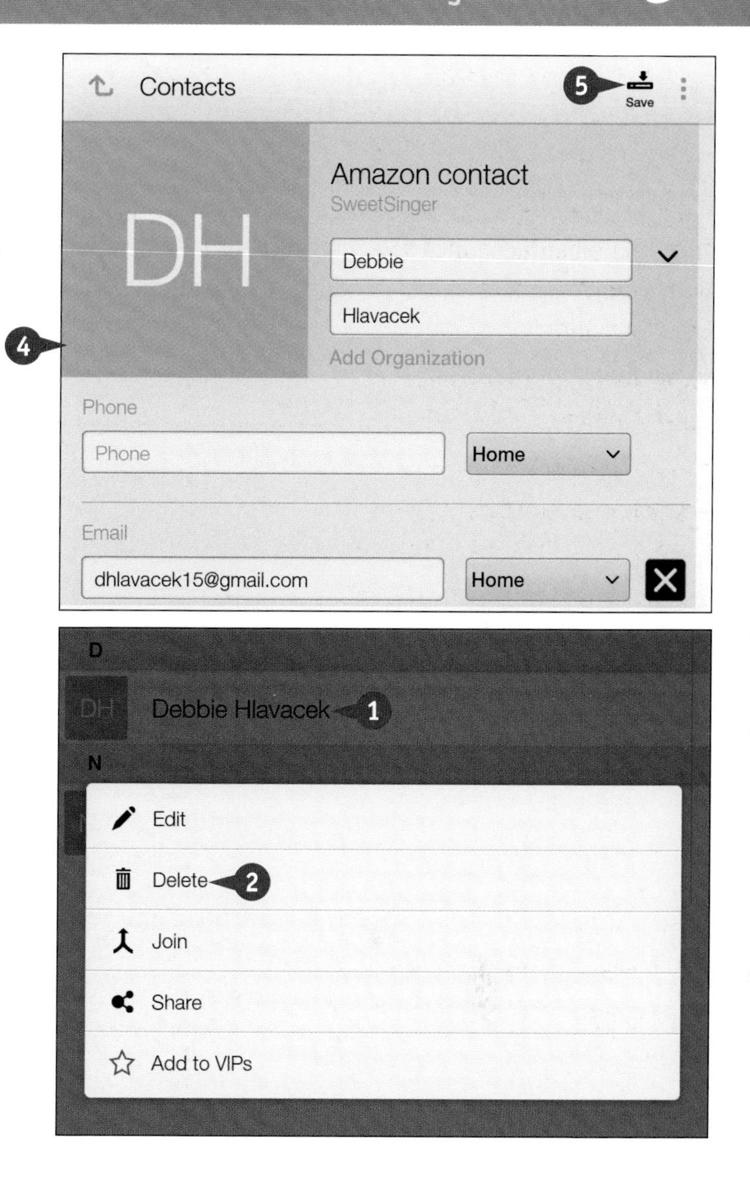

Delete a Contact

1. Tap and hold a contact to display the option menu.
2. Tap **Delete**.

   A dialog box appears, asking you to confirm the deletion.
3. Tap **OK**, and the Contacts app removes the contact from the list.

TIP

What happens if I tap the Share command that appears when I tap and hold a contact's name?

The Contacts app creates an electronic business card file (.vcf) for the contact and attaches it to an email message A, preparatory to sending the card to any recipient you choose.

Combine Contacts

You can combine two contact records in the same account into one on your Fire tablet. When examining your contacts, especially after importing contacts as described in the section "Import Contacts," you commonly find multiple versions of the same contact record. You can easily clean up your Contacts list by combining those records — a process known in the Contacts app as *joining* contacts.

You can join two records at a time, if you have more than two versions of the same contact, and join multiple times. And, if you make a mistake, you can split a contact.

Combine Contacts

1. Follow steps **1** and **2** in the section "Open the Contacts App."
2. Swipe up to scroll through your contacts, looking for repeats.

A This contact has a name that includes a middle initial.

B This record looks like it is a duplicate.

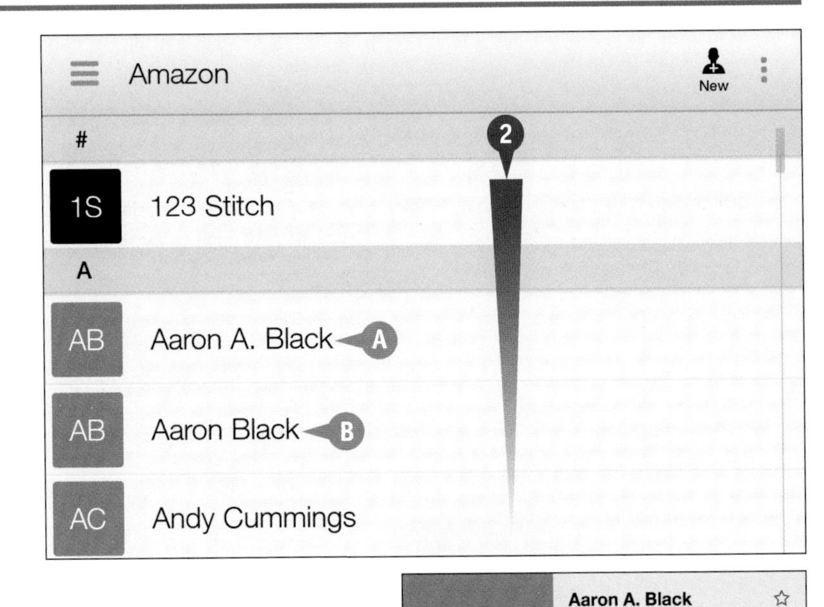

C This record shows a work title and a company name.

D This version of the contact record shows no middle initial or work title and a different company name and a company address and phone number.

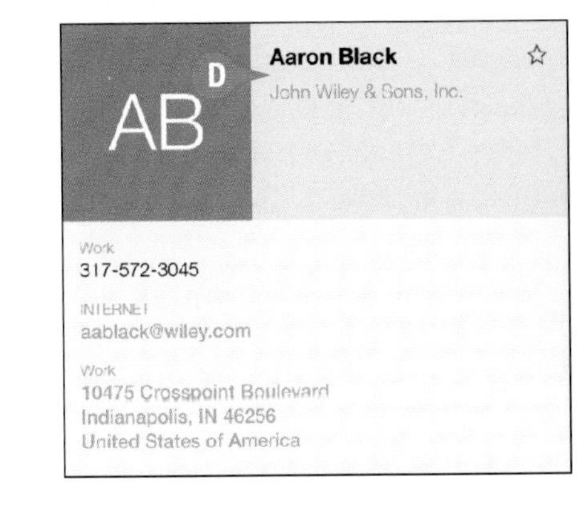

3. Press and hold the contact whose record you want to keep.
4. Tap **Join**.

The Join Contacts list appears.

5. Tap the contact whose record you want to combine with the contact you selected in step **3**.

TIP

What if I make a mistake when I combine two contacts?
You can split the two contacts again. Press and hold the newly joined contact and tap **Edit** to open the contact's record. Then, tap ⋮ (A) and tap **Split** (B).

continued ▶

If you decide to join two records, review each record to determine which one has the most information that you want to keep. Do not worry, however, about losing information from either record; the Contacts app does a nice job of combining all the information in the two records.

During the process of joining records, the Contacts app tries to guess — and usually does so accurately — the contact record to join. After you join the records, only one entry remains in the list of contacts.

Combine Contacts (continued)

The Contacts list reappears, without the contact you selected in step **5**.

6. Tap the remaining contact record, which is the contact you selected in step **3**.

The remaining contact record is updated with information from the record you selected in step **3**.

A. In this example, the remaining record now excludes the middle initial in the contact name, adds a work title and phone number, and updates the business name.

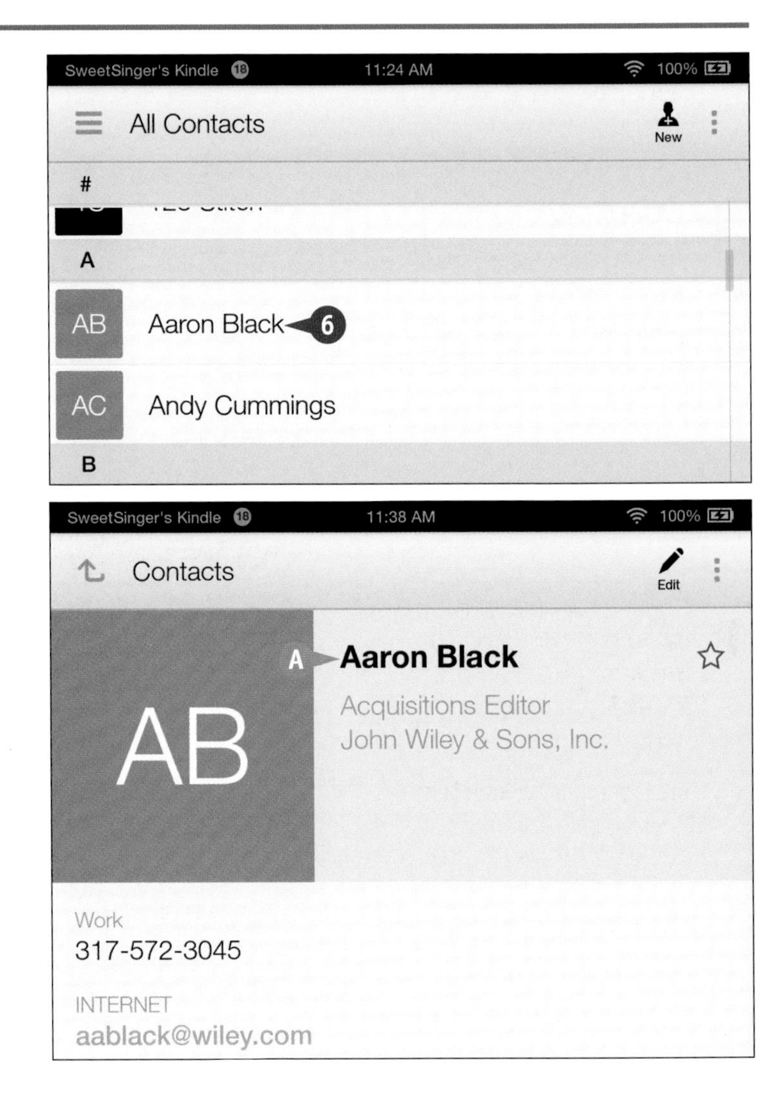

Search for a Contact

As your Contacts list grows, finding the right contact might seem like a daunting task, but your Fire tablet enables you to easily search for any contact on the device. Although you can choose the account in which you think the contact exists, doing so is not necessary. The Contacts app's search function searches all accounts even if you are not displaying the All Contacts view.

You can search for any word stored in a contact record; you are not limited to searching for a contact's name. For example, you can search for a company name and view all contact records that contain that company name.

Search for a Contact

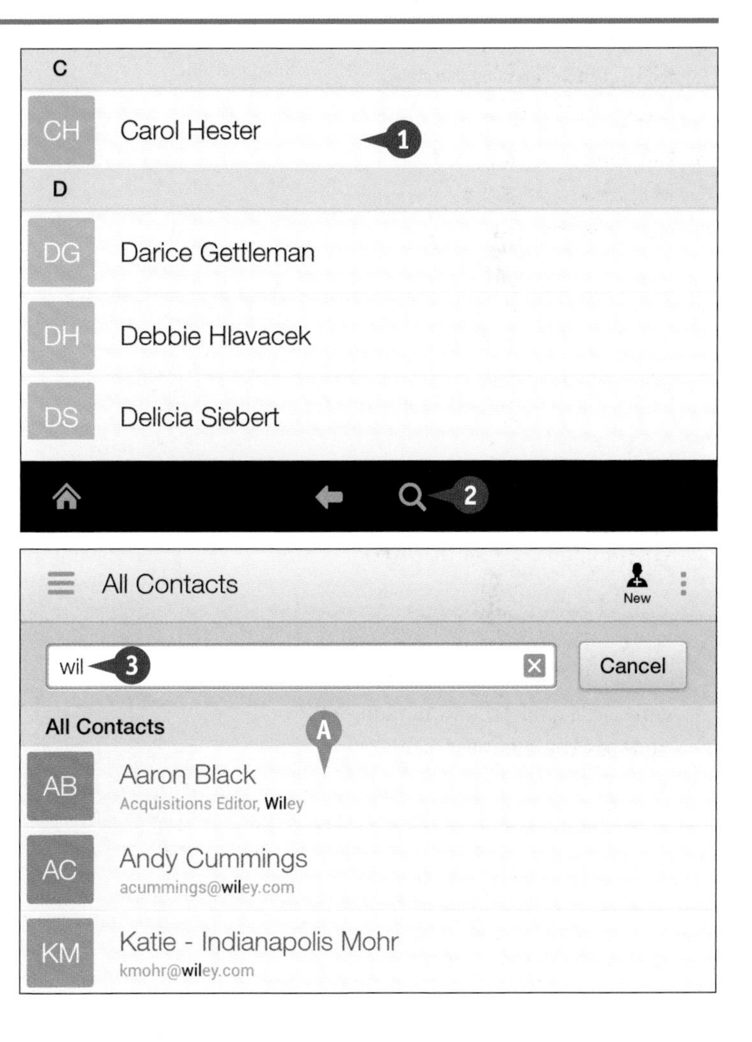

1. Follow steps **1** and **2** in the section "Open the Contacts App."

Note: To view All Contacts, tap the **Navigation** button (☰) and then tap **All Contacts**.

2. Tap the **Search** button (🔍).

The Search box appears.

3. Type some characters associated with the contact for which you want to search.

Ⓐ Matches appear below the Search box.

Establish Settings for Contacts

You can control the general behavior of the Contacts app. You can control whether the Contacts app synchronizes contacts across Amazon devices and services, and whether contacts on your Fire tablet synchronize with Facebook. You also can control whether contacts sort in the Contacts list in "first name, last name" order or in "last name, first name" order. You can even control the way the Contacts app displays contact names: first name first or last name first.

Establish Settings for Contacts

1. Follow steps **1** and **2** in the section "Open the Contacts App."
2. Tap the **Navigation** button (☰).

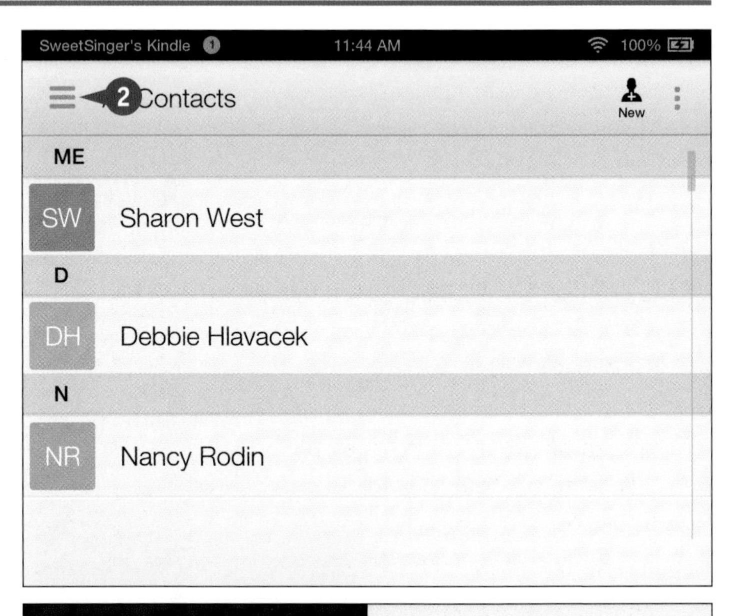

The Navigation panel appears.

3. Tap **Settings**.

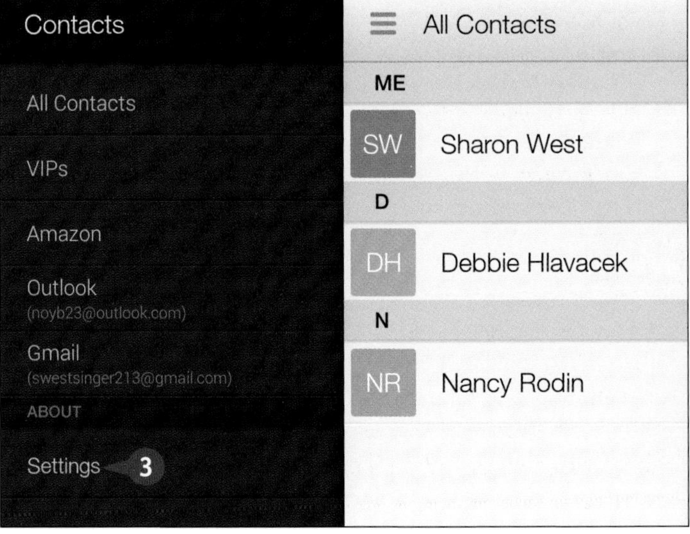

The Email, Contacts, Calendars settings screen appears.

4 Tap **Contacts General Settings**.

The Contacts General Settings screen appears.

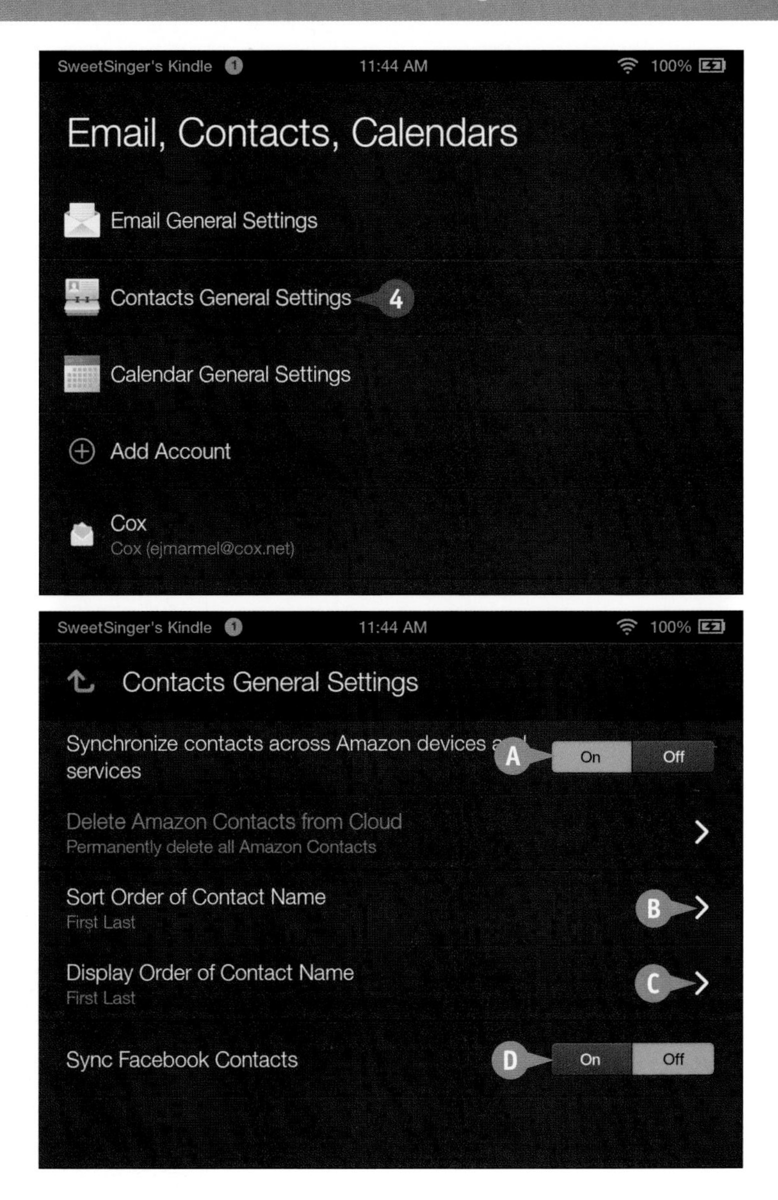

A You can control whether the Contacts app synchronizes contacts across Amazon devices and services.

B You can tap > to control the order in which contacts sort in the list.

C You can tap > to control the way the Contacts app displays contact names: first name first or last name first.

D You can control whether contacts on your Fire tablet synchronize with Facebook.

TIP

What is the Delete Amazon Contacts from Cloud option and why is it unavailable?
This option enables you to permanently delete all Amazon contacts from the Amazon Cloud. The option is unavailable as long as the **Synchronize contacts across Amazon devices and services** option is enabled, because that option controls whether the Fire tablet saves your contacts to the Amazon Cloud. If you opt to turn off this option, the Kindle prompts you to choose to either keep your Amazon contacts on your device or delete them from your device.

CHAPTER 10

Using the Calendar

Your Fire tablet comes with a Calendar app that you can use to track calendar-related information. Calendar is not a standalone app; it needs to sync with a web-based account such as Outlook.com, Gmail, or Hotmail. Once you add a web-based email account, the Fire tablet Calendar app functions as described in this chapter.

Open the Calendar App 210
Change Calendar Views 212
View or Hide Calendars 214
View an Event 215
Create an Event 216
Edit an Event. 218
Include Facebook Events 220

Open the Calendar App

You can use the Calendar app that comes with your Fire tablet to keep track of scheduled events in your life. Although Calendar is included with the Fire tablet, it is not an independent app; you cannot store events on it unless you have set up a web-based email account, such as a Gmail, Outlook.com, or Hotmail account. See Chapter 8 for details on setting up email accounts.

If you have not set up a web-based email account, you can use Calendar only to view dates.

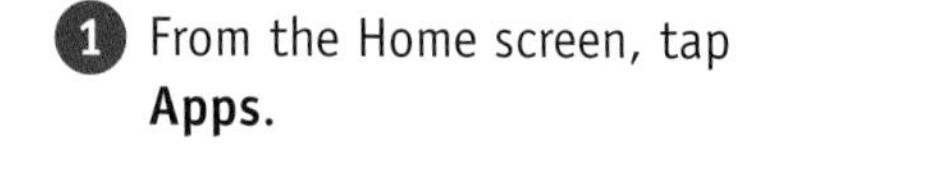

Open the Calendar App

1. From the Home screen, tap **Apps**.

   The Apps content library appears.

2. Tap **Calendar**.

The Calendar app opens.

Ⓐ The current view appears here.

Ⓑ In the Week view, the current week is selected.

Ⓒ The horizontal bar represents the current time.

3 Tap the **Home** button (🏠).

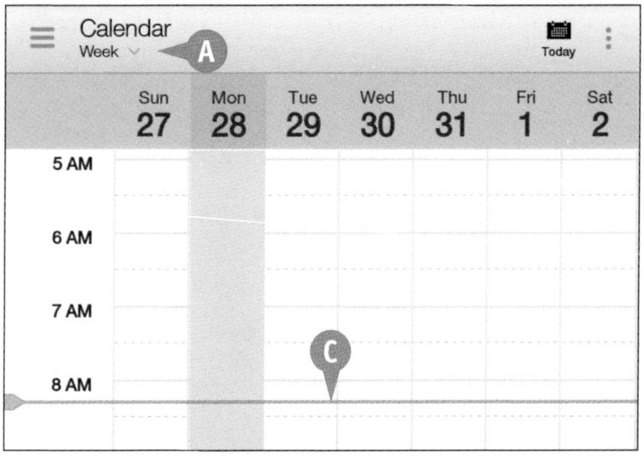

The Carousel appears.

Ⓓ The Calendar app appears in the Carousel.

TIP

Is there an easier way to open the Calendar app?
Yes. After you have opened the Calendar app, it appears in the Carousel. Or, you can swipe up on the Home screen to display the Favorites section, where you can tap a shortcut to the app Ⓐ.

Change Calendar Views

You can view the calendar in a variety of ways: one week, one day, or one month at a time, or you can simply view calendar events in list format.

In the Day, Week, and Month views, a Navigation bar appears across the bottom of the app; you can swipe in either direction to view the next or preceding days, weeks, or months, and you can tap in the Navigation bar to switch to a different day, week, or month. In List view, your calendar events display the description, day, date, and time of the event.

Change Calendar Views

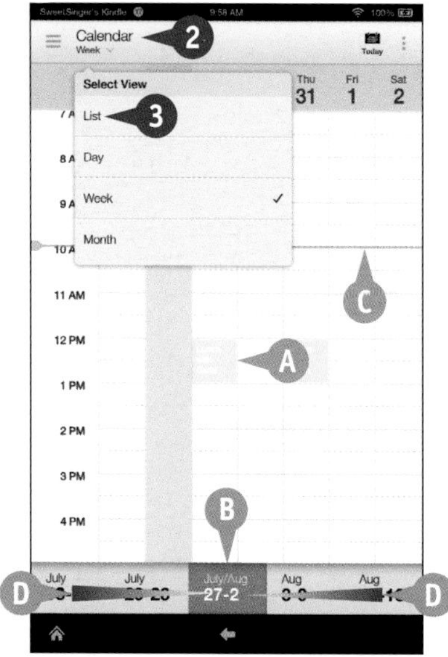

1. Follow steps **1** and **2** in the section "Open the Calendar App" to open the Calendar app in Week view.
   - (A) Events on the calendar look like this.
   - (B) The current week appears selected.
   - (C) If you are viewing the current week in Week view, this horizontal bar represents the current time.
   - (D) You can swipe here and tap to select a different week.
2. Tap **Calendar** to display the Select View menu.
3. Tap **List**.

   The Calendar app displays calendar events in list format.
4. Tap **Calendar**.
5. Tap **Day**.

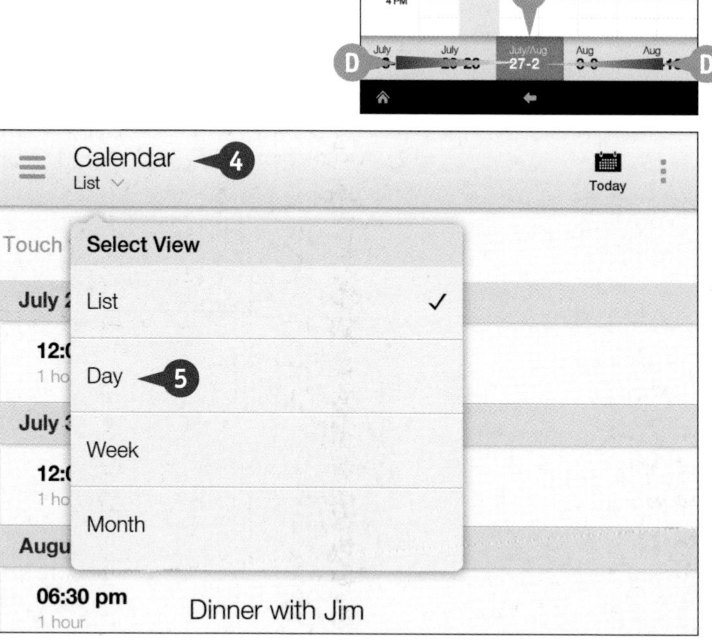

The Calendar app displays calendar events for the current day.

Ⓔ You can swipe left or right in the calendar to skip forward or backward a day at a time.

Ⓕ The currently selected day appears here.

Note: The current time appears in the Day view only if you are viewing the current day.

Ⓖ You can swipe here and tap to select a different day.

6 Tap **Calendar**.

7 Tap **Month** to display calendar events for the current month.

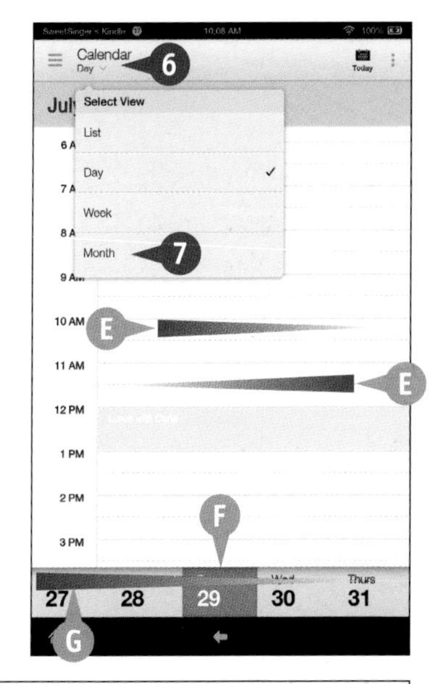

Ⓗ Yellow bars represent calendar events.

Ⓘ The currently selected month appears here.

Ⓙ You can swipe in either direction to view other months and tap any month to view that month's events.

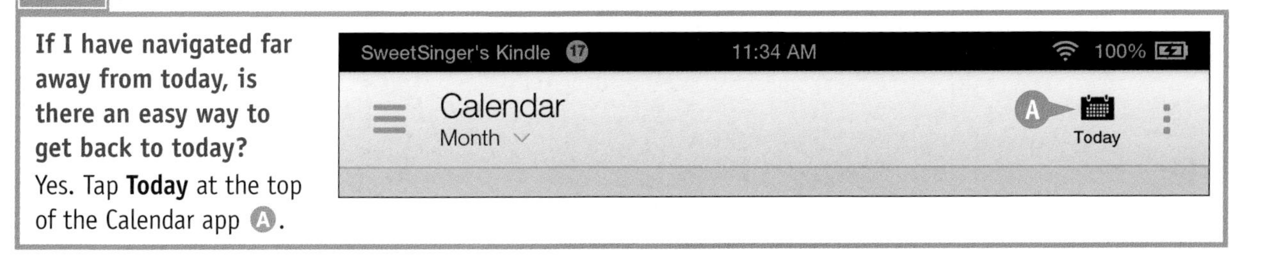

TIP

If I have navigated far away from today, is there an easy way to get back to today?

Yes. Tap **Today** at the top of the Calendar app Ⓐ.

View or Hide Calendars

If you have multiple web-based email accounts that sync to your Fire tablet, you can select the calendars of those accounts that you want the Calendar app to show. Each web-based email account comes with a calendar on which you can store events, and some provide more than one calendar. On your Fire tablet, you can choose which calendar's events appear in the Fire tablet Calendar app, or you can opt to view all calendars so that the Calendar app displays all events stored on all your calendars.

View or Hide Calendars

1. Follow steps **1** and **2** in the section "Open the Calendar App" to open the Calendar app in Week view.
2. Tap the **Navigation** button (☰).

The Navigation panel appears.

A. Check marks (☑) beside a calendar indicate that events on that calendar are visible in the Calendar app.

3. Tap any calendar to display its events.

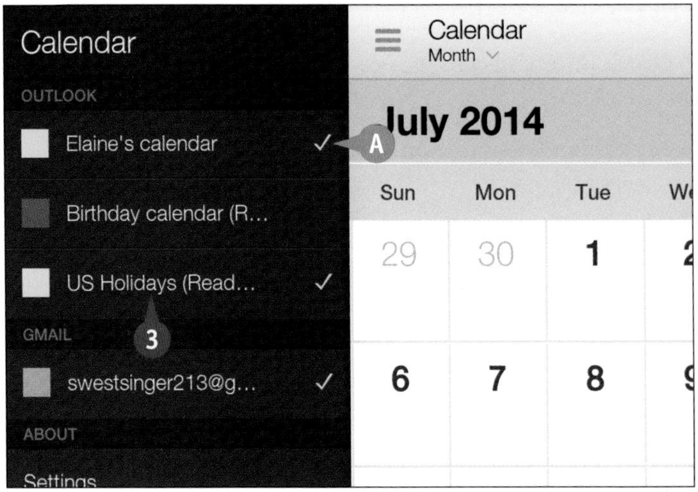

View an Event

You can view the details of any calendar event. By default, the Calendar app identifies events with a yellow bar in any view other than the Day view; to see the details of an event, you must start in Day view. In this view, some basic information appears at the event's time, including its title, start time, end time, and location — if you have entered that into the calendar. For more on entering calendar information, see the section "Create an Event." You can view all the details stored about the event without editing the event.

View an Event

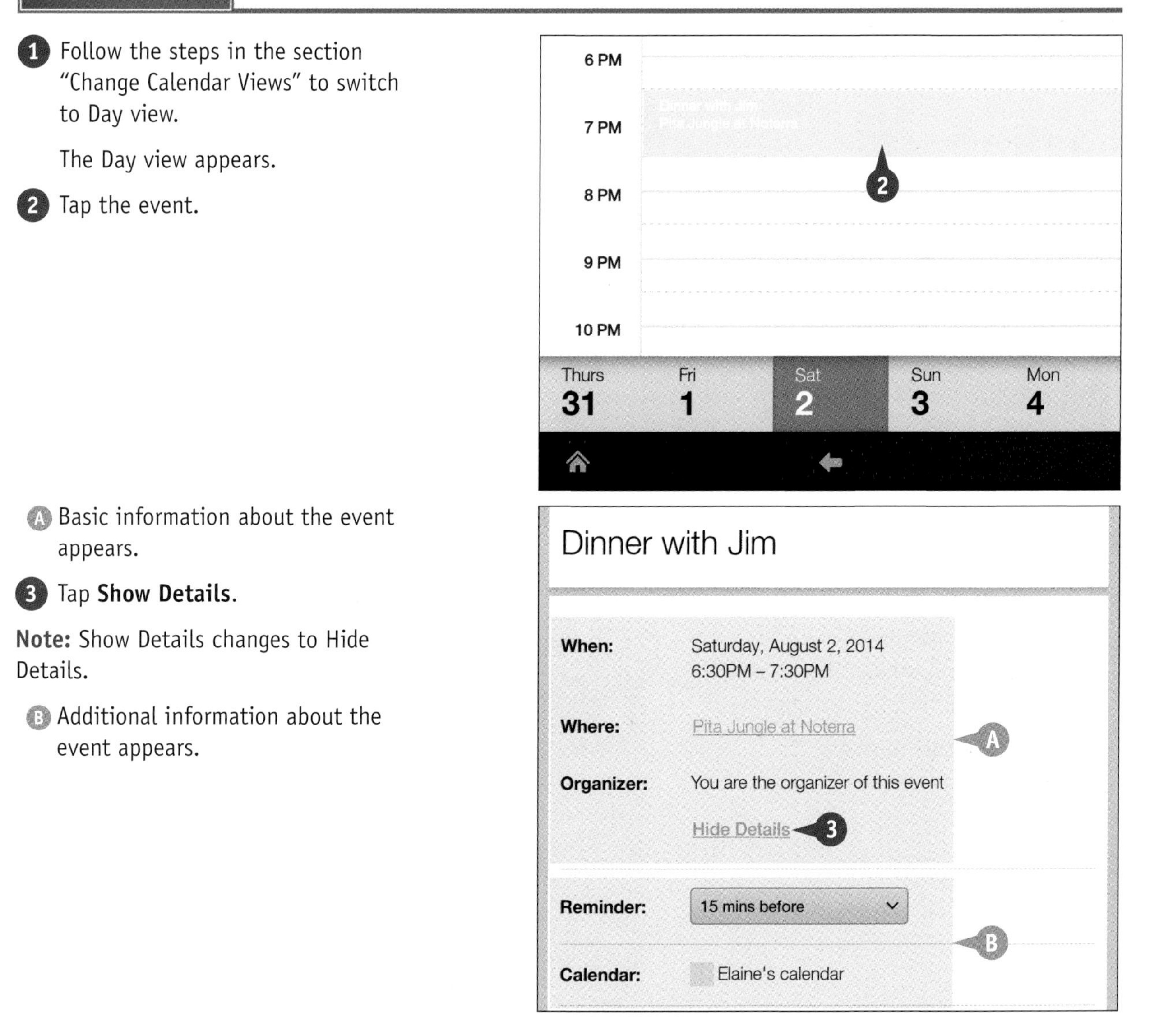

1. Follow the steps in the section "Change Calendar Views" to switch to Day view.

   The Day view appears.

2. Tap the event.

A. Basic information about the event appears.

3. Tap **Show Details**.

Note: Show Details changes to Hide Details.

B. Additional information about the event appears.

Create an Event

From any calendar view, you can create a new event. When you do so, you can define the name of the event, its start date and time, and, if appropriate, its end date and time. You also can type location information and set a reminder alarm that sounds at any time you specify before the event starts.

You can invite people in your Contacts list to attend the event, and, if you find it necessary, you can set up the event to repeat at an interval you specify.

Create an Event

1. Follow steps **1** and **2** in the section "Open the Calendar App" to open the Calendar app in Week view.
2. Tap ⋮.
3. Tap **New Event**.

The New Event window appears.

4. Type a title for the event.

A. You can type the event's location here.

5. Select a start time and date and, if appropriate, an ending time and date.

B. You can tap this option to set up a recurring event.

C. You can tap ⌄ to set the reminder time and the calendar for the event.

6. Tap ⊕ to invite a contact to the event.

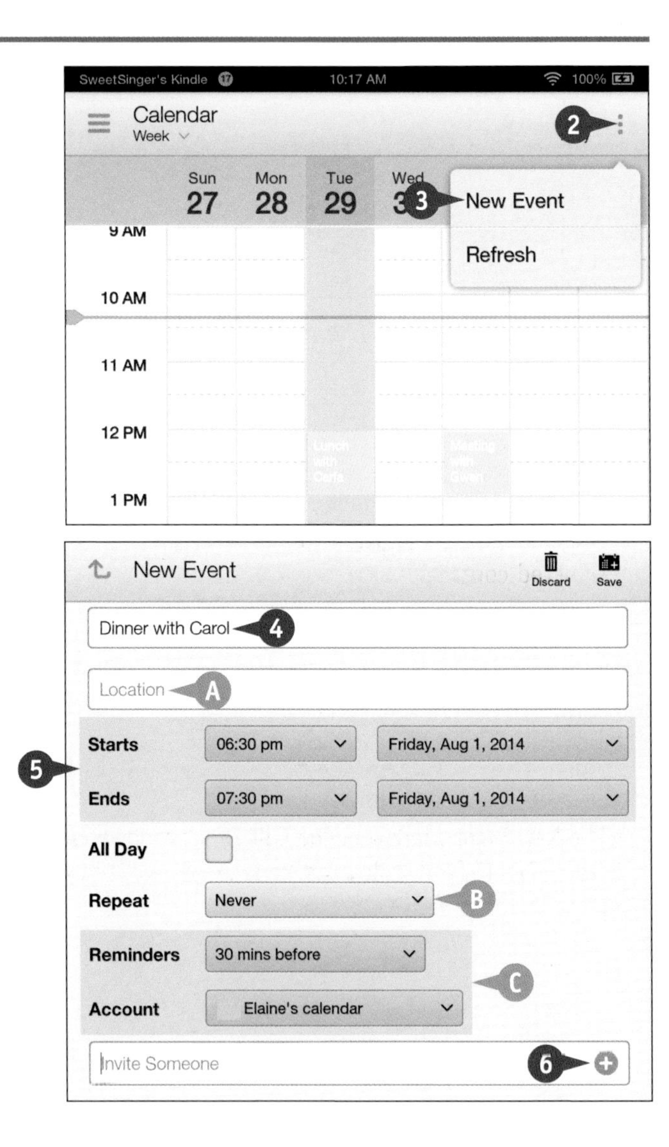

A list of your contacts appears.

D You can type here to search for a contact.

7 Tap a contact's name.

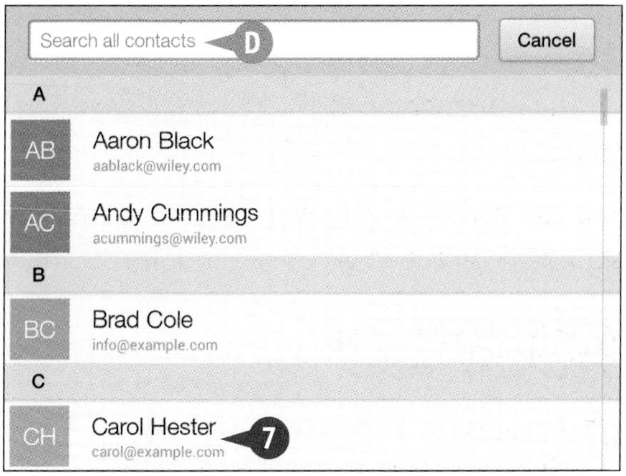

The New Event window reappears.

E The selected contact appears here.

8 Repeat steps **6** and **7** to add another contact.

F You can type any notes about the event here.

9 Tap **Save**.

The Calendar app saves the event, displays it on the calendar, and sends an email invitation to all selected contacts.

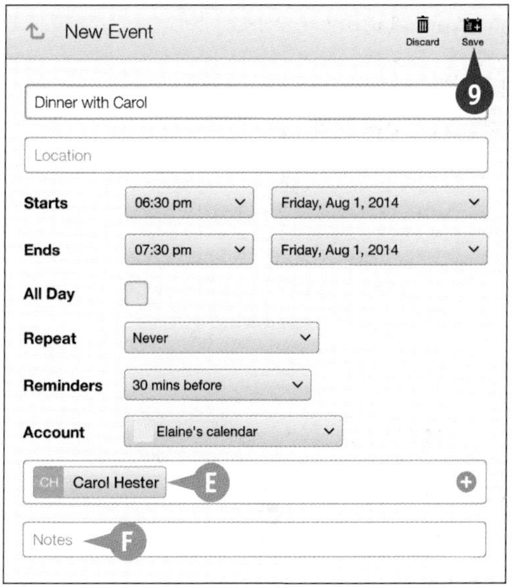

TIP

How do I set up a recurring event?

In the New Event window or the Edit Event window (see "Edit an Event" for details), tap **Repeat** (⌄) A and tap any choice other than Never.

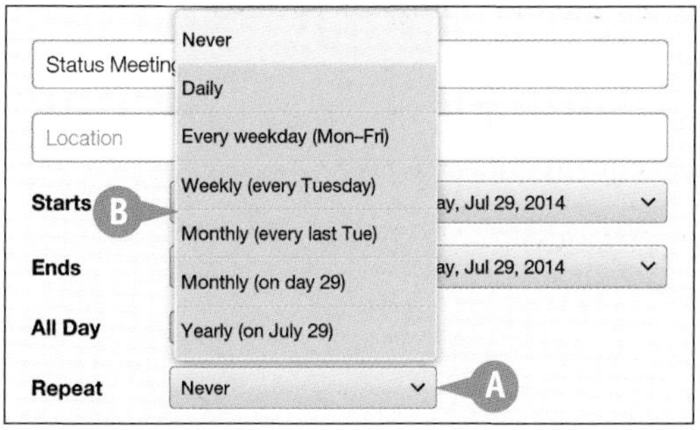

Edit an Event

After you create an event, invited participants may need you to change it (something that they cannot do themselves), or low attendance may require you to do so. As the event's organizer, you can change any field of the event, including its start and end times, title, and location. Doing so means that your participants are sent a second invitation, and the event updates on the calendar. If circumstances arise that make the meeting time or place impossible, you can delete an event, which also notifies any contacts of the cancellation.

Edit an Event

1. Follow steps **1** and **2** in the section "Open the Calendar App" to open the Calendar app in Week view.
2. Tap the event you want to edit.

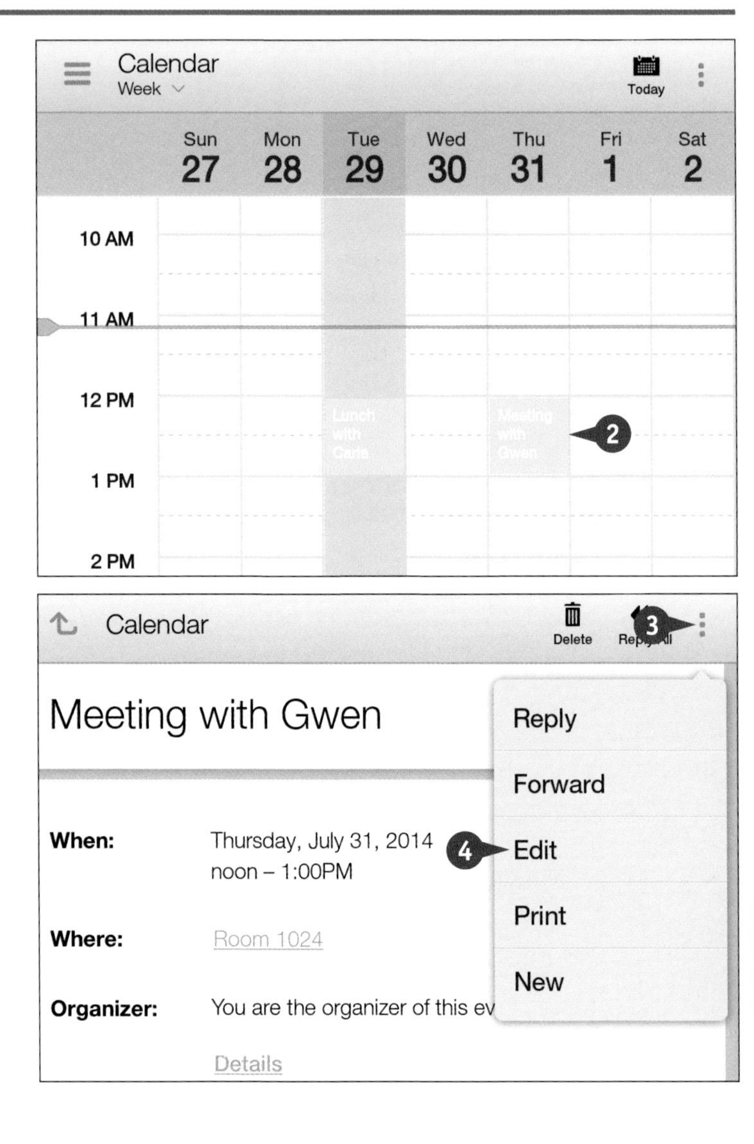

A preview of the event details appears.

3. Tap ⋮.

4. Tap **Edit.**

The Edit Event screen appears.

5. Make changes as appropriate.

This example changes the event time.

6. Tap **OK** if necessary.
7. Tap **Save**.

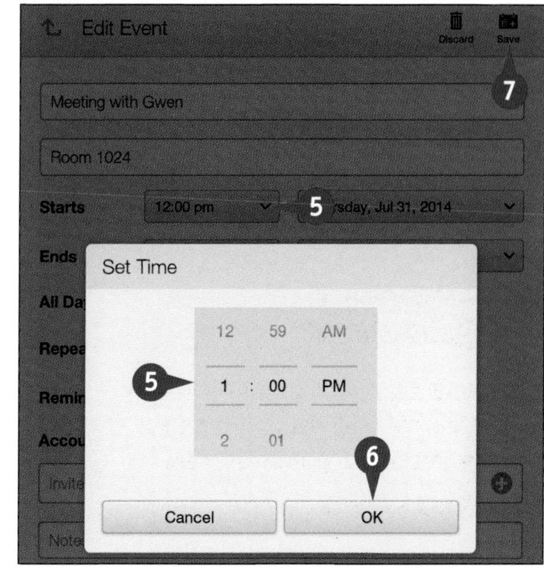

The Calendar app saves the event's changes and redisplays the calendar.

A The event in this example appears at its new time.

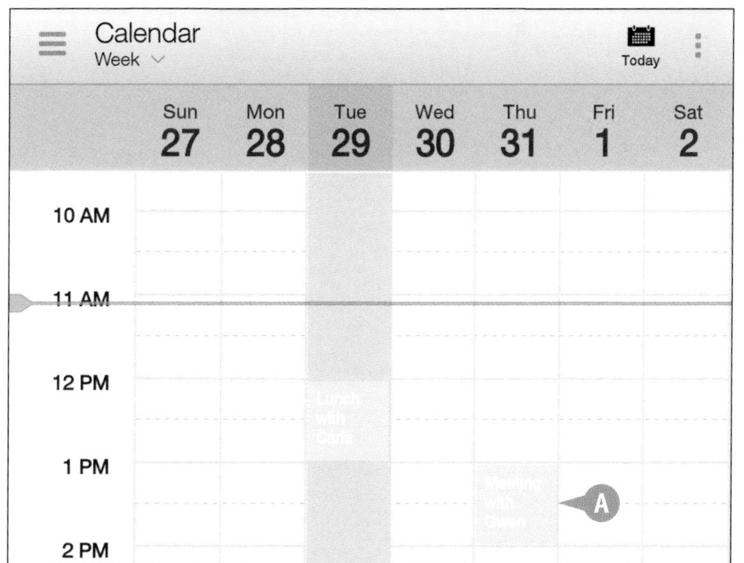

TIP

How do I delete an event?

To delete an event, tap the event. On the screen that appears, tap the **Delete** button (🗑) A.

Include Facebook Events

If you set up a Facebook account on your Fire tablet, you can opt to synchronize events on your Facebook calendar so that they also appear in the Kindle's Calendar app. For details on setting up a Facebook account on your Fire tablet, see "Connect to Social Networks" in Chapter 11.

The synchronization is two-way and happens automatically; that is, events you place on your Fire tablet calendar appear on Facebook, and vice versa. You can manually synchronize as described in "Open Settings" in Chapter 12. If need be, you can stop the syncing process altogether.

Include Facebook Events

1. Follow steps **1** and **2** in the section "Open the Calendar App" to open the Calendar app in Week view.
2. Tap the **Navigation** button (☰).

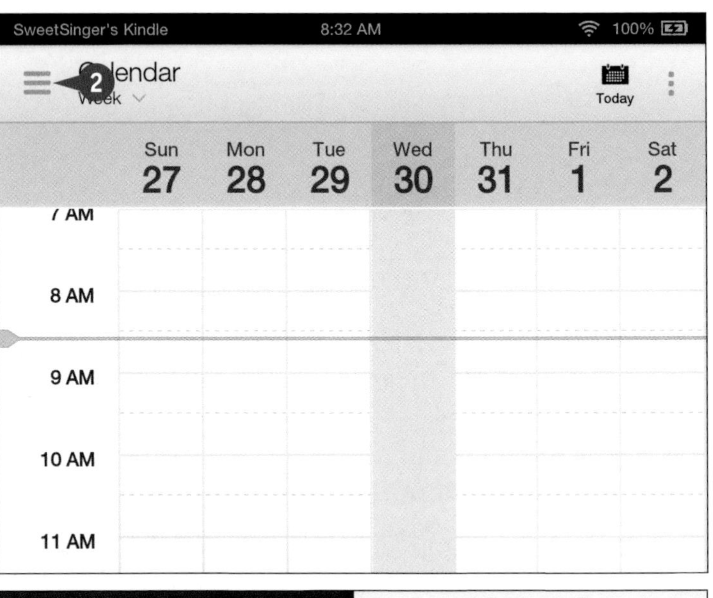

The Navigation panel appears.

3. Tap **Settings**.

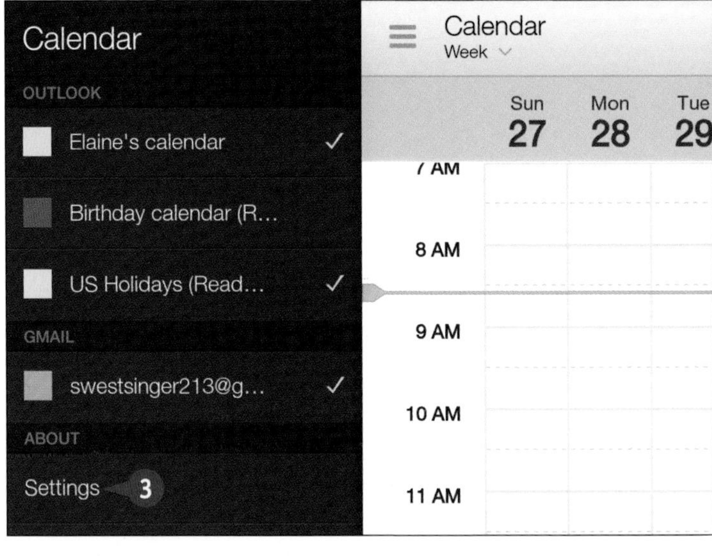

The Email, Contacts, Calendars settings page appears.

4. Tap **Calendar General Settings**.

The Calendar General Settings page appears.

5. Tap **On** to synchronize Facebook events with your Fire tablet calendar, and synchronization occurs automatically.

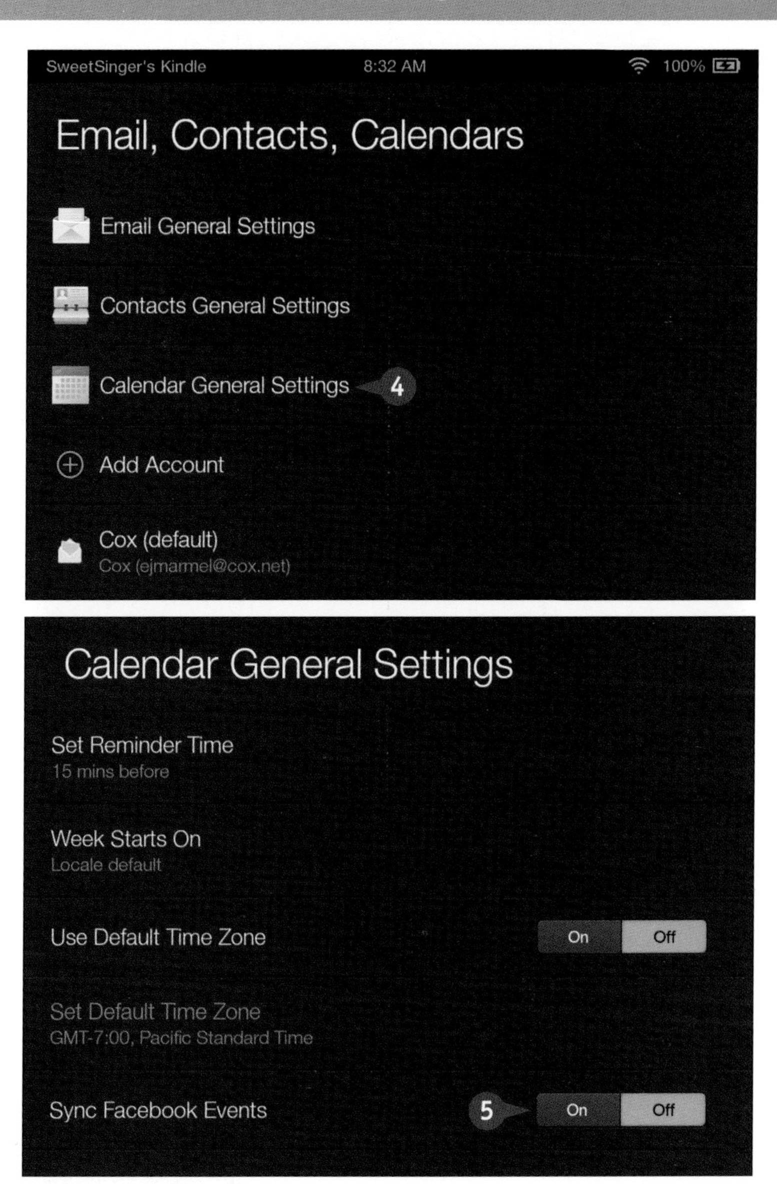

TIP

Can I stop synchronizing events between my Fire tablet and Facebook?

Yes. You can turn synchronization off by tapping **Off** (A) on the Calendar General Settings page, or you can disconnect your Facebook account from your Fire tablet entirely, as described in Chapter 11.

CHAPTER 11

Going Online

You can go online to browse the Internet using the Silk browser app that comes with the Fire tablet working in Silk efficiently can help optimize your browsing experience. You also can make Internet-based phone calls using the Skype app, and connect to and synchronize with your Facebook account.

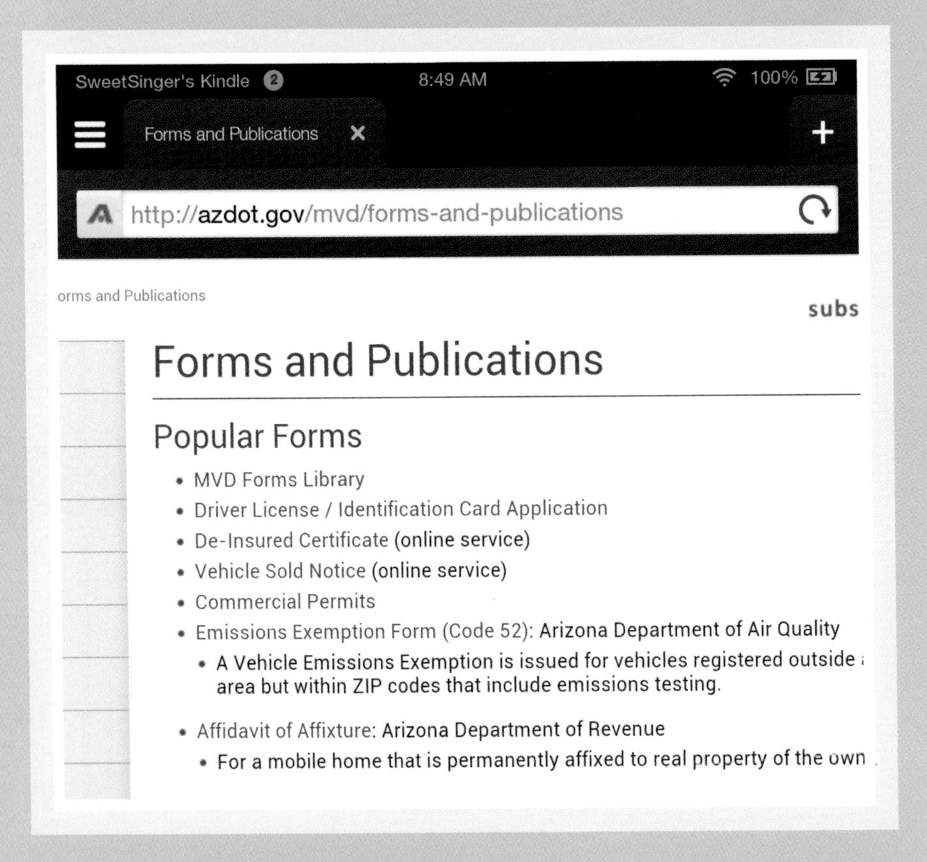

Open Silk 224
Understanding the Silk Screen 225
Open a New Tab 226
Bookmark a Page. 227
Navigate Using a Bookmark. 228
Using Reading View 229
Request Another View 230
Search a Page 232
Search the Web 234
Set the Default Search Engine. 236
View Browsing History 238
Review Silk Settings 239
Clear Browser Information 240
Download and Open a Document 242
Make Phone Calls Using Skype 244
Connect to Social Networks 246

Open Silk

Your Fire tablet comes with a web browser called *Silk* that you can use while connected to the Internet. The Silk browser has no set home page like other browsers; the first time you open Silk, you see the Most Visited page. When you subsequently open the browser, it displays the last page you viewed in your previous browsing session. Silk is a full-fledged browser; you can type addresses of websites to visit or search the web using the Bing, Google, or Yahoo! search engines, as described later in this chapter.

Open Silk

1. From the Home screen, tap **Web**.

Note: You might need to swipe to the left on the Home screen's Navigation bar to see Web. Alternatively, you can tap **Silk** in the Favorites section of the Home screen.

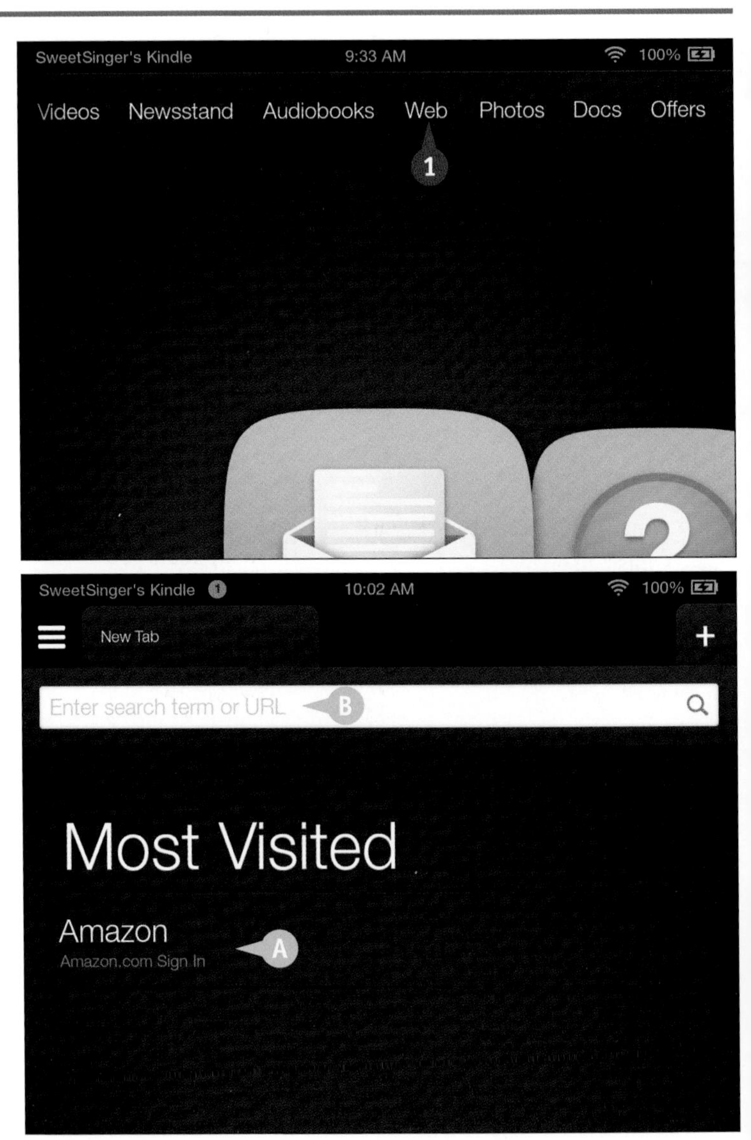

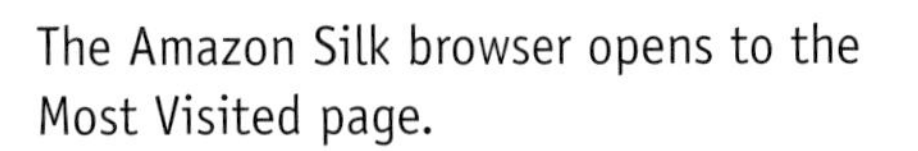

The Amazon Silk browser opens to the Most Visited page.

Note: The Most Visited page appears the first time you open the Silk browser and when you open a new browser tab. When you close the Silk browser and reopen it, the last website you viewed in your previous browsing session appears.

- **A** You can tap a website here.
- **B** If you prefer, tap here and type to search the web.

CHAPTER 11

Understanding the Silk Screen

The Silk browser contains all the tools you need to browse the web. You can navigate to websites, switch between websites, display a website in full-screen mode, and access additional page options. Some websites support zooming in or out of the site's content. To zoom, use two fingers and slide outward to enlarge the view. Slide inward to reduce the view. See the sections "Search the Web" and "Open a New Tab" for further details on these options.

A Address Bar

Displays the current website address. Tap in the bar and type URLs to visit the sites.

B Refresh Button

Refreshes the current page to display any updates to the page.

C Web Page Tab

Shows the current website name. You can open multiple web pages using these tabs.

D Options Bar

Contains further navigation tools.

E Home Button

Closes the Silk browser.

F Back Button

Displays previously viewed pages starting with the current page and moving to the earliest page in the order viewed.

G Forward Button

Becomes available after tapping the Back button and displays the current page followed by later pages.

H Full Screen Button

The Silk browser fills the entire screen and the Options and Address bars disappear. You redisplay them and exit full-screen mode by tapping .

I Menu Button

Displays additional options for the current web page.

J Search Tool

Opens the Address bar as you view any web page.

Open a New Tab

You can use tabs in the Silk browser to open multiple web pages and switch among them. You can open up to ten tabs at one time.

Tabs appear in the Tab bar across the top of the Silk browser window. You can close tabs at any time, and work with them in different ways. For example, you can close the current tab, close all other tabs except the current tab, close all tabs, add the website of a tab as a bookmark, or share the website with others.

Open a New Tab

1. Complete the steps in the section "Open Silk."
2. Tap + to open a new tab.

   The Most Visited page appears.

   Ⓐ Your new tab appears in the Tab bar.

Note: To switch to a different tab, tap it. You might need to swipe left or right in the Tab bar to bring the tab you want in view.

   Ⓑ You can tap ✕ in the current tab to close that tab.

3. Press and hold any tab.

   Ⓒ This menu appears; from here you can close the tab you selected in step **3**, close all other tabs except the tab you selected in step **3**, close all tabs, add the website of the tab you selected in step **3** as a bookmark, or share the website with others.

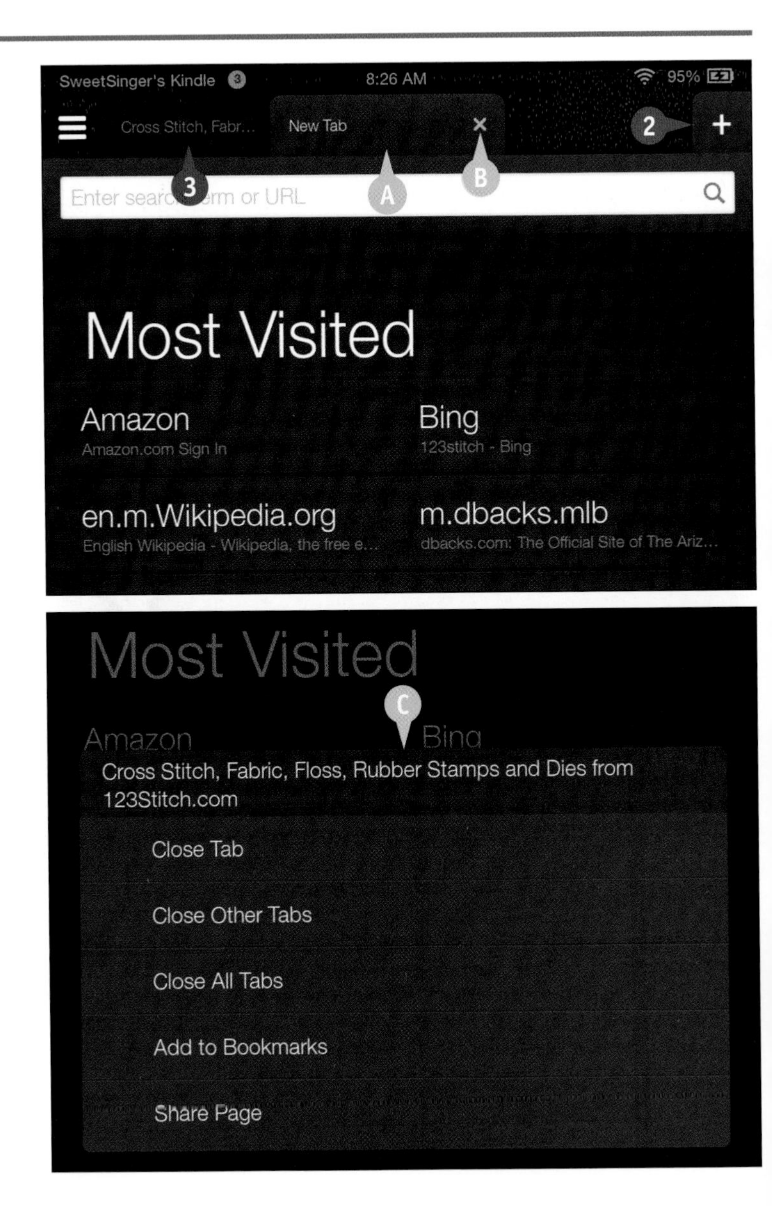

Bookmark a Page

You can add a *bookmark* for a web page in the Silk browser. Using bookmarks, you can quickly and easily redisplay a particular web page. Think of a bookmark in the Silk browser the same way as you would a physical bookmark in an actual book — as a means to mark your place.

As you create a bookmark, the website you are marking suggests a name, but you can change that name to something you can more easily recognize. Also, you can create as many bookmarks as you want, and you learn to use them in the next section, "Navigate Using a Bookmark."

Bookmark a Page

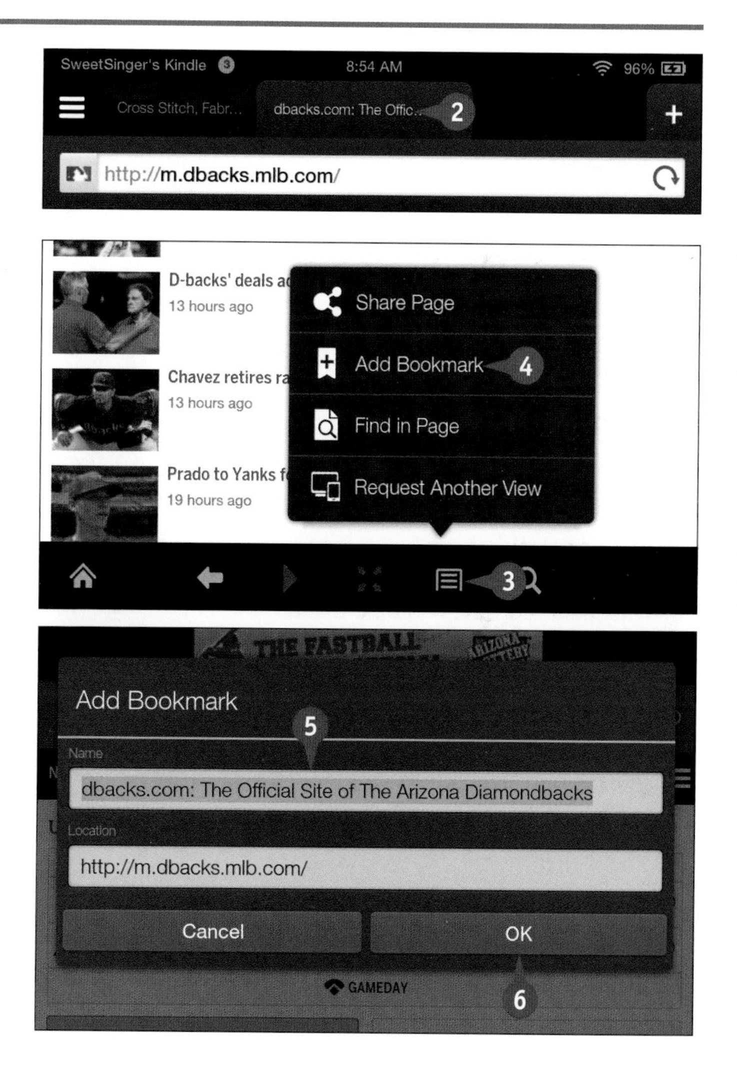

1. Complete the steps in the section "Open Silk."
2. Display the web page you want to bookmark.
3. Tap ▤.
4. Tap **Add Bookmark**.

The Add Bookmark dialog box appears.

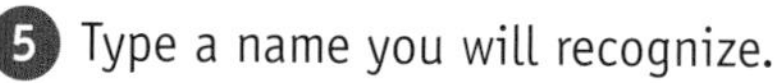

5. Type a name you will recognize.
6. Tap **OK**.

Silk saves the bookmark.

Note: See the next section to learn how to use the bookmark.

Navigate Using a Bookmark

After you create bookmarks for various websites, you can use them to quickly and easily visit those sites. All your bookmarks appear on the Silk browser's Bookmarks page and are organized, by default, in alphabetical order by title. You can opt to organize your bookmarks by order viewed, with the last site accessed appearing first, or by the number of times you have visited sites, with the site you have visited most appearing first.

By default, bookmarks appear as icons on the Bookmarks page, but you can view bookmarks in a list, which enables you to simultaneously see more bookmarks.

Navigate Using a Bookmark

1. Complete the steps in the section "Open Silk."
2. Tap the **Navigation** button (☰) to display the Navigation panel.
3. Tap **Bookmarks**.

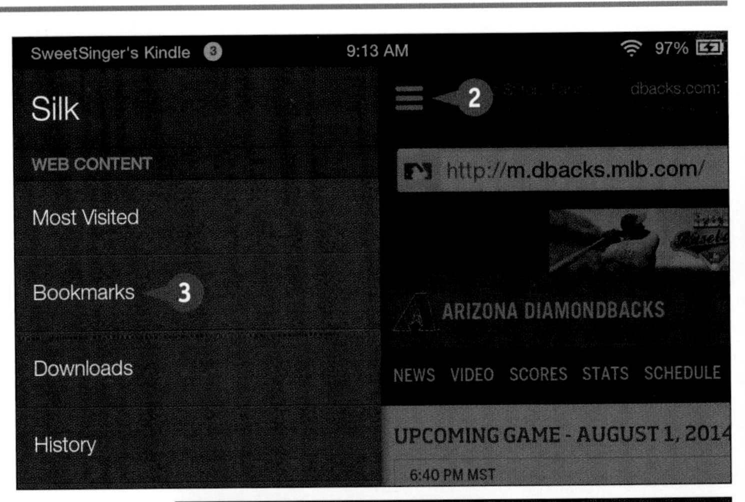

The Bookmarks page appears.

- Ⓐ Bookmarks appear as icons and, by default, are organized alphabetically by title.
- Ⓑ You can tap here to display other ways you can organize bookmarks.
- Ⓒ You can tap here to display bookmarks in a list instead of as icons.

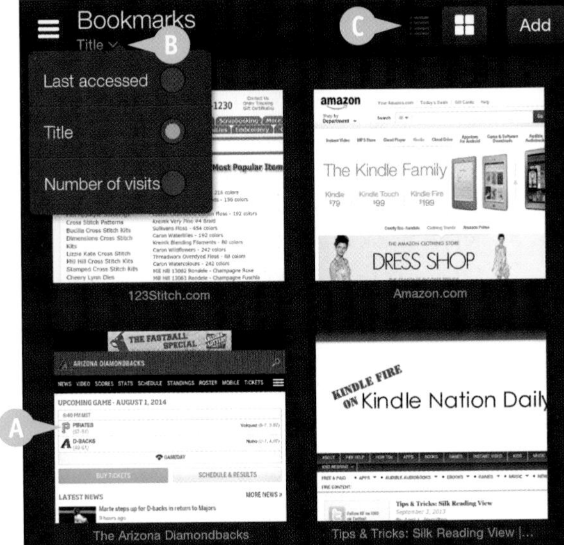

CHAPTER 11

Using Reading View

Silk's Reading View feature eliminates all pictures from a webpage and redisplays the page using text only. Reading View enables you to focus on what you are reading without distractions and without having to scroll through a lot of images to get to the text you want to read. When you are ready, you can easily redisplay the images that appeared on the page originally.

Reading view is not available for all websites; when it is available, you see a green Reading View button beside the Address bar.

Using Reading View

1. Complete the steps in the section "Open Silk."
2. Navigate to a website you want to visit.

   The Reading View button appears if the website offers the feature.
3. Tap **Reading View**.

The site's page reappears displaying only text.

A You can tap ⊗ to return to the original view of the page.

B You can tap ▬ to redisplay the Options bar and the Address bar. On the Address bar, a black-and-white version of the Reading View button appears. You can tap that version of the Reading View button to redisplay the original view of the page.

online.wsj.com

A

Gas Explosions in Taiwan Kill at Least 25

Underground explosions in Taiwan's second-largest city triggered fires that ripped through the streets. The WSJ's Jake Lee speaks with Eva Dou about the situation on the ground.

TAIPEI—Deadly explosions caused by a gas leak overnight killed at least 25 people and injured 257 in the southern Taiwanese city of Kaohsiung, according to government officials.

Underground explosions in Taiwan's second-largest city triggered fires that ripped off manhole covers on roads and cratered large boulevards, local television footage showed. Roads exploded with flames, overturning cars and collapsing houses. Many streets are still littered with rubble and impassible by ambulances.

Economic Minister Chang Chia-juch said Friday that officials are still unable to determine what caused the blast, though an initial investigation indicated the leak could have occurred in an underground pipeline that transports propene, a highly flammable, nearly odorless petrochemical used for polyesters. Kaohsiung is one of B n's centers of petrochemical producti

Request Another View

Many websites have two versions of their site: one designed for the large screens typically associated with desktop computers, and another designed for use on mobile devices. In some cases, if you navigate to a website on a mobile device, you automatically see the mobile version of the website. If a mobile version is available but you do not see it, you can use the Request Another View command to switch to the mobile version.

You also can use the Request Another View command to switch to the desktop version from the mobile version.

Request Another View

1 Complete the steps in the section "Open Silk."

2 Navigate to a website.

Note: This section uses *The Wall Street Journal* website.

3 Tap the **Menu** button (▤).

The Silk menu opens.

4 Tap **Request Another View**.

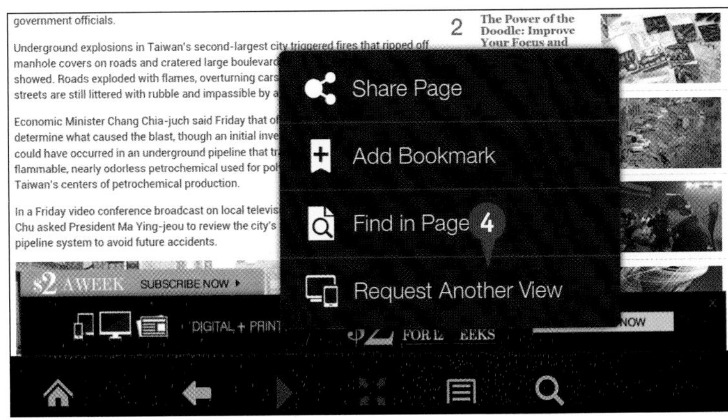

The Request View For menu opens.

5. Tap a view (■ changes to ◙); this example switches to the mobile version of the website.

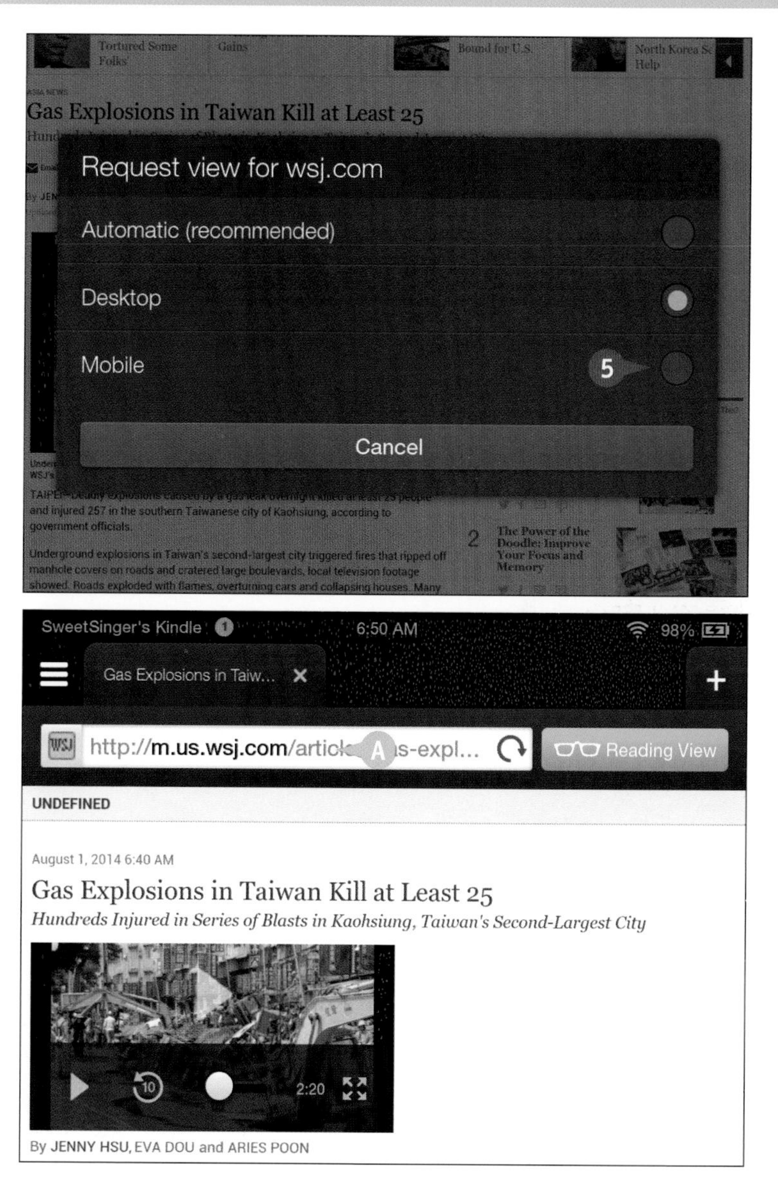

The version of the website you requested appears.

A. Note that mobile website addresses typically begin with *m*.

TIP

Why should I switch to a mobile website while using my Fire tablet?
Mobile websites are designed specifically to function on mobile devices, removing incompatible plug-ins such as Adobe Flash, and decreasing the time needed to load each web page. Therefore, while using your Fire tablet, you will probably find your web browsing experience optimized when you view mobile websites. You can, of course, switch to a desktop version of any website. If you prefer to use a desktop version and that site supports zooming, you can zoom in to enlarge the text. Place two fingers on your Fire tablet and then slide them apart to zoom in.

Search a Page

You can search any web page for specific phrases and keywords. After you display the page and provide the search term, the Silk browser temporarily highlights all words on the page that match all or part of the term. To highlight fewer words, you provide more specific information in your search term. For example, if you type **explo**, the Silk browser will highlight *explode, explodes, explosions, explore, explores, explorer*, and *explorers* if those words appear on the page. But, if you type **explode**, the Silk browser will highlight only *explode* and *explodes*.

Search a Page

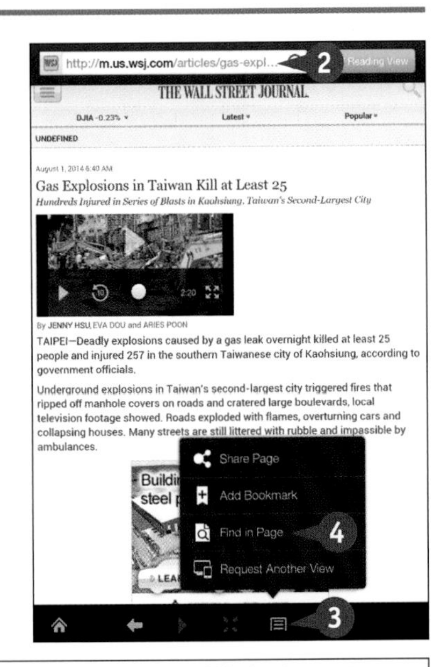

1. Complete the steps in the section "Open Silk."
2. Navigate to a web page.
3. Tap ▤.
4. Tap **Find in Page**.

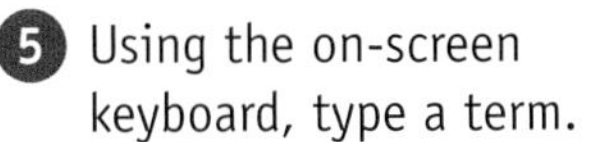

5. Using the on-screen keyboard, type a term.
6. Tap **Done**.

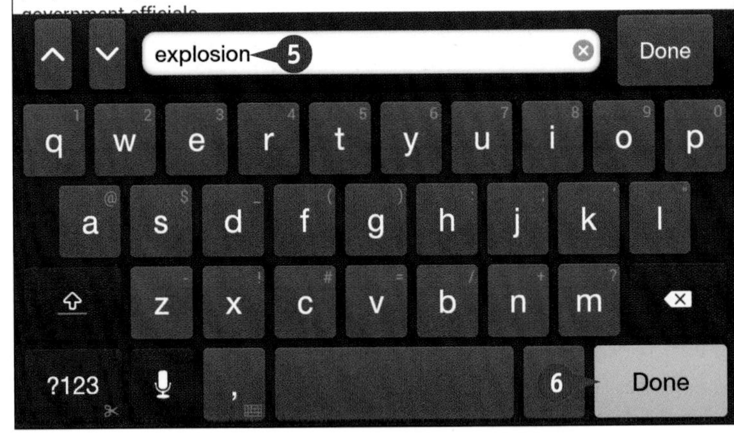

Words that match the search term appear highlighted.

A The currently selected word appears in orange; other matching terms appear in yellow.

B You can tap these buttons to select the next or previous word that matches the search term.

7 Tap **Done**.

Silk cancels the search and removes highlighting from the page.

August 1, 2014 6:40 AM

Gas Explosions in Taiwan Kill at Least 25

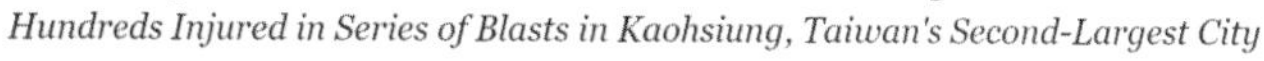
Hundreds Injured in Series of Blasts in Kaohsiung, Taiwan's Second-Largest City

By JENNY HSU, EVA DOU and ARIES POON

TAIPEI—Deadly explosions caused by a gas leak overnight killed at least 25 people and injured 257 in the southern Taiwanese city of Kaohsiung, according to

TIP

How does the page look as I select the next or previous word that matches the search term?

As you move from word to word, the selected word appears highlighted in orange A whereas all other matches appear highlighted in yellow B.

Search the Web

You can search the entire Internet for anything you want, including products, services, and information. Remember, though, that just because you see something in print does not make it true; trust information you find on the Internet only after you have established its veracity.

You search the web using a search engine; by default, Silk on your Fire tablet uses Bing as the search engine, but you can change to a different search engine, as described in the section "Set the Default Search Engine."

Search the Web

1. From any page, tap the **Search** button (🔍).

Note: This example starts on the Most Visited page.

The on-screen keyboard appears.

A. A list appears of bookmarked sites, sites you have already visited, and searches you have already made.

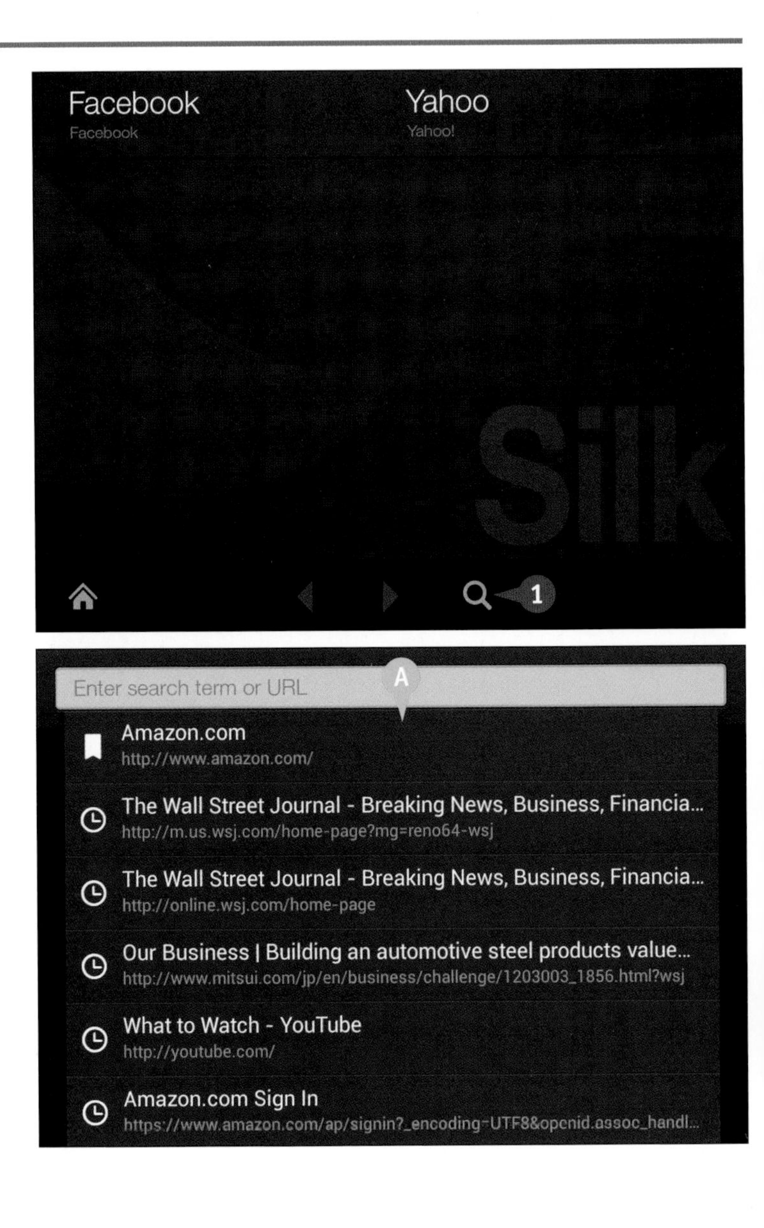

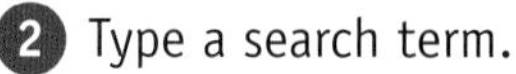

2 Type a search term.

B As you type, a list of search terms containing the words you have typed appears.

C You can swipe up or down as needed to scroll through the list.

3 Tap an item in the list.

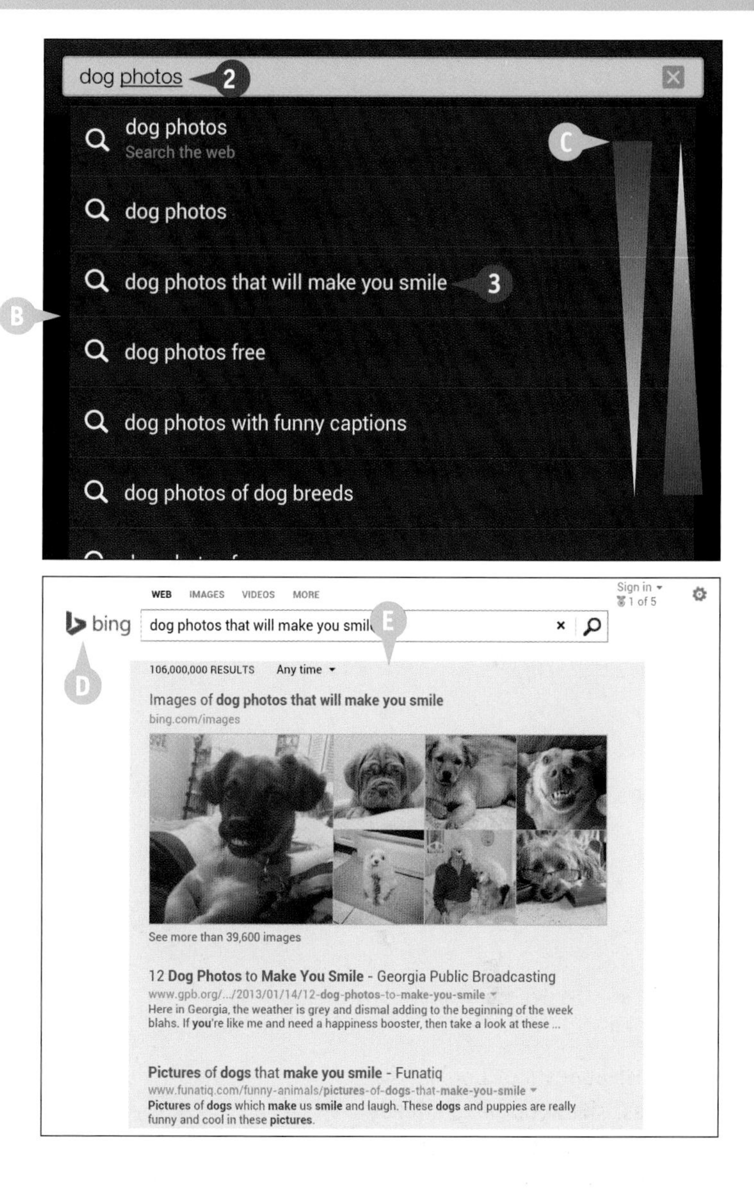

D The default search engine's page appears.

E Links that match the search term you selected appear on the page.

TIP

What should I do if no term in the list matches the term for which I want to search?

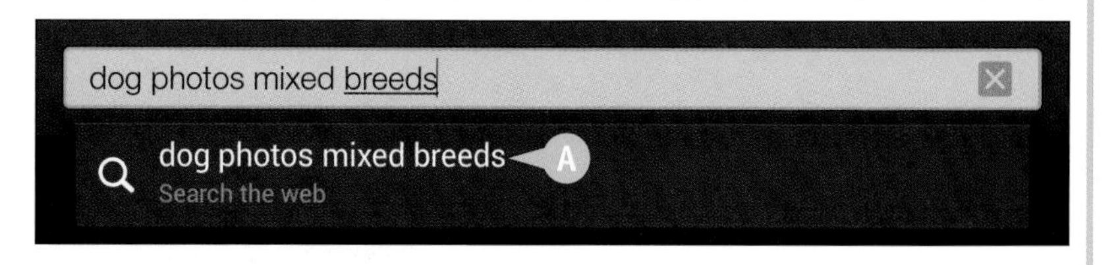

Continue typing to finish entering the term A. When you finish typing, your term will be the only one in the list. Tap it or tap **Go** on the bottom right of the on-screen keyboard.

Set the Default Search Engine

By default, the Silk browser on your Fire tablet uses the Bing search engine, but you might prefer to use another search engine permanently. Silk enables you to set Bing, Google, or Yahoo! as your default search engine.

Search engines are programs that search and catalog content on the Internet; when you type a term, the search engine displays links it has found during its cataloging process. The number of links that appear depends on the search engine you use and how well it does its job.

Set the Default Search Engine

1. Tap the **Navigation** button (☰) to display the Navigation panel.
2. Tap **Settings**.

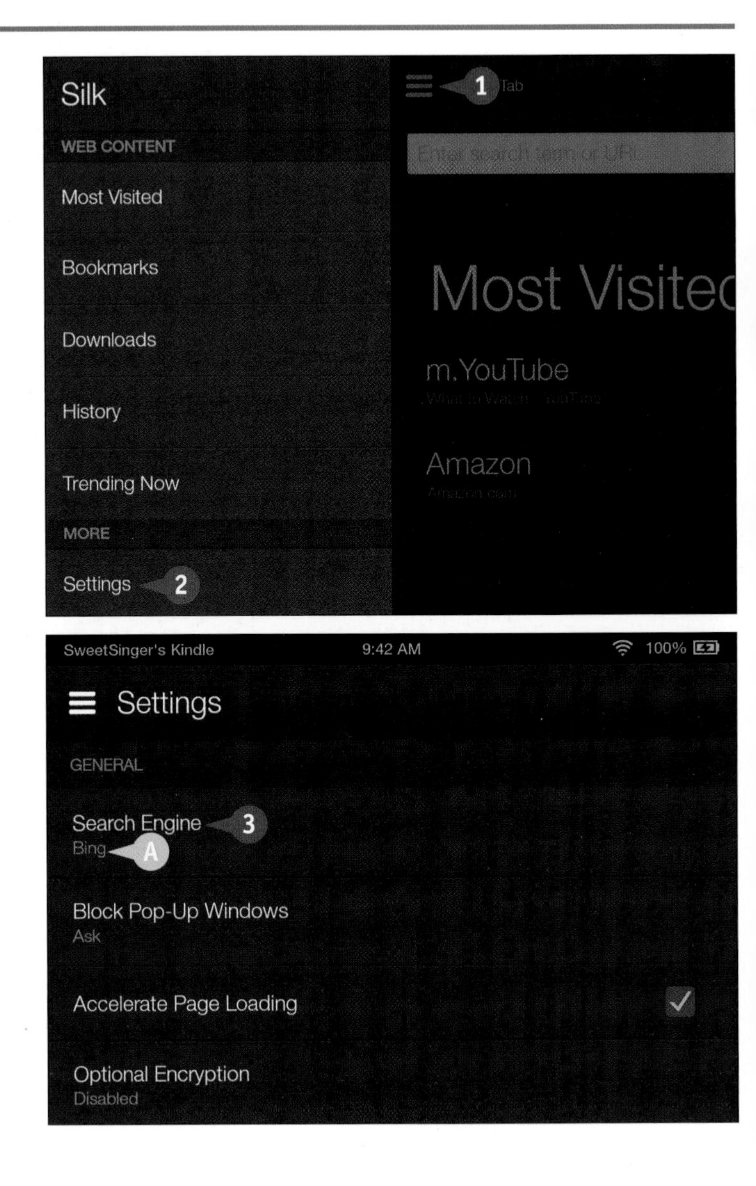

The Settings page appears.

A. The currently selected search engine appears here.

3. Tap **Search Engine**.

The Search Engine dialog box appears.

4 Tap the search engine you want to use as the default (■ changes to ◙).

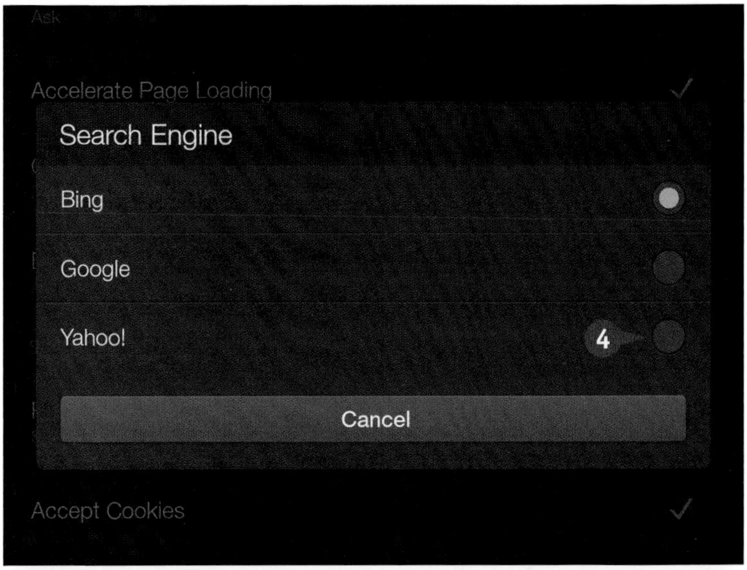

The Settings page reappears.

B The result of your change appears here.

Note: When you search the Internet as described in the section "Search the Web," the search page provides results in the new default search engine.

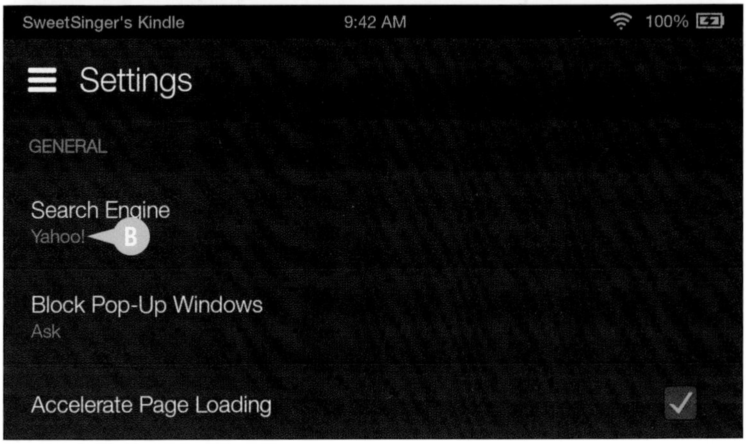

TIP

Can I search using some other search engine besides Yahoo!, Google, or Bing?

Yes and no. Although you cannot set any other search engine to be your default search engine, you can use any search engine. And, if you bookmark that search engine for easy access, you essentially create a viable substitute for the default. Navigate to the search engine's web page, and then create a bookmark for the page as described in the section "Bookmark a Page." Then, to use the search engine, navigate to the bookmarked page as described in the section "Navigate Using a Bookmark."

View Browsing History

Reviewing browsing history can come in handy when you remember that you saw something on the Internet — a bargain, information on a product, a news story, or something else — but you cannot remember exactly where you saw it. By reviewing your browsing history, you might be able to identify the website containing the information and revisit the site.

The Silk browser organizes sites you have visited by day; so, if you thought you saw the information on a particular date, you can easily narrow down your search.

View Browsing History

1. Tap the **Navigation** button (☰) to display the Navigation panel.
2. Tap **History**.

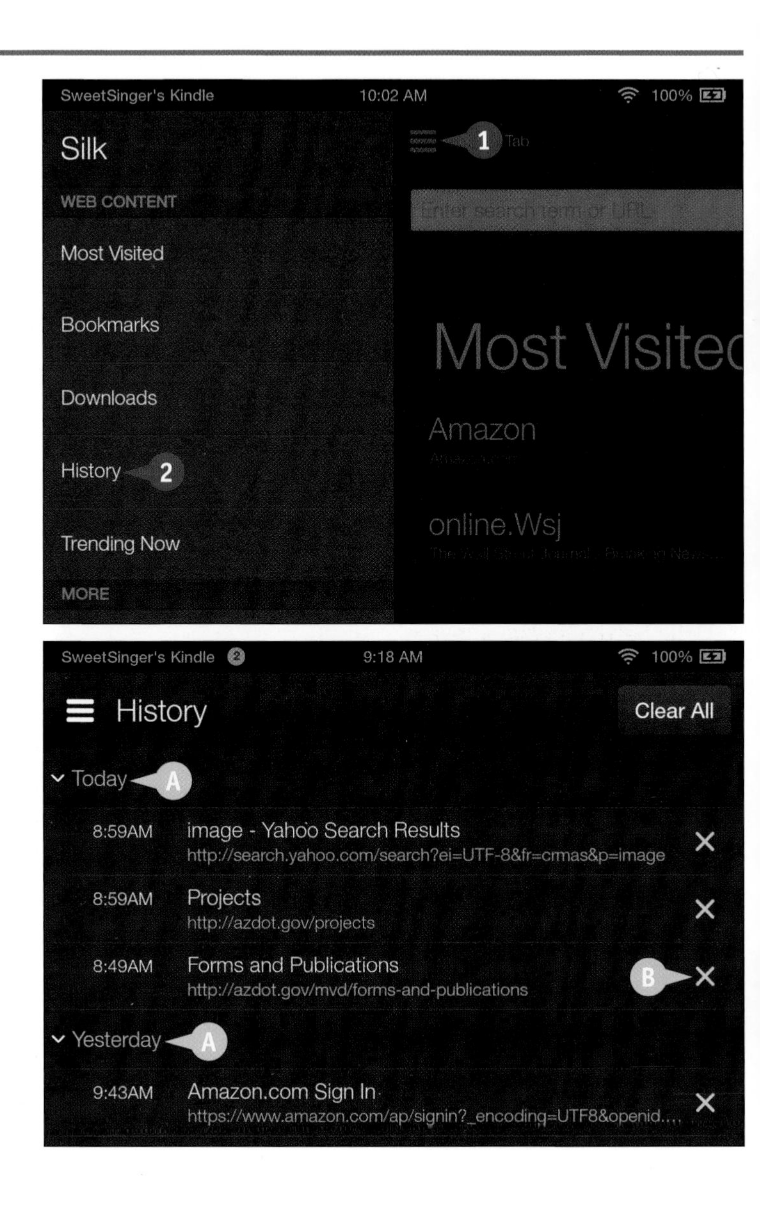

The History page appears.

- **A** Sites you have visited are organized by date.
- **B** You can delete any individual site by tapping the Close button (☒) beside it and then tapping **Delete marked items** at the bottom of the screen.

Review Silk Settings

You can control Silk's behavior under some circumstances. For example, Silk sends your requests for web pages either to the original server where the page resides or to the Amazon Cloud servers — whichever is more efficient — and does not, by default, encrypt the website addresses. If you opt to encrypt the website addresses, Silk encrypts the requests that go through the Amazon Cloud servers; be aware, however, that encrypting can slow down page loading.

Other settings you can control include deciding whether Silk remembers passwords you type, accepts cookies, provides your location to websites that request it, or prompts you before downloading information.

Review Silk Settings

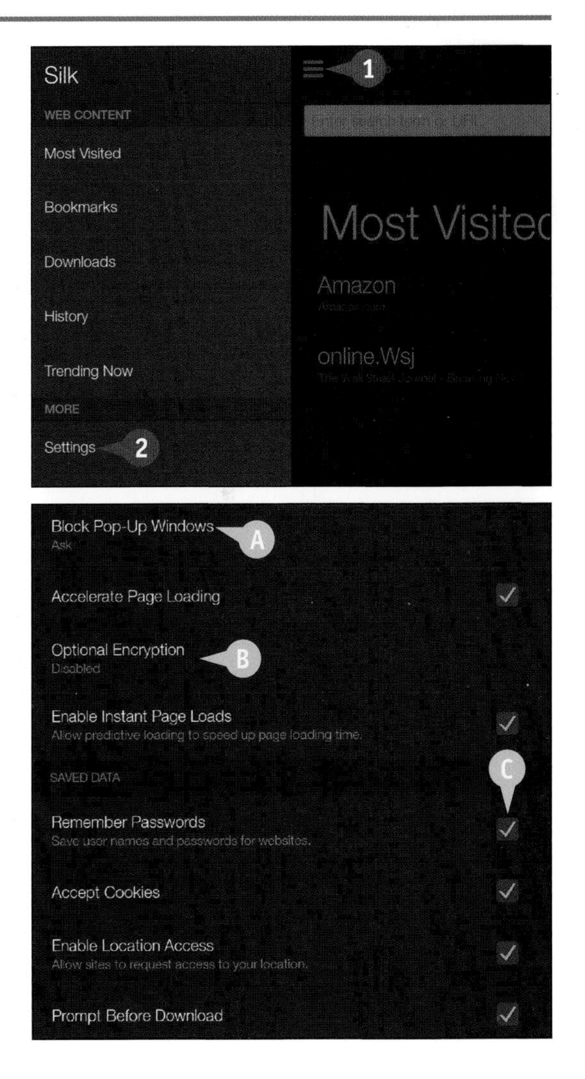

1 Tap the **Navigation** button (☰) to display the Navigation panel.

2 Tap **Settings**.

The Settings page appears.

A You can tap **Block Pop-Up Windows** to control how Silk handles pop-up windows.

B You can tap **Optional Encryption** to enable encryption.

C If you tap these check boxes, Silk does not remember passwords you type, accept cookies from websites, provide your location to websites that request it, or prompt you before downloading information.

Clear Browser Information

You can clear information that Silk stores as you browse, which can be particularly helpful if Silk begins to behave in unexpected ways. For example, if a web page you visit seems to have incorrect information on it, clearing the *cache* — an area where Silk stores information to speed up your browsing experience — may fix the problem.

In particular, you can clear the history of websites you visit, passwords you store, and cookies that websites place on your Fire tablet when you visit them. In addition, you can clear the location information you provide to websites that request it, as well as Silk's cache.

Clear Browser Information

1. Tap the **Navigation** button (☰) to display the Navigation panel.
2. Tap **Settings**.

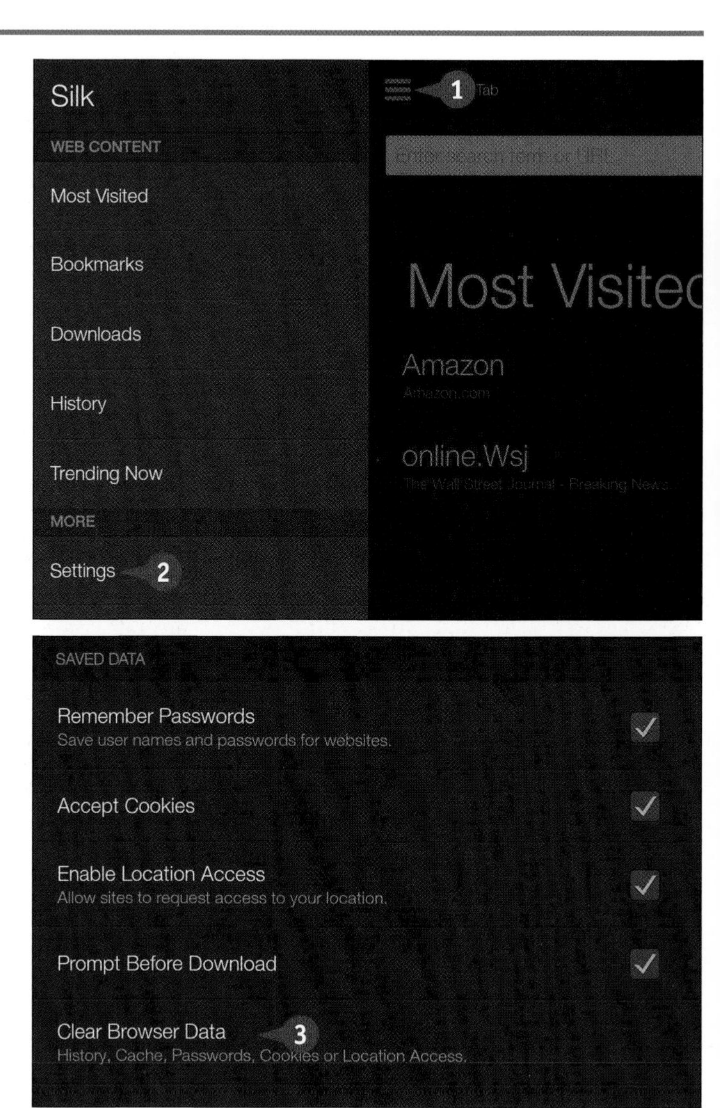

The Settings page appears.

 Tap **Clear Browser Data**.

The Clear Browser Data dialog box appears.

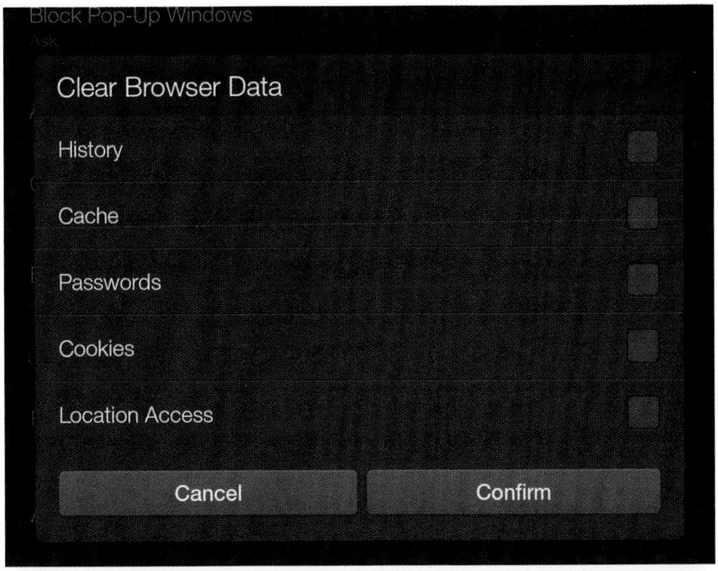

4. Tap items you want to delete (■ changes to ☑).
5. Tap **Confirm**.

   Silk deletes the selected items.

Note: You will not notice the effects of your changes until you start using Silk again. For example, if you clear your history and then display the History page, as described in the section "View Browsing History," no websites will appear on the History page until you visit more sites.

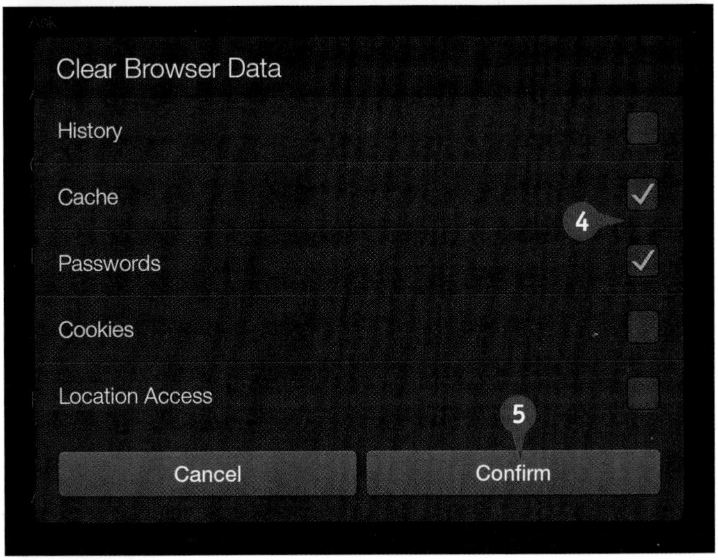

TIPS

Why should I clear cookies?
Cookies are typically harmless bits of information that a website stores on your Fire tablet to improve your browsing experience for that site. On occasion, if you notice Silk slowing down, clearing cookies might ultimately help speed up browsing. Any websites you revisit after clearing cookies will simply place a new cookie on your Fire tablet.

Should I clear passwords?
If you believe someone else will use your Fire tablet it might be a good idea to clear website passwords; otherwise, anyone who uses your Fire tablet will be able to log into any website for which you have saved a password.

Download and Open a Document

You can download and save a copy of a document you find on the Internet to your Fire tablet. Most documents found on the Internet are *portable document format* (PDF) documents, and the Amazon Kindle app — the app you use to read books — automatically opens these types of documents if you tap them. When you download and save a document via Silk, your Fire tablet stores the document in the Silk Downloads folder and in the Docs content library. You also can download and save images you find on the Internet.

Download and Open a Document

Download a Document

1. In Silk, navigate to the website where the document resides.
2. Tap the document's link.

The Download File dialog box appears.

3. Tap **OK**.

Starting Download and Download Complete messages appear.

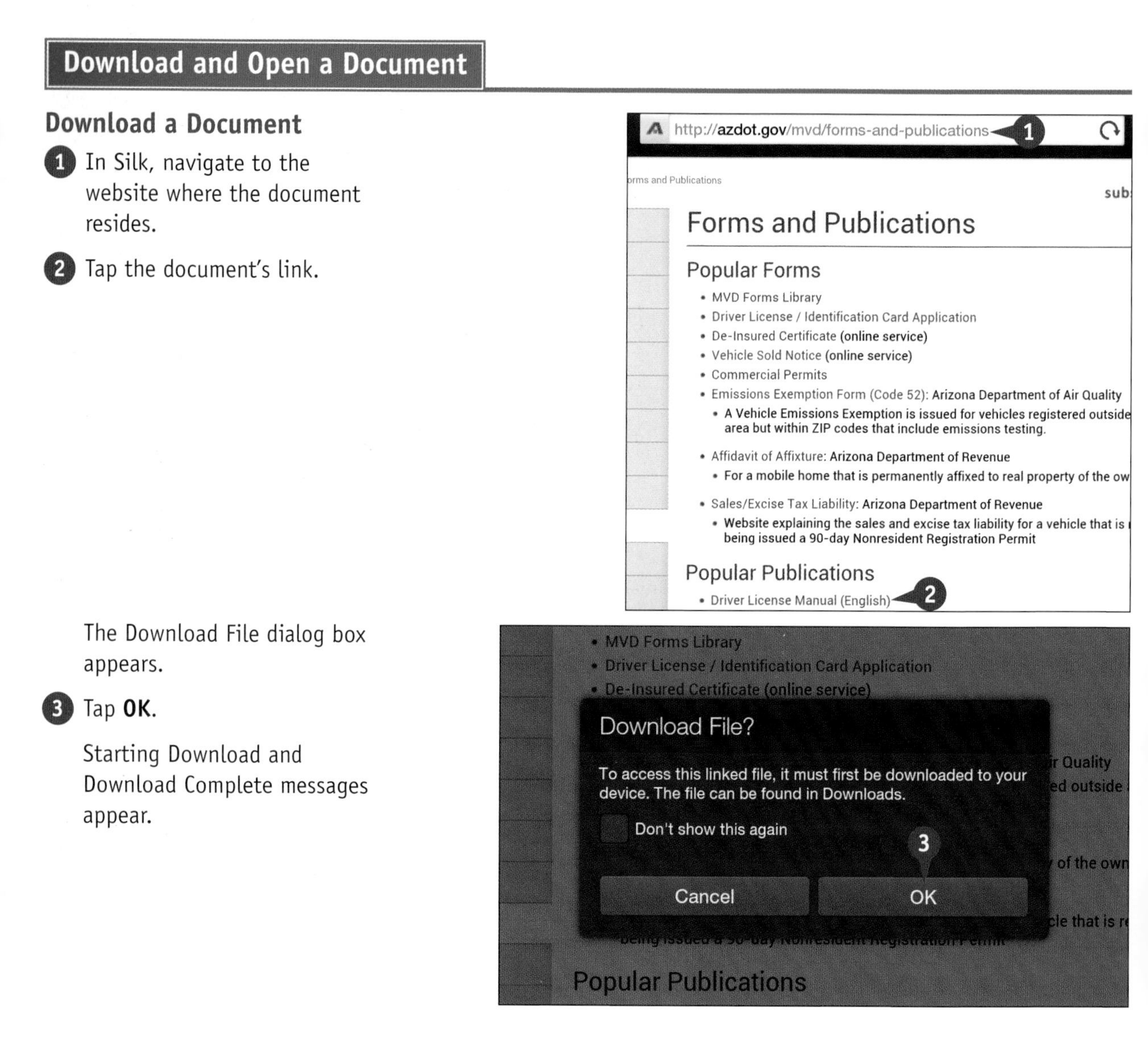

Open a Downloaded Document

1. In Silk, tap the **Navigation** button (☰).

   The Navigation panel appears.

2. Tap **Downloads**.

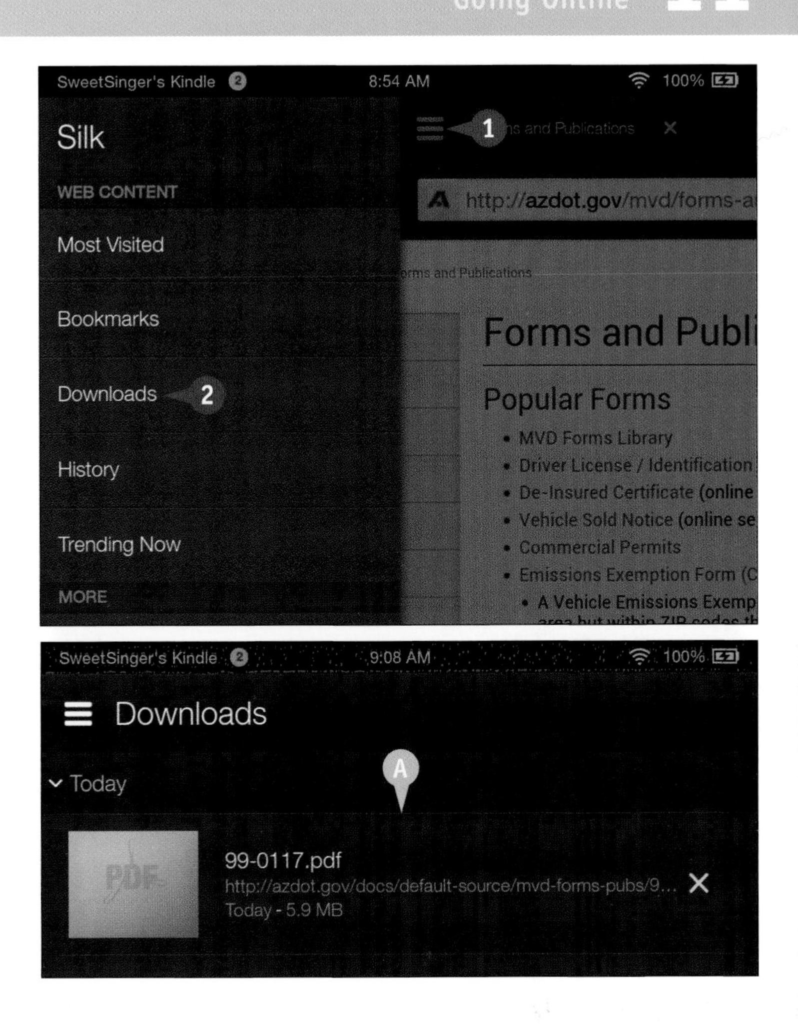

The Downloads page appears.

Ⓐ Documents and images you download appear on this page, organized by date.

TIP

How do I download images from the Internet?
Navigate in Silk to the page displaying the image, then press and hold it. From the menu that appears, tap **Save Image** Ⓐ. The image appears on the Silk Downloads page and also in the Photos content library.

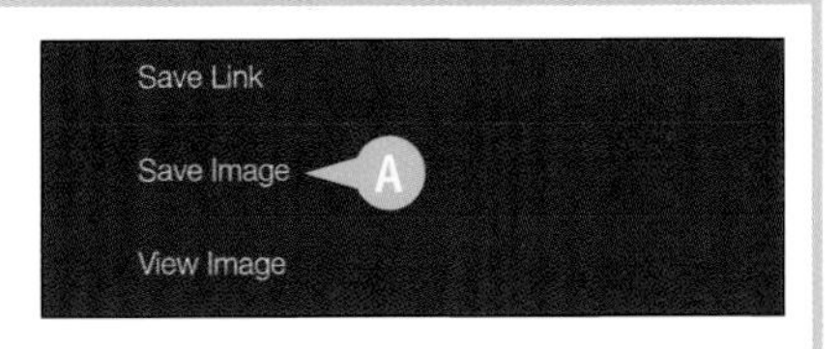

Make Phone Calls Using Skype

You can use the Skype app to make phone or video calls via Internet protocol. This section shows you how to initiate a Skype call. To call people who do not use Skype, you must have Skype credits, available on the Skype website.

To make calls using the Skype app, you create a Skype account or use a Microsoft account to sign in. By default the Skype app keeps you signed in, but you can manually sign out (for security purposes) as well as change the default behavior so that you are not always signed into the Skype app.

Make Phone Calls Using Skype

1. From the Home screen, tap **Apps** to display the Apps content library.
2. Tap **Skype**.

The Skype Sign in screen appears.

3. Choose a method to sign in; you can use a Microsoft account or your Skype name associated with your Skype account.

Ⓐ If you want, you can tap **Create account** to create a Skype account.

The appropriate sign-in screen appears; supply your credentials and sign in.

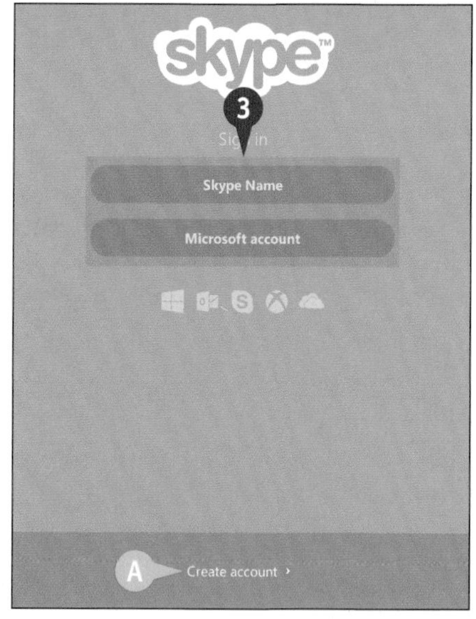

The Skype app opens.

B You can tap the Contacts button (▣) to add a contact name or number.

C You can tap the Text Message button (▣) to create and send a text message.

D You can tap the **Profile** button (▣) to set up and view your profile.

E You can tap **Echo/Sound Test** to verify a proper Skype connection; tap the handset to start the test and follow the verbal instructions.

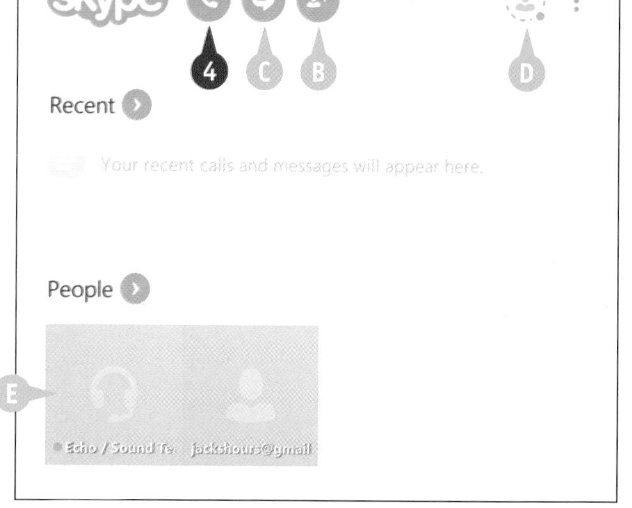

4 Tap the **Phone Dial Pad** button (▣) to display the phone dial pad.

5 Tap the phone number you want to call.

6 Tap the handset to place the call.

Note: To end the call, tap the handset again.

TIP

How do I sign out of Skype?

Tap the **Profile** button (▣) in the upper-right corner of the Skype app window. Then, tap **Sign out** A. To change the defaults so that you do not remain signed in, tap ⋮ and then tap **Settings**. Then, tap the **Sign in automatically** option.

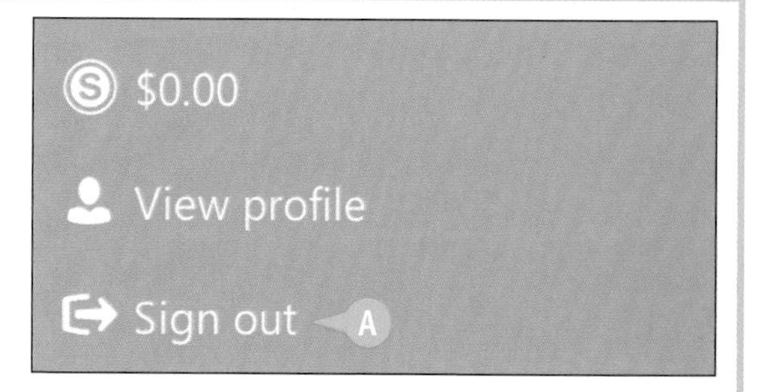

Connect to Social Networks

You can connect your Fire tablet with your Facebook and Twitter social network accounts. Connecting with your Facebook account means you can also synchronize Facebook events with the Calendar app on your Fire tablet, enabling you to view events in both places.

Connecting your Facebook and Twitters accounts to your Fire tablet is very much like setting up email accounts, described in Chapter 8. To link the accounts to your Fire tablet, you need know nothing more than your Facebook and Twitter login information.

Connect to Social Networks

1. Swipe down from the top of any screen.

   The Quick Settings panel appears.

2. Tap **Settings**.
3. From the Settings screen, tap **My Account**.

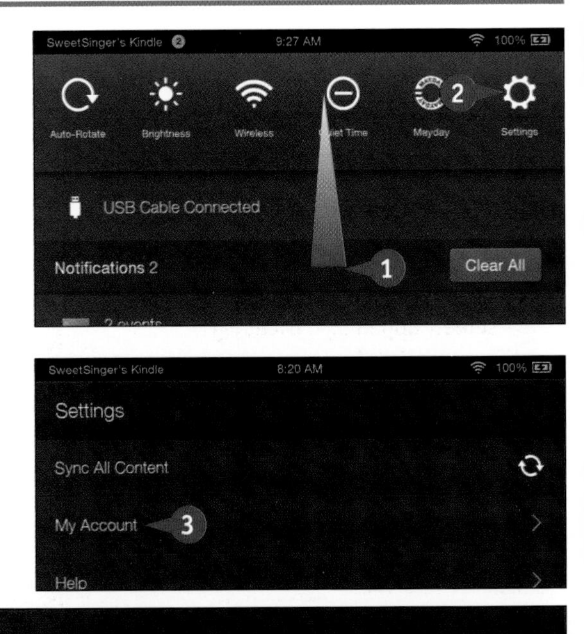

   The My Account page appears.

4. Tap **Social Network Accounts**.

The Social Network Accounts screen appears.

5. Tap **Facebook**.

A. You can tap **Twitter** to set up your Twitter account and follow steps **5** to **7** in this section to complete the process.

The Connect Your Facebook Account screen appears.

6. Type your username or email address.
7. Type your password.
8. Tap **Connect**.

A screen appears, indicating that you give Amazon permission to use Facebook information; tap **Connect**.

Your Fire tablet connects to your Facebook account and redisplays the Social Network Accounts screen.

TIP

If I change my mind and opt not to link my Fire tablet with my Facebook account, can I undo the link?

Yes. Complete steps **1** to **3** in this section to display the Social Network Accounts page. Then, tap **Unlink** (A).

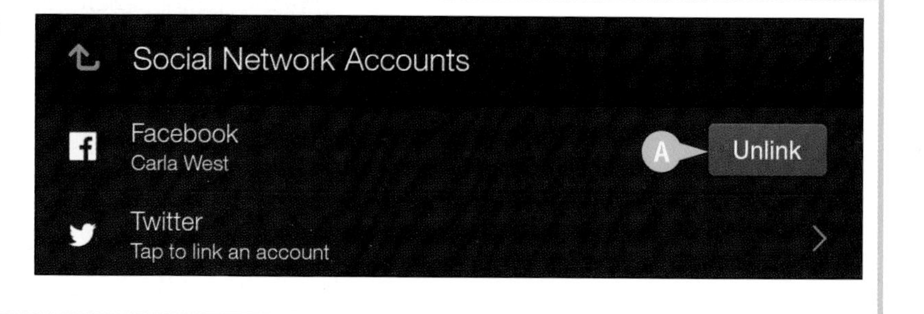

CHAPTER 12

Customizing Settings

You can customize your Fire tablet behavior using various settings. For example, you can manage the lighting of the display and control the types of sounds you hear and their relative volume level. You also can connect to any wireless network and, for added security, establish a personal identification number (PIN) that the tablet requires on its lock screen.

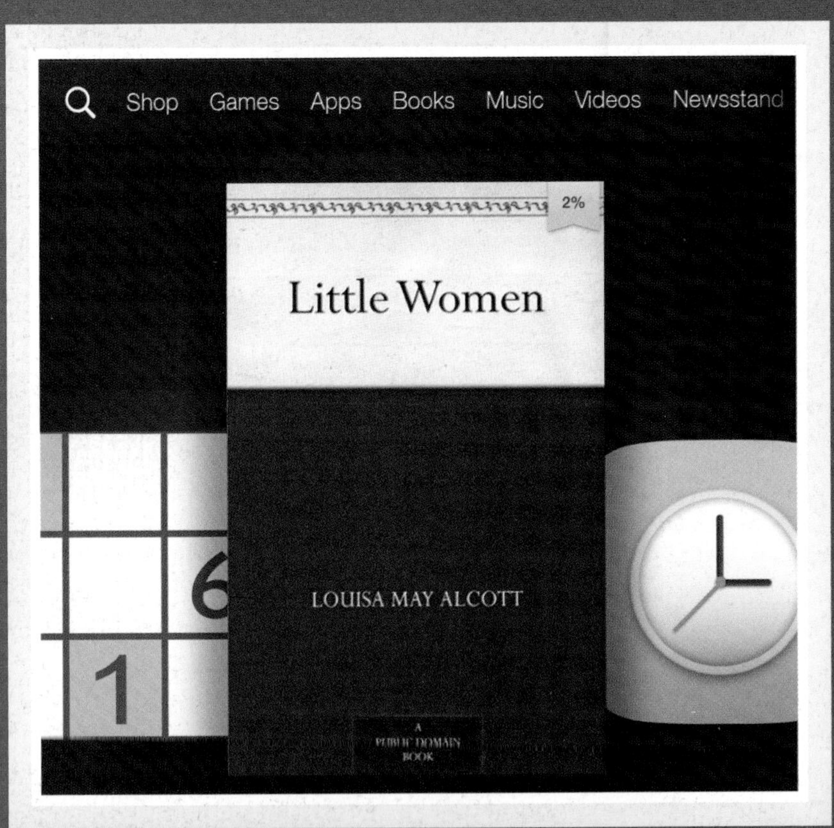

Open Settings 250
Manage Display and Sounds Settings 251
Show or Hide Home Screen Recommendations 252
Manage Notifications. 254
Connect to a Wireless Network 258
Work with a Lock Screen Password 260
Check for Software Updates. 262

Open Settings

All the settings you can control on your Fire tablet are accessible from the Settings screen. From this screen, you can manually synchronize content, examine and change your Amazon account settings, set up parental controls, manage display and sound settings, and show or hide Home screen recommendations. You can also connect to a wireless network, examine and set device behavior, check for software updates, set a password for the tablet's lock screen, and more.

Some of these settings were discussed in previous chapters in this book; the rest of the most important settings are discussed in this chapter.

Open Settings

1. Swipe down from the top of any screen.

   The Quick Settings panel appears.

2. Tap **Settings**.

   The Settings screen appears.

A. You can tap the Synchronize button (⟳) to manually synchronize all content on your Fire tablet.

   From the Settings screen, you tap a particular setting to examine or change it.

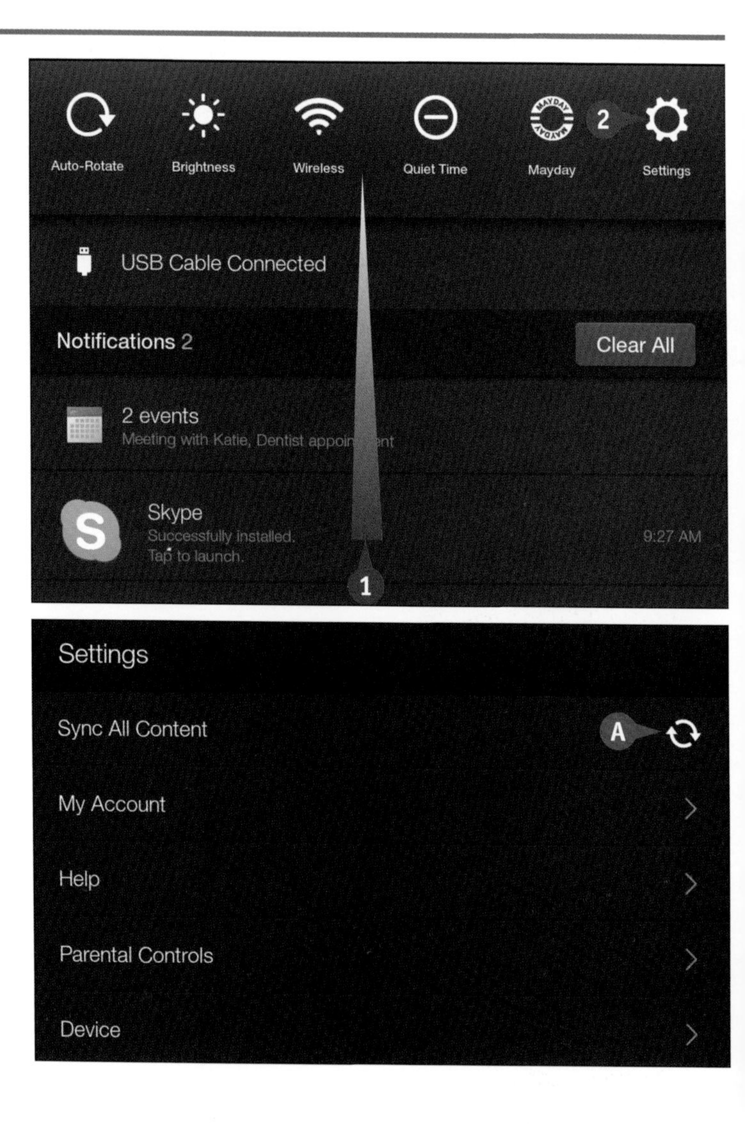

Manage Display and Sounds Settings

CHAPTER 12

You can manage the sound your Fire tablet makes when notifications arrive and the volume of that sound. You also can opt to use the Auto-Brightness feature, which automatically adjusts display brightness based on surrounding lighting conditions, or you can manually control the brightness of your Fire tablet display. In addition, you can control the elapsed time before your Fire tablet goes to sleep.

From the Display & Sounds screen, you also can set up an alternate, Wi-Fi-ready device such as a television set to display the tablet screen — a useful feature when streaming movies.

Manage Display and Sounds Settings

1. Complete the steps in the section "Open Settings" to display the Settings screen.
2. Tap **Display & Sounds**.

Notifications & Quiet Time
Display & Sounds
Language & Keyboard
Accessibility
Security
Legal & Compliance

- A Dragging this slider bar increases or decreases sound volume.
- B You can tap ▸ to select the notification sound.
- C Tapping **On** to turn on the Auto-Brightness feature.
- D If you do not turn on the feature, you can drag the Display Brightness slider to control screen brightness.
- E Tapping ▸ sets up a Wi-Fi-enabled device to display your Fire tablet screen.
- F Tapping ▸ controls how much time must elapse without any user action before your Fire tablet goes into sleep mode.

Display & Sounds
Volume
Set volume for music, video, games, and other media
Notification Sound
Set the sound that plays when an application sends a notification
Auto-Brightness
Dynamically adjust display brightness based on surrounding light conditions
On Off
Display Brightness
Display Mirroring
Display your Kindle screen on your TV or media streaming device
Display Sleep
15 Minutes

Show or Hide Home Screen Recommendations

By default, in portrait orientation, your Fire tablet displays recommendations on the Home screen below the Carousel. If you swipe through the items on the Carousel, recommendations based on the type of item in the foreground of the Carousel appear in the area below it. For example, if a book or game title appears in the foreground of the Carousel, similar types of books or games appear as recommendations.

You can opt to show these recommendations or hide them if they annoy you or for any other reason.

Show or Hide Home Screen Recommendations

1. From the top of any screen, swipe down.

   The Quick Settings screen appears.

2. Tap **Settings**.

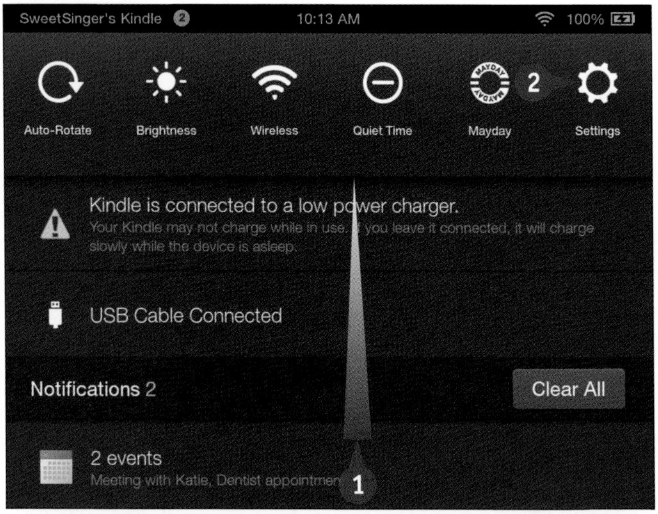

   The Settings screen appears.

3. Tap **Applications**.

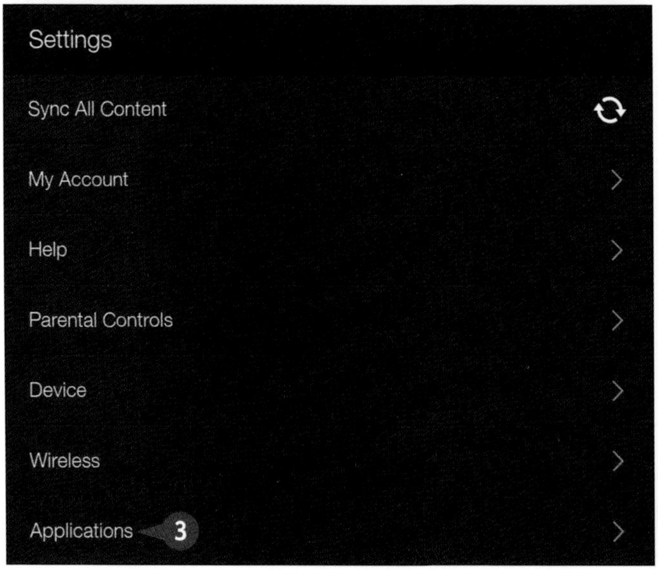

SweetSinger's Kindle 2 10:13 AM 100%
Auto-Rotate Brightness Wireless Quiet Time Mayday Settings
Kindle is connected to a low power charger.
Your Kindle may not charge while in use. If you leave it connected, it will charge slowly while the device is asleep.
USB Cable Connected
Notifications 2 Clear All
2 events
Meeting with Katie, Dentist appointment

Settings
Sync All Content
My Account
Help
Parental Controls
Device
Wireless
Applications

The Applications settings screen appears.

4 Tap **Home Screen**.

The Home Recommendations screen appears.

5 Tap **Hide** to hide Home screen recommendations.

A Once you turn off Home screen recommendations, you can tap **Show** to redisplay them.

TIP

Can you show me an example of recommendations?
The recommendations shown here A are for books similar to *Little Women*. You can eliminate a particular recommendation if you press and hold the recommendation and then tap **Not Interested** from the menu that appears.

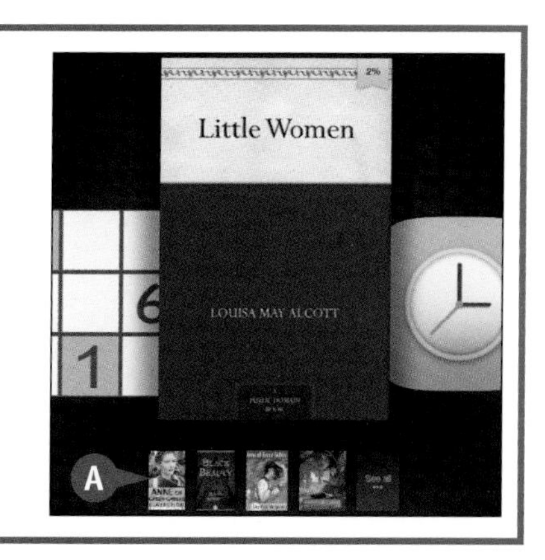

Manage Notifications

You can manage the visual and audible way your Fire tablet handles notifying you of events that occur, such as email reception, app updates, or calendar event reminders. By default, the Fire tablet plays a sound and displays a number in a circle in the notification tray for each notification. In some cases, notifications also pop up on-screen when an event occurs.

For each app, you can turn off notifications and you can tell the Fire tablet not to play a sound when an event occurs to avoid being disturbed.

Manage Notifications

Control Notifications

Ⓐ When notifications are enabled, this symbol appears beside your name.

1. Swipe down from the top of any screen.
2. Tap **Settings**.

The Settings screen appears.

3. Tap **Notifications & Quiet Time**.

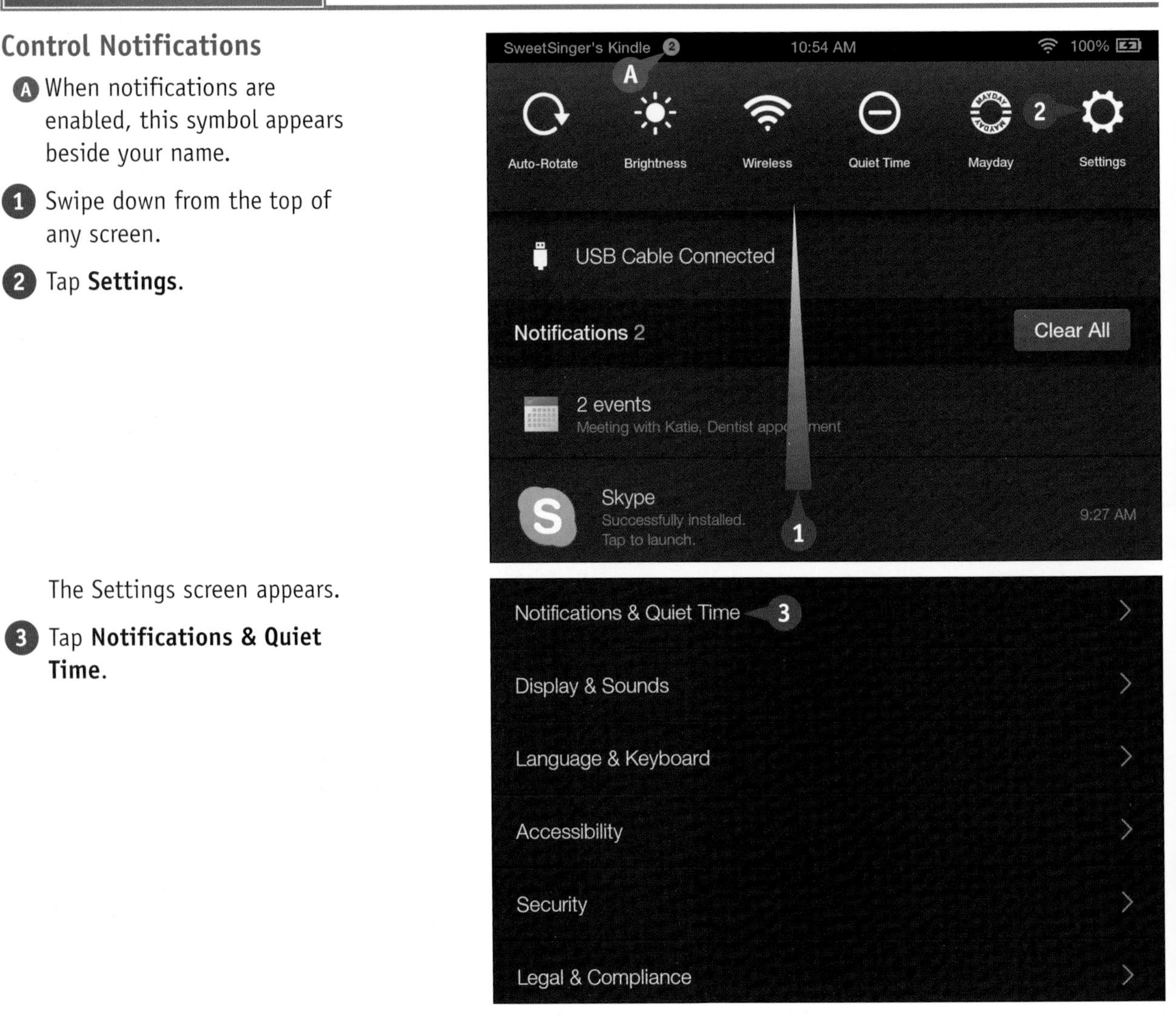

The Notifications & Quiet Time settings screen appears.

B Each app on your Fire tablet appears under the Choose How Applications Notify You area; you can see the current notification settings below each app name.

4 Tap an app; this section uses the Email app as an example.

The app's notifications settings appear.

C You can tap **Off** to hide notifications from the notification tray.

D You can tap **Off** to mute sounds when a notification for the app arrives.

TIP

How do I view notifications?

Swipe down from any screen; notifications appear on the Quick Settings screen. To dismiss any notification, swipe it right or left. To change settings for an app's notifications, press and hold the notification **A**. A menu with options appears **B**.

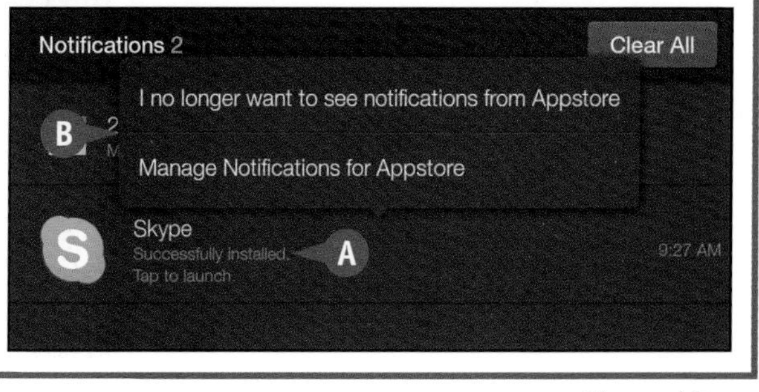

continued ►

In addition to managing notification settings, you can use Quiet Time to disable all notification sounds and pop-ups. When you enable Quiet Time, the notifications symbol still appears at the top of the screen, but your experience while using your Fire tablet is not interrupted by those sometimes annoying beeps and pop-up messages.

You can automatically enable and disable Quiet Time at scheduled intervals. For example, to prevent sounds from disturbing your sleep, you might find it useful to automatically enable Quiet Time at night when you go to bed and automatically it disable it in the morning.

Manage Notifications (continued)

Using Quiet Time

1. Complete steps **1** to **3** in the "Control Notifications" subsection to display the Notifications & Quiet Time settings screen.

   A. The settings in the Choose How Applications Notify You section are the ones functioning when Quiet Time is disabled.

2. Tap **Quiet Time**.

   The Quiet Time settings screen appears.

3. Tap **On**.

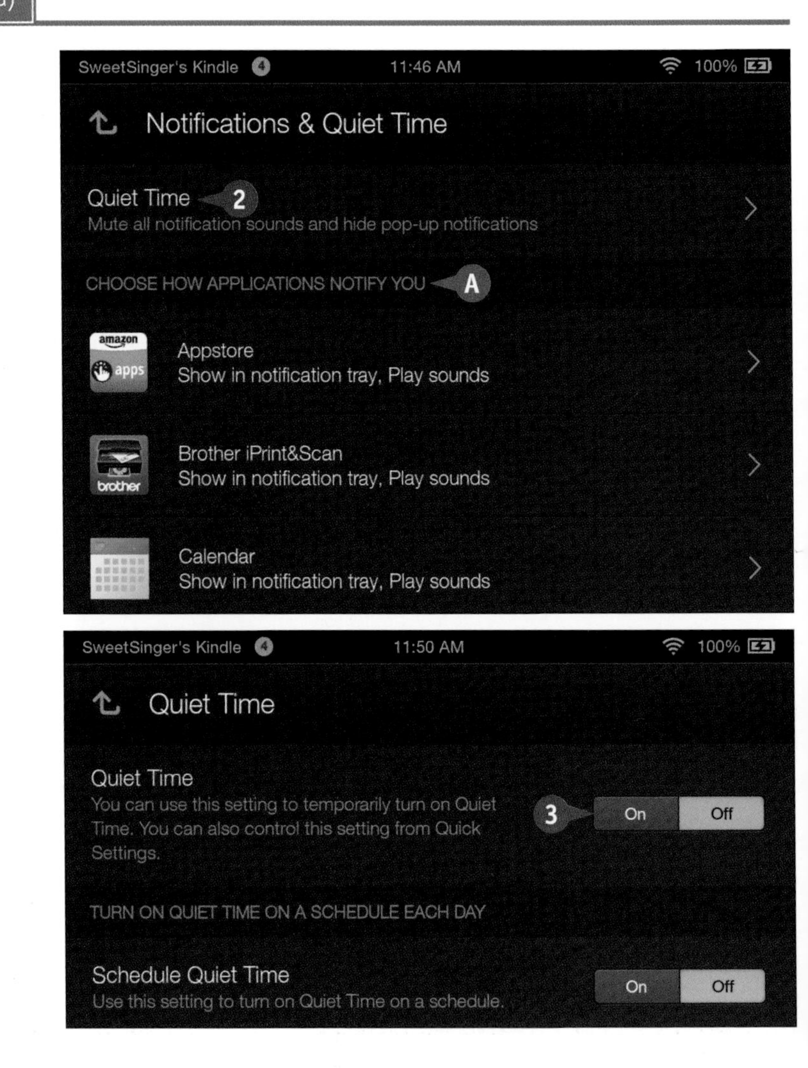

The Fire tablet enables Quiet Time.

B This icon (⊝) indicates that Quiet Time is enabled.

C You can check these boxes (■ changes to ☑) to automatically enable Quiet Time during certain activities.

4. Tap **On** to set up a schedule for Quiet Time.

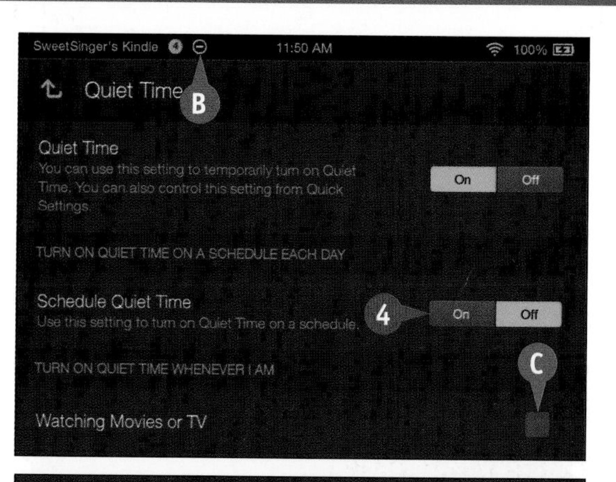

The Schedule Quiet Time dialog box appears.

5. Tap the hour, minute, and AM/PM indicator to set the start of Quiet Time.

6. Tap the hour, minute, and AM/PM indicator to set the end of Quiet Time.

7. Tap **Set Time**.

The Fire tablet stores your Quiet Time schedule.

You can tap the **Home** button (🏠) in the lower-left corner of the screen to redisplay the Home screen.

TIP

Is there an easy way to turn Quiet Time on and off?

Yes. Swipe down from the top of any screen to display Quick Settings **A**. Then, tap **Quiet Time** **B**. When you enable Quiet Time, its icon in the Quick Settings menu bar appears orange instead of white.

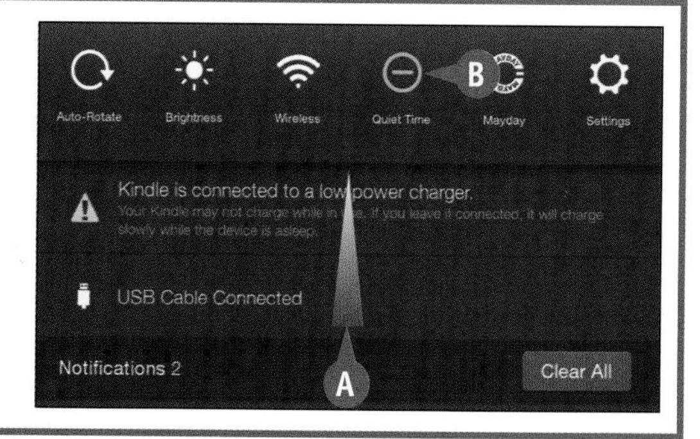

Connect to a Wireless Network

You can connect your Fire tablet to any wireless network so that you can browse the Internet and check email from anywhere. Many coffee shops, restaurants, hotels, airports, and even government areas such as parks and highway rest stops provide access to public Wi-Fi. In many cases, access is free, but some locations charge you to use their networks.

If you visit a friend, you can connect the Fire tablet to his or her private Wi-Fi network; typically, such networks are password-protected and your friend must give you the password, as shown in this section.

Connect to a Wireless Network

1. Complete the steps in the section "Open Settings" to display the Settings screen.
2. Tap **Wireless**.

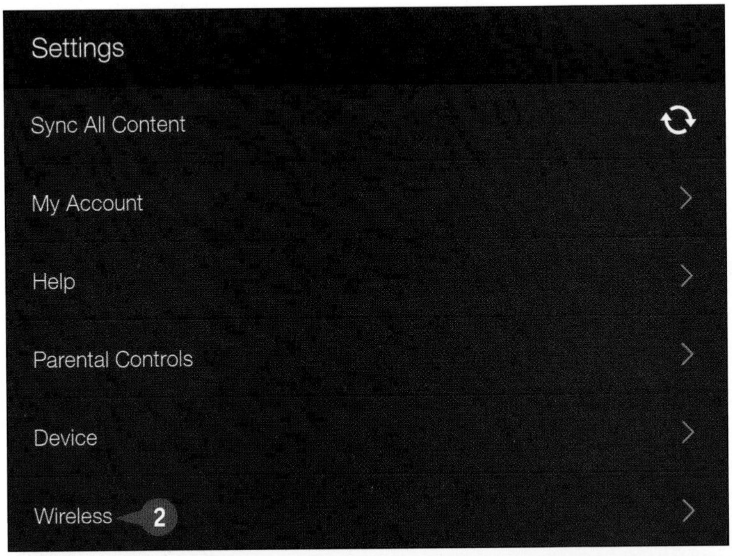

Settings
Sync All Content
My Account
Help
Parental Controls
Device
Wireless 2

The Wireless settings screen appears.

3. Tap **Wi-Fi**.

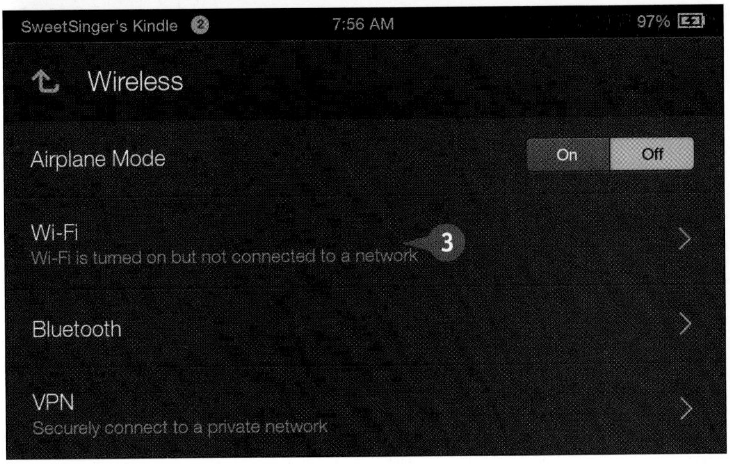

SweetSinger's Kindle 2 7:56 AM 97%
Wireless
Airplane Mode On Off
Wi-Fi
Wi-Fi is turned on but not connected to a network 3
Bluetooth
VPN
Securely connect to a private network

The Wi-Fi screen appears.

Ⓐ Available wireless networks appear in the Wi-Fi Networks area.

Ⓑ The lock symbol in a network connection (🔒) indicates that the network is password-protected.

4. Tap the wireless network to which you want to connect.

Note: This section assumes you want to connect to a password-protected network.

The Password box appears.

5. Type the password for the network.

6. Tap **Connect**.

The network authenticates the password and your Fire tablet connects to the network.

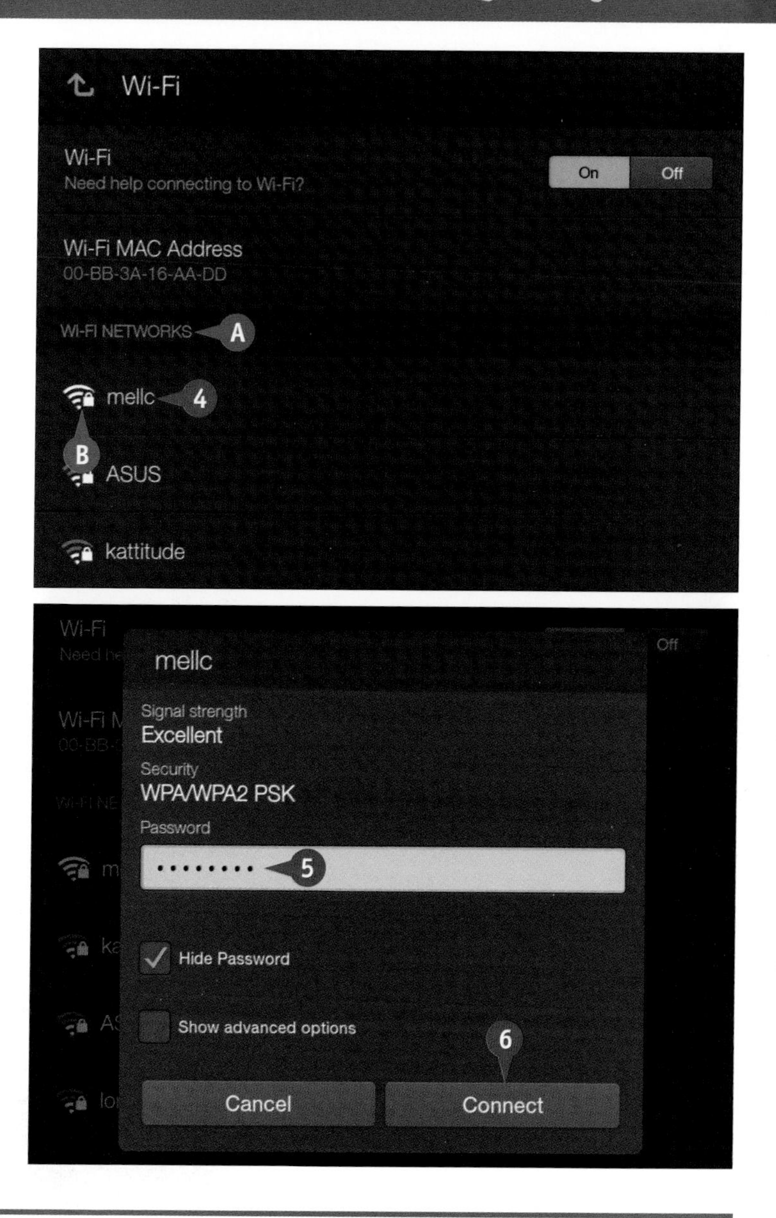

TIP

Should I take any precautions when using public Wi-Fi?

Both the pro and con of public Wi-Fi networks is that anyone can use them because they are not password-protected. To stay safe, connect only to networks provided by reputable establishments such as national hotel and restaurant chains, and do not connect to networks run by unknown operators. And, when connected to an unsecured or public Wi-Fi network, do not transmit any private information, like bank or email passwords. When you finish using a public network, tell the Fire tablet to forget the network by tapping the network on the Wi-Fi screen and, in the dialog box that appears, tap **Forget**.

Work with a Lock Screen Password

You can set up a *personal identification number* (PIN) on your Fire tablet. When you do so, the Fire tablet prompts you for it on the Lock screen, which appears whenever you wake up the Fire tablet or turn it on.

The PIN must be numeric and have a minimum of four numbers. However, you can create a longer PIN to make device more secure. To use the PIN effectively, you can tap the tablet's Power button each time you finish using it to put the device into sleep mode.

Work with a Lock Screen Password

Set a Password

1. Complete the steps in the section "Open Settings" to display the Settings screen.
2. Tap **Security**.

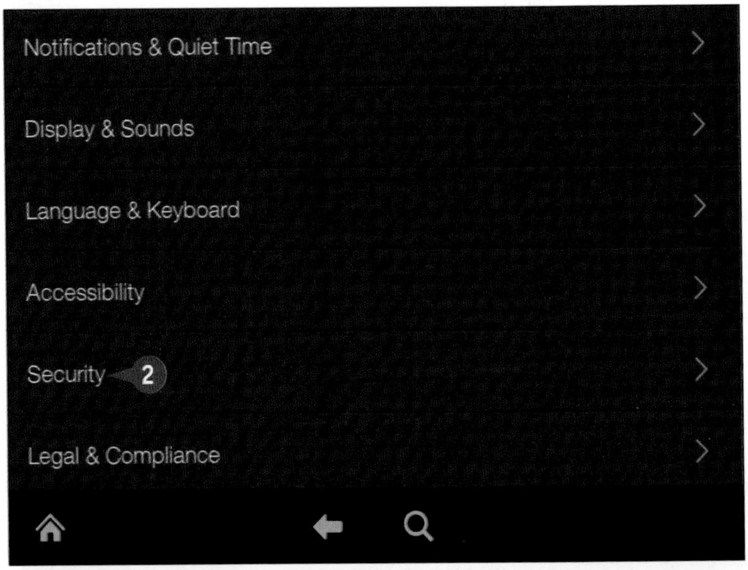

The Security settings screen appears.

3. Tap **On**.

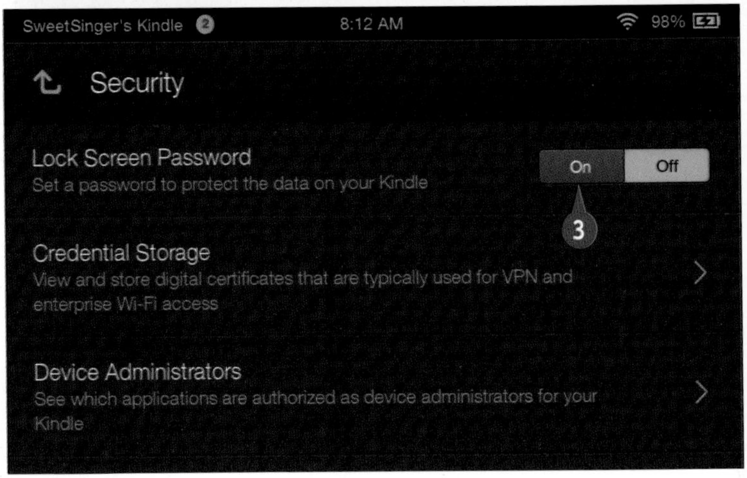

The Lock Screen Password screen appears.

4. Using the on-screen keypad, type a numeric personal identification number (PIN) at least four characters long.
5. Retype the PIN.
6. Tap **Finish**.

The PIN you set is saved.

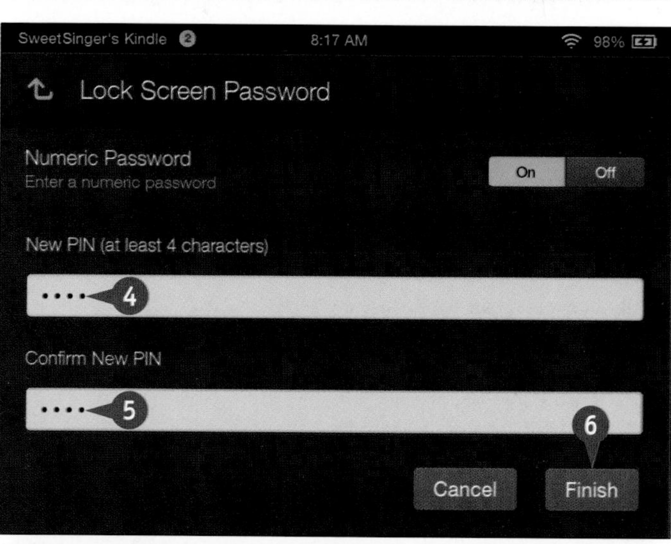

Using the PIN

1. Lightly press the Power button on the back of the tablet to display the Lock screen and swipe to start using the tablet.

Note: To find the Power button and start using the Fire tablet see "Examine the Hardware" in Chapter 1.

A prompt for the PIN appears.

2. Use the keypad to type the PIN.
3. Tap **OK**.

The Home screen appears.

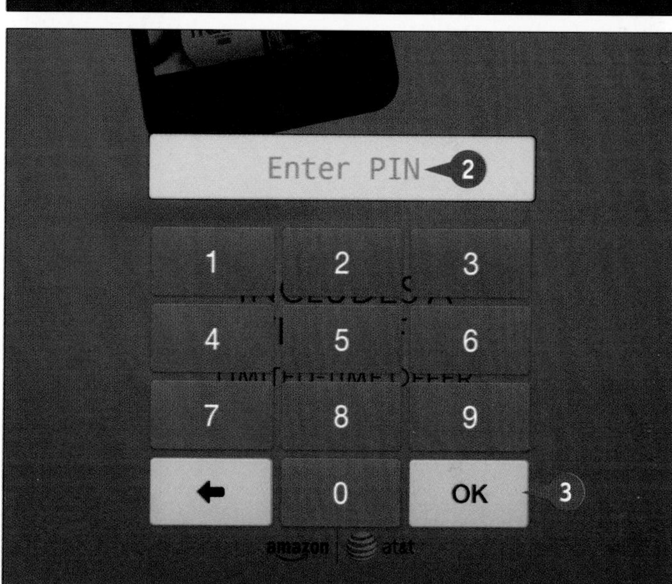

TIP

If I decide that I do not want to use a PIN, can I remove it?

Yes. Complete steps **1** and **2** in the subsection "Set a Password," then tap **Off**. The Fire tablet prompts you to supply the PIN to ensure that you are authorized to remove it; type the PIN Ⓐ and tap **Finish** Ⓑ.

Check for Software Updates

By default, your Fire tablet uses its Wi-Fi connection to periodically connect to Amazon servers and check for updates to the system software. If you do not regularly connect your Fire tablet to a wireless network, or do so for only a short time, it cannot or may not have time to update. Keeping your Fire tablet software up-to-date helps keep your device running smoothly.

If you connect to a wireless network, as described in the section "Connect to a Wireless Network," you can check for updates.

Check for Software Updates

1. Complete the steps in the section "Open Settings" to display the Settings screen.
2. Tap **Device**.

The Device settings screen appears.

3. Tap **System Updates**.

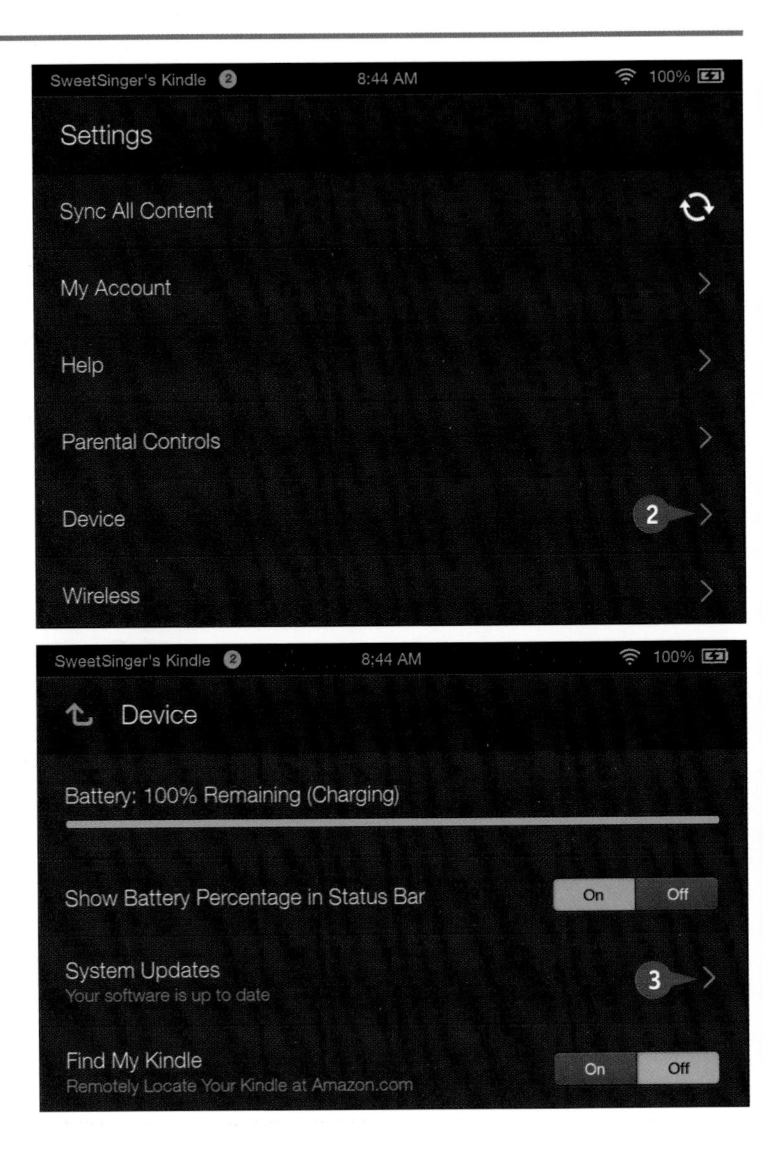

The System Updates screen appears.

 Tap **Check Now**.

The tablet connects to the Amazon servers and checks for updates.

Ⓐ The result of the check appears in the Updates area.

Ⓑ The version of system software currently installed on your Fire tablet appears here.

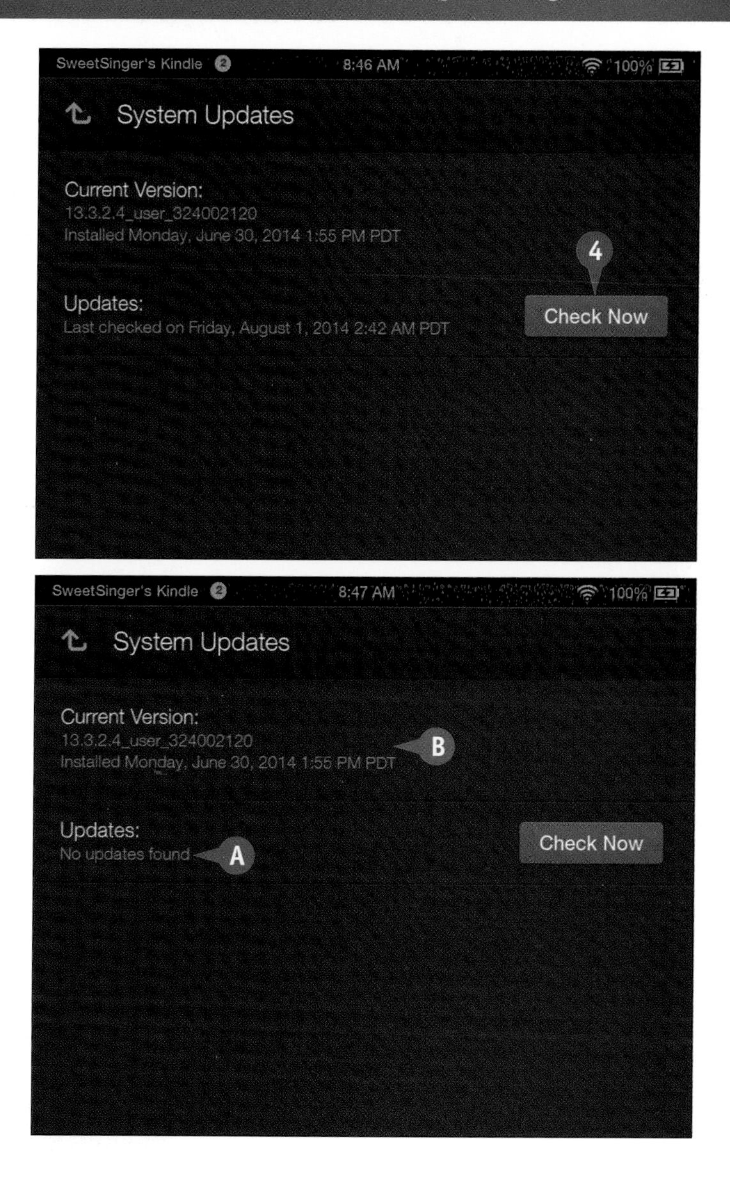

TIP

When would I check for updates?

If your Fire tablet begins to behave in unexpected ways and you have not connected to a wireless network for a while, you should consider updating. If you want, you also can check in the Amazon Kindle Forums to identify the latest version of the software and compare it to the one currently installed on your Fire tablet. If your device is using an older version of the system software, then you can update as described in this section.

Index

Symbols and Numerics

?123 key, 13, 27
1-Tap Archive feature, 58–59
4G LTE connectivity, 4

A

Aa View button, Books content library, 124, 128, 139
ABC key, 13, 27
accessibility features, 5
accounts
  Amazon.com
    creating, 8–9
    linking to Audible.com, 53
    registering tablet to, 14, 15
  Audible.com, 53
  email
    Calendar app, 210
    contacts associated with, viewing, 195
    default, setting, 187
    manual setup, 160–161
    multiple, working with, 164–165
    setting up, 158–159
    settings for specific, 186–187
    switching between, 165
    synchronizing contacts with, 194
    viewing in Navigation panel, 163
Actions button, Amazon, 47, 59
Add a City screen, Clock app, 65
Add a Credit or Debit Card option, Amazon Your Account page, 9
Add a new approved e-mail address option, Amazon, 183
Add Account wizard, 158–159, 161, 164
Add All Kids' Titles button, Kindle FreeTime app, 77
Add an Alarm screen, Clock app, 67
Add Another Child button, Add Child Profile screen, 76
Add Bookmark dialog box, Silk browser, 227
Add Child Profile screen, Kindle FreeTime app, 74, 75, 76
Add Contact window, Email app, 196, 197
Add Files option, Cloud Drive page, 104
Add More Fields option, My Local Profile screen, 193
Add Narration button, Bookstore, 132
Add Organization link, My Local Profile screen, 192
Add Photo option, My Local Profile screen, 193
Add Timer screen, Clock app, 70, 71
Add to Cart option, Amazon, 39
Add to Collection window, 147
Add to Home option, 56
Add to Wish List option, Amazon, 39
Add Your Amazon Books option, Goodreads on Kindle app, 63
Address bar, Silk browser, 225, 229
Airplane mode, 22, 23
alarms, 66–67, 69, 71
All Cities view, Clock app, 64, 65
All Contacts view, Contacts app, 205
Allow In-App Purchases option, 93
alternative characters, typing, 27
Always option, when opening attachments with apps, 181
Amazon Appstore for Android
  apps, shopping for, 42–43
  games, shopping for, 40–41
  in-app purchasing, 92–93
  printer plug-in, installing, 60–61
  viewing particular categories in, 43
Amazon Cloud Drive
  automatic uploading of photos and videos to, 113
  downloading content, 103
  storage space, 4
  streaming videos from, 99
  transferring music to computer from, 49
  uploading to via PC, 102–105
Amazon Cloud Player, 48
Amazon Coins, 36–37, 41
Amazon GameCircle, 90–91, 93
Amazon Instant Video, 50–51, 98
Amazon Prime, 5, 98, 143
Amazon Silk browser. ***See*** Silk browser
Amazon Tech advisor, 19, 32
Amazon.com
  account, creating, 8–9
  Audible.com, linking account to, 53
  cancelling subscriptions, 47
  documents, receiving via email, 182–183
  home page, 9
  lending ebooks, 143
  OverDrive service, 143
  permanently removing content from, 59
  registering Kindle with, 14, 15
  Shop by Department page, 38–39
  subscriptions, managing, 152–153
  uploading to Cloud Drive via PC, 102–105

annual subscriptions, 151
App Settings screen, 93
Applications settings screen, 92, 93, 252–253
Apply option
  Email app, 168
  Photos content library, 111
Approved Personal Document E-mail List section, Amazon, 183
apps. *See also specific apps*
  email attachments, opening with, 181
  Favorites, adding to, 56
  magazine and newspaper, 150
  overview, 5
  printer plug-in, installing, 60–61
  removing, 57–59
  shopping for, 42–43
Apps content library, 42, 60, 62, 72, 80
Appstore option, Applications settings screen, 92
Archive button, 1-Tap Archive feature, 59
As a Business Card option, Microsoft Outlook, 199
Attach Photo option, Compose window, 176
attachments, email
  adding, 176–177
  opening, 180–181
  removing, 177
  saving, 181
Audible.com, 52, 53, 132
audio books, shopping for, 52–53
Audiobooks content library, 52
Audiobooks Store, 52–53
Auto-Brightness control, 23, 251
automatic uploading to cloud, 113
AutoPlay window, PC, 96, 106
auto-renewal, subscriptions, 151, 153
Auto-Rotate option, 22
Auto-Save option, Photos content library, 113

B

Back arrow
  explained, 21
  Photos content library, 111
  X-Ray feature, 135
Back button, Silk browser, 21, 225
background color, Books content library, 125
battery, 4, 7, 24–25
Bcc field, Compose window, 173, 176
Bing Translator, 137
Block Pop-Up Windows option, Silk browser, 239
Bluetooth, 23
bookmarks
  in ebooks, 142
  Silk browser, 227–228, 237
Bookmarks button, Books content library, 127
Bookmarks page, Silk browser, 228
books, audio, 52–53. ***See also*** Books content library; ebooks
Books content library
  bookmarks, 142
  Cloud Collections, 144–147
  highlighting, 138–139
  Immersion Reading, 131, 133
  notes, 140–141
  Popular Highlights feature, 139
  reading books, 120–123
  reading view, changing, 124–127
  shopping for books, 44
  Smart Lookup feature, 136–137
  Text-to-Speech feature, 128–130
  X-Ray feature, 134–135
Bookstore, 45, 131–133
Born Today option, IMDb app, 84
borrowing ebooks, 143
BrailleBack app, 5
brightness controls, 22–23, 251
browsing history, 238. ***See also*** Silk browser
buttons, Options bar, 21
Buy Album button, Music Store, 49
Buy button
  Amazon Instant Video store, 51
  Bookstore, 132
  Music Store, 49
Buy for Free button, Bookstore, 45, 132
Buy Issue button, Newsstand storefront, 47
Buy More Coins option, Amazon Coins screen, 37
Buy Tickets wizard, IMDb app, 83
buying content. ***See*** shopping for content

C

cache, Silk browser, 240
Calendar app
  events
    creating, 216–217

Calendar app *(continued)*
- deleting, 219
- editing, 218–219
- Facebook, 220–221
- recurring, 217
- viewing, 215

opening, 210–211
viewing or hiding calendars, 214
views, changing, 212–213

Calendar General Settings page, 221
calls, making with Skype app, 244–245
camera, 4, 10, 112, 113
Camera app, 112
Camera button, Photos content library, 108, 112
Camera Roll option, Photos content library, 108
Cancel Subscription option, Amazon, 47
Carousel
- Favorites section as alternative to, 56
- Kindle FreeTime app, 78
- overview, 17, 18
- recommendations, 252–253

cart, Amazon, 39
cases, for tablet, 10
Cc field, Compose window, 173, 176
celebrity information, IMDb app, 84–85
charging, 6–7
Check Box button, Photos content library, 108, 115
Check Now option, System Updates screen, 263
check-ins, Yelp app, 87
Child Profile, Kindle FreeTime app, 74–77
Choose How Applications Notify You area, Notifications & Quiet Time settings screen, 255, 256
city clocks, 64–65
cleaning screen, 10
Clear All option, notifications, 26
Clear Browser Data dialog box, Silk browser, 241
Clear Player option, Music content library, 95
clearing browser information, 240–241
clipboard, 28, 29
Clock app
- alarms, setting, 66–67
- clocks, setting, 64–65
- Nightstand mode, 68, 69
- stopwatch, 68
- Timer feature, 68, 69, 70–71

Closed Captioning feature, 5
Cloud Collections
- adding to, 147
- creating, 144–147
- deleting, 147
- editing, 145
- overview, 144

cloud dictation service, 30–31
Cloud Drive. ***See*** Amazon Cloud Drive
Cloud Drive option, Photos content library, 108, 115, 116
Cloud Drive page, Amazon, 104–105
Cloud option
- Books content library, 121
- content libraries, 20
- Music content library, 49
- Videos content library, 99

Cloud Player, Amazon, 48
Coins, Amazon, 36–37, 41
Collections, Cloud. ***See*** Cloud Collections
Combined Inbox option, Email app, 165
Complete Action Using dialog box, 193
Compose window, Email app, 173, 175, 176, 179
computer
- charging tablet through, 7
- contacts, importing from, 198–199
- copying media from, 106–107
- transferring music from, 96–97
- transferring music to, 49
- uploading to Cloud Drive via, 102–105

Confirm Account screen, 14
Confirm option, Clear Browser Data dialog box, 241
Connect option, Mayday screen, 19
Connect Social Networks page, 15
Connect Your Facebook Account screen, 247
connectivity, Fire tablet, 4
Contact Profile, setting up, 192–193
contacts. ***See also*** Contacts app
- Gmail, 191
- inviting to Calendar app events, 216–217
- sending email to, 172–173
- VIP, 163, 197

Contacts app
- adding contacts, 194–197
- Contact Profile, setting up, 192–193
- deleting contacts, 200, 201
- editing contacts, 200–201
- email message, adding contacts from, 196–197

importing contacts, 198–199
joining contacts, 202–204
opening, 190–191
searching, 205
settings for, 206–207
Contacts button, Skype app, 245
Contacts General Settings screen, 207
Contacts window, 194–195, 197
content. ***See also*** shopping for content; *specific content*
adding to Favorites, 56
copying from computer, 106–107
for Kindle FreeTime Child Profile, 76–77
removing from tablet, 57–59
uploading to Cloud Drive via PC, 102–105
content libraries. ***See also*** *specific content libraries*
Kindle FreeTime app, 78
1-Tap Archive feature, 59
opening, 20–21
overview, 20
switching to other content, 21
Continue Shopping option, Amazon, 39
conversations, email, 185
cookies, clearing, 241
copying
media from computer, 106–107
music from computer, 97
text, 28–29
Create Account option
Register Your Kindle screen, 14
Skype Sign in screen, 244
Create Collection dialog box, 146
Create Contact Under Account menu, Contacts app, 199
Create New Contact option, Email app, 197
cutting text, 28–29

D

Daily Goals & Time Limits button, Kindle FreeTime app, 77
Day view, Calendar app, 212–213, 215
Deals, Yelp app, 87
Decrease Font button, Books content library, 125
default email account, 187
default search engine, setting, 236–237
Delete Amazon Contacts from Cloud option, Contacts app, 207
deleting
Calendar app events, 219
Cloud Collections, 147
contacts, 200, 201
content from Amazon.com account, 59
content from Cloud, 57
email messages, 167
History page sites, 238
notes, in books, 141
photos or videos, 111, 114–115
delivery frequency, subscriptions, 150
desktop versions, websites, 231
destination folder, Cloud Drive page, 104, 105
Device option, Photos content library, 108–109, 115, 116
Device settings screen, 24–25, 57–58, 262
dictating text, 30–31
Dictionary Smart Lookup card, 136
Display & Sounds area, Settings screen, 251
Display this Badge option, Amazon GameCircle, 91
documents
downloading and opening with Silk browser, 242–243
receiving via email, 182–183
Download All option, Music content library, 49
Download File dialog box, Silk browser, 242
downloading
books, 121
Cloud Drive content, 103
email attachments, 180
videos, 99
Downloads page, Silk browser, 243
Drafts folder, Email app, 173

E

ebooks
bookmarks, 142
borrowing, 143
Cloud Collections, 144–147
Goodreads on Kindle app, 62–63
highlighting, 138–139
Immersion Reading, 45, 131–133
notes, 140–141
Popular Highlights feature, 139
reading, 120–123
reading view, changing, 124–127
shopping for, 44–45
Smart Lookup feature, 136–137
Text-to-Speech feature, 128–130
X-Ray feature, 134–135
Echo/Sound Test, Skype app, 245

Edit Event screen, Calendar app, 219
Edit Profile option, Goodreads on Kindle app, 63
editing
Calendar app events, 218–219
Cloud Collections, 145
contacts, 200–201, 203
notes, in books, 141
photos, 110–111
electric power adaptor, 6
Email, Contacts, Calendars screen
adding accounts, 160, 164
Calendar General Settings, 221
Contacts General Settings, 207
Email General Settings, 185
reviewing account settings, 186
email accounts. ***See also*** Email app
Calendar app, 210
contacts associated with, viewing, 195
default, setting, 187
manual setup, 160–161
multiple, working with, 164–165
setting up, 158–159
settings for specific, 186–187
switching between, 165
synchronizing contacts with, 194
viewing in Navigation panel, 163
Email app
accounts, adding, 158–161
attachments
adding, 176–177
opening, 180–181
removing, 177
saving, 181
checking for new messages, 174
contacts, adding from message, 196–197
creating and sending messages, 172–173
deleting messages, 167
documents, receiving, 182–183
exploring, 162–163
forwarding messages, 175
general settings, 184–185
managing messages from Inbox, 171
moving messages to another folder, 168–169
multiple accounts, working with, 164–165
reading messages, 166
replying to messages, 178–179
searching for messages, 170
settings for specific accounts, 186–187
email conversations, showing, 185
Email General Settings screen, 185
Email option, Share To menu, 117
Empty Trash option, Email app, 167
encrypting, with Silk browser, 239
Enter Page Number or Location dialog box, Books content library, 123
events, Calendar app
creating, 216–217
deleting, 219
editing, 218–219
Facebook, 220–221
recurring, 217
viewing, 215
Exit FreeTime option, Kindle FreeTime app, 79
Explore by Touch feature, 5
External Market Links setting, App Settings screen, 93

F

Facebook
adding friends to Goodreads on Kindle, 62
connecting to, 246–247
events, in Calendar app, 220–221
Facebook option, Share To menu, 117
Favorites, 16, 18, 56
Featured Apps category, Amazon Appstore for Android, 43
Find in Page option, Silk browser, 232–233
Finish button, tutorial, 17
Fire tablet. ***See*** Kindle Fire tablet
First Episode Free option, Videos content library, 51
Flag option, Email app, 171
focal point, camera, 113
folders
Amazon Cloud Drive, 104, 105
Email app, 163, 168–169
font size, Books content library, 124–125
fonts, Books content library, 126–127
Forget option, Wi-Fi screen, 259
formatting, email, 179
Forward button, Silk browser, 21, 225
Forward Contact option, Microsoft Outlook, 199
forwarding messages, Email app, 175
4G LTE connectivity, 4
Free button, Amazon Appstore for Android, 43, 61
free movies and TV shows, 51

free periods, subscriptions, 151
FreeTime app. *See* Kindle FreeTime app
From item, Email app Search area, 170
frozen screen, 11
Full Screen button, Silk browser, 21, 225

G

GameCircle, Amazon, 90–91, 93
games
  deleting, 57
  shopping for, 40–41
  starting new, 41
Games content library, 40, 41, 57, 90
geographic location, in IMDb app, 81
Get App button, Amazon Appstore for Android, 41, 43, 61
Get Started button
  Kindle FreeTime setup wizard, 73
  tutorial, 15
Gmail contacts, 191
Go to Cart option, Amazon, 39
Go to Inbox option, Setup Complete! screen, 159
Go to Page or Location option, Books content library, 122
Go to Wikipedia option, Wikipedia Smart Lookup card, 137
Go to X-Ray option, X-Ray Smart Lookup card, 137
Goodreads on Kindle app, 62–63, 140

H

hardware, examining, 10
headset jack, 10
hearing impairments, accessibility features for, 5
Help icon, Home screen, 32
Hide Details option, Calendar app, 215
Hide option, Home Recommendations screen, 253
hiding calendars, 214
highlighting, in books, 138–139
Highlighting toolbar, Books content library, 138, 139, 140
History page, Silk browser, 238, 241
Home button
  explained, 21
  Silk browser, 225
Home page, Amazon, 102, 103
Home Recommendations screen, 253
Home screen
  exploring, 18
  Favorites, 56
  IMDb app, 80–81
  recommendations, 18, 252–253

I

IMDb app
  celebrity information in, 84–85
  exploring, 80–81
  movie times, finding, 82–83
  tickets, buying, 83
Immersion Reading feature, 45, 131–133
Import from storage option, Contacts app, 198
Import/Export Contacts menu, Contacts app, 198
importing contacts, 198–199
inactive subscriptions, 153
in-app purchasing, turning off, 92–93
Inbox, Email app
  checking for new messages, 174
  Combined Inbox option, 165
  deleting messages from, 167
  forwarding messages from, 175
  managing messages from, 171
  moving messages to other folders, 168–169
  opening messages in, 166
  overview, 162
  switching between accounts, 165
Inbox check frequency dialog box, 187
Increase Font Size button, Books content library, 124
Increased Spacing button, Books content library, 126
insertion point marker, text fields, 27
interactive magazines, 151
Internal storage option, Windows Explorer, 96, 106
Internet
  Silk browser
    bookmarks, 227–228
    browsing history, viewing, 238
    clearing, 240–241
    default search engine, setting, 236–237
    documents, downloading and opening, 242–243
    opening, 224
    Reading View, 229
    Request Another View command, 230–231
    screen, understanding, 225
    searching web, 234–235
    searching web pages, 232–233

Internet *(continued)*
settings for, 239
tabs, 226
Skype app, 244–245
social networks, connecting to, 246–247

J

Join Contacts list, Contacts app, 203
joining contacts, 202–204
Just once option, when opening attachments with apps, 181

K

Keep option, Newsstand content library, 155
keyboard, on-screen, 27
Keyboard button, 21, 27, 31
Kindle Fire tablet
charging, 6–7
functionality, 4–5
hardware, examining, 10
setting up, 12–17
turning on and off, 11
unboxing, 6
Kindle FreeTime app
setting up, 72–77
using, 78–79
Kindle FreeTime Unlimited, 72, 73, 76
Kindle Owners' Lending Library, 143

L

language, choosing, 12
laps, Stopwatch feature, 68
lending ebooks, 143
Link Now button, Audible.com, 53
List view, Calendar app, 212
listening to music, 94–95
Loan this title option, Amazon.com, 143
location, in IMDb app, 81
location number, Books content library, 121, 122–123
Location-Based Services button, 23
lock screen
password for, 260–261
unlocking, 12
when charging, 7
Lock Screen Password screen, 261
locking tablet, 11
lyrics, 94, 95

M

magazines
buying or subscribing to, 46–47
interactive, 151
keeping issues on device, 155
subscriptions, 150–154
Manage Content & Subscription screen, Kindle FreeTime app, 76, 77
Manage Your Content and Devices page, Amazon, 47, 59, 153, 183
Manage Your Content option, Kindle FreeTime app, 73
margins, Books content library, 125–126
Mark Read option, Email app, 171
Mark Unread option, Email app, 171
Mayday feature, 19, 32
Menu button
explained, 21
Silk browser, 225, 230
messages. ***See*** Email app
micro-B USB connector, USB cable, 7
microphone, 10
Microphone button, on-screen keyboard, 30
Microsoft Outlook, creating vCards in, 199
mobile printing, 60
mobile websites, 230–231
Month view, Calendar app, 213
monthly subscriptions, 151
More Actions button, 105
More Settings option, Books content library, 129, 139
Most Visited page, Silk browser, 224
Most-Viewed Stars on IMDb screen, IMDb app, 84
Move option
Email app, 168, 169
files, 105
movies. ***See also*** personal videos
buying or renting, 50–51
free, 51
IMDb app, 80–83
tickets, buying, 83
watching, 98–99
music
listening to, 94–95
shopping for, 48–49
transferring from computer, 96–97
transferring to computer, 49
Music content library, 48, 49, 94
Music folder, Windows Explorer, 96, 97
Music Store, 48–49, 94

My Account page, 246
My Local Profile screen, Contacts app, 192–193
My Rating star, Goodreads on Kindle app, 63

N

name, wireless network, 13
Narration Speed button, Books content library, 129, 130
Navigation bar
  Calendar app, 212
  explained, 18
  Kindle FreeTime app, 78
Navigation panel
  Books content library, 122, 132
  Calendar app, 214
  Clock app, 65
  Contacts app, 191, 195
  content libraries, 21
  Email app, 163, 165, 169
  Goodreads on Kindle app, 62–63
  IMDb app, 80
  Music content library, 94
  Photos content library, 115
New Event window, Calendar app, 216–217
New option
  Contacts app, 194
  Email app, 172
Newer option, Email app, 166
newspapers
  buying or subscribing to, 46–47
  keeping issues on device, 155
  subscriptions, 150–154
Newsstand content library, 46–47, 155. ***See also*** subscriptions
Newsstand Subscription Settings option, Manage Your Content and Devices page, 153, 154
Next button, Music content library, 95
Nightstand mode, Clock app, 68, 69
No, I am a new customer option, Amazon Sign In page, 8
Not Interested option, Home Screen recommendations, 253
notes, in books, 140–141
notifications
  managing, 26, 254–255
  Quiet Time, 256–257
  sounds for, 251
  viewing, 255
Notifications & Quiet Time settings screen, 26, 255, 256
number pad, on-screen keyboard, 27

O

Older option, Email app, 166
On Device option
  Books content library, 120
  content libraries, 20
  Videos content library, 99
onboard user guide, 32–33
1-Tap Archive feature, 58–59
on-screen keyboard, 27
Open device to view files option, AutoPlay window, 106
Open window, 105
Optional Encryption option, Silk browser, 239
Options bar
  common buttons on, 21
  content libraries, 20
  Nightstand mode, 69
  Silk browser, 225
Outlook, Microsoft, creating vCards in, 199
OverDrive service, 143

P

page, going to in Books content library, 122–123
page view, magazines and newspapers, 150
paperclip icon, Email app, 180
parental controls password, 72, 73, 79
Password Required box, In-App Purchasing settings screen, 93
passwords
  clearing in Silk browser, 241
  email, 159
  for lock screen, 260–261
  parental controls, 72, 73, 79
  wireless network, 13, 259
past issues of subscriptions, 151, 155
pasting
  media from computer, 107
  music to Kindle, 97
  text, 28–29
Pause button
  Books content library, 130, 133
  Music content library, 95
  Stopwatch feature, 68
  Timer feature, 71
payment method, setting up for Amazon account, 9
PC. ***See*** computer
People options, Goodreads on Kindle app, 63

percentage display, battery, 24–25
personal identification number (PIN), 260–261
personal videos. *See also* movies
- automatic uploading to cloud, 113
- copying from computer, 107
- defined, 107
- deleting, 114–115
- recording, 113
- viewing, 108–109

Phone & Email option, Mayday screen, 33
phone calls, with Skype app, 244–245
Phone Dial Pad button, Skype app, 245
photos
- attaching to email, 176–177
- automatic uploading to cloud, 113
- Contact Profile, adding to, 193
- copying from computer, 106–107
- deleting, 114–115
- downloading, 243
- editing, 110–111
- for Kindle FreeTime Child Profile, 75
- printing, 115
- sharing, 116–117
- taking, 112–113
- viewing, 108–109

Photos content library
- camera, displaying, 112
- deleting items from, 114–115
- editing in, 110–111
- sharing, 116–117
- viewing photos, 108–109

physical products, shopping for, 38–39
PIN (personal identification number), 260–261
Play button
- Audiobooks Store, 53
- Books content library, 129, 130, 133
- Music Store, 49

plug-in, printer, 60–61
POP3 email account, setting up, 160–161
Popular Highlights feature, 139
pop-up windows, Silk browser, 239
power adaptor, 6
Power button, 10, 11, 261
Power off option, 11
Previous button, Music content library, 95
Prime, Amazon, 5, 98, 143
Prime Instant Video, 98
printer plug-in, installing, 60–61
printing, 61, 115
privacy settings, subscriptions, 154
private Wi-Fi, 258–259
profile
- Amazon GameCircle, 91
- contact, 192–193
- Kindle FreeTime app, 74–77

Profile button, Skype app, 245
Progress bar, Books content library, 122, 128, 130, 133
public libraries, borrowing ebooks through, 143
public Wi-Fi, 258, 259
publications, buying or subscribing to, 46–47. *See also* subscriptions
punctuation marks, when dictating, 31

Q

Quick Settings, 19, 22–23, 26. *See also* Settings screen
Quiet Time, 22, 23, 256–257

R

rating books, Goodreads on Kindle app, 63
Read and Listen Now button, Bookstore, 133
Read shelf, Goodreads on Kindle app, 63
Reader Settings page, 129, 139
Readers to Follow area, Goodreads on Kindle app, 62
reading
- books, 120–123
- email messages, 166

Reading toolbar, Books content library, 122, 124, 128, 130, 142
Reading View, Silk browser, 229
recommendations, Home Screen, 18, 252–253
Record button, camera, 113
recording
- personal videos, 113
- text, 30–31

recurring events, Calendar app, 217
Refresh button, Silk browser, 225
Register Your Kindle screen, 14
registering tablet to Amazon account, 14, 15
Registration page, Amazon, 9
regular patrons, Yelp app, 87
Remove button
- Clock app All Cities view, 65
- Favorites section, 56
- 1-Tap Archive feature, 59

Remove Flag option, Email app, 171
Remove from Carousel option, 18
removing. *See also* deleting
content from tablet, 57–59
highlighting, in books, 139
notes, in books, 141
renting movies, 50–51
Repeat option
Calendar app events, 217
Music content library, 95
Reply All option, Email app, 179
replying to messages, Email app, 178–179
Request Another View command, Silk browser, 230–231
Request View For menu, Silk browser, 231
resolution, screen, 4
Return This Book option, Amazon, 143
reviews, Yelp app, 86, 87
rotation, screen, 22

S

saving
Calendar app events, 217, 219
changes to contacts, 201
Contact Profile, 193
email attachments, 181
new contacts, 195, 197
notes, in books, 140, 141
photos from Internet, 243
Schedule Quiet Time dialog box, 257
screen
Auto-Rotate option, 22
brightness controls, 22–23, 251
cleaning, 10
frozen, 11
sizes, Fire tablet, 4
Screen Reader, 5
Search button, explained, 21
Search Engine dialog box, Silk browser, 237
search engines, 236–237
searching
Amazon Appstore for Android, 40, 42, 43, 60
Amazon Instant Video store, 50
Amazon Shop by Department page, 38
Audiobooks Store, 52
Bookstore, 45, 132, 133
Contacts app, 205
content libraries, 20
Email app, 170
Goodreads on Kindle app, 63
IMDb app, 84
Music Store, 48
Newsstand storefront, 46
with Silk browser
overview, 225
in web pages, 232–233
web searches, 234–235
user guide, 33
Yelp app, 86
Security settings screen, 260
Select files to upload option, Upload Files to Your Cloud Drive window, 104
Select Photo window, Kindle FreeTime app, 75
Select View menu, Calendar app, 212
sending email, 172–173
Send-To-Kindle email address, 182, 183
Sent folder, Email app, 173
Set Alarm button, Clock app, 67
Set as VIP option, contacts, 163, 197
Set Date screen, Kindle FreeTime app, 74
Set Time option, Schedule Quiet Time dialog box, 257
Set up my profile option, Contacts app, 192
Settings screen
Amazon GameCircle, 91
Auto-Save option, 113
Clock app, 71
Device area, 24–25, 57–58, 262
Display & Sounds area, 251
general, 92
Home Screen recommendations, 252–253
IMDb app, 81
lock screen password, 260–261
notifications, 254–255
opening, 250
overview, 250
Quiet Time, 256–257
Silk browser, 236, 237, 239, 240
software updates, 262–263
wireless network, connecting to, 258–259
Settings tab, Manage Your Content and Devices page, 183
Setup Complete! screen, Email app, 159, 161
setup process, 12–17

setup wizard, Kindle FreeTime app, 73
Share button
- Contacts app, 201
- Photos content library, 108, 111

Share To menu, Photos content library, 117
Share your Content area, Kindle FreeTime app, 76
sharing
- contacts, 201
- notes, in books, 140
- photos, 116–117

shipping, with Amazon Prime, 5
Shop Amazon option, 38
Shop content library, 38
shopping cart, Amazon, 39
shopping for content
- Amazon Coins, 36–37
- apps, 42–43
- audio books, 52–53
- ebooks, 44–45
- games, 40–41
- movies, 50–51
- music, 48–49
- physical products, 38–39
- publications, 46–47

Show Battery Percentage in Status Bar button, Device settings screen, 25
Show Details option, Calendar app, 215
Show folders option, Email app, 163, 165
Show Formatting option, Email app, 179
Show labels option, Email app, 163
Show option, Home Recommendations screen, 253
showtimes, in IMDb app, 82–83
Showtimes & Tickets screen, IMDb app, 82
Shuffle button, Music content library, 95
Shutter button, camera, 113
shutting off, 11
Sign in automatically option, Skype app, 245
Sign in screen
- Amazon, 8, 102, 152, 182
- email, 159
- Skype, 244

Sign out option, Skype app, 245
signature, email, 187
Silk browser
- bookmarks, 227–228, 237
- browsing history, viewing, 238
- clearing, 240–241
- default search engine, setting, 236–237
- documents, downloading and opening, 242–243
- Go to Wikipedia option, 137
- opening, 224
- Reading View, 229
- Request Another View command, 230–231
- screen, understanding, 225
- searching web, 234–235
- searching web pages, 232–233
- settings for, 239
- tabs, 226

Skype app, 244–245
sleep mode, 251
Smart Lookup feature, 136–137
snoozing alarm, 67
Social Network Accounts screen, 247
social networks, 14, 15, 246–247
software functionality, 5
software updates, 262–263
Sort menu, X-Ray feature, 134–135
sound, 4, 251
spacing between lines, Books content library, 126
speakers, 10
Split option, Contacts app, 203
Start button, Stopwatch feature, 68
Start Using IMDB option, IMDb app, 80
Status bar, 18
Stop Recording button, camera, 113
stopwatch, 68
storage
- email, 187
- Fire tablet, 4, 15, 97

Storage screen, 58
Store option
- Apps content library, 42, 60
- Audiobooks content library, 52
- Books content library, 44, 133
- Games content library, 40
- Music content library, 48, 94
- Newsstand content library, 46
- Videos content library, 50

streaming videos, 98, 99
subject, forwarded messages, 175
Subscribe now button, Newsstand storefront, 47

Subscribe to FreeTime Unlimited option, Kindle FreeTime app, 73
subscriptions
  cancelling, 47
  general discussion, 150–151
  keeping issues on device, 155
  Kindle FreeTime Unlimited, 72, 73
  managing, 152–153
  overview, 46–47
  privacy settings, 154
  verifying existing, 151
swipe down gesture, 17
swipe left gesture, 16
swipe up gesture, 16
synchronization
  Calendar app events and Facebook, 220–221
  Contacts app, 207
  controlling, 187
Synchronize button, Settings screen, 250
System Updates screen, 262–263

T

table of contents, user guide, 33
tablet. ***See*** Kindle Fire tablet
tabs, Silk browser, 225, 226
"Terms of Use" screen, Music Store, 49
text
  copying and pasting, 28–29
  dictating, 30–31
Text Message button, Skype app, 245
text view, magazines and newspapers, 150
Text-to-Speech feature, 128–130
theaters, in IMDb app, 82–83
tickets, movie, 83
time, in Calendar app, 211. ***See also*** Clock app
time limits, Kindle FreeTime app, 77
timeline bar, Photos content library, 108
Timer feature, Clock app, 68, 69, 70–71
Today option, Calendar app, 213
trailers, 51, 81
Translation Smart Lookup card, 137
Trash folder, Email app, 167
Trivia option, IMDb app, 85
Turn off auto-renewal option, Amazon, 153
turning tablet on/off, 11
tutorial, 15, 16–17
TV option, Videos content library, 99
TV section, IMDb app, 81
TV shows, 51, 98–99
Twitter, connecting to, 246–247
Twitter option, Share To menu, 117

U

unboxing Fire tablet, 6
Unlink option, Social Network Accounts screen, 247
unlocking tablet, 11
Unread messages folder, Email app, 163
updates, software, 262–263
Updates area, System Updates screen, 263
Upload Files to Your Cloud Drive window, Amazon, 104
uploading to Cloud Drive via PC, 102–105
USB cable, 6–7, 96, 106
user guide, 32–33

V

vCards, 198–199
video calls, with Skype app, 244–245
videos. ***See*** movies; personal videos
Videos content library, 50, 98
Videos option, Photos content library, 108
View inactive subscriptions option, Manage Your Content and Devices page, 153
View on IMDb.com option, IMDb app, 85
views, Calendar app, 212–213
VIP contacts, 163, 197
vision impairments, accessibility features for, 5
voice recognition software, 30–31
volume, adjusting in Settings screen, 251
volume buttons, 10, 113

W

Want to Read menu button, Goodreads on Kindle app, 63
Watch Now option, Videos content library, 99
Web icon, Home screen, 224. ***See also*** Silk browser
web searches, Silk browser, 234–235. ***See also*** Internet
web-based email account, 210
Week view, Calendar app, 211, 212
weight, Fire tablet, 4
Whispersync, 5, 90–91
Wide Margin button, Books content library, 125
Wi-Fi screen, 259
Wikipedia Smart Lookup card, 137

Windows Explorer, PC, 96–97, 106–107
wireless network
  checking on, 99
  connecting to, 13, 258–259
  connectivity, 4
Wireless settings screen, 23, 258

X

X-Ray button, Books content library, 127
X-Ray feature for ebooks, 134–135
X-Ray for Music feature, 94, 95
X-Ray Smart Lookup card, 136, 137

Y

Yelp app, 86–87
Your Account page, Amazon, 9, 59, 182
Your Cloud Drive option, Amazon, 103
Your Devices tab, Amazon, 183
Your Video Library option, Videos content library, 98

Z

zooming
  camera, 113
  in Silk browser, 225, 231

31901055787776